A Land Transformed
THE ARABIAN PENINSULA, SAUDI ARABIA
AND SAUDI ARAMCO

Camels make their way toward the Tuwayq Escarpment in central Saudi Arabia in search of fodder, providing a millennia-old connection with the past.

A LAND TRANSFORMED

THE ARABIAN PENINSULA,
SAUDI ARABIA AND SAUDI ARAMCO

EDITED BY

Arthur P. Clark

Muhammad A. Tahlawi

AUTHORS

William Facey

Paul Lunde

Michael McKinnon

Thomas A. Pledge

CONTRIBUTING EDITORS

Thomas A. Pledge, Helen El Mallakh, James P. Mandaville,
Kay Hardy Campbell

THE SAUDI ARABIAN OIL COMPANY (SAUDI ARAMCO)
DHAHRAN, SAUDI ARABIA

Terraces sculpted to the contours of a valley near Abha in 'Asir Province in southwestern Saudi Arabia make use of every bit of cultivable land.

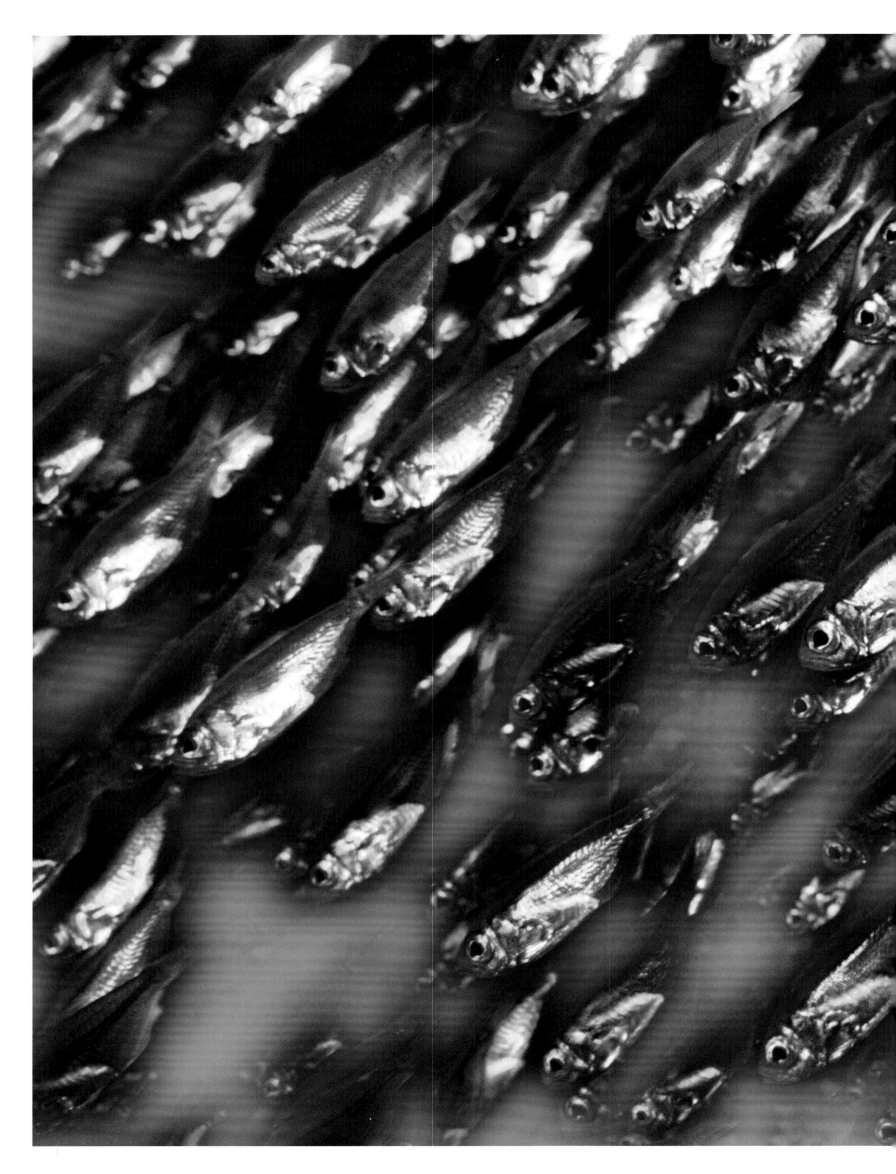

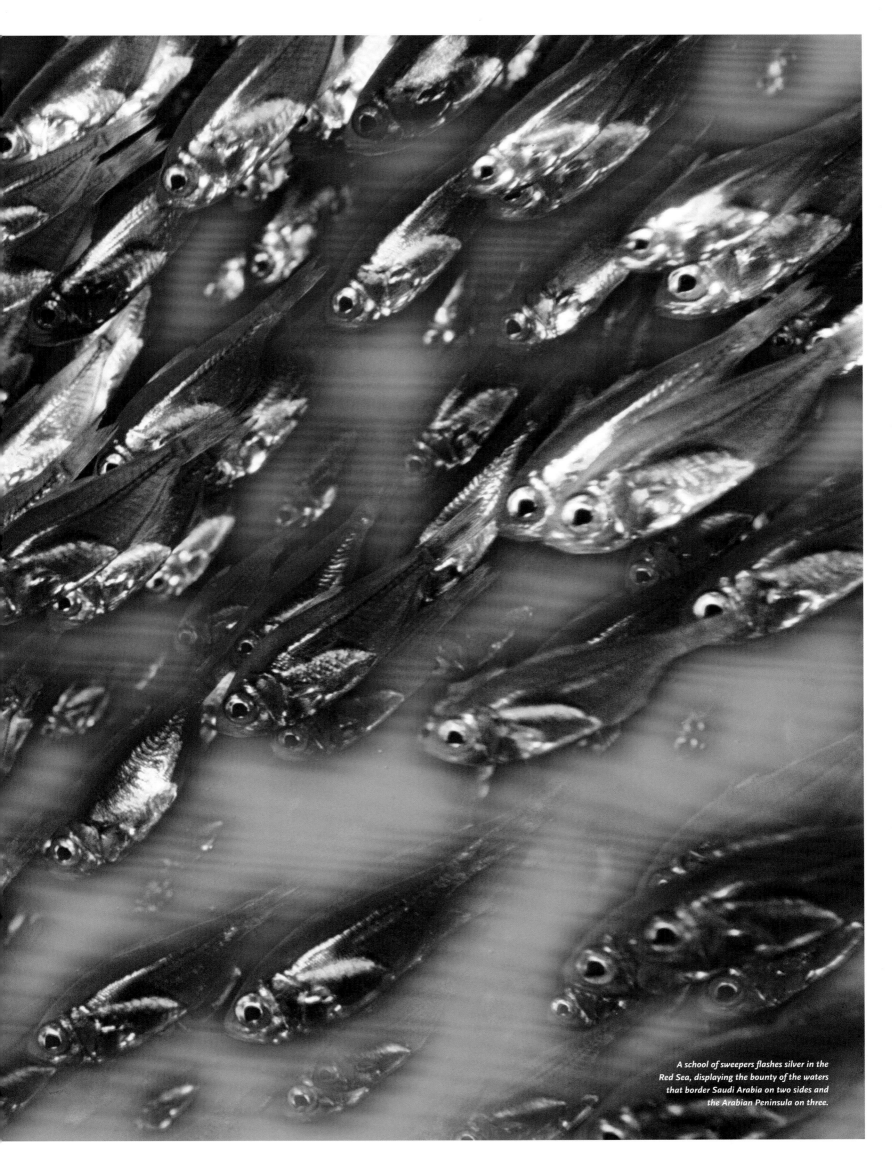

A school of sweepers flashes silver in the
Red Sea, displaying the bounty of the waters
that border Saudi Arabia on two sides and
the Arabian Peninsula on three.

For information about permission to reproduce selections from this book, or to acquire additional copies of this book, write to the Director, Public Affairs Department, Aramco Services Company, 9009 West Loop South, Houston, Texas 77096.

ISBN-13: 978-0-9601164-0-9
ISBN-10: 0-9601164-0-0
Library of Congress Control Number: 2006928339

ARAMCO SERVICES COMPANY
Houston, Texas
2006

PRINTED BY Dai Nippon Printing Co., Ltd. in Singapore.
DESIGNED BY Pentagram Design, Austin, Texas.

TABLE OF CONTENTS

199 CHAPTER 8
TAPPING THE TREASURE

Pilgrims clad in two seamless white garments called the ihram take part in the hajj, which draws more than 2 million pilgrims to Makkah during the 12th month of the Islamic calendar.

This gleaming pump station on the East-West Crude Oil Pipeline system is one of several that send cargo 1,200 kilometers (740 miles) across the Arabian Peninsula from Abqaiq in the east to Yanbuʻ on the Red Sea.

*Chrome, marble, mirrors and glass
mix in a kaleidoscope of colors at the
Al-Hamra Shopping Mall in Jiddah.*

A newly painted doorway at al-Dir'iyah, the ancestral home of the Al Sa'ud family, provides a pathway into the history of the First Saudi State (1744-1818), a predecessor of the Kingdom of Saudi Arabia.

PREFACE

A LAND TRANSFORMED IS A FRESH APPROACH TO A PUBLICATION initiated in the late 1940s. At that time, Aramco (the Arabian American Oil Company), Saudi Aramco's predecessor, found itself moving through a period of tremendous growth that involved the rapid expansion of a multinational work force comprised largely of Saudis and Americans. To provide the newcomers with basic information about the Middle East in general, and Saudi Arabia and its petroleum industry in particular, the company in 1950 issued a series of five spiral-bound booklets entitled *Handbook for American Employees.*

In 1952, Aramco published a revised, hardbound edition consisting of two volumes: *Aramco and World Oil* and *The Arabia of Ibn Saud.* A one-volume edition, further revised, appeared in 1960 as the *Aramco Handbook.* When the company produced the fourth edition in 1968, it was apparent that the book had become much more than a "handbook" for employees; accordingly, it carried the subtitle *Oil and the Middle East.* A richly illustrated fifth edition appeared in 1980 under the name *Aramco and Its World,* with the subtitle *Arabia and the Middle East.* It was followed, in 1995, by the sixth edition, entitled *Saudi Aramco and Its World.*

A Land Transformed may thus be considered the seventh edition of a groundbreaking publication first printed more than half a century ago. In the 1950s, most Westerners considered Saudi Arabia and the rest of the Middle East to be exotic lands, and comprehensive, up-to-date books about the area hardly existed. In the 21st century, although global communications and broadened education have helped make more people aware of the Arab world's history and its contributions to the world's spiritual and intellectual heritage, the bridges of understanding remain incomplete.

As reflected in its subtitle, *The Arabian Peninsula, Saudi Arabia and Saudi Aramco,* this volume brings with it a refined concentration. While there has been an outpouring of books that concentrate on Islam and the Arab and Muslim worlds, the Arabian Peninsula remains a less well-focused part that picture — even though the role of oil in the world economy and political events have pushed it to center stage.

We hope that this volume will add to an understanding of the Arabian Peninsula for readers who may have no direct connection with the region, Saudi Arabia or Saudi Aramco, but who desire to learn something about those subjects. For those who are already familiar with those topics, we hope it provides new insights into a land whose energy resources make it critical to the well-being of nations and whose contributions to civilization — most notably Islam and the Arabic language — remain as vital as ever.

INTRODUCTION

THE MIDDLE EAST IS THE PLACE WHERE ASIA, AFRICA AND Europe meet. It has no precise boundaries. Some people center the Middle East in the oil-rich lands of Iran, Iraq, Kuwait and Saudi Arabia. Others define it as encompassing some 20 Arabic-speaking countries stretching from the Arabian Gulf and across northern Africa to the Atlantic Ocean. Still others consider Turkey, Iran, Pakistan and Afghanistan, four non-Arabic-speaking nations, to be part of the Middle East.

By any definition, the Arabian Peninsula is the heart of the Middle East. It is the central focus of this volume. Saudi Arabia stands out as the largest country in this area, and the one with the largest cache of proven oil reserves, by far.

Much research has been devoted to developments crucial to mankind that occurred on the periphery of the Arabian Peninsula, and for good reason. Agriculture began in Mesopotamia some 8,000 years ago. Two millennia later, the first of several civilizations rose in Mesopotamia, the Levant and the Nile Valley, with the attendant development of laws, crafts, kingship and writing. From the wider Middle East came basic elements of mathematics, the wheel and the arch, and sciences such as astronomy and medicine.

Less attention was paid to the more remote, harder-to-reach Arabian Peninsula. Two of the world's three great monotheistic religions, Judaism and Christianity, were born in the area just northwest of the Arabian Peninsula. The third—Islam—was revealed in Arabia itself, the location of the faith's Holy Cities, Makkah and Madinah. This land was also the birthplace of Arabic, the language in which the Holy Quran was revealed to the Prophet Muhammad some 1,400 years ago. Much earlier than that, merchants, caravaneers and sailors had forged the framework for organized commerce between the Indian Ocean on the east and the Mediterranean Sea on the west, making Arabia a hub of international trade.

Scholars from across the Middle East, many of them Muslim, saved the philosophical, scientific and practical knowledge of the Greeks and Romans from extinction after Europe sank into the Dark Ages. The works of Aristotle, Plato and others, translated into Arabic, and then into Latin, were reintroduced to Europe starting in the 11th century, forming the basis of pre-modern Western scientific and philosophical thought.

A Land Transformed relies on recent research to bring a new understanding to events in the Arabian Peninsula, many of which have had an impact far beyond its boundaries. Like-wise, this volume views the energy industry from a local as well as a global perspective. In addition, it sets out a variety of subjects for treatment independent of the main text.

This book covers thousands of years. Compressing such a volume of information into a readable narrative required many omissions and, occasionally, a narrow focus on particular details to the exclusion of other significant material. The authors and editors strove for a balance that they hope will appeal to the general reader and, at the same time, succeed in presenting information based on sound scholarship and, wherever possible, on firsthand knowledge of the events, places and people discussed. Like its predecessors, *A Land Transformed* is dedicated to bringing to its readers a greater awareness of a land and culture that have contributed much to the artistic, scientific, philosophical and economic evolution of both East and West.

A FEW COMMENTS ABOUT THE ARABIC LANGUAGE WILL BE helpful to readers. Arabic personal names and place names are spelled according to a system used by Saudi Aramco, which closely follows a generally accepted system of transliteration from Arabic to English.

One Arabic consonant which has no counterpart in English is the letter *'ayn,* which is generally represented by an inverted apostrophe ('). It often appears in personal or place names, such as Al Sa'ud or Ka'bah. But when an Arabic word has acquired a common English-language usage, the popular form is used, such as Saudi Arabia (instead of Sa'udi Arabia).

It may also be helpful to explain several common Arabic words that are used repeatedly in this book. The word *al-* (joined to the following word, and with a small *a* unless it begins a sentence) is the definite article and corresponds to the English "the." The similar *Al* (always with a capital *A* and never joined to the following word) means "House (or family) of," as in Al Sa'ud, the name of the ruling family of Saudi Arabia. *'Abd* means "servant of," and in conjunction with one of the attributes of God is very commonly used to form Arabic personal names such as 'Abd Allah ("Servant of God") or 'Abd al-Rahman ("Servant of the Merciful"). The word *ibn,* sometimes pronounced bin, means "son of" or "descendant of the House (or family) of," as in Ibn Sa'ud or Ibn Khaldun. Its plural is *banu* or *bani* ("sons of"), as in Banu Musa or Bani Hilal. The word *abu* (sometimes spelled *abi,* depending on its grammatical position) means "father."

CHAPTER 1

A LAND TRANSFORMED

Finance Minister 'Abd Allah al-Sulayman (left) and
Lloyd Hamilton, representing Standard Oil of California,
sign the epoch-making oil Concession Agreement on
May 29, 1933, at the Khuzam Palace outside Jiddah.

"PUT YOUR TRUST IN GOD AND SIGN!"

THE KING WAITED, CASTING HIS EYE AROUND HIS ASSEMbled advisors.

It was an oppressively hot day in May 1933 — typical summer weather in Jiddah, the famously sweltering Red Sea port that served as the new Kingdom of Saudi Arabia's gateway to the outside world. King 'Abd al-'Aziz Al Sa'ud and key aides had gathered to approve the oil Concession Agreement that Finance Minister 'Abd Allah al-Sulayman had negotiated with Standard Oil of California, or Socal.

The minister had read the entire contract out loud. At the silence signaling the end of the recitation, the King sought his advisors' opinions. He did not expect comment or dissent, and none was offered.

"All right," he said to al-Sulayman. "Put your trust in God and sign!"

So dawned a new era in the Kingdom's history. Its vast significance, however, can only be appreciated in retrospect. At the time, few would have risked serious money on Saudi Arabia's oil prospects. The world economy was languishing in the doldrums of the Great Depression, and revenues from the pilgrimage to Makkah, the nation's major source of income, had slumped by 80 percent since 1930, reflecting a slide in the number of foreign pilgrims from 100,000 in 1926 to around 20,000 in 1933.

True, the country had just, in September 1932, been proclaimed the Kingdom of Saudi Arabia, an event that

Previous spread: (Left)The bustling old city center of Riyadh in 1949 comprised the main mosque, market and palace, the official Saudi seat of government, from which this photograph was taken. By the mid-1950s, the old mud-brick center had been demolished to make way for concrete buildings. (Right) Riyadh today is a modern metropolis of more than 4 million people, boasting multi-lane highways and many eye-catching buildings such as the Kingdom Tower (center).

3

King 'Abd al-'Aziz is seated in his palace in Jiddah in 1937, at the dawn of the oil era. Exploration had commenced in 1933, but it would be five long years before the first commercial oil strike.

to Socal. The territory, today called the Eastern Province, is now renowned as the home of the world's largest known oil reserves. But Holmes and his syndicate failed to follow through, and the concession lapsed in 1927.

With hindsight, this looks like the most fabulous lost opportunity of all time. Yet the decision was reasonable enough in the 1920s, given the state of geological knowledge. No one, least of all King 'Abd al-'Aziz, held out much hope for the Kingdom's oil prospects, and indeed he had to wait until 1938 for some good news. Even then, success almost eluded the American prospectors: after five years of hard work and thwarted hopes, it finally all hung on geologist Max Steineke's deduction that Dammam Well No. 7—now called the "Prosperity Well"—should be drilled a little deeper.

ADAPTING TO CHANGE

FROM THAT SMALL BUT FATEFUL DECISION FLOWED ALL the rapid economic development that was to transform Saudi Arabia after World War II. The pace of change contrasted starkly with the long, slow evolution that had characterized centuries past, and the oil industry itself drove much of this transformation in the early years.

In Saudi Arabia, the 1930s and 1940s were the swan song of the old days and the old ways. By the late 1940s, nomadic camel-herders, settled farmers and craftsmen, merchants and mariners who had taken pride in making a living in one of the harshest environments on earth were starting to adapt to unfamiliar modern comforts, new livelihoods, new levels of state support and routine contact with foreigners.

Photographs taken before mid-century show the tail-end of traditional life in Saudi Arabia as it had been lived for centuries, even millennia. While it would be misleading to think that they reveal a timeless, unchanging state of affairs, they vividly capture the end of one era and the beginning of another.

The hardship from which Saudis have emerged within living memory is striking. In the early 1930s, Saudi cities had no electricity, paved roads, modern schools or hospitals. Such austerity can only have been tolerated by a people extremely well adapted to doing without. If there is one craft that best represents the ability to conjure utility and beauty out of the simplest materials, it is the richness and inventiveness of traditional Arabian architecture, an aspect of Saudi culture that is clearly portrayed in much early photography.

While Saudi society has forged many fundamental changes in recent decades, it has maintained an unbroken link with its roots through Islam and the Arabic language, two of mankind's most powerful and enduring legacies.

marked the culmination of King 'Abd al-'Aziz's grand vision of reuniting its regions under Saudi rule for the first time since the early 19th century. That project had absorbed all his talents and energies since his recapture of Riyadh in 1902. Moreover, the beginnings of technical modernization were already visible, if only around the royal court, in the shape of motor vehicles, telephones and wireless telegraphy. But the outlook was bleak. The larger the state became, the greater the number of people who depended upon the wisdom and largesse of the traditional Arabian ruler—and there was not enough of the latter to go around. The King had to borrow from the merchants. Although Socal had agreed to pay £5,000 a year for the concession, and provide a £50,000 loan in gold (about $250,000), this would go only a little way toward satisfying his people's expectations.

The skeptics included the King himself, for he had seen it all before. As early as 1922 he had been alerted to the possibility of oil by Major Frank Holmes, an ebullient New Zealand mining engineer. Holmes's Eastern and General Syndicate had been granted a concession to prospect for oil in al-Ahsa, more commonly known as al-Hasa, the very area that was, in May 1933, about to be granted

American geologist Max Steineke enjoys the King's hospitality at Badi'ah Palace in Riyadh in 1937. When Westerners began to visit Riyadh regularly in the 1930s, it was considered good form that they don Saudi dress. Today, it is rare to see a Westerner in Saudi clothing, but many Saudis move easily between the dress of either world.

The annual heritage festival at Janadriyah, near Riyadh, features exhibitions like traditional dancing amid structures representing the Kingdom's architecture. This building represents a traditional style in mountainous 'Asir Province in the southwest.

As guardians of Makkah and Madinah, the holy places of Islam, and as hosts of the *hajj*, or Muslim pilgrimage, Saudis have a special feeling about themselves and their place in the world. The Saudis have expended enormous effort and expenditure in developing and improving facilities in the two Holy Cities, particularly during the tenure of King Fahd ibn 'Abd al-'Aziz, who reigned from 1982 to 2005.

Saudi Arabia's sense of itself as the heartland of Islam and the Arabs has made the country a unique example of rapid change. Saudis have striven to preserve key aspects of their heritage from foreign influence and opinion. Thus, rapid material progress and the revolution in consumerism have taken place against a background of official, societal and personal efforts to retain traditional values.

Saudis have welcomed modern buildings, motor transport, air conditioning, medicine and a varied, imported diet, while other aspects of modern life — including telephones, cameras and television — have found acceptance after initial resistance. In other areas, such as the organization of family and public life, Saudis in general have adopted a much slower pace of change. In recent years, a lively debate has emerged among Saudis on issues that were previously considered sensitive, such as the role of women in a modern society.

LANDSCAPE AND GEOLOGY

ARABS FROM MOROCCO TO SAUDI ARABIA ITSELF CALL the Arabian Peninsula *Jazirat al-'Arab*, the "Island of the Arabs." Almost an island, the peninsula is surrounded by seas on three sides and by desert on the north. Its latitude just north of the trade winds zone determines its climate. Arabia falls largely within the great Saharan-Arabian-Sindian desert belt that stretches from the Atlantic in the west to India in the east, so the popular image of Saudi Arabia as mainly desert is not far off the mark.

However, the country's sheer size means that it encompasses a wide variety of deserts. They range from the towering sand dunes of the Rub' al-Khali, or Empty Quarter, to the rolling pink crescents of sand in the Great Nafud, and the longitudinal sand ridges of the Dahna. Western Najd and the Dibdibah in the northeast feature barren gravels, while eroded sandstone massifs stand out in the northern Hijaz and Hisma. In the northern Hijaz, these contrast with the black lava fields found throughout the region.

Although the Kingdom contains no great rivers, a glance at the map quickly points up two key features of its location. It lies close to the ancient cradles of civilization in Egypt,

5

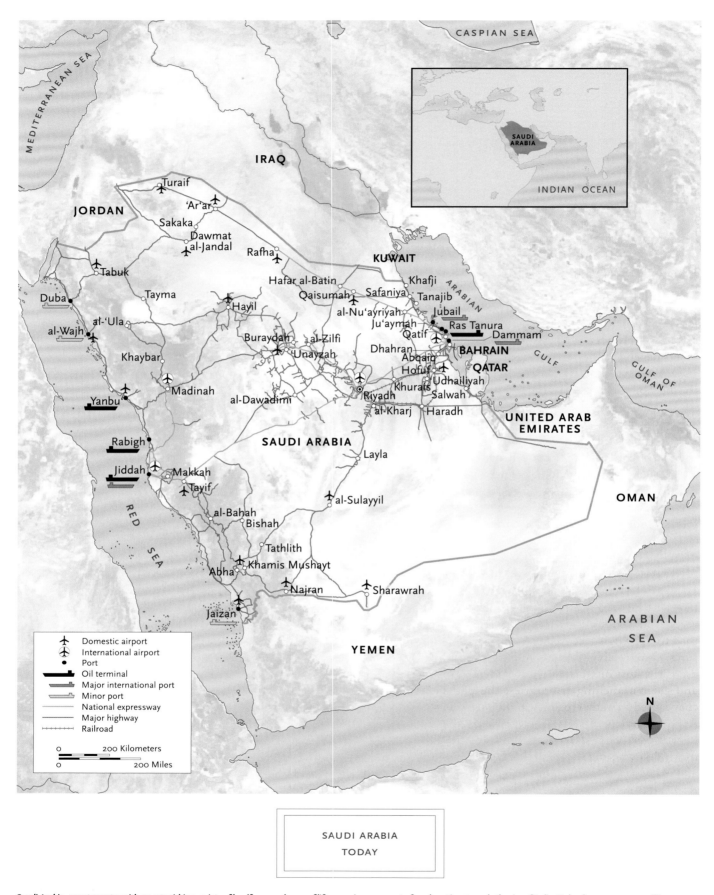

CASPIAN SEA

INDIAN OCEAN

SAUDI ARABIA

IRAQ

JORDAN

Turaif
'Ar'ar
Sakaka
Dawmat
al-Jandal
Rafha
Tabuk
Tayma
Duba
al-'Ula
al-Wajh
Khaybar
Yanbu
Rabigh
Jiddah
Makkah
Tayif
al-Bahah
Bishah
Tathlith
Abha
Khamis Mushayt
Jaizan
Najran

KUWAIT

Hafar al-Batin
Qaisumah
Khafji
Safaniya
Tanajib
al-Nu'ayriyah
Jubail
Ju'aymah
Ras Tanura
Qatif
Dammam
Dhahran
BAHRAIN
Abqaiq
Hofuf
QATAR
Udhailiyah
Khurais
Salwah
Hayil
Buraydah
al-Zilfi
Unayzah
Madinah
al-Dawadimi
Riyadh
al-Kharj
Haradh
SAUDI ARABIA
Layla
al-Sulayyil
Sharawrah

ARABIAN
GULF

GULF OF
OMAN

UNITED ARAB
EMIRATES

OMAN

RED
SEA

YEMEN

ARABIAN
SEA

N

Domestic airport
International airport
Port
Oil terminal
Major international port
Minor port
National expressway
Major highway
Railroad

0   200 Kilometers
0   200 Miles

SAUDI ARABIA

TODAY

Saudi Arabia, a vast country with an astonishing variety of landforms and ways of life, occupies 70 percent of a subcontinent nearly the size of India. Its land area, some 2.25 million square kilometers (865,000 square miles), is about a quarter the size of the United States, and it slightly exceeds the area of France, Germany, the United Kingdom, Ireland, Spain, Portugal, Italy, Denmark, Holland and Belgium together.

Syria, Iraq and Iran. And the peninsula as a whole, while forming a formidable barrier between the Mediterranean and the Indian Ocean, is bounded to the east and west by seas, providing excellent opportunities for communication and commerce. Both these factors have been fundamental in determining Arabia's history.

Dramatic mountain ranges are also a feature of Arabia. The vast mountain chain of the Hijaz and 'Asir runs along the Kingdom's entire western side. The most southerly peaks rise to 3,000 meters (nearly 10,000 feet) and catch the monsoon rains of summer that also make neighboring Yemen the garden of Arabia. South of the Empty Quarter, barren highlands fringe the coast of southern Arabia, concealing the fertile Hadhramaut region of Yemen. Farther east in Oman, the summer monsoon just catches the mountains in the vicinity of Salalah. The spine of northern Oman is formed by Arabia's other mountain range, the Hajar. Here, rainfall is just sufficient to replenish the aquifers tapped by the ancient underground *falaj* systems — on which Oman's historic settlements depend.

One can view the Arabian Peninsula and the bed of the Arabian Gulf together as a tray, slightly tilted so that it is higher on the western, mountainous side and slopes gently toward the east. The eastern regions of this shelf were covered by a giant sea that ebbed and flowed over millennia. It was here, in layers of carbonate rocks laid down by marine organisms in that sea, that oil explorers finally found Saudi Arabia's oil and gas riches.

Water Sources — Ancient and Modern

Large sections of Arabia have little or no vegetation, so its surface geology is relatively easy for geologists to read. Among its features, easily visible from an aircraft window, are the *wadi*s, or normally dry streambeds, and their branching tributaries; the paths they carved by water erosion are evidence that Arabia experienced several wet phases in the distant past. Large *wadi*s peter out into areas of windblown sand. Beneath, it's likely there are older sands washed down by the *wadi* itself, and it is from such erosion that the great deserts of Saudi Arabia were originally formed. These ancient river systems carried surface runoff during earlier, wetter climatic periods. Saudi Arabia owes its plentiful underground water resources to rain that fell on the exposed western ends of sedimentary strata that dip downwards to the east and flowed underground into the deep aquifers

lying beneath impervious rock layers. These must be used with care, however, for they are nonrenewable.

Shallow aquifers, formed by more recent rainy intervals, have been critical to Arabia's people in their struggle to adapt to their demanding land. Rain-fed farming is possible only where annual rainfall exceeds about 200 millimeters (eight inches) a year, and such bounty exists only in the highlands of 'Asir, Yemen and Oman. Elsewhere, for example in the oases of Najd, farmers have relied on wells. The only exceptions to this rule are the oases of al-Kharj and al-Aflaj in central Saudi Arabia, where natural sinkholes in the limestone gave direct access to aquifers until overextraction depleted the flow, and al-Hasa and Qatif in the east where, until recently, water was forced to the surface by natural artesian pressure. In Qatif and other places, farmers also tapped groundwater sources by building underground channels of the type called a *falaj* or *qanat*.

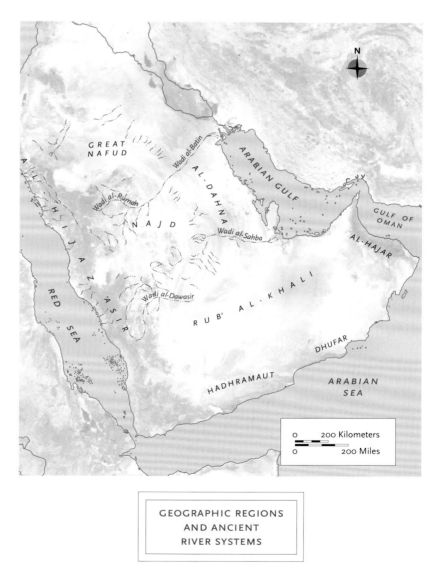

GEOGRAPHIC REGIONS
AND ANCIENT
RIVER SYSTEMS

During rainy epochs, three great river systems traversed central Arabia: the Wadi al-Rumah/Wadi al-Batin that debouched in the Kuwait area; the Wadi al-Sahba that broke through the Tuwayq Escarpment south of Riyadh and now loses itself in the sands toward the Qatar Peninsula; and the Wadi al-Dawasir that also broke through the Tuwayq Escarpment to lose itself in the western Rub' al-Khali.

The first American oil prospectors came ashore at the little fishing port of Jubail, north of Qatif, in September 1933. Little changed by the late 1940s, when this picture was taken, Jubail is today one of the Kingdom's main industrial cities. It is located 100 kilometers (62 miles) north of Saudi Aramco's headquarters in Dhahran.

THE LAND THE OILMEN ENTERED

IT IS ALMOST IMPOSSIBLE FOR A VISITOR TO SAUDI ARABIA today to imagine himself back in the physical world of the 1930s, when Socal's geologists arrived in the Kingdom. And it is unlikely those oilmen or the Saudis who worked with them could have imagined that their enterprise would by the mid-1940s grow into the Arabian American Oil Company (Aramco) and then — in 1988 — into the Saudi Arabian Oil Company, or Saudi Aramco, responsible for managing the world's largest-known crude oil reserves.

The country that the oil prospectors entered in the 1930s was virtually unknown to anyone outside the Muslim world. While the places that had most contact with outsiders, Makkah and Madinah, were exceedingly well-known to Muslims at large, that wasn't so for most Westerners.

NAJD—HEARTLAND OF SAUDI ARABIA

RIYADH, THE CAPITAL, IS NOW A MODERN METROPOLIS of more than 4 million people covering some 1,800 square kilometers (695 square miles), but in the 1930s it had only just begun to expand outside the mud-brick walls enclosing a Najdi town four-fifths of a kilometer (half a mile) across at its widest. One could stroll across it from gate to gate, through the center dominated by the old royal palace, the *suq*, or marketplace, and the great mosque, in just 15 minutes.

The city was growing, however, from a tiny base to 30,000 in 1930 and around 47,000 in 1940. Its palm groves to the north, west and south were largely intact and the Wadi Hanifah, now absorbed into the western part of the city, was about three kilometers (two miles) away. Concrete was unknown, since there was no way of transporting cement in quantity from the coast, and paved roads were a thing of the future.

Rudimentary development was beginning to make itself felt, as Riyadh was the capital of a new state with far-flung borders. For the first time, foreign officials were paying visits to the King in Riyadh, rather than Jiddah, though it would not be until the 1980s that the diplomatic corps made the move. In the 1930s Riyadh, the seat of government of the Saudi domain since 1824, was used to playing host to thousands of people who had business with the King: nomads and townsfolk pledging allegiance and receiving a gift in return; members of the burgeoning royal household; supplicants bringing grievances for adjudication; and the diversifying number of government employees and those seeking government jobs. As King 'Abd al-'Aziz's chief steward, Ibn Shalhub, who was responsible for catering to the ever-flowing stream of guests, declared proudly to Lebanese-American writer Amin Rihani in 1922: "Every king in the world is supported by his people; but the people of Najd are supported by their king!"

Other important Najdi towns such as 'Unayzah, Buraydah and Hayil were growing, too, but in a different way than the Kingdom's capital. They flourished as centers of trade, agriculture and livestock, and the basic crafts that supported life in a desert environment. The date palm was the staff of life, by virtue of its fruit, fiber and wood products; vegetables, fruits and fodder crops flourished in its partial shade.

Constant irrigation was vital, and in summer Najdi oasis towns rang day and night with the creaking and squealing of *sawani*, or well wheels, as draught animals plodded back and forth drawing up water. Access to shallow sources of groundwater meant that Lower Najd had been settled since ancient times, giving rise to a sturdy, isolated and fiercely independent people who tended to dominate the nomadic Bedouin with whom they coexisted and exchanged foodstuffs.

Hayil, a major town of northern Najd, was brought into the Saudi realm in 1921.

The accumulation of groundwater, combined with modern irrigation technology, allows crops to be grown at the base of the Tuwayq Escarpment.

The great limestone Tuwayq Escarpment, the "backbone of Arabia," faces west, its cliffs rising in places almost 300 meters (1,000 feet) above the plain. It is cut by steep gorges giving access to the plateau above.

NAJD

Najd means "high, flat and solid land" in Arabic, and as a name it denotes all of central Arabia — the region enclosed by the mountains of the Arabian Shield to the west, the Great Nafud desert to the north, the sand sea of the Empty Quarter to the south and the Dahna sand strip to the east that separates it from the Eastern Province. It is chiefly Bedouin country in its western reaches, where the *wadis* draining the Arabian Shield have yet to develop beyond small tributaries. Farther east, however, as they coalesce into larger *wadis* and encounter the barrier of the Tuwayq Escarpment, groundwater has accumulated, enabling settlements to grow. The north-south arc of the Tuwayq plateau is itself drained by large *wadis*, the most notable the Wadi Hanifah.

The scene in Riyadh's old market, seen here in one of the earliest color photographs taken in the capital city, in the mid-1940s presented much the same vista as in earlier times.

KING 'ABD AL-'AZIZ HISTORICAL CENTER

The park-like King 'Abd al-'Aziz Historical Center provides a striking reflection of Saudi Arabia, past and present, in the heart of Riyadh. Opened on 5 Shawwal 1419 (January 22, 1999) to inaugurate national festivities celebrating the 100th *Hijri* anniversary of the recapture of Riyadh by 'Abd al-'Aziz Al Sa'ud, it holds a complex of traditional, Najdi-style buildings. They include the new Saudi Arabian National Museum and the King 'Abd al-'Aziz Center for Research and Archives.

The center stands on the site of the Murabba' royal compound, built by the King in the late 1930s outside Riyadh's city walls, and where he lived from 1938 until his death in 1953. Craftsmen renovated some of the original mud-brick structures, including the *Diwan* (now known as Murabba' Palace), where the King worked and held court, several associated palaces for the royal family and the King 'Abd al-'Aziz Mosque. In practical terms, the Murabba' compound served as government headquarters. Planners also preserved a section of its thick, mud-brick wall and a square watchtower.

The National Museum and the King 'Abd al-'Aziz Center for Research and Archives face each other across a large *maydan*, or public square, that welcomes residents and visitors late into the evening. The center as a whole forms a green island in the midst of a bustling capital city, offering residents and visitors opportunities to relax, socialize and learn. In all, the facility covers some 40 hectares (100 acres), almost evenly divided between structures and irrigated parkland.

The National Museum, fronted by a sweeping 170-meter (560-foot) wall of yellow Riyadh limestone, features eight main galleries and covers 17,000 square meters (183,000 square feet). A unique gallery focuses on Arabia as the place where Islam was revealed to the Prophet Muhammad, and as the home of the Holy Cities of Makkah and Madinah.

Museum multimedia presentations about long-vanished cities enhance displays of artifacts from archeological sites around the Kingdom. These allow visitors to "enter" places such as the metropolis in Qaryat al-Faw in the southwest, for example, to discover how people lived more than 2,000 years ago. A team of Saudi scholars drafted text, identified artifacts for displays and multimedia treatment, and advised on exhibit development. All subjects are treated in Arabic and English.

Saudi Aramco is represented in several galleries. In fact, the large meteorite at the entry to the first exhibit on "Man and the Universe" was retrieved by a company team on an expedition to the Rub' al-Khali desert in 1965. The gallery includes a display describing how oil reservoirs of the Eastern Province were formed, discovered and produced. Among the photographs is one of early drilling on the Dammam Dome on the Gulf coast, where the oil strike in 1938 launched Saudi Arabia's petroleum industry.

The King 'Abd al-'Aziz Center for Research and Archives is built on the "footprint," or foundation outlines, of the original Murabba' Palace. The center offers men and women the opportunity to study the history, geography and arts, as well as the intellectual and architectural heritage, of Saudi Arabia and the wider Arab and Muslim worlds. Its Memorial Hall holds a collection of artifacts covering the life of King 'Abd al-'Aziz; a glass-walled annex shows some of the technological introductions in the Kingdom during his reign — including several of his automobiles.

The King 'Abd al-'Aziz Historical Center includes the new Murabba' branch of the King 'Abd al-'Aziz Library. Like the rest of the center, the library offers a rich cultural and historical focus for the city, the Kingdom and the rest of the world.

(Left) The spectacular Saudi Arabian National Museum forms part of the King 'Abd al-'Aziz Historical Center complex on the old Murabba' Palace site in Riyadh.
(Right) A gateway to the Murabba' Palace complex, built in 1936–37 as King 'Abd al-'Aziz's new headquarters.

A date harvester climbs to work in Qatif Oasis in the late 1950s. Dates have been cultivated in the al-Hasa and Qatif oases since the beginnings of oasis agriculture at least 5,000 years ago.

THE EASTERN PROVINCE

Saudi Arabia's two coasts have been open to outside influences ever since man began to venture upon the seas and discover his neighbors. In the east, the Arabian Gulf coast witnessed man's earliest-known long-distance trading voyages, and the Eastern Province's experience of civilization goes back at least 5,000 years to the era of Dilmun and Magan and their links with the Sumerians of southern Iraq.

The province's oases of al-Hasa and Qatif are remarkable places. Along with the northern side of the island of Bahrain, they form some of the largest natural oases in the world and have been cultivated since the dawn of oasis agriculture in the region before 3000 BC. They are blessed with large quantities

of water that once came to the surface in large spring pools and were canalized by farmers to their gardens. Water was so abundant that farmers grew rice extensively in the past.

Up the coast from Qatif, Jubail was just a small fishing village when the first oilmen came ashore in 1933. It is now, with Yanbuʻ on the Red Sea, one of the two industrial powerhouses of the Kingdom. The oil and petrochemicals industry has changed the face of the Eastern Province, a transformation in which Aramco played a major part in the first decades. Spending on education, health, housing, water, drainage and agriculture accelerated so rapidly that, combined with the mushrooming of service businesses and private housing, new population centers at Dammam, Dhahran and al-Khobar close to the first oil discovery soon

13

BEFORE THE OIL ERA

Al-Hasa was once the name of the region now called the Eastern Province and, until oil was discovered nearby, al-Hasa Oasis was the chief economic and political center of the area. It has three large towns, Hofuf, al-Mubarraz and al-'Uyun, and more than 50 villages scattered through an ocean of date palms and other cultivation. Natural water pressure in the oasis has been falling in recent decades as more and more water is drawn from spring-fed pools by mechanical pumping, and the area under cultivation has shrunk accordingly. On the coast, the people of Qatif and the adjacent island of Tarut possess similar water resources, but their livelihoods have had a maritime dimension, too, in trade, fishing and pearling.

(Clockwise from left) Uniquely in Arabia, rice was once cultivated in al-Hasa Oasis on a large scale; wheat, barley and a wide range of vegetables and fruit and fodder have been grown in Saudi Arabian oases for many centuries. Pearling was the main economic activity all along the Arabian shore of the Gulf before the oil era, as highlighted by this pearl diver holding his harvest. Traditional potters still work today in al-Hasa Oasis.

OLD JIDDAH

Jiddah was for centuries the chief port of the Red Sea, serving both trade with India and the pilgrimage. It is renowned for its Red Sea architecture: elaborate tall buildings of coral stone and plaster adorned with intricate wooden *mashrabiyah* screens and balconies. In 1916, British officer T.E. Lawrence expressed his admiration for the city and its architecture in these words: "The style of architecture was like crazy Elizabethan half-timber work in elaborate Cheshire fashion.... House-fronts were fretted, pierced and pargetted.... Its winding, even streets were floored with damp sand ... silent to the tread as any carpet."

eclipsed the old centers of al-Hasa and Qatif. The seat of government was moved from Hofuf to Dammam in 1953, and today Dammam, Dhahran and al-Khobar are merging into a single conurbation.

THE HIJAZ AND THE HOLY CITIES

THE MESSAGE OF ISLAM WAS REVEALED TO THE PROPHET Muhammad between 610 and 632 and is embodied in the Holy Quran and the *sunnah* (the words and actions of the Prophet). The revelations took place in the Hijaz, around his hometown of Makkah, and in Madinah, more than 400 kilometers (250 miles) to the north. Muslims believe Muhammad is the final prophet and messenger of God in a line stretching back through Jesus and Moses to Abraham, and even beyond to Noah and Adam.

Muhammad believed that his mission was one of bringing humankind back to the religion of Abraham, the builder of the Ka'bah—*Bayt Allah*, or the "House of God"—in a barren valley where Makkah grew up. Makkah thus possesses an inexpressible sanctity for Muslims. With the establishment of the *hajj* by the Prophet in his lifetime, it became the focus of faith for the ever-growing number of converts to Islam.

All roads led to Makkah, both overland and by sea. The trade between India and Egypt had in antiquity passed up the Red Sea to ports on the African side, but with the coming of Islam, Jiddah, as the port of Makkah, began to attract not just pilgrims but the sea trade from India. With the arrival of steamships in the mid-19th century, more and more pilgrims came on ships rather than by land. While steam dealt a blow to Jiddah's role as a trading center by enabling ships to sail directly to Suez in the north, bypassing the port, it greatly increased its pilgrim business.

In 1924, as part of his campaign to reunify the country under the leadership of the House of Sa'ud, 'Abd al-'Aziz Al Sa'ud entered Makkah peaceably, taking power from the *sharif* of Makkah. In a gesture of pan-Islamic brotherhood, he announced to the people: "Our most cherished desire is that the land of Islam be open to all Muslims." This proved no empty promise, as 'Abd al-'Aziz went on to devote much money and energy to the improvement of conditions for pilgrims and to extending the *haram*, the common name for the Sacred Mosque that includes the Ka'bah. By January 1926, he had taken Jiddah and Madinah.

Jiddah was the most cosmopolitan city in what today is Saudi Arabia. Even so, when Socal lawyer Lloyd Hamilton arrived in 1933 to negotiate the oil concession accord with 'Abd Allah al-Sulayman, Jiddah was still contained within its old walls, its atmosphere one of ancient heat exhaustion and its tall streets a fantastic array of Red Sea buildings.

Nowadays Jiddah, like Riyadh, has expanded beyond all recognition. Despite its sprawling growth over recent decades into one of the largest container ports and commercial hubs in the Middle East, remnants of the much earlier port city remain in the old downtown area. When

Before the age of photography, Europeans had only a hazy notion of what the two Holy Cities of Islam, Makkah and Madinah, looked like. This visualization of Makkah was by a Briton, Charles Hamilton Smith (1776-1859).

it was absorbed into the new and growing state, the Hijaz brought with it the religious and cultural weight of the holy places; it was also able to reap the benefits of the oil wealth that soon followed. Its ports and towns have seen the same development effort as the rest of the Kingdom.

'ASIR AND THE SOUTHWEST

SOUTH OF MAKKAH, THE HIJAZ MOUNTAINS RISE TO THE ancient garden city of Tayif, long a summer residence of kings and popular with today's Saudi tourists. From here, a great escarpment marches southward, parallel to the Red Sea coast, into Yemen. Its plateau descends gently eastward to southern Najd and the Empty Quarter. Its western face gives way to steep and jagged foothills whose ranges and deeply cut *wadi*s drain to the coastal plain of Tihamah below. The mountains of the southwest—the highlands of the southern Hijaz, al-Bahah and 'Asir, and the foothills of Tihamah—contain Saudi Arabia's most rugged and remote landscapes, and the most diverse of the Kingdom's people.

The forbidding nature of the terrain for centuries sealed off this region from outside influences, and the first Westerners to explore it in detail were the Englishman Harry St. John B. Philby in the 1930s and his countryman Wilfred Thesiger in the 1940s. The origins of settlement in 'Asir are shrouded in mystery, but over thousands of years its people have terraced their green mountainsides, built their villages and established weekly markets.

Jazan, more commonly known as Jaizan, was for centuries the chief port of the Tihamah region. It has now been developed as the Kingdom's third Red Sea port after Jiddah and Yanbu'. The government recognized the agricultural

ARCHITECTURE OF 'ASIR AND TIHAMAH

'Asir's architecture is outstanding. As a general rule, the farther south one travels the taller the buildings become, from single-story hamlets south of Tayif to the tower-houses of Abha, Sarat 'Abidah and Najran. Stone and mud are used for building, and in recent times modern industrial paints have enjoyed a riotous vogue.

On the Tihamah plain, one steps back into the Red Sea world. Here, peasant farming communities live in distinctive villages of brushwood compounds and circular houses. Huge *wadis* have built up great alluvial fans that are ideal for crops such as sorghum, millet and sesame.

(Top) This brushwood-and-rope house is typical of Saudi Arabia's southern Red Sea coast, known as Tihamah. (Above) This small farmhouse is built in the distinctive mud-layer technique of Wadi Najran, close to the Kingdom's border with Yemen.

A woman separates warp threads while weaving on a simple Bedouin ground-loom in Qatif. Colorful carpets like this are sold at the weekly market, or suq, in the Arabian Gulf coast town.

HANDICRAFTS

Handicrafts offer unique insights into the Arabian Peninsula. They tell the story of an exceptional people fashioning beautiful and useful goods while living under difficult environmental conditions with limited natural resources. The uniting factor among handicrafts throughout the Arabian Peninsula is their functionality. They provided shelter and protection, met homemaking needs and — in the case of women's jewelry — served as a valuable decorative asset.

While Arabia was influenced by African, Persian, Levantine and Turkish craft styles, traditional handicrafts had a tenacity of their own and retained their authenticity for hundreds of years. By the 1970s, manufactured goods — which were often imported — began to replace long-established handicrafts in Saudi Arabia, as a result of economic growth and increased urbanization. However, traditional craftwork remains a part of Saudi culture.

Handicrafts varied among the Bedouins, villagers and city dwellers, who often traded with one another. For example, Bedouins sold some craft items in villages to replenish their stocks of coffee, rice, sugar and cardamom. Thus, craft types and styles were shared across the peninsula. Regional and geographic conditions affected the kinds of materials used for crafts. Crafts along the trade and pilgrimage routes were the most likely to be influenced by external sources. In the interior, harsher living conditions meant there was less craft variety.

In contrast to weavers in Central Asia and Persia, those in Arabia produced items with very simple designs. This was particularly true for villagers and nomadic communities. Weavings took the form of rugs, tent walls and roofs, animal coverings and blankets. Most had geometric designs including wide stripes, triangles, diamond shapes or tribal marks, known as *wusum* (sing. *wasm*). Although most handicrafts in Arabia date back many years before Islam, the influence of Islamic principles is obvious. For example, depictions of humans or animal figures are virtually absent.

Weavings were brightly colored in red, orange, white, yellow and brown, achieved by using indigenous plant dyes such as henna, indigo, saffron, pomegranates and onion skins, or dyes imported from India and Indonesia. Wool came from sheep, camels and goats. Weavings were used extensively in Bedouin tents, but as early as the turn of the 20th century some Bedouins purchased basic tent strips readymade and then stitched them together and added finishing touches.

Rugs used on the tent floor were another valued craft item. In addition to small prayer rugs, Bedouins generally had up to three main rugs per tent. Vividly colored sheep's-wool rugs are distinguished by their stripes, geometric patterns and black edging. Other weavings included saddlebags, blankets and utility bags. Camels were traditionally caparisoned with brightly woven bands and sashes. A distinct handicraft was the leather or woven cushion on the front of the camel saddle called a *mirakah*, which served as a leg and knee pad for the rider.

Gold and silver jewelry has featured prominently in the Arabian woman's life over the centuries, not just as adornment, but also as part of her personal wealth, a sign of social and marital status, and what were believed to be amuletic powers. Fine jewelry is still highly prized and Saudi women wear both modern and traditional styles. Men generally do not wear jewelry, and what little they wear, such as rings, is made of silver—not gold—in accordance with Islamic principles.

Factory-made jewelry has now replaced much that was once created and sold by local silversmiths and goldsmiths. The most renowned silversmiths, from Najran in southwestern Saudi Arabia and from Yemen, transformed silver into relief decorations, filigree, twisted metal coils, chain links and talismans. They also embedded semiprecious stones of blue (turquoise), red (coral), green (malachite) and yellow (carnelian and amber) in silver items.

Pearls, harvested by hardy divers off the east coast of Arabia, were a major part of the jewelry industry. Indeed, pearls from the Gulf were highly valued around the world. The largest market for Gulf traders was India, but they even had offices in capitals like Paris.

Coins and beads, and Maria Theresa *thaler* coins imported from Austria adorn many antique Bedouin necklaces. Diamonds and other precious gems were used in later jewelry designs. Silver containers for kohl, black eye makeup, were also prized.

The date palm provided not just food but fiber for a wide range of products, including mats, baskets and fans. This man weaves strips from palm-leaf to be made into mats and baskets at the annual Janadriyah Festival near Riyadh.

Relatively few handicrafts were made of wood, due to limited supplies. Indigenous woodcrafts relied on date palm and acacia trees. Ports receiving wood from Africa and India were wooden handicraft centers. The largest handcrafted wooden items were seafaring and pearling dhows. Faint traces of this once great but diminishing industry can still be seen in cities on the Gulf and the Red Sea.

Doors and gates in cities and towns were often incised with geometric patterns painted yellow, red, green and blue. Intricate wooden window screens known as *mashrabiyah* were popular on the Red Sea coast, capturing cooling breezes while providing privacy. Highly decorated, compartmentalized chests called *sanduq mubaiyyat* were made in India, and Madinah and Makkah as well. Today, they are made throughout the Kingdom. Incense burners were crafted from clay and wood. Incense is used as an aromatic in homes and as a way to perfume clothing, a tradition that continues from pre-Islamic times.

Artisans decorated the *khanjar* (dagger) and the *sayf* (sword), creating elaborate hilts and sheaths adorned with silver, brass, embroidery and sometimes semiprecious stones. However, the blades were imported from Damascus and Yemen owing to the local scarcity of metal. Today, these weapons are used for ceremonial and decorative purposes.

The Bedouins were well known for their leatherwork. They developed innovative tanning techniques to produce items to carry and store water, including portable drinking troughs for animals. They used leather from the hides of camels, sheep, goats and antelopes to make sandals, baby litters and back carriers, coffee bean bags, falconry gear, bellows and food bags.

Oasis folk in eastern Arabia wove baskets and mats from palm fronds, and large, round mats used for trays under food, seats and displaying merchandise were very popular. In fact, every part of the palm tree was used to provide necessities for daily life. The people of the 'Asir mountains and Tihamah coastal plain in southwestern Saudi Arabia are known for their colorful baskets and for woven wear including wide-brimmed hats.

Pottery is made around the peninsula and Hofuf, the capital of al-Hasa Oasis, is well known for its pottery tradition. Typically, pieces are crafted on a wheel and decorated in a simple style, then sun-dried or baked into more durable items in communities with a kiln.

Given the high value placed on the art of calligraphy, it is not surprising that crafts have been affected. This is reflected in the manufacture and ornamentation of the *Kiswah*, the covering of the Ka'bah at Makkah, which is replaced annually. In 1926, King 'Abd al-'Aziz Al Sa'ud established a factory in Makkah staffed with highly skilled artisans to create the *Kiswah*; prior to that time, other Muslim countries had sent the precious covering to the Holy City as a gift.

Traditional handicrafts inform many styles and tastes in contemporary Saudi Arabia. Saudis are staying connected with their past by incorporating traditional expressions into clothing, carpets and jewelry, while many homes and buildings reflect traditional styles in their design and furnishings.

The minaret of the Mosque of 'Umar ibn al-Khattab at Dawmat al-Jandal in al-Jawf — from ancient times the cross-roads of northern Arabia — is one of the oldest in the Kingdom.

potential of 'Asir early on: Dams have been built and farming encouraged in the highlands around Abha and in Tihamah, particularly on the vast alluvial fan that spreads around Jaizan, Sabya and Abu 'Arish.

THE NORTH

NORTH OF THE GREAT NAFUD DESERT, SAUDI ARABIA borders on Jordan and Iraq. For centuries, the crossroads of this vast region has been the al-Jawf depression, lying just north of the Nafud and commanding the southeastern end of Wadi al-Sirhan. Here, routes converged from Najd to the south and from Jordan and Iraq to the northwest and northeast. Al-Jawf is home to the two historic settlements of Dawmat al-Jandal and Sakaka, the administrative capital of al-Jawf Province.

Assyrians, Nabataeans and Romans all at different times held sway over al-Jawf, and the great ancient fortress of Qasr Marid in Dawmat al-Jandal traces its origins at least to Nabataean times 2,000 years ago. One of the Kingdom's most ancient mosques, named for the second caliph of Islam in the 7th century, 'Umar ibn al-Khattab, still stands in Qasr Marid's shadow, and Dawmat al-Jandal was the site of a celebrated market in early Islamic times.

For centuries until recent times, the people of al-Jawf owed their livelihoods to trade and agriculture on the Najdi model, irrigating their palms from animal-drawn wells. In the late 19th and early 20th centuries, al-Jawf was contested between the powerful nomadic tribe of Shammar of Hayil in northern Najd and the Ruwalah who ranged the Syrian desert as far as Damascus and Palmyra. The region was incorporated into the growing Saudi domain by 'Abd al-'Aziz Al Sa'ud in 1922.

Al-Jawf served as an important camping ground for tribes of the Syrian desert, such as the Ruwalah, during the harsh summer months. To the south, the great sand desert of the Nafud, like a sea, is at once a barrier and a means of communication with Najd. But unlike the Rub' al-Khali, the Nafud catches winter rains from the Mediterranean, and its towering dunes are thus a rich source of grazing and firewood in the winter months. Neolithic remains at the single oasis in the Nafud, at Jubbah in the southern sands, testify to a very long habitation of this area by man. Today's tribespeople can take advantage of a wide range of government services in the form of water points, veterinary expertise, education and health care, and are encouraged to settle in large new towns such as Tabarjal in Wadi al-Sirhan.

Since the late 1940s, northern Arabia has been served by the highway between the Eastern Province and Jordan that followed the Trans-Arabian Pipeline, which carried oil to the Mediterranean. Settlements along this route, including Turaif, 'Ar'ar and Rafha, have since grown in importance. This road superseded the traditional routes crossing the northern region, such as the *Darb Zubaydah*, the medieval pilgrim thoroughfare from Iraq to Makkah.

A tribesman and his laden camel make their way over the sands of the Eastern Province around 1950.

THE BEDOUIN

The nomads and semi-nomads who roamed central, northern and eastern Arabia herded camels, goats and sheep. The great camel-rearing tribes traveled farthest and valued the distinctively Bedouin virtues of courage, generosity and the ability to mediate in disputes. The tribes and individuals displaying such qualities in their most exalted form were regarded as *asil*, or "noble." They prized desert life and tended to look down on semi-nomads and settlers. These camel-rearing tribes, especially in northern Najd where pasture becomes progressively more abundant, also reared horses.

Nomadic pastoralism is a highly specialized way of life, conducted in extremely harsh conditions. The nomads covered vast distances on their annual round in search of pasture; this might take them outside their "home range," or *dirah*, of wells and camping grounds. The Al Murrah of the Rub' al-Khali might range as far as Najran in the west or Iraq in the north. Northern tribes, like the 'Anazah and Ruwalah, roamed the Syrian desert north of the Nafud. The Ruwalah occasionally contested the oases of al-Jawf with the Shammar of Hayil.

The great tribes of Najd, such as the Qahtan, Dawasir, 'Utaybah, Mutayr and Subay', used the oases on the Hijaz borderlands and in Lower Najd. In summer, they congregated for the two or three hottest months around their desert wells or on the outskirts of the oases, where some tribespeople participated in the date harvest. Sometimes, a nomadic tribe owned date palms in an oasis, and a powerful tribe might even take complete control of a town. Great tribes like these established relations with outside powers, and this in turn bolstered the position of the ruling clan.

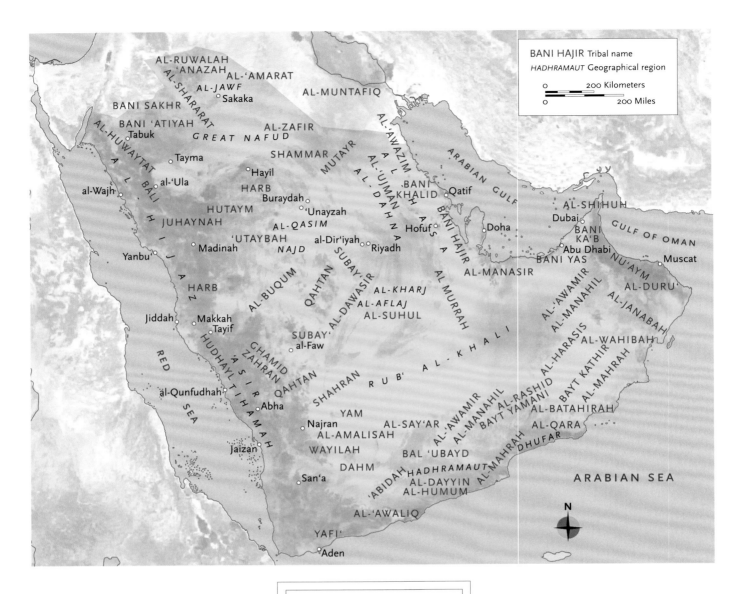

MAP LEGEND:
BANI HAJIR Tribal name
HADHRAMAUT Geographical region

0 — 200 Kilometers
0 — 200 Miles

TRIBES OF ARABIA
ON THE EVE OF UNIFICATION
{ EARLY 20TH CENTURY }

NOMADIC TRIBES AND DIVERSE TOWNSPEOPLE

THE NOTION THAT SAUDI ARABIA WAS IN THE PAST PEO-
pled entirely by nomadic Bedouin tribes is a misconcep-
tion, for nomads have probably never been in a majority in
Arabia and their lives have always intertwined with their
settled neighbors. The nomads depended on the people of
the oases and villages as markets for their animal products,
exchanging them for foodstuffs and other essentials. The
townspeople, in turn, relied upon the Bedouin for transport
and for alliances in time of war. A strong town with an effective ruler could exert control over the nomads in its district
and even subject them to taxation and military levy.

Whether settled or nomadic, the basis of society in inland
Saudi Arabia has been essentially tribal. Typically, a tribe
included both nomadic and settled sections up to the recent
past, and there was always interchange between the two. Saudis
are proud of their tribal past and many claim a tribal lineage.
In addition, Saudi Arabia's homogeneous mix includes non-
tribal people in ancient ports and linked inland towns, some
cultivators in the older oases, peasants on the Tihamah coast,
and even non-Arab people from all over the Islamic world
whose forefathers settled in the Holy Cities over the centuries.

FORGING A NEW STATE

WHEN FRENCH PRESIDENT CHARLES DE GAULLE VISITED
the Kingdom in 1965, he asked if Saudi Arabia was a nation
or a collection of tribes. His ambassador replied: "It is a collection of tribes in the process of becoming a nation." This
insight highlights the relative youth of the modern Saudi

The face of old Saudi Arabia:
An arduous life before oil,
under the unforgiving Arabian sun, etched a landscape
of physical hardship onto
this elderly man's features.

state, forged by King 'Abd al-'Aziz's campaigns of unification between 1902 and 1930.

The great challenge and achievement of the Saudis since the discovery of oil has been to manage change in a way that has caused minimum disruption to traditional values. Naturally, there have been problems over the decades. Challenges of the kind that Saudi Arabia has had to meet as a traditional society adapting to rapid modernization are bound to cause difficulties. On balance, the policy of managing social and political change cautiously has proved to be a wise one.

A characteristic of this caution is that every monarch since the death of King 'Abd al-'Aziz in 1953 has been one of his sons: Sa'ud (1953-64), Faysal (1964-75), Khalid (1975-82), Fahd (1982-2005) and 'Abd Allah. Saudi monarchs wield supreme power and appoint the Council of Ministers. The King also appoints the *Majlis al-Shura*, the Consultative Council, a 150-member body that advises the Council of Ministers. In early 2005, the first elections for half the members of local municipal councils took place in the cities and towns of the Kingdom's 13 administrative districts. The structure of government is tempered by a very traditional respect for consensus, informed by the ideal of the ruler as protector of his people. Furthermore, Islamic tradition sets various standards for the ruler, such as consultation. Most of all, there is a strong recognition of the Muslim ruler's obligation to provide for the public welfare. These ideals have inspired the provision of generous social welfare to Saudis in the form of free health care and education, as well as housing support and pensions.

The trend of the last 250 years — especially in the seven decades since the signing of the oil Concession Agreement in Jiddah — has been toward the triumph of settled values over those of nomadism. Many Bedouin have been drawn into settled occupations, and even the few who are still nomadic use trucks to transport their animals between government-sponsored watering points, send their children to government schools and visit government health clinics. One result of this process has been to overlay old allegiances to tribe or district with a strong sense of Saudi nationhood.

Today's Saudis are overwhelmingly settled, with years of economic progress resulting in mass urbanization. This extends beyond the mere fact that they live in towns and cities. It characterizes also their attitudes and expectations: Most Saudis now earn their livelihoods in the highly specialized ways typical of advanced urban societies, and share their material expectations with a cosmopolitan expatriate community.

Today's generation takes seriously the need to adjust to modern influences in its own way, relying upon Islam and tradition as a guide. It is a process with attendant doubts and difficulties. Healthy debate on change occurs in many forms. As in any society undergoing adjustment, some individuals cannot resist an extreme response. But for most Saudis, the geographical, political and economic influence that the Kingdom wields in the peninsula and the wider Arab world has merely added to the sense of historic responsibility they feel as the direct descendants of the original Arabs and the ancestors of the first Muslims.

The challenge to come: A new generation of Saudis, male and female, has benefited from the programs of universal education, health care and housing provided by the state. They will play their part in shaping the future of their country.

Chapter 2

Arabia before Islam

A fragment of a colorful wall fresco from Qaryat al-Faw, up to 2,000 years old, offers a vivid glimpse of the people of that time.

THE PEOPLE
OF ARABIA

THE ARABIAN PENINSULA TAKES ITS NAME FROM ITS INHAB-
itants, the Arabs. Nearly 3,000 years ago, the first people
known as Arabs lived in an area taking in today's northern Saudi Arabia and the Syrian Desert, bordered by the
broad arc of arable land known as the Fertile Crescent. They
formed nomadic camel-breeding tribes that were linked with
oases that also served as cult centers. They were by no means
the only inhabitants of Arabia at that time, but by the 7th
and 8th centuries after Christ's birth the people who carried
Islam from the Arabian Peninsula over most of the civilized
world had all come to think of themselves as Arabs.

Over the preceding centuries, the distinctive civilization
of kingdoms and caravan cities they had created played a
vital role in the trade between the Indian Ocean and the
classical Mediterranean world of Greece and Rome. They
left records of their accomplishments in the remains of
tombs and temples, palaces and paintings. They also left
imprints of their languages—including the precursor of
Arabic—carved on rocks. However, the record of early
man's presence in Arabia goes back much longer, to the
stone tools left at campsites in the distant past.

*Previous spread: (Left) The earliest rock art of Arabia records a time when its
environment was more hospitable. During the New Stone Age, c. 7000-2000 BC,
people could live by hunting and gathering even as settled life was evolving. This
finely carved scene depicts a wild ass or onager, now extinct in the Middle East, at
Jabal al-Mulayhiyah south of Hayil. (Right) Writing developed in Arabia possibly
more than 3,000 years ago as settlements grew up, and thousands of graffiti in
pre-Islamic scripts can still be seen on rock faces throughout northern and western
Saudi Arabia. This inscription in bronze from Najran, in the Sabaean script and
language of ancient Saba or Sheba in Yemen, is more than 1,700 years old.*

29

Finely chipped Neolithic arrowheads like these are a common find in central and southern Saudi Arabia, even in the arid wastes of the Nafud and Empty Quarter.

Primitive hand axes, such as this one from a site near al-Dawadimi in central Najd, date back hundreds of thousands of years.

NEOLITHIC TOOLS

By the 4th–3rd millennia BC, central Arabia's Neolithic people had developed into advanced hunters and gatherers. Some were beginning to settle and experiment with newly domesticated crops, while others pursued a more mobile life of hunting and, increasingly, herding of cattle, goats and sheep. Metals were still unknown, and stone tool-making reached a high degree of sophistication.

IN THE BEGINNING

ARCHEOLOGISTS TODAY CAN TRACE THE ARABIAN PENINSULA's earliest inhabitants to the Early Paleolithic period, or Early Old Stone Age, more than a million years ago. Tool sites near Najran in southwestern Saudi Arabia close to the border with Yemen, and in al-Jawf in the north, testify to the presence of hunting and gathering groups using crude pebble tools typical of early human groups in East Africa. Further discoveries may one day link Arabia to the story of even earlier human activities in Africa.

Such ties would not be surprising. The Arabian Peninsula split off from Africa beginning some 36 million years ago, riding the slowly expanding Great Rift that created the Red Sea. Even today at the Red Sea's mouth, a mere 32 kilometers (20 miles) separate Yemen from Africa, so it appears likely there was easy access to Arabia.

Sites with more sophisticated hand axes, scrapers and picks provide the next evidence of hunter-gatherers in Arabia. These have been discovered all over the Kingdom except in the Eastern Province. They date back 1 million to 150,000 years and reflect the so-called Acheulean tradition. A major Acheulean site lies near al-Dawadimi, some 240 kilometers (150 miles) west of Riyadh, near the remains of a large lake.

In the Middle Paleolithic period, or Middle Old Stone Age, a wider range of blades, points and flakes show broader, more sophisticated stone-chipping skills linked to the ability to use a growing range of natural resources, and hence to a more complex lifestyle. These tools date back as far as 100,000 years and are associated with the Neanderthal people elsewhere in the Middle East and Europe. Such sites are also widespread in the Kingdom—once again with the exception of the Eastern Province. Their absence in the east may relate to the fluctuation of sea levels in the Arabian Gulf resulting from the advance and retreat of ice during the Ice Ages in the Northern Hemisphere over the last 120,000 years.

In fact, glaciers covered parts of what is now Saudi Arabia twice in the far distant past. Geologists reckon the first ice incursion occurred roughly 435 million years ago and the second around 280 million years ago, well before early man appeared. This is when Africa, including today's Saudi Arabia, was part of a super-continent called Gondwanaland that lay in the Southern Hemisphere.

Closer to the present day, from 70,000 to 35,000 years ago, Arabia experienced increasing aridity, which may have spelled the end of its Middle Paleolithic people. A sustained wet phase followed until around 18,000 years ago. Remains of antelope, buffalo and hippopotamus dating to this time are evidence of a rich landscape of savannah and lakes, even in today's bone-dry Empty Quarter.

The last Ice Age peaked around 18,000 BC. Then a new phase of global warming set in, melting the glaciers and dramatically affecting sea levels worldwide. At the maximum extent of the ice cap, the Arabian Gulf basin had been

The major Paleolithic site at Saffaqah, southeast of al-Dawadimi in central Najd, has yielded more than 11,000 stone tools of Acheulean type, between 1 million and 150,000 years old.

a continuation of the Tigris/Euphrates river system. As the ice in more northern latitudes melted, sea levels rose and water began to fill the Gulf basin.

THE NEOLITHIC REVOLUTION

THE FADING OF THE ICE AGE APPEARS TO HAVE BEEN ACCOMpanied by a period of aridity in Arabia lasting until around 10,000 BC. Then a wetter climate set in again, perhaps the result of a northward shift in the Indian Ocean monsoon system. Shallow lakes reappeared in the Empty Quarter during this period, which lasted from around 8000 BC to 4000 or 3000 BC and which some archeologists call the "Neolithic Wet Phase."

During this time, a profound change began. It originated in the Fertile Crescent, running from the Mediterranean coast through today's Jordan, southern Turkey, greater Syria and Iraq to Iran. Here, hunters and gatherers began to sow wild forms of wheat, barley, beans and lentils, and to herd goats, sheep and cattle. This process of plant and animal domestication involved selective breeding, which engendered progressively higher-yielding sources of food. This new relationship between man and his environment is often called the Neolithic Revolution.

People learned to store their surplus crops. Permanent villages appeared, populations increased and society became more stratified. Individuals began to specialize in crafts such as pottery and copper-working, and leaders emerged who often represented the community's link with its gods. Between 4000 and 3000 BC, the first cities began to grow up on the Tigris and Euphrates rivers in Mesopotamia and along the Nile in Egypt, laying the foundations for business and social life that continue today.

Northern Arabia's Neolithic inhabitants were influenced by such developments. They began to make pottery and finely chipped spearheads and arrowheads. By the 4th millennium BC, they had started to use raw copper to make tools and ornaments. They continued to hunt and herd, moving seasonally with their livestock to fertile grazing grounds. Numerous stone circle sites mark their huts and enclosures. Fortified hills such as Jabal Bunayyan near Sakaka in northern Saudi Arabia may date to this period.

The peoples of the Syrian Desert and northern Arabia are particularly interesting because, in the 3rd and 2nd millennia BC, they appear in the records of Mesopotamian city-states. Referred to as MAR-TU or Amorites, they were probably among the forefathers of the Aramaeans and Arabs of the same region in the later 2nd and early

Text within the image:

||∩∩
||∩∩∩

ARRIVÉE D'UNE FAMILLE ASIATIQUE EN ÉGYPTE.

[BENI HACEN¹. XII° DYNASTIE.]

E. Prisse d'Avennes.

This tomb painting from the Egyptian site of Beni Hasan, dating to the Middle Kingdom, shows A-amu or "Asiatic" immigrants in around 1800 BC – possibly North Arabian donkey nomads, at a time when use of the domesticated camel had not yet become widespread.

1st millennia BC. Other predecessors of the Arabs in this region, donkey nomads from Sinai, Palestine and Jordan, appeared in Egypt around 1800 BC.

In central Arabia south of the Nafud desert, Neolithic hunters and gatherers also appear to have taken up herding, while continuing to hunt with the bow and spear. These people may have left the earliest and finest rock art of Arabia, near Bir Hima in the southwest, at al-Hanakiyah in northwestern Najd and at Jubbah in the Nafud.

A remarkable Neolithic site lies near King Khalid International Airport, north of Riyadh. Here, by the wells of al-Thumamah, circular drystone walls mark a large village believed to date to the 5th or 4th millennia BC. Tools such as stone querns for grinding grain and long, finely flaked stone spearheads suggest a mixed foraging, herding and hunting economy. As this is unlikely to have been an isolated phenomenon, it testifies to a way of life that must have been evolving in the better-watered parts of Lower Najd before 3000 BC.

On the Gulf coast, hunter-gatherers had developed into cattle-herders with settlements by 5000 BC. They had also come into contact with the pottery-making 'Ubayd people of southern Iraq. Sites have yielded distinctively decorated 'Ubayd potsherds, as well as clay sickles for harvesting cereals, cattle and fish bones, and oyster shells — the latter pointing to the origins of the pearl-fishing of later times. Pieces of reed-impressed plaster recovered at coastal sites testify to simple huts similar to the palm-thatch *barastis* once common in the region. Such 'Ubayd-influenced shore settlements imply short-hop seafaring along the coast to the head of the Gulf in small boats, perhaps like the palm-

Huwayriyah fishing boats, made of palm-leaf stalks, survived in the Gulf until recently and trace their origin to Neolithic times at least 6,000 years ago.

frond *huwayriyah* vessels that were familiar until recent times. Inland, finds of 'Ubayd pottery overlying Neolithic stone tools at 'Ayn Qannas in al-Hasa Oasis suggest that al-Hasa, together with Qatif Oasis on the coast, may be the oldest continuously settled area of Saudi Arabia.

BRONZE AGE ARABIA

THE TERM BRONZE AGE IS A USEFUL SHORTHAND RUBRIC FOR the first great civilizations of the ancient world because making bronze — an alloy of copper and tin—appears to dovetail with other complex technical and social developments that distinguished these pioneering cultures. The first great Bronze Age societies evolved in Mesopotamia and Egypt. Their hallmarks included a highly centralized administration, cities, colossal sacred structures such as ziggurats and pyramids, long-distance trade, craft specialization, instruments of exchange and mankind's earliest known writing systems.

In Arabia, recent investigations show that Yemen was acquiring characteristics of Bronze Age civilization by 3000 BC. Sites in the Najran region suggest that a settled village culture was emerging in the foothills of 'Asir. Given the natural advantages of the rain-fed mountain environment in the area, archeologists may eventually reveal a development from Neolithic to Bronze Age there similar to that in Yemen.

It is in the east, however, that archeologists can confirm Arabia's first exposure to the great river societies. It is reflected in the Dilmun civilization, which grew up around 3000 BC in the maritime oases of Qatif on the mainland and on the Bahrain archipelago, less than 50 kilometers (30 miles) away. Dilmun culture was also almost certainly represented in the inland oasis of al-Hasa and the remote oasis of Yabrin, some 240 kilometers (150 miles) farther south.

Dilmun's merchants acted as middlemen in the trade between Sumer to the north (in today's Iraq), Magan to the south (in what are now Oman and United Arab Emirates), Meluhha (the Indus Valley civilization) and southern Iran. The village farming people of Magan mined and smelted copper for export. They funneled copper and probably diorite, a black stone used to make statues of Mesopotamian gods and kings, into Dilmun's trade network. This Gulf-centered trade highlights another important trend in Arabia's past: seafaring.

Dilmun's own exports included dates, onions, cloth and perhaps pearls or beads, described in texts as "fish-eyes." In the later stages of their society, Dilmun's merchants were surprisingly modern, using business methods such as a standard system of weights and measures, silver as a medium of exchange, banking and insurance. This commerce fueled eastern Arabia's first economic boom.

It is likely that Bahrain emerged as the chief center of Dilmun after 2500 BC. No large city site like that found on Bahrain has yet been discovered on the Arabian mainland. But by the early 3rd millennium Sumerian influence was conspicu-

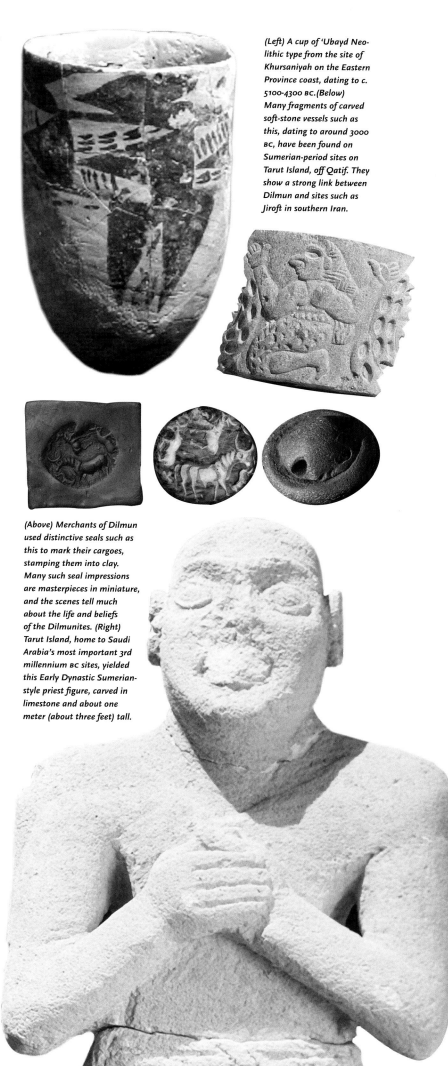

(Left) A cup of 'Ubayd Neolithic type from the site of Khursaniyah on the Eastern Province coast, dating to c. 5100-4300 BC. (Below) Many fragments of carved soft-stone vessels such as this, dating to around 3000 BC, have been found on Sumerian-period sites on Tarut Island, off Qatif. They show a strong link between Dilmun and sites such as Jiroft in southern Iran.

(Above) Merchants of Dilmun used distinctive seals such as this to mark their cargoes, stamping them into clay. Many such seal impressions are masterpieces in miniature, and the scenes tell much about the life and beliefs of the Dilmunites. (Right) Tarut Island, home to Saudi Arabia's most important 3rd millennium BC sites, yielded this Early Dynastic Sumerian-style priest figure, carved in limestone and about one meter (about three feet) tall.

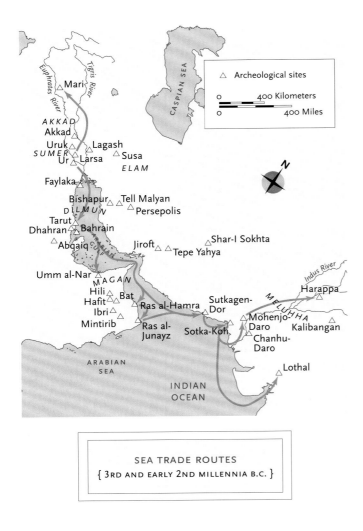

SEA TRADE ROUTES
{ 3RD AND EARLY 2ND MILLENNIA B.C. }

ous on the coast, where Tarut Island, just off Qatif, was set-tled from early on. The fort at its heart, dating from a much later Portuguese presence on the island, appears to stand over important settlement remains of the Dilmun period.

Near Abqaiq, complexes of tumuli stood on ridgelines overlooking the remains of a large lake and drainage chan-nel, possibly a "river" flowing from al-Hasa Oasis to the Gulf — attesting to the much greater abundance of natural artesian water in ancient times than today.

Dilmun's status was as sacred as it was secular for the Sumerians and their successors in Mesopotamia. The Sume-rians associated it with the origins of their civilization and immortality. Enki, their god of the sweet waters under the earth, presided over the *Apsu*, or Abyss. This is a telling con-cept because the oases of al-Hasa, Qatif and Bahrain were remarkable until recently for the fresh water that welled up from underground aquifers; at Qatif and Bahrain, this was true both on land and under the sea. The Sumerians saw Dilmun as the Land of the Rising Sun and the abode of the immortal Ziusudra. It was a "pure place" to which agri-culture, irrigation and many of the arts of mankind traced their origins — a prototype Garden of Eden.

The famous Sumerian epic of Gilgamesh tells the story of a hero-king who, pursuing the flower of eternal youth,

travels to a place "set in the midst of the sea" that has been identified with Dilmun. He is directed to plunge into the sea (perhaps at one of the submarine freshwater springs) where he finds the flower. Then a serpent devours the bloom, rob-bing Gilgamesh of immortality. The hero returns to his city of Uruk resigned to his earthly lot.

Dilmun's economy seems to have run into the doldrums in the mid-18th century BC when Mesopotamia fell prey to political disruption, the Indus Valley civilization faded and Magan's export business withered as new sources of cop-per appeared. After that, Dilmun appears in the cuneiform records as a colony of successive rulers of Mesopotamia. Locally, there were soon problems with neighboring tribes-men called Ahlamu raiding mainland Dilmun settlements.

Brilliantly crafted trade goods disappeared and cities fell into decline. However, it is likely that other basic activities such as local trading, the evolution of oasis agriculture and, almost certainly, the domestication of the camel continued.

THE 2ND MILLENNIUM BC: CAMEL DOMESTICATION, NOMADS AND SETTLERS

DIRECT EVIDENCE FOR PROFOUND CHANGES IN INNER ARABIA during the 2nd millennium BC remains elusive, but an idea of the significance of this period can be reached by compar-ing what came before with what came after. By the early 1st millennium BC, camel-herding Arab tribes were a political force in northern Arabia and perhaps in central and western Arabia as well. Equally important, by then the system of oasis agriculture based on the date palm and irrigation seems to have taken root all over central and northern Arabia. In short, the two economic mainstays of the desert-dwelling Arabians right up to the 20th century appear to be in place.

How did this come about? The earliest archeological evi-dence in Arabia for this type of oasis farming comes from the United Arab Emirates and Oman where, shortly after 3000 BC, the date palm, wheat, barley and sorghum were already under cultivation. The spread of oasis agriculture to other parts of Arabia could be accounted for by climate change. Toward the end of the 3rd millennium, as aridity intensified, life would have become more difficult for herd-ers and hunters in inner Arabia. Semi-settled cattle-herding seems to have died out, as it did to the west in the Sahara. Some groups probably gravitated to the better-watered areas — the oases and *wadi*s — and became farmers.

In more arid areas, hunters and herders would have been forced to increase their mobility. The camel, hitherto a wild animal hunted for its meat, was probably first domesticated in southern Arabia as a milk provider in the 3rd millennium BC. However, the full camel nomadism of the Arab Bedouin involves using the animal not just for its milk but also for riding and load-carrying. Such symbiosis between camel and man had to be in place all over Arabia before camels could be used for purposes like the trans-peninsular caravan trade

The mound or "tell" beneath the fort in the center of Tarut Island, off Qatif, forms one of Saudi Arabia's most intriguing archeological sites, reaching back at least to 3000 BC. When this picture was taken around 1950, the island retained much of its ancient character of palm-frond hamlets nestling among dense palm groves.

that flowered in the 1st millennium BC. Thus, the spread of this camel-dependent lifestyle to all parts of Arabia probably took place throughout the 2nd millennium. The first firm documentary record of the large-scale domestication of the one-humped camel occurs in the 9th century BC.

Southern Arabia also experienced major changes. By the early 1st millennium BC, the city-state of Saba (Sheba) was established in Yemen, larger political units were emerging and the distinctive South Arabian alphabetic script was in use. This alphabet shares features with Northwest Semitic scripts of the eastern Mediterranean cities. Precisely when and how such a link arose is still a matter of speculation, as archeological evidence from western Arabia for contact between the two regions is lacking.

However, a discovery in Saudi Arabia in the 1960s may have closed the gap a little. Archeologists located a great Late Bronze Age trading town at Qurayyah in the Midian region in the far northwest. It dates to around 1300 BC and featured a heavily fortified hilltop. Archeologists have shown that Qurayyah was linked with the Egyptian copper mines in Sinai. Camel figurines found at Qurayyah suggest involvement in a caravan trade, while its pottery ties it to sites in Palestine and possibly Yemen. It is tempting to think that Qurayyah may be the first link in a chain connecting the Levant and Egypt with southern Arabia. The origins of the ancient city of Tayma (Tema), 200 kilometers (125 miles) to the southeast, also appear to date to this period, which scholars call "Midianite."

The First "Arabs"

BOTH THE BIBLE AND ASSYRIAN SOURCES DEPICT TRIBALLY organized, nomadic camel-herders living in inaccessible parts of the North Arabian and Syrian deserts between the 10th and 7th centuries BC. They have their own deities and are linked to settled oases such as "Adummatu" and "Tema," which can clearly be identified with Dawmat al-Jandal in al-Jawf and Tayma.

These people are occasionally described as Arabs, but they are referred to more often by the names of individual tribes. The earliest biblical use of the term "Arab" occurs in II Chronicles, where Solomon, the 9th-century BC prophet and king, is said to have received gold and silver from "all the Arab kings and the provincial governors." However, this account may have been written four or five centuries after the events it purports to describe. The first known Assyrian reference is more reliable: It records the victory of King Shalmaneser III over a coalition that included Ahab the Israelite and "Gindibu the Arab and his 1,000 camels" at the battle of Qarqar in Syria in 853 BC.

A sequence of Assyrian inscriptions features Arab tribes, the most prominent of which are the Qedarites, whom the Assyrians vanquished and drew into their system of imperial borderland control in the 8th and 7th centuries BC. Their way of life as militarily active camel-herders linked with oasis settlements marks them out as typically Bedouin,

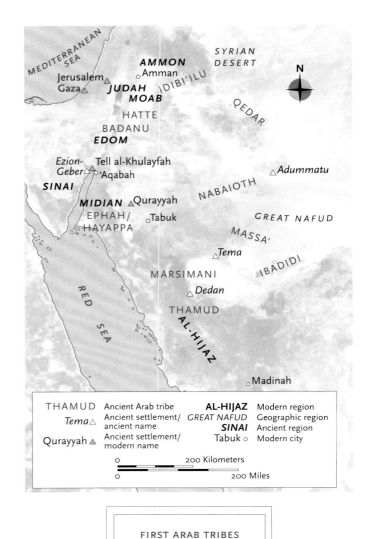

THAMUD — Ancient Arab tribe
Tema△ — Ancient settlement/ ancient name
Qurayyah ▲ — Ancient settlement/ modern name
AL-HIJAZ — Modern region
GREAT NAFUD — Geographic region
SINAI — Ancient region
Tabuk ○ — Modern city

0 ———— 200 Kilometers
0 ———— 200 Miles

FIRST ARAB TRIBES
{ EARLY 1ST MILLENNIUM BC }

already following a pattern that persisted in central and northern Arabia into the 1900s. The cultural continuity is striking, except that their leaders often seem to have been women and their tents circular.

The biblical writers, like the Arabs after them, represented supposed relations between peoples by genealogical links between ancestors, revealing what appears to be an earlier stratum of tribes in northern and western Arabia. The genealogies in Genesis 10 and 25 are clear on one point: that the sons of Ishmael (Isma'il in Arab and Muslim traditions), who was the son of Abraham from Hagar, are destined for a nomadic life in the desert. Both Qedar and Nabaioth—Arab tribes of later times—are represented as sons of Ishmael. In later Arab and Muslim tradition, Isma'il is the ancestor of the northern Arabs. At manhood, he joined his father Abraham in building the Ka'bah at Makkah.

Another notable point is that some of the Arab tribes from the 8th century BC were often required to pay the Assyrians tribute, some of which took the form of large amounts of aromatic resins. These resins—frankincense and myrrh — were undoubtedly obtained from the southern parts of Arabia. This implies that the tribes were already performing their historic role as middlemen in an overland trade between the Indian Ocean and the Levant.

The nomadic Arabs were not the only Arabian groups engaged in this long-distance trade. Settled people such as those at Saba, Dedan and Midian are also recorded to have been involved. Saba is believed to be Sheba, the well-known city of ancient Yemen, while Dedan and Midian were located in agricultural areas in the mountains of western Arabia and strategically placed on the trade route from southwestern Arabia.

What little is known of the dialects of the people of northern and western Arabia, whether settled or nomadic, points to them being mutually intelligible, but it is unlikely that the settled people were regarded specifically as "Arabs" at this early time. For outsiders at least, Arabs were identifiable by their camel nomadism, their warrior qualities, their emphasis on kinship and perhaps by their devotion to certain deities. Today, and for the past several centuries, it is the Arabic language, in addition to their tribal lineage, that is the touchstone.

With time and growing prosperity, these early Arabs diversified away from nomadism and oasis life. They settled in the cities of the Levant, took up various occupations and gradually loosened their ties with camel pastoralism. It was only later, after the dawn of Islam in the 7th century after Christ's birth, that language began to outweigh other criteria as the hallmark of "Arabhood," enabling anyone to identify himself as an Arab by virtue of his mother tongue.

KINGDOMS AND CARAVAN CITIES

FOR NEARLY A THOUSAND YEARS, BEGINNING AROUND 600 BC, the people of what is now Saudi Arabia enjoyed commercial prosperity and independence. Two major themes characterize this era: interaction with powerful neighbors outside the Arabian Peninsula; and the emergence of strong, prosperous trading cities and states within it. During this time, Arabia's people created a distinctive civilization of their own, leaving a record in the major pre-Islamic archeological sites of Saudi Arabia. This was a golden era, during which the Arabs coexisted with several great empires of antiquity, the Persian, Greek and Roman.

By 500 BC, Arabia was being drawn rapidly into the international nexus of ancient commerce. The growing wealth of Greece and the eastern Mediterranean was beginning to attract the luxury goods and raw materials of India and East Africa and of southern Arabia itself, for that was the source of most frankincense and much myrrh. To outsiders, the peninsula posed a formidable barrier between two great economic areas, the Mediterranean and the Indian Ocean. The people of Arabia had the skills to transport such goods over the vast, waterless tracts of the peninsula, and they exploited this advantage.

Assyrian troops attack camel-riding Arab tribesmen in retreat, c. 653-51 BC. One of the earliest-known depictions of desert Arabs, this detail is part of a relief mural found in one of the Assyrian royal palaces.

Who Is an Arab?

Who is, and who was, an Arab? The term "Arab" does not signify a particular ethnic group or way of life. The modern Arab world is a vast region stretching from Morocco on the Atlantic to Iraq in the east. It takes in the whole of North Africa, Sudan, the Arabian Peninsula and most of the Fertile Crescent. The Arab League has 22 member states, with a total population of some 300 million people. In addition there are substantial Arab communities in Europe, North and South America, Australia and elsewhere.

The people known as Arabs today spring from a diverse range of racial, ethnic and socioeconomic backgrounds. They range from Bedouin camel nomad to international businessman, from Yemeni mountain farmer to Iraqi cleric, and from Moroccan tapestry maker to Omani dhow sailor.

Although the great majority of Arabs are Muslims, being a Muslim does not make one an Arab. In fact, the majority of Muslims today are non-Arabs. On the other hand, there are Arab Christians, some of whom trace their lineage to the provinces of the Byzantine Empire before the revelation of Islam to the Prophet Muhammad.

The deciding factor in Arab identity is one's mother tongue: Arabic. Those born into an Arabic-speaking milieu with Arabic as their first language are identified, and often identify themselves, as Arabs.

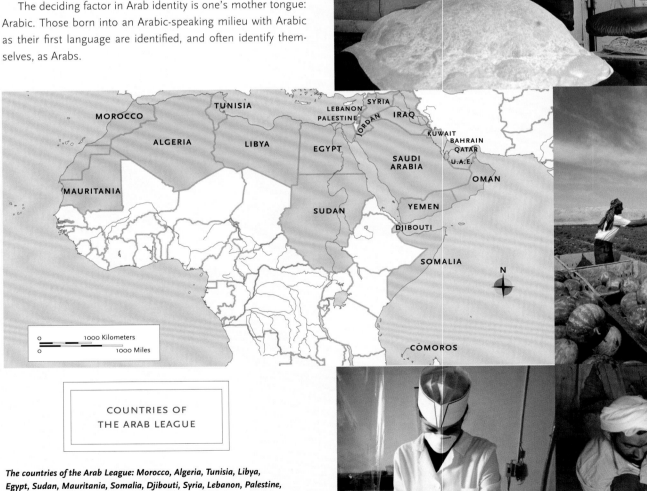

COUNTRIES OF
THE ARAB LEAGUE

The countries of the Arab League: Morocco, Algeria, Tunisia, Libya, Egypt, Sudan, Mauritania, Somalia, Djibouti, Syria, Lebanon, Palestine, Jordan, Iraq, Saudi Arabia, Kuwait, Bahrain, Qatar, United Arab Emirates, Oman, Comoros and Yemen. Some people in some of these states do not speak Arabic as their first language.

Beirut (Berytus)
Homs (Emesa)
Palmyra
Damascus
MEDITERRANEAN SEA
Jarash
Bostra
Ctesiphon
Jerusalem
Amman (Philadelphia)
Gaza
al-Hirah
al-'Arish
Petra
Kaf
Ithrah
Suez
'Aylah
NABATAEA
Dawmat al-Jandal (Adummatu)
Ubullah (Apologos)
SINAI
Qurayyah
Charax
al-Bid'
Tabuk
GREAT NAFUD
Leuke Kome
Madain Salih (Hegra/al-Hijr)
Tayma (Tema)
Hayil
al-Wajh
al-'Ula (Dedan)
Coptos ("Port of Hegra"?)
Thaj
Qatif
Khaybar (Khibra)
Tarut
ARABIAN GULF
Edfu
al-Nuqrah
Buraydah
al-Dur (Ommana?)
GULF OF OMAN
al-Qusayr al-Qadim
Gorda?
'Unayzah
HGR/Hajar/Gerrha?
al-Buraymi
Suhar
Madinah (Yathrib)
Rustaq
Berenike
al-Jar
Wadi Masil
NAJD
al-Kharj (Khidrimah)
Muscat
Mahd al-Dhahab
Riyadh (Hajar al-Yamamah)
Yabrin
al-Jiwa Oases
Izki
Possible ancient route through Rub' al-Khali
Wadi Al-Dawasir
Layla
RED SEA
Makkah
Turabah
Tayif
al-Khamasin
RUB' AL-KHALI
Thumala
Qaryat al-Faw (Qaryat Dhat Kahl)
Tathlith
Jarash
Bir Hima
'Athr
Najran
Taqah (Samhar/Moscha)
Sa'dah
N
MAIN
Jaizan
QARNAW
SAYHAD
al-'Abr
Tarim
Shibam
Adulis
Sirwah
Marib
HADHRAMAUT
Sayhut
San'a'
SABA
Timna
Bir 'Ali (Qana)
ARABIAN SEA
Aksum
HIMYAR
Muza
Mukha
Aden (Eudaimon Arabia)

○ Modern towns on ancient locations
△ Archeological sites
Ctesiphon Ancient place name
Yabrin Modern place name
Kingdom of Hajar/Gerrha
QARNAW Ancient kingdom
200 Kilometers
200 Miles

PRE-ISLAMIC TRADE
ROUTES
{ 100 COMMON ERA }

Caravan provisioning centers grew up at the oases and some became major settlements: Adummatu, Tema and Dedan are early examples. Nomads and settlers all over what is today Saudi Arabia and the desert enclosed by the Fertile Crescent of cultivable land to the north grew to depend on each other in the operation of the increasingly lucrative overland trade. Newly available linguistic evidence, in the form of some 40,000 graffiti on rocks and a few formal inscriptions associated with the major sites, reveals a range of related and mutually intelligible Ancient North Arabian dialects and scripts within Saudi Arabia. From one of these—Old Arabic, which is a shadowy presence in a few of the later texts—classical Arabic was developed as a written language in the early centuries of Islam.

The zenith of the Arabian overland trading network was marked by two kingdoms controlling the termini of this trade—Gerrha in the east, and the Nabataean kingdom based in Petra, in today's Jordan, and in Madain Salih in northwestern Saudi Arabia.

Settled cultures achieved ascendancy throughout Arabia as the riches of the overland trade stimulated the development of centralized societies combining commercial and military power. Trade peaked in the early centuries of the Roman Empire when, from 30 BC to around 200 years after the birth of Christ, it pulled in vast quantities of luxury goods, largely spices and aromatics, from Yemen, East Africa, India and even faraway China. The frankincense and myrrh of Arabia Felix—as Yemen was known to the Romans—were among the most prized.

After amassing considerable wealth, the merchants of Arabia Felix also came to play a pivotal part in the commerce of the Indian Ocean. They bought and transshipped goods from the sea trade, feeding them into the network of overland routes through today's Saudi Arabia to the growing markets of Mesopotamia and the eastern Mediterranean. The Nabataeans of Petra, the Gerrhaeans of eastern Arabia and the rulers of Palmyra in the northern Syrian Desert dominated these networks. They owed their power to the webs of allegiance they built up among the nomadic tribes that provided camel transport and among the settled people of the oases along the caravan routes. Important caravan towns evolved throughout Arabia, with agents, markets and transport facilities. Merchants amassed wealth, and rulers who could provide protection grew powerful.

Such entities highlight a typically Arabian process of state formation. A tribe is a mutual aid group bound together by ties of kinship. A person's honor, possessions and life are protected through those ties. A state, by contrast, exercises a right to adjudicate disputes and maintain law and order among all its citizens, irrespective of tribal bonds; it may employ full-time officials and soldiers to enforce regulations and judgments. It may also include other associations, such as guilds of craftsmen and merchants that cut across traditional kinship ties, as well as groups such as cultivators with no tribal affiliation.

Settlements in Arabia developed from purely tribal structures into varying degrees of statehood throughout the pre-Islamic period, not so much overriding the tribes that formed them as encapsulating them unchanged. The most developed of these societies were the markedly centralized kingdoms of Yemen such as Saba, Ma'in, Qataban and Hadhramaut. All retained their tribal traditions, as did the "states" in what became Saudi Arabia, including Qaryat al-Faw in the south, the Nabataeans of Petra and Madain Salih, and probably Gerrha.

Petra, in the Greco-Roman Levant, was renowned in the ancient world, and its spectacular ruins are equally so today. Less well-known are the principalities along the trade routes farther south, in today's Saudi Arabia. They were little-known in antiquity, and remained obscure until the 1960s and '70s when they came under sustained investigation by archeologists. Until that time, Saudi Arabia and indeed the Arabian Peninsula as a whole were represented by an enormous blank on the archeological map of the Middle East, on which the grander neighboring ancient civilizations took pride of place.

A much clearer picture is available today of the distinctive civilization that evolved in the special conditions of Arabia before Islam. Ancient caravan towns such as Thaj, Madain Salih, al-Khuraybah (ancient Dedan) near al-'Ula, Tayma, Qaryat al-Faw and Najran have all yielded dramatic finds.

Patterns of trade were subject to political and economic conditions along the routes. The relative ascendancy of the

Frankincense trees still grow in the wadis and hills of Dhufar in southern Oman and Yemen.

Frankincense is an aromatic gum resin. It weeps from tree species of the genus Boswellia *when it is cut.*

FRANKINCENSE

Frankincense and myrrh were two of the most highly prized aromatics in the ancient world. Valued for their fragrance and their medicinal and preservative properties, they were used in many luxury products. Frankincense was burned in great quantities, a use that still forms part of the ritual of some Christian churches. Today, frankincense is popular in Arabia as an air freshener, as a fumigant for clothes and the body, and even as a chewing gum. The ancient world's frankincense came from southwest Arabia and Somalia, and its export to the Levant and Mediterranean brought great wealth to the states of Arabia Felix, such as Saba/Sheba and Hadhramaut.

Gulf and Red Sea as trade routes also proved important factors. Perhaps most significant were developments in maritime technology. For example, around 100 BC Greek sailors in the Red Sea discovered how to use the powerful winds of the monsoon seasons to sail directly from Egypt to India and back, bypassing Yemen with their cargoes. This would have adversely affected the amount of overland trade. Nonetheless, it continued to flourish, until finally the economic slump in the Roman Empire in the 3rd century after Christ's birth dealt a blow to land and sea trade alike.

NAJRAN

NAJRAN BELONGED CULTURALLY AND GEOGRAPHICALLY TO the civilization of Arabia Felix, of which it was perhaps the northernmost outpost. Imperial Rome was intrigued by tales of the wealth of Arabia Felix, but its dreams of conquest resulted in just one, ultimately doomed, campaign. Roman General Aelius Gallus marched through Najran in 24 BC, but his plan to conquer all of southwestern Arabia faltered when he ran short of water and supplies, and his army was forced to retire. By this time, Najran had already served the caravan trade northward for centuries. It covered

(Top) This fine bronze lion's head was found at Najran and probably dates to the early centuries after the birth of Christ. It may have been part of a line of lions that adorned the top of a wall or gateway. (Above) This bronze inscription in Sabaean script was found at Najran with the lion's head.

some 28 hectares (70 acres), most of it today uneven ground marking tumbled mud buildings.

Some four centuries later, Christianity had become a force in the Roman world and beyond. Najran became a Christian center and there were churches in Aden and San'a and Hadhramaut in Yemen, and on the island of Tarut in the Arabian Gulf. There were also Judaic influences in the Najran area. In 523, Dhu Nuwas, a Judaized Yemeni ruler, killed many Christians in Najran, an event referred to in the 85th *surah*, or chapter, of the Quran as the massacre of al-Ukhdud, "the trench." This is still the name of the site and is believed to refer to the city's moat.

BIR HIMA

BIR HIMA IS A GROUP OF WELLS LYING 90 KILOMETERS (56 miles) north of Najran. From here, caravans continued along the inland desert route north through the Hijaz borderlands on the peninsula's western side, via the oases

of Tathlith, Bishah and Turabah, or traveled northeast to Qaryat al-Faw and then on to the Gulf.

Bir Hima and Jabal Qarah, the mountain range that runs north from it, contain some of the richest rock art sites in Saudi Arabia. The art spans all periods of the pre-Islamic past from the animal depictions of the Neolithic period to inscriptions from the age of caravan trade.

THE HIJAZ AND ʻASIR

IT SEEMS LIKELY THAT CARAVANS HAD A CHOICE OF TWO MAIN routes on Arabia's western side. One became known as *Darb al-Fil*, or "Elephant Road," in memory of the failed elephant-borne expedition against Makkah by the Abyssinian Abraha in 570, the year of the Prophet Muhammad's birth. *Darb al-Fil* followed the crest of the escarpment through al-Bahah to Tayif and Makkah. From there, caravans could travel a coastal path, or a route through several oases and the gold mines of Mahd al-Dhahab on the inland side

of the mountain range to Yathrib, today's Madinah. The other route went inland from Najran and Bir Hima, skirting Tayif and making for Mahd al-Dhahab before going on to Yathrib. The important pre-Islamic port of ʻAthr lies on the coastal plain of Tihamah, just north of the modern harbor of Jaizan.

King Nabonidus of Babylon conquered Yathrib in the 6th century BC. More than 1,000 years later, in 622, the Prophet Muhammad took refuge here with his followers from Makkah. Ever since, it has been known as *Madinat al-Nabi*, "The City of the Prophet," or more simply as Madinah. From here, caravans proceeded north via Khaybar or Wadi al-Hamd, to al-ʻUla or Tayma.

Inscriptions and graffiti throughout southern ʻAsir and on the Tihamah coastal plain show that the people there belonged to the same ancient cultural sphere as the far south of Arabia. Unlike the far south, however, ʻAsir boasts no ruins of great pre-Islamic cities, just as today it is a region of villages and local markets.

"Abu Lawhah," as it is known by local residents, is the largest of the great Nabataean tombs at Hegra (al-Hijr), now known as Madain Salih. Madain Salih is Saudi Arabia's most spectacular ancient site.

AL-ʿULA AND MADAIN SALIH

AL-ʿULA IN THE NORTHERN HIJAZ WAS HOME TO SEVERAL SETtlements controlling the trade along the main route north. Saudi Arabia's most spectacular archeological sites are concentrated in and north of the red sandstone gorge in which it is located.

The earliest, Dedan, dates to before 600 BC. Like Tayma to the northeast, it is mentioned in the Bible and Assyrian inscriptions. It is likely that Dedan's rulers established contacts with Egypt. Minaean inscriptions show that traders from Maʿin in Yemen had an outpost here.

About 150 BC, the Nabataeans extended their influence from Petra to take control of Wadi al-ʿUla. They established Hegra (al-Hijr)—today's Madain Salih—some 25 kilometers (15 miles) to the north. Originally a nomadic tribe, the Nabataeans settled and formed a state toward the end of the 4th century BC. They meant their funerary architecture to live on, and at Petra and Madain Salih they created two of the glories of the ancient world. The Nabataeans also made notable advances in agriculture, water use, ceramics and masonry. Saudi Arabia's Department of Antiquities is undertaking an extensive survey and excavation of the remains of the large walled Nabataean town at Madain Salih.

Nabataean sites are dotted throughout northwestern Saudi Arabia and Jordan, and in the Sinai and the Naqab (Negev) deserts. Although ancient Arabians preferred to trade by land, they were not entirely reluctant sailors, and Karkuma is a possible location for the "Port of Hegra" mentioned by the Greek geographer Strabo. The ancient port of Leuke Kome was probably located farther north, on the well-watered coastal plain at ʿAynunah.

One hundred six years after the birth of Christ, Rome annexed Petra and its territories. The northern Hijaz briefly formed part of Rome's provincial administration of the region, but it does not appear that this outlasted the 2nd century.

TAYMA

THE REMOTE OASIS OF TAYMA LIES ABOUT 110 KILOMETERS (70 miles) northeast of Madain Salih. The road to Tabuk, the next caravan staging post, passes through Tayma's ancient city walls, as it has done since before 500 BC when the city served the earliest camel caravans carrying incense and luxury goods

The ruins of ancient Dedan lie near the town of al-ʿUla. Today known as al-Khuraybah, they predate nearby Hegra/Madain Salih, and are overlooked by a row of simple rock-cut tombs in the red sandstone cliff face, among them these two "Lion Tombs." Dedan flourished from the 7th to the 1st centuries BC.

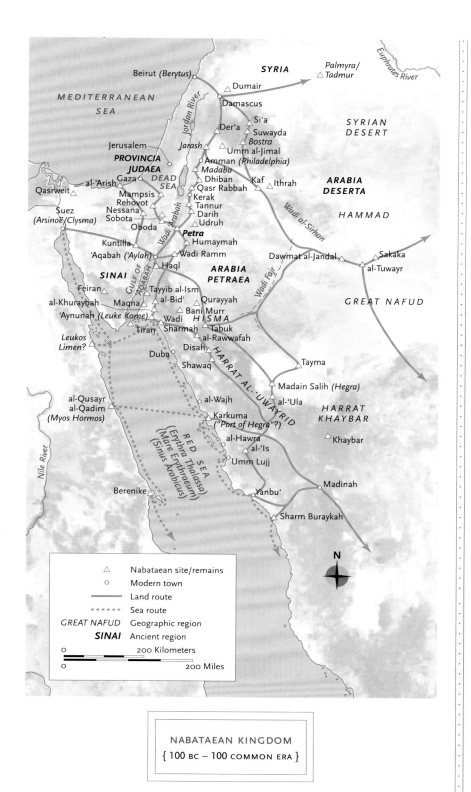

NABATAEAN KINGDOM
{ 100 BC – 100 COMMON ERA }

THE TAYMA STONE

The famed Tayma Stone was discovered by the French explorer Charles Huber in 1880 and remains one of the most important Aramaic inscriptions ever found. It now resides in the Louvre Museum in Paris and probably dates to the mid-5th century BC. It records the introduction of a religious cult of the god Salm of Hagam into Tayma.

to the Mediterranean. Another route from Tayma went north to al-Jawf and to Wadi al-Sirhan and Syria.

Tayma rose to prominence as a great walled city in the mid-1st millennium BC. In the 550s BC, Tayma was the arena for one of the most puzzling episodes in Arabian history: After capturing towns including Dedan and Yathrib, Nabonidus, the last Neo-Babylonian king, abandoned the splendors of Babylon to make Tayma his residence. Tayma

had a grand reputation as a cult center of the Moon god, Sin. Nabonidus, a devotee of Sin, had fallen afoul of the religious establishment at Babylon and decided to take refuge at this remote sanctuary of his deity.

Later, like other north Arabian settlements, Tayma came under Nabataean control. Like al-Jawf, it may have briefly formed part of Rome's Province of Arabia when Nabataea fell to Rome.

AL-JAWF AND WADI AL-SIRHAN

THE ANCIENT OASIS TOWN OF DAWMAT AL-JANDAL STOOD AT the junction of trade routes from the Hijaz, Syria and Iraq. Known as Adummatu in the annals of the Assyrian kings, it was a prominent center of the early Arabs, and it remained important under the Nabataeans. The oasis retained its tribal and commercial prominence into the Early Islamic period in the 7th century.

QARYAT AL-FAW

QARYAT AL-FAW WAS A KEY CITY ON THE ROUTE RUNNING from Najran to eastern Arabia. More is known about this metropolis than any other pre-Islamic site in Saudi Arabia because it has been excavated for many seasons by archeologists from Riyadh's King Sa'ud University. It features an extensive residential area and a palace, a temple and a fortified market, along with field systems, wells and underground tombs marked by towers. Sophisticated metalwork, statuary, jewelry, ceramics, glass, textiles, foodstuffs and colorful frescoes all testify to a sophisticated and highly organized tribal state.

Called Qaryat Dhat Kahl in ancient times, it was founded as early as the 4th century BC and its heyday dates to the first four centuries after the birth of Christ. It was ruled by a king and later was a center of the tribal confederation of Kindah that came to dominate central Arabia.

(Clockwise from left) A bronze charioteer statuette provides a glimpse into the past at Qaryat al-Faw. Qaryat al-Faw has produced some of the finest gold jewelry found on pre-Islamic Arabian sites. This fresco fragment from Qaryat al-Faw shows a cheetah or leopard, with an inscription in Sabaean script.

50

The city boasted a fortified *suq*, or market, with its own well and workshops. Like many Arabian *suq*s, it was separated from the residential areas of town. There were also subsidiary *suq*s, along with caravanserais. The houses were substantial and had arrangements for removing waste, which was probably used on the land.

Although barren today, one can imagine Qaryat al-Faw as an oasis: The remains of extensive field systems and many wells, underground cisterns and *qanat*s conjure up a picture of shady date palm groves, and gardens of fruits, vegetables, grain crops and even frankincense trees.

SOUTHERN NAJD

AROUND 80 KILOMETERS (50 MILES) NORTH OF QARYAT AL-Faw, the caravans passed through the great gap where the Wadi al-Dawasir breaks through the Tuwayq Escarpment. Remains of settlements have been found in Wadi al-Dawasir, by the ancient lakes of al-Aflaj and Layla, in al-Kharj southeast of Riyadh and even in the oasis of Yabrin on the edge of the Empty Quarter.

Al-Kharj lies at the confluence of major *wadi*s from central Arabia and is still relatively well-watered today. Shortly before the dawn of Islam, it attained prominence as the center of the kingdom of al-Yamamah, a tribal state controlling the route through southern Najd between the Eastern Province and Yemen.

GERRHA

THE GREAT L-SHAPED OASIS OF AL-HASA WITH ITS MAIN TOWN of Hofuf in today's Eastern Province was probably the chief rest and reprovisioning site on the route from southwest Arabia to the Gulf and Mesopotamia. The oasis, with its ocean of palms, large spring-fed pools and myriad channels of fresh water, must have beckoned like a mirage to caravaneers.

It was inevitable that somewhere nearby a city would grow up to control this trade. The Greeks called it "Gerrha." This was possibly a corruption of Hajar, the old name of al-Hasa; Qarah, a village in today's al-Hasa; or al-'Uqayr, the old port of the oasis. While overland trade flourished, Gerrha prospered and maintained its independence. Around 205 BC, its citizens even bribed one of Alexander the Great's successors, Antiochus, to leave the city alone. Alexander himself had nursed ambitions to invade Arabia, but his death in Babylon in 323 BC derailed that plan.

The Gerrhaeans appear to have played the same role in eastern Arabia as the Nabataeans did in the northwest, and there is evidence that the two kingdoms did business with each other. Gerrha was the regional focus of trade by land and possibly by sea, for it was positioned to take delivery of goods from India via the Gulf and organize their transport across central Arabia to the Nabataeans and the Mediterranean.

Although inscriptions and coins testify to Gerrha's existence, its location remains an archeological mystery. Con-

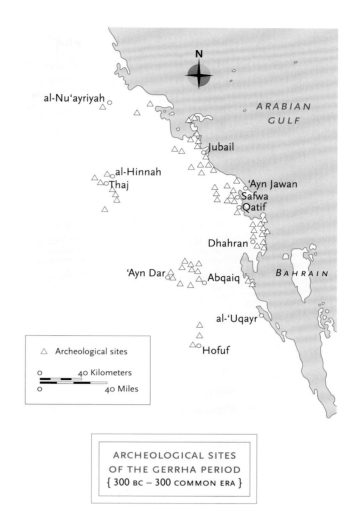

ARCHEOLOGICAL SITES
OF THE GERRHA PERIOD
{ 300 BC – 300 COMMON ERA }

temporary Greek and Roman authors tantalize readers with depictions of a city of fabulous wealth.

Over the last century, several sites have been proposed for Gerrha, and al-Hasa Oasis lays the strongest claim. It was certainly the population and food production center of the region, and probably the political and commercial center, too. Trade routes from Yemen, Najd and modern-day Iraq converged here, meeting routes from Qatif and the Gulf coast. Hajar is known to have been the capital of the oasis (also named Hajar) in late pre-Islamic and Early Islamic times. So, if the name Gerrha could be proved to be derived from South Arabian *HGR* (Hajar, meaning a walled city with gates and towers) and Aramaic Hagara, that would clinch the identification.

But no major city site of this period, particularly not one that would fit the connotation of *HGR*, has been found in the oasis. The lack of obvious archeological remains may be due to the fact that it, like Qatif to the north, has been continuously inhabited and farmed since Gerrha's era, so much may have been obliterated, especially if buildings were made of sun-dried mud.

The Greek geographer Ptolemy, writing around 150 years after the birth of Christ, placed Gerrha on the coast and named several other towns in the area, including "Phigeia," which may have been Thaj to the north. Whatever the precise limits of the Gerrhaean state, it represents, after the Dilmun period, the second climax of prosperity in the history of al-Hasa.

Like the Nabataeans, the Gerrhaeans were vulnerable to competition from sea routes. In the Gulf, the Parthians, who ruled Persia for more than four and a half centuries beginning around 240 BC, controlled the sea trade to Mesopotamia. They learned to extend the range of direct sailing, bypassing ports in eastern Arabia. Perhaps as a result, overland trade from the Gulf to the Mediterranean shifted

to the north in the 1st century after the birth of Christ. By the early 3rd century, the Parthians appear to have imposed a ruler on eastern Arabia, perhaps with the intention of controlling the land trade through it, too.

QATIF

QATIF ON THE GULF COAST WAS AN ALTERNATE STOP FOR CARA-vans traveling north. Little archeology has been carried out here, but its ancient history is probably much like that of al-Hasa Oasis. An added maritime flavor brought Greek,

Thaj is one of the largest city sites in Saudi Arabia and has yielded a wealth of archeological material, including coins of "Kings of HGR," many camel figurines and incense burners, and this golden treasure.

Persian and Mesopotamian influences, especially to neighboring Tarut Island.

The oasis was an obvious target and a natural base for the Persians from across the Gulf, first the Parthians and then the Sasanians. *Qanat*s and tombs, such as the one at 'Ayn Jawan near Safwa, point to Persian influence. Archeological remains confirm that the cultivated coastal strip supported by the oasis was much more extensive than today, reaching all the way to Dammam and Dhahran where, as at Abqaiq and al-Kharj, there was once an extensive tumulus field. Qatif Oasis has been seen by some as another strong candidate for the location of Gerrha.

THAJ

THAJ IS THE ONLY KNOWN SITE IN THE EASTERN PROVINCE whose walled remains fit the meaning of *HGR*. It is also the sole site in the region where coins of the kings of *HGR* have been found. Furthermore, the evidence for the location of Gerrha given by the Greek and Roman geographers can be made to fit Thaj as well as al-Hasa Oasis.

Thaj was a town of exceptional size and prosperity during its heyday, which spanned about 400 years from the early 4th century BC. The site covers 80 hectares (200 acres), larger than Qaryat al-Faw. Thaj has not been extensively inhabited since pre-Islamic times, and its stone construction has led to an impressive degree of preservation.

CENTRAL AND NORTHERN NAJD

NO GREAT TRADE ROUTE CITIES HAVE BEEN DISCOVERED ANYwhere in central and northern Najd, though some overland trade, particularly that between the Gerrhaeans and the Nabataeans, must have passed that way. In recent centuries, the eastern side of Lower Najd has supported many settled farming communities. Among these, 'Unayzah, Buraydah, al-'Uyaynah, al-Dir'iyah and Riyadh became politically powerful. Any earlier settlements in these places would probably have been obliterated by later building and oasis farming, especially if, as is likely, they were made of sun-dried mud.

Oasis farming and settlement must have been well-established by the 3rd and 2nd millennia BC, but settlements of the 1st millennium BC and earlier remain to be identified. There are later legends of the "vanished" or "lost" Arabs. The tribes of Tasm and Jadis, for example, were settled cultivators said to have lived in Wadi Hanifah and al-Kharj, that region encompassing modern-day Riyadh. The tribes are said to have quarrelled in the 4th century after Christ's birth, and the Tasm invited the Himyarites of Yemen to intervene. Both the Tasm and Jadis were destroyed and their settlements abandoned. When they were repopulated by Bani Hanifah in the 5th century, the remains—towers, fortresses and irrigation systems—were said to be still visible.

Such tales may hold a kernel of historical truth. The "vanished" Arabs appear to belong to the period of the great trad-

Groundwater has been available in limestone solution holes at various places in eastern Najd since earliest times, enabling settlements to grow. The most dramatic are at al-Kharj, southeast of Riyadh. This photograph shows one of the sinkholes in the mid-20th century, when the water was still near the surface. They have since been depleted by mechanical pumping.

ing towns dating from before the 3rd century. Residents of Najd and eastern Arabia today seem to trace their origins to tribes such as the Bani Hanifah that replaced the earlier residents when they moved into central and eastern Arabia during the four centuries before Muhammad's birth. The stories of the "vanished Arabs" may thus point to settled occupation of Lower Najd as a whole during the era of overland trade.

THE "AGE OF IGNORANCE"

WHATEVER THE ACHIEVEMENTS OF THE AGE OF OVERLAND trade, that era disappeared almost totally from the collective memory of the Arabs. One reason was the coming of Islam in 622. Muslim historians tended to ignore this period, dismissing the centuries immediately preceding the dawn of Islam as the *Jahiliyah*, or "Age of Ignorance." Historians use this term, which is derived from the root word *jahl*, to imply ignorance of Islam, but its core meaning is passion ungoverned by wisdom.

A century or so after the revelation of Islam, the *Jahiliyah* poets were recognized as a source of classical Arabic and worthy of linguistic research. Otherwise, the pre-Islamic Arabs were regarded by Muslim tradition as pagans who had turned their face from the One God of Abraham to worship various gods, many of them local, tribal or embodied in natural features, such as rocks or trees. The most obvious remains from the period, such as those of abandoned

The site of 'Ukaz, near Tayif, was renowned for the great annual fair held there in the pre-Islamic era. Desert poets recited their odes (qasidahs) celebrating the glorious deeds of times past, the qualities of princes, and the joys and hardships of desert life. The fair began on the first day of Dhu al-Qa'dah and lasted several weeks, during which the scattered nomads and settled people of Arabia could gather, without fear of bloodshed, to negotiate disputes, do business and exchange the news.

Madain Salih, were of importance only as examples of the destruction visited upon unbelievers as a consequence of their blasphemy and rejection of God's message as delivered to them through his messengers.

The *Jahiliyah* marked the end of several centuries of prosperity in Arabia, as overland trade fell off and caravan towns declined. The scene was set for this process during the 1st and 2nd centuries by the migration of various Arab tribes from the southwest into the Hijaz, the Syrian Desert, eastern Arabia and Oman, as well as Yemen. It is from this time that the collective memories represented by Arab traditions mostly begin. Byzantium, Abyssinia, Sasanian Persia and Yemen all became embroiled in conflicts in the peninsula, making this a period of political weakness in contrast to the previous centuries of prosperity. Finally, monotheistic faiths began to rival the old pagan Arabian deities and cults.

Three external factors caused the Arabian economic decline. First, the slow shift from overland trade to trade by sea caused commerce to shrink. In the 3rd century, economic problems in the Roman world brought on by inflation resulted in a sharp slump in demand for the luxury products of the Indian Ocean and Arabia Felix. Then, in the 4th century, the emperor Constantine adopted Christianity as the official religion of the Roman Empire. This led to a sharp drop in the use of incense for religious observances, choking a main engine of peninsular commerce.

The oasis towns along the caravan routes would have continued to play important roles in agricultural production during this period, even as their commercial and political power fell. The bigger settlements held large annual markets that drew both townspeople and nomads. They included Yathrib, Tayif, Khaybar, Wadi al-Qura (al-'Ula), Dawmat al-Jandal and al-Yamamah. Al-Hasa and Qatif continued to play important roles in production and exchange.

Some towns took on status as "sacred enclaves" where hostilities were suspended so that influential local families might settle tribal disputes. Their prestige derived from their position as the guardians of sanctuaries in places including Makkah, Tayif, Yathrib and Dawmat al-Jandal. The tribes themselves fell under increasing control of Yemeni, Persian and Byzantine rulers. The Kindah tribal confederation was appointed client ruler of the neighboring Arabs by the Himyarites of Yemen and, by the mid-5th century, came to dominate most of central Arabia.

To the north, the Arabs in the Syrian Desert fell under the domination of the rival Roman and Persian empires. Emperors in Byzantium, Rome's successor in the East, entrusted the border region of the western Syrian Desert to a series of warrior clans at the head of Arab tribal confederations. These acted as buffer "states" against Sasanian Persia's desert allies to the east. To counteract them, the Sasanians maintained the Lakhmids (commonly referred to as al-Manadhirah) as client lords of a powerful tribal confederation that intervened in the affairs of the tribes of eastern Arabia.

The Sasanians also attempted to control the commerce of the Gulf and Indian Ocean. They worked to strangle trade in the Red Sea, a rival artery of commerce controlled by the Byzantines from the 4th century. They involved themselves more deeply in eastern Arabia, campaigning across the peninsula at least once, and made alliances with the tribes controlling the land route through eastern Arabia and southern Najd. Finally, in 570, they took control of Yemen by sea. At the same time, they installed a governor in al-Hasa Oasis to enforce direct rule in eastern Arabia.

Arabia's people were both nomadic and settled, and tribal states as well as confederations continued to appear. A good example was Bani Hanifah of al-Yamamah where two settlements, al-Khidrimah (al-Kharj) and Hajr al-Yamamah (Riyadh), flourished before Islam as protectors of the overland trade and producers of grain and dates.

By the early 7th century, a new center of influence was emerging in western Arabia at Makkah, where the members of the Quraysh tribe skillfully used their status to weave a network of alliances among the other tribes. In doing so, they made Makkah an important commercial and political center. In 602, Persia and Byzantium became embroiled in a 25-year war that weakened both empires, to the advantage of the tribes of the northeast. They demonstrated their emerging strength around 605 when a coalition of Bakr ibn Wail tribes soundly defeated a Persian army in battle near the border of what today is Iraq—a foretaste of events to come.

RELIGION DURING THE *JAHILIYAH*

DURING THE *JAHILIYAH*, MANY INHABITANTS OF ARABIA, AND those of Makkah in particular, believed that Makkah and the Ka'bah were sacred. They revered the Ka'bah, held by Muslims to have been built by the Prophets Abraham and Ishmael, as the House of God. Traditional Arabian cults were pagan and animist, ascribing supernatural powers to natural features such as rocks and trees—and sanctuaries were dedicated to various idols. There were sanctified months during which hostilities were suspended and pilgrimage to the Ka'bah was performed.

The Prophet Muhammad was born into an extended merchant family of the Quraysh tribe of Makkah that had formed a commonwealth to protect its trade with Yemen and Syria. So, far from being a product of the desert, Islam was revealed to the Prophet in the essentially settled context of a commercial and cult center. The Quraysh tribe was able to confer divine sanction on its commonwealth at the Ka'bah, of which it was the protector, although the Ka'bah was now a sanctuary crowded with and surrounded by various idols.

With the revelation of Islam to the Prophet Muhammad, Makkah became the hub of a revolution in Arabian affairs that would influence much of the known world: the attempt to replace kinship loyalties with the universal ideal of the brotherhood of all Muslims, whatever their origins, before God.

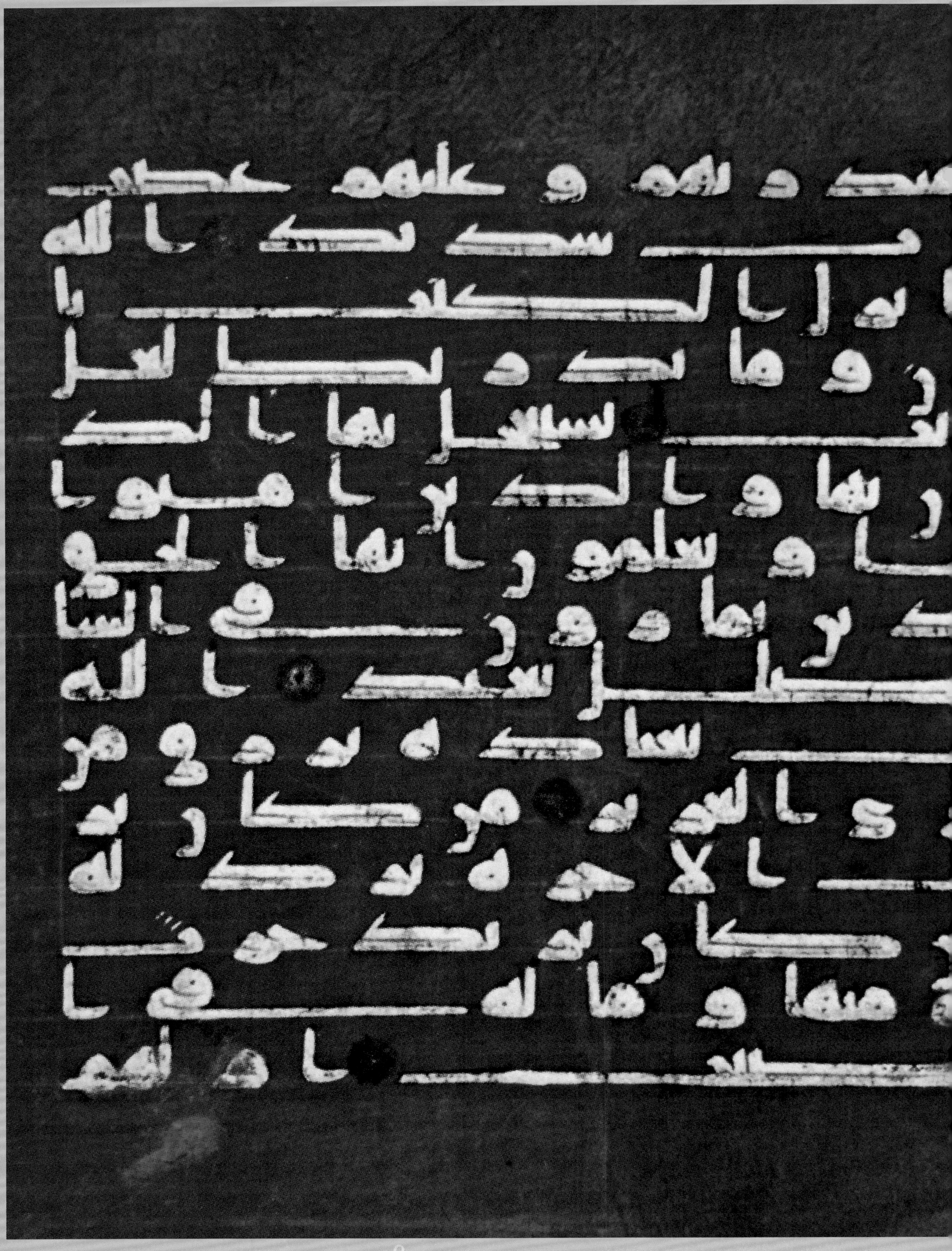

بسم الله ... و كله ... د وهو ...

الله ... سك ...

لا ... الكل ... ا

و ما ... د ... ها ...

لسا ... ها ... ها ...

ها ... ا ... ها ... ها ...

ها ... ها ... علمو ...

ها ... در ... احد ...

... ها ... ا

... ها ... و ... ه ...

... كا ... مر ... و ... الو ... الا ...

اله ... د ... د ... و ... كا ... د

... ها ... كو ... كار ... د ...

ا ... ه ... ها ... وها ...

لهم ... ا ... ا

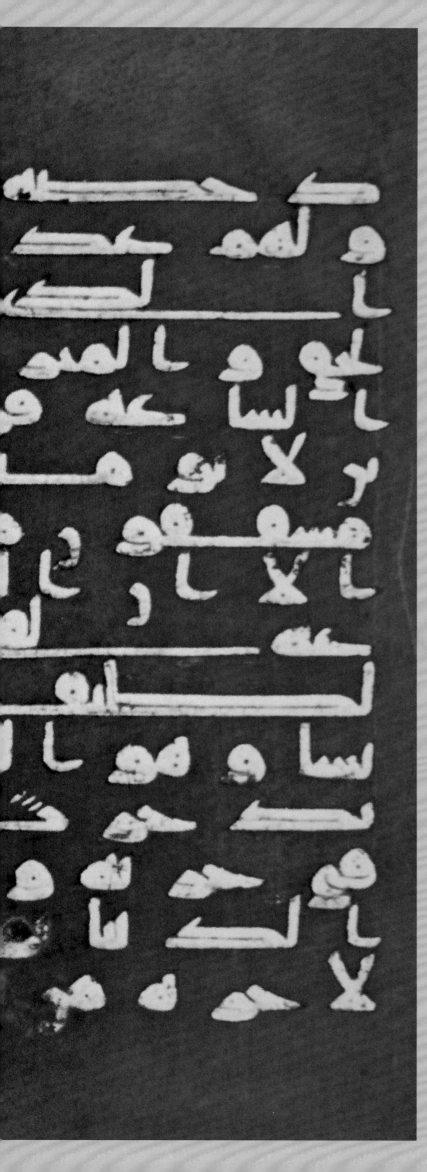

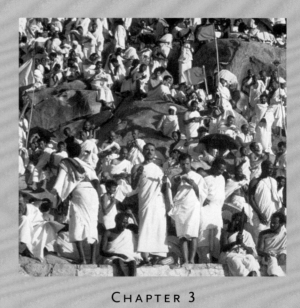

The Sacred Mosque in Makkah today can accommodate up to 1 million worshipers. Here, pilgrims perform the tawaf, circling the Ka'bah in one of the rituals of hajj.

58

CONTRIBUTIONS TO WORLD CIVILIZATION

WHAT IS SAUDI ARABIA'S MOST IMPORTANT CONTRIBUTION TO the world? Many people today might say, "Oil."

While it is true that the Kingdom contains the world's largest-known oil reserves, that resource will one day run out. Long after the last barrel of oil has been produced in Saudi Arabia, Muslims from around the world will continue making the *hajj*, the annual pilgrimage to Makkah and to the other sacred sites in its vicinity, as they have done for some 1,400 years. And they will still face in the direction of Makkah five times a day to say their prayers in Arabic, whatever their native tongue.

For Muslims the world over—and they number more than 1.2 billion people or a fifth of mankind—the territory today named Saudi Arabia is the heartland of Islam. Its great contributions to civilization are Islam and Arabic, the language in which the Quran, the Muslim scripture, was revealed to the Prophet Muhammad.

To understand the profound effect of Islam on Arabian society, and then on the world, one must look back to Arabia at the time when the faith was revealed. In 7th-century Arabia, the idea of a loyalty higher than one's extended family, or the tribe, was revolutionary. Identity and social position were determined by tribal affiliation. Survival in a difficult environment with very limited resources depended

Previous spread: (Left) This page from an early 9th-century Quran written in the kufic script is thought to have been commissioned by the Caliph al-Mamun (813-17). Written in gold on indigo-dyed parchment, it is a masterpiece of fine book production. (Right) In the central rite of the hajj, pilgrims "stand" at 'Arafat in worship and supplication.

on the solidarity of individuals who shared the same blood and descent. Conflicts over water rights and pasturage were endemic, as were the blood feuds they engendered, often lasting for generations. Tribesmen supported each other in adversity without question; banishment from the tribe was equivalent to a death sentence.

Tribal coalitions and alliances were not unknown, but they were commonly short-lived and did not affect tribal identities. The early history of the *ummah*, the community of believers, coincides with the story of the development of a Muslim identity that replaced tribal affiliation with loyalty to brothers and sisters in the faith. In many ways, this process was the extension of the tribal ideal of group solidarity to the entire Muslim community. In the process, Islam, first revealed to mankind in a small city in the western region of Arabia, became the universal religion it is today.

The Life of the Prophet Muhammad

MUHAMMAD IBN 'ABD ALLAH WAS BORN IN Makkah in or about the year 570. His father 'Abd Allah ibn 'Abd al-Muttalib died before Muhammad was born and his mother Aminah died when he was six—losses that gave him a lifelong concern for the plight of orphans.

Muhammad was raised first by his grandfather 'Abd al-Muttalib, chief of the Hashim clan of the tribe of Quraysh, and then by his uncle Abu Talib. When he was 25, he married a widow named Khadijah bint Khuwaylid, for whom he had worked as a commercial agent, organizing and even accompanying caravans to Syria. In the 40 years that preceded the revelation of Islam to him, Muhammad was known among his fellow Makkans for his honesty, virtue, modesty and wisdom. He was also known as one who disagreed with the concept of paganism and the accompanying worship of idols.

THE FIRST REVELATION
TRADITION RECORDS THE PRESENCE IN MAKKAH OF MONOTHEists called *hunafa*, who made a practice of going on retreat in caves on the surrounding mountainsides. Muhammad did this as well, setting aside one month a year for reflection. While he was on retreat in a cave on the slopes of Mount Hira overlooking Makkah, the Archangel Gabriel appeared to Muhammad holding forth a scroll and urging him to "Read." The year was 610.

Muhammad, who was illiterate, was terrified. He pleaded three times that he was unable to read. Gabriel then recited the words to Muhammad and Muhammad repeated them after him. These verses were the first five of what is now the 96th *surah* of the Quran:

> Read, in the name of your Lord who created,
> Created humanity from a clot of blood!
> Read, for your Lord is most generous,
> Who taught by the pen,
> Taught humanity what it knew not.

Shaken by his experience and doubting his senses, Muhammad returned to his home and confided in Khadijah, who questioned him closely about the circumstances. Convinced of the reality of what had occurred, and that the revelation was indeed divine, she reassured her husband. Other revelations followed at irregular intervals, asserting the Oneness of God, demanding that mankind abandon polytheistic beliefs and warning of severe punishments for those who did not hearken. These first revelations are short, densely worded and urgent.

For a time, Muhammad confided the continuing revelations only to his family and closest friends. After Khadijah, who was the first to accept the faith, early believers included Abu Bakr al-Siddiq, Muhammad's lifelong friend and the first man to accept his message, and Muhammad's cousin

TRIBES AT THE TIME OF
THE PROPHET
{ 570 – 632 }

'Ali ibn Abi Talib. Then followed Zayd, a slave Muhammad had freed and adopted as his son. Other early converts were 'Umar ibn al-Khattab and 'Uthman ibn 'Affan, who, like 'Ali, eventually succeeded Muhammad at the head of the *ummah*.

Three years after the first revelation, Gabriel conveyed to Muhammad God's command to preach openly. He began to call people to Islam, which means "submission"—submission to the will of God—and preach against polytheism publicly. Muhammad gained new adherents, and enemies, as news of him and his message began to spread throughout Arabia. Leaders of Quraysh became worried, for they were the custodians of the Ka'bah and the *haram*, the holy precinct surrounding it. While they had no objection to the idea of a new religion, they feared both for their authority and the loss of revenues from the cult center. They began to persecute Muhammad's followers.

In 615, Muhammad advised a number of his followers to seek refuge across the Red Sea with the Negus, the Christian ruler of Abyssinia, today's Ethiopia. Muhammad stayed in Makkah, where he was protected by his relationship to his uncle Abu Talib. His humbler followers, like the Abyssinian Bilal, the first to give the *adhan*—the call to prayer that summons the faithful to their devotions—suffered greatly.

PERSECUTION AND THE *HIJRAH*

MUHAMMAD'S REFUSAL TO CEASE PREACHING IN THE NAME OF the One God and attacking polytheism made his position in Makkah increasingly untenable. On the death of Abu Talib around 619, he lost the protection of the leader of the House of Hashim. His beloved wife Khadijah, another powerful source of comfort and support, died that same year. He considered seeking help in Tayif, in the mountains east of Makkah, but he was shunned and driven out by the devotees of the cult center there.

In 620, Muhammad met a group of men from one of the settled Arab tribes of Yathrib, a large oasis some 400 kilometers (250 miles) north of Makkah. Impressed by his message, they offered him their protection should he seek it. Two years later, fearing for the safety of his followers, he sent them to Yathrib to take refuge from their persecutors.

On the night of July 16, 622, Muhammad and his friend Abu Bakr left Makkah for Yathrib, closely followed by a detachment of Makkans bent on their death. They passed the night in a cave and while they slept a spider spun its web across the cave's mouth. Spotting the unbroken web, the Makkans rode on and Muhammad and Abu Bakr were able to elude their pursuers and reach Yathrib safely.

Muhammad's historic journey from Makkah to Yathrib is known as the *Hijrah*, a word that means "migration" or "exodus." In the tribal world, it has the stark connotation of breaking with one's kin group. Those who migrated from Makkah to Yathrib in 622 are called the *Muhajirun*, "those who made the *Hijrah*" or the "emigrants." Those who welcomed, accommodated and supported them in Yathrib are called the *Ansar*, or "supporters." Islamic tradition has

THE PRAYER RUG

According to the accounts of his contemporaries, the Prophet Muhammad either prayed on the bare ground or simply spread out his cloak to protect his clothing when he prayed. In later years, the custom of using a cloth or mat to protect the clothing while praying became widespread. By the 14th century, the *sajjadah*, or prayer rug, called *namazlık* in Turkish and *ja-yi namaz* in Persian, had become popular, although no examples from so early a date survive. These small rugs could be conveniently carried and used anywhere. Larger examples, called *saff*, woven with multiple *mihrabs*, were used in the home so the family could pray side by side. The finest materials were used to produce the famous prayer rugs like this 18th-century masterpiece from the little town of Gördes in eastern Turkey. The central portion depicts the *mihrab*, the niche in a mosque that indicates the *qiblah*, the direction of Makkah, toward which worshipers direct their prayers. Two columns support the *mihrab*, and a mosque lamp hangs at the apex of the arch.

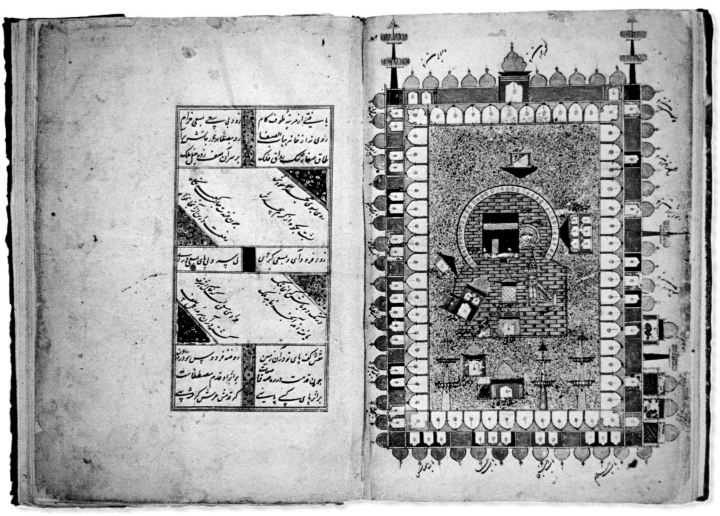

This little manuscript describes, in Persian verse, the history of the foundation of Makkah and the rites of the pilgrimage. The illustration shows the Ka'bah and Sacred Sanctuary. The manuscript, by an otherwise unknown author named Gulam 'Ali, was completed in Makkah in 1582.

lovingly preserved the names of both the *Muhajirun* and the *Ansar*. They were the nucleus of the first Muslim community and *ummah*, and a primary source for the teachings, deeds and sayings of the Prophet which reflect his way of life, or *sunnah*, and direct the lives of Muslims to this day.

The *Hijrah* marked the shift from a persecuted minority religion to an organized, autonomous Islamic community. Muslims very early recognized the *Hijrah* as the turning point in their history, and 622 was taken as the first year of the Muslim lunar calendar, known from the event with which it begins as the *Hijri* calendar.

THE FIRST MUSLIM COMMUNITY IN MADINAH

THE EARLIEST ISLAMIC POLITICAL DOCUMENT IS KNOWN AS the Constitution of Madinah, for Madinah was the name by which Yathrib became known after Muhammad's arrival. The full name in Arabic is *Madinat al-Nabi,* or "The City of the Prophet," and it is also known as *al-Madinah al-Munawwarah*, "The Enlightened City." Muhammad resided here until his death. The Constitution of Madinah, the text of which is preserved in one of the earliest biographies of the

Prophet, regulated relationships between the *Muhajirun,* the *Ansar* and the rest of the inhabitants of Madinah.

The constitution also defined the role of non-Muslims in the community. Three Jewish tribes formed part of the community. They were *dhimmi*s, people who were given a commitment of protection and cohabitation so long as they observed the laws. This established an important precedent for the treatment of subject people during the later Muslim conquests. Like the Muslims, they were subject to a yearly tax. They retained their status as non-Muslims, but were considered associate members of the *ummah*.

A major part of the constitution is concerned with what might be termed rules of engagement. The Muslim community of Madinah was on high alert because of the threat from Quraysh of Makkah. All internal disputes were to be resolved according to the teachings of God as conveyed and interpreted by His Messenger, Muhammad.

This Constitution of Madinah marked a radical break with the past. Faith, not blood relationship, defined the group. All members of the *ummah*, whatever their origins, were equal. Tribesmen who would not accept this new state of affairs were

THE FIVE PILLARS OF ISLAM

Faithful Muslims submit unreservedly to God's will and obey His precepts as set forth in the Quran and transmitted to mankind through the teachings of Muhammad, His Messenger. Muslims must accept five primary obligations which Islam imposes. These Five Pillars of Islam are: the profession of faith (*shahadah*), devotional worship or prayer (*salah*), obligatory alms-giving (*zakah*), fasting (*sawm*) and the pilgrimage to Makkah (*hajj*).

The *shahadah* is the acceptance and utterance of the statement, "There is no god but God; Muhammad is the Messenger of God"—in Arabic the euphonious "*La ilaha illa Allah; Muhammad rasul Allah.*" In this way, a Muslim expresses complete acceptance of, and total commitment to, the message of Islam.

The second pillar, *salah*, requires Muslims to pray five times daily—dawn, noon, afternoon, sunset and evening—while facing toward the Ka'bah, the House of God, in Makkah. Prayer is simple and personal, but also communal; the wording of the prayers and other parts of the ritual are set out in detail.

The *zakah*, the third pillar, enshrines the duty of social responsibility by which well-to-do Muslims must concern themselves about those less fortunate. It prescribes payments of fixed proportions of a Muslim's possession for the welfare of the community in general and for the needy in particular, whether Muslims or non-Muslims. All Muslims are also encouraged to make voluntary contributions to the needy called *sadaqah*.

The fourth pillar is fasting during Ramadan, the ninth month of the Muslim lunar year. Abstention from eating and drinking, as well as sexual continence, is obligatory every day between dawn and sunset. Ordained in the Quran, the fast is an act of deeply personal worship. Its object is the subjection of the passions and the purification of one's being so that the soul is brought nearer to God. Fasting is also an exercise in self-control and self-denial whereby one learns to appreciate the pangs of hunger that the poor often feel. Refraining from cursing, lying, cheating and abusing or harming others—behavior condemned in Islam—is further emphasized during Ramadan in consideration of the high spirituality of the month. Muslims break their fast at sunset and, later in the evening, perform voluntary nocturnal worship (*tarawih*) and throng the streets in moods at once festive and communal.

Those who are ill or on an arduous journey may fast another time. Those for whom fasting is impossible may forego it; they should give stipulated alms to the needy.

The last 10 days of Ramadan are particularly sacred. They include the anniversary of the night on which Muhammad received his first revelation from God—"the Night of Power"—and the appearance, on the final day, of the new moon announcing the end of Ramadan and the celebration of '*Id al-Fitr*, the "Feast of the Breaking of the Fast." Islam has instituted *zakat al-fitr*, a levy in the form of provisions or money for the poor.

The fifth pillar of Islam is the *hajj*. For those Muslims who are able to travel to Makkah, the pilgrimage is the peak of their religious life. The *hajj* is a worldwide migration of the faithful and a remarkable spiritual event that, according to Islamic tradition,

dates back to Abraham, was affirmed by Muhammad and systemized by Muhammad's own pilgrimage.

The *hajj* proper is made between the eighth and 13th days of Dhu al-Hijjah, the 12th month of the Muslim year. A Muslim approaches Makkah, bathes, trims nails and hair, discards jewelry and headgear, and puts on the *ihram* dress: two white, seamless garments for men, and a simple dress and headcovering for women, that symbolize purity. In donning it, pilgrims pronounce the *talbiyah*: "Here I am, O God, at Thy Service"—in Arabic "*Labbayk!*" They may then enter the *haram*, the sacred precinct surrounding Makkah, and then Makkah, where they perform the *tawaf*—the circling of the Ka'bah—and the *sa'y*—walking between two hills at al-Mas'a in Makkah. The *sa'y* is a reenactment of a frantic search for water by Hagar when she and Abraham's son Ishmael were left in the valley of Makkah until the Archangel Gabriel led them to the Well of Zamzam. All this can be part of the '*umrah*, or "lesser pilgrimage"; this is often a prelude to the *hajj*, but it may be performed separately any time of the year.

The major *hajj* rites begin on the eighth day of Dhu al-Hijjah when pilgrims pour out of Makkah to Mina where, as the Prophet did, they meditate overnight. The next day, they proceed to 'Arafat, farther outside Makkah, and pray and meditate in "the standing," a few precious hours of profound self-examination, supplication and penance. Some pilgrims also visit other pilgrims or the Mount of Mercy, where Muhammad gave his farewell sermon. The standing is the culmination of a Muslim's devotional life.

After sunset, the pilgrims move to Muzdalifah to gather pebbles for the "stoning of the devil" and then pray and sleep. The third day of the *hajj*, at Mina, they enact a repudiation of evil by throwing the pebbles at three pillars held by many to represent Satan. According to one tradition, it was in this area that Satan urged Abraham not to perform God's command to sacrifice his son Ishmael. '*Id al-Adha*, the worldwide Feast of Sacrifice, also begins at Mina. Pilgrims sacrifice animals to commemorate Abraham's willingness to sacrifice his son and to symbolize a Muslim's willingness to give up what is dearest.

Men now clip their hair or shave their heads and women clip a symbolic lock to mark partial deconsecration. They may also remove the *ihram* dress.

In Makkah, the rites are concluded by the *tawaf* of the return, the circling of the Ka'bah seven times, an act implying that all human activity must have God at the center. The pilgrims then worship in the courtyard of the Sacred Mosque at the Place of Abraham. They are now *hajjis*, those who have completed the *hajj*. Most also attempt to kiss, touch or salute the *Hajar al-Aswad*, the Black Stone of the Ka'bah, a fragment of polished rock revered as a sign sent by God and a remnant of the original structure built by Abraham and Ishmael. Many also make the *sa'y*.

Pilgrims return to Mina between the 11th and 13th days, cast their remaining pebbles at the three pillars and then make a farewell circling of the Ka'bah. Some may also visit the Mosque of the Prophet in Madinah before returning to their homes.

A European Muslim family in Jiddah gathers for the iftar, the meal served after sundown to break the fast of Ramadan.

THE *HIJRI* CALENDAR AND THE TWO FESTIVALS

In the 7th century, wrote the historian al-Biruni, the Caliph 'Umar ibn al-Khattab, who had conquered Persia and driven the Byzantines from Syria, found that administration of the new Islamic empire required extensive correspondence with his far-flung regional governors and generals. That, in turn, involved him in the problem of calendars; in attempting to date the correspondence, he learned that the various systems of dating then current were both complicated and linked to other religions and states. As they were both impractical and unacceptable for one reason or another, a new calendar system based on the advent of Islam was established.

After consulting with his companions, 'Umar decided to use the year of the *Hijrah*, the Prophet's emigration from Makkah to Madinah, as the starting point of the Islamic era and to begin the new calendar from the day of Muhammad's departure from Makkah: July 16, 622. Year One of the Islamic calendar thus corresponds to the years 622–23 of its Gregorian counterpart. The Western method of designating Islamic dates is by the abbreviation AH, for Anno Hegirae, or "Year of the *Hijrah*."

Relying on a number of passages in the Quran (*Surahs* ix: 36-37, and x: 5), 'Umar established the new Islamic calendar on the basis of a lunar year. This system contrasts with most other calendars. One lunar month, or the cycle between two new moons, contains 29 days, 12 hours, 44 minutes and 2.8 seconds. A lunar year of 12 months thus contains 354 days and 11/30 of a day.

The difference between the 354- or 355-day lunar year and the astronomical solar year of 365 and 1/4 days accounts for the difficulty of converting dates from the Islamic (*Hijri*) calendar to the Gregorian calendar and vice versa. One method is to use the following equation on the basis that every 32 Gregorian solar years are approximately equal to 33 Muslim lunar years.

$$GY = 622 + (32/33 \times AH) \quad \text{or} \quad AH = 33/32 \times (GY - 622)$$
(GY = GREGORIAN YEAR,   AH = HIJRAH YEAR)

It should be remembered that these formulas give only the year in which the corresponding year began. For example, AH 1426 began on February 10, 2005.

Some other guides for approximate conversion are: a Gregorian century equals 103 *Hijrah* years; and 100 *Hijrah* years equal 97 Gregorian years. The 12 months of the Islamic year are: Muharram, Safar, Rabi' al-Awwal (Rabi' I), Rabi' al-Thani (Rabi' II), Jumada al-Ula (Jumada I), Jumada al-Akhirah (Jumada II), Rajab, Sha'ban, Ramadan, Shawwal, Dhu al-Qa'dah and Dhu al-Hijjah.

In theory, the months contain 30 or 29 days alternately, with the odd-numbered months generally containing 30 days and the even-numbered months generally containing 29 days. However, the actual length of each month depends on when the new moon is sighted, as this marks the beginning of the month and the sighting of the next new moon marks its end.

The lunar year is completely unrelated to the seasons because each year begins roughly 11 days earlier in the Gregorian year than the previous one. Thus, any one of the months of the Islamic year may occur in any season. If your birthdate is Rajab 15, you might mark the occasion one time in July and 15 years later in February. As a result, schools in Saudi Arabia close for the summer holiday in any three consecutive months that may fall in that season; and Ramadan, the month of fasting, may occur in winter, spring, summer or autumn, making a complete cycle every 33 Gregorian years.

Similarly, Muslim festivals, unlike Christmas, for example, may occur in any season. In addition to the difference in timing, there are major differences with regard to festivals. In Western countries, holidays celebrate a variety of religious, historic, social and military events. In Saudi Arabia, a country that strictly follows the doctrines of Islam, the main holidays that are recognized and observed are the two religious feasts: 'Id al-Fitr and 'Id al-Adha.

'Id al-Fitr, or "The Festival of the Breaking of the Fast," occurs on the first day of the month of Shawwal and marks the end of Ramadan, the month of fasting. Like 'Id al-Adha, it is celebrated by public worship and exchanges of gifts and visits. As it marks the successful completion of God-ordained fasting, 'Id al-Fitr is a particularly joyous festival.

'Id al-Adha, or "The Festival of the Sacrifice," falls on the 10th day of Dhu al-Hijjah and marks the end of the hajj. It is celebrated with the sacrifice of a sheep or goat—or sometimes, if the family can afford it, a camel or a cow—which is then divided among the family offering the sacrifice, and relatives, friends and the poor. Public worship is also performed by the whole community. Like 'Id al-Fitr, in most countries the festival lasts three days. During this time, most people dress in new clothes, exchange presents, visit friends and relatives, and may serve special foods and sweets.

Both festivals are primarily religious occasions, designed for expression of communal solidarity as well as individual satisfaction and fulfillment at having carried out two major duties of the faith. They are characterized by the giving of alms to the poor and generous gifts (generally of money) to one's younger relatives.

Beginning in 2005, Saudi Arabia also began observing National Day as a public holiday. This holiday, which commemorates the unification of the country under the name of the Kingdom of Saudi Arabia, follows neither the Hijri nor the Gregorian calendar, but rather the solar zodiacal calendar.

In fact, King 'Abd al-'Aziz issued a Royal Decree on September 19, 1932, announcing the new name of the country and chose the first day of Libra as the day it would take effect. He picked that date because the sign and the symbol of Libra, the scales, symbolize justice and equality—two of the principles closest to his heart. The date, which stays virtually the same every year, also was convenient for foreign governments and diplomats, making it easier for them to send congratulatory messages to the Government of Saudi Arabia and for envoys abroad to hold receptions.

The solar zodiacal calendar is also used in Saudi Arabia to define the government's fiscal year. Beginning with 1989, it was decided that each fiscal year should commence on 11 Capricorn, corresponding to January 1, and end on 10 Capricorn of the following year, December 31. Since January 1, 1989, fiscal years have corresponded exactly with Gregorian calendar years.

Gregorian calendar indicated in black type

OCTOBER 2005

RAMADAN 1426

Hijri calendar names and dates in red type

Friday, or yawm al-Jum'ah, is the day of congregational prayer for Muslims the world over.

yawm al-Sabt Saturday	yawm al-Ahad Sunday	yawm al-Ithnayn Monday	yawm al-Thulatha Tuesday	yawm al-Arba'a Wednesday	yawm al-Khamis Thursday	yawm al-Jum'ah Friday
1	2	3	☾ NEW MOON 1 / 4	2 / 5	3 / 6	4 / 7
5 / 8	6 / 9	7 / 10	8 / 11	9 / 12	10 / 13	11 / 14
12 / 15	13 / 16	14 / 17	15 / 18	16 / 19	17 / 20	18 / 21
19 / 22	20 / 23	21 / 24	22 / 25	23 / 26	24 / 27	25 / 28
26 / 29	27 / 30	28 / 31	☾ NEW MOON 1 / 'Id al-Fitr	2	3	4

These are the last three days of the month of Sha'ban, which is the 8th month of the Hijri calendar.

The Hijri month begins and ends with the rising of the new moon.

'Id al-Fitr is joyously celebrated throughout the Muslim world when the new moon is sighted at the end of Ramadan, ending the month of fasting.

These are the first days of the month of Shawwal, the 10th month of the Muslim calendar.

65

Masjid al-Fath *(the "Mosque of Conquest") outside Madinah was built by the Umayyad Caliph 'Umar II (717–20) to mark the site of a Muslim victory over the pagans of Makkah. The mosque was erected on the western slope of Jabal Sil' on the site where the Prophet's tent was pitched during the battle.*

expelled. This proved the case with the Jewish tribes, whose relationship with the Muslim immigrants deteriorated, ending in open conflict. Survivors were forced out of the oasis.

Another major step affirming the status of the emerging *ummah* came after drafting the Constitution of Madinah. It was the composition of a series of letters that the Prophet sent to the rulers of Persia, Byzantium and Ethiopia and the Governor of Egypt, inviting them to embrace Islam. None accepted the invitation.

BATTLES WITH QURAYSH

IN 624, THE MUSLIM FORCES CONFRONTED THE MAKKAN Confederation at the Battle of Badr, southwest of Madi-

nah. Outnumbered three to one, the Muslims managed to achieve a resounding victory over the Makkans, gaining much prestige among the tribes. A Makkan force of 3,000 men defeated the Muslims the following year at Uhud, a ridge outside Madinah, where Muhammad himself was wounded. It is a tribute to his leadership and authority that this loss did not dishearten his followers.

Three years later, the Makkans attacked Madinah with 10,000 men. This was the famous Battle of the Ditch, in which the Muslims introduced a new defense. They dug a trench too wide for Makkan cavalry to clear without being exposed to archers in Madinah. After a 40-day siege, the Makkans were forced to withdraw.

THE FIRST ATTEMPT TO REVISIT MAKKAH

IN 628, MUHAMMAD GATHERED HIS FOLLOWERS AND MOVED toward Makkah to visit the Holy Ka'bah and perform *'umrah*, an abridged form of *hajj*. Quraysh refused him entry and negotiated a treaty at a place called al-Hudaybiyah. The treaty allowed Muslims to come to Makkah to perform *'umrah* for three days the following year and the adversaries agreed to a 10-year truce. Makkan caravans were granted the right to pass freely through Muslim territory. In return, the Makkans recognized the Muslim community of Madinah as an autonomous and legitimate political entity.

Muhammad and his followers revisited Makkah in 629 to perform *'umrah*. The prayers and actions of the Prophet at this time and at the *hajj* he performed three years later established these rites for all time.

In 630, the Makkans reneged on the treaty reached at al-Hudaybiyah and Muhammad took the city without bloodshed. Since Makkah capitulated without fighting, it was granted immunity from looting. This established a legal precedent for dealing with enemies who did not take up arms against the Muslim armies. Muhammad destroyed the idols inside and around the Ka'bah, restoring it to its Abrahamic purity.

When Muhammad was capturing Makkah, two of the city's shrewdest leaders, 'Amr ibn al-'As and Khalid ibn al-Walid, embraced Islam. This was a momentous event, for in a few years these two men would lead the armies that conquered much of the Byzantine Empire and all of Sasanian Persia—the superpowers of the era. 'Amr ibn al-'As and Khalid ibn al-Walid, the latter known as the "Sword of Islam," were generals and strategists who rank with the world's greatest. Their victories against the vastly superior professional armed forces of the Byzantines and Sasanians seem in retrospect little short of miraculous. 'Amr ibn al-'As conquered Palestine, Egypt and Libya, while Khalid ibn al-Walid defeated the Sasanian army in Iraq and took Damascus from the Byzantines. Once again, Muhammad used his skills as a leader and his authority to facilitate the effective incorporation of these new Muslims into the *ummah*. If Islam was to survive and prosper, it needed as many competent adherents as possible, and they had to be accepted as equals to the earlier converts to win their support.

THE DEATH OF THE PROPHET

WHEN MUHAMMAD DIED IN MADINAH AT MIDDAY ON JUNE 8, 632, after a short illness, the Muslim community suddenly lost its Prophet, leader, friend, guide and counselor. There would be no more divine revelations to guide the *ummah*.

Some refused to believe that Muhammad could be dead. Finally, Abu Bakr, his closest friend and the father of 'Aishah, Muhammad's third wife who had attended him on his deathbed, stepped forward. He addressed the distraught crowd that had gathered before their humble dwelling with the words, "Whoever worshiped Muhammad, let him know

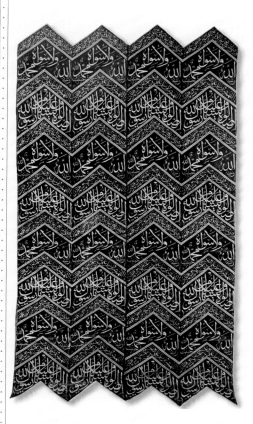

THE RIGHTLY GUIDED CALIPHS

The first four caliphs, the successors of the Prophet Muhammad as leaders of the *ummah*, presided over the critical period which saw the transformation of the Muslim state from a simple community of believers in the Arabian Peninsula to a world empire. The top band of beautifully rendered calligraphy on this woven silk brocade panel, produced in Ottoman Turkey in the 17th century, contains a benediction on those four "Rightly Guided" caliphs – Abu Bakr, 'Umar, 'Uthman and 'Ali – and their companions, while the second, broader band asserts the Uniqueness of God. The next two bands call down blessings on all the prophets and on the Prophet Muhammad.

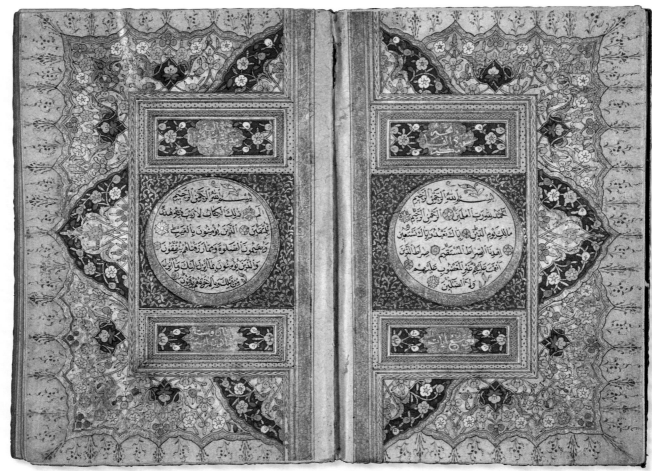

The skill and technical competence of Ottoman calligraphers and illuminators are reflected in the opening pages of this 17th-century Ottoman Quran.

THE HOLY QURAN

The core of Islam's divine message is kept safe and intact in a book: the Holy Quran. Muslims consider the Quran (sometimes spelled "Koran") to be the Word of God as transmitted by the Archangel Gabriel, in Arabic, through the Prophet Muhammad. It is the final revelation, as Muhammad is regarded as the final prophet—"the Seal of the Prophets." The Muslim view is that the Quran supersedes and seals earlier revelations; it is regarded as their summation and completion. As expressed in Verse 62 of *Surah 2, al-Baqarah* ("The Heifer"):

> *Those who believed [in the Quran],*
> *And those who followed the Jewish [scriptures],*
> *And the Christians and the Sabians —*
> *Any who believed in God*
> *And the Last Day,*
> *And did righteousness,*
> *Shall have their reward*
> *With their Lord: on them*
> *Shall be no fear, nor shall they grieve.*

In a very real sense, the Quran is the mentor of millions of Muslims, Arab and non-Arab alike. It shapes their everyday life, anchors them to a unique system of law and inspires them by its guiding principles. For some 1,400 years, this Holy Text has illuminated the lives of Muslims with its eloquent message of uncompromising monotheism, human dignity, righteous living, individual responsibility and social justice. For countless millions, it has been the single most important force in guiding their religious, social and cultural lives. The Quran is the cornerstone on which the edifice of Islamic civilization has been built.

The text of the Quran was delivered orally by the Prophet Muhammad to his followers as it was revealed to him. The first verses were revealed in or about 610 and the last revelation dates from the last year of his life, 632. Muhammad's followers at first committed the Quran to memory and then, as instructed by him, to writing. Although the entire contents of the Quran, the placement of its verses and the arrangement of its chapters date back to the Prophet, as long as he lived he continued to receive revelations. Consequently, the Holy Text could only be collected as a single corpus after the death of Muhammad.

The contents of the Quran differ in substance and arrangement from the Old and New Testaments. Instead of presenting a straight historical narrative, as do the Gospels and the historical books of the Old Testament, the Quran treats, in allusive style, spiritual and practical as well as historical matters.

The Quran is divided into 114 *surahs*, or chapters, and the *surah*s are conventionally assigned to two broad categories:

those revealed at Makkah and those revealed at Madinah. The *surahs* revealed at Makkah at the beginning of Muhammad's mission tend to be short; they stress, in highly moving language, the eternal themes of the unity of God, the necessity of faith, the punishment of those who stray from the right path and the Last Judgment, when all man's actions and beliefs will be judged. The *surahs* revealed at Madinah are longer, often deal in detail with specific legal, social or political situations, and sometimes can only be properly understood with a full knowledge of the circumstances in which they were revealed.

The *surahs* are divided into *ayahs*, or verses, and, for purposes of pedagogy and recitation, the Quran as a whole is divided into 30 parts. These, in turn, are divided into short sections of nearly equal length to facilitate study and memorization.

The *surahs* themselves vary in length. The longest, *Surah 2*, has 282 verses; the shortest, *Surahs 103, 108 and 110*, have only three. With some exceptions, the *surahs* are arranged in the Quran in descending order of length, the longest at the beginning and the shortest at the end. The major exception to this arrangement is the opening *surah*, "*al-Fatihah.*" It contains seven verses and serves as an introduction to the entire revelation:

> In the Name of God, the Merciful, the Compassionate.
> Praise be to God, Lord of the Worlds;
> The Merciful, the Compassionate;
> Master of the Day of Judgment;
> Thee only do we worship, and Thee only we ask for help.
> Guide us to the straight path,
> The path of those on whom Thou has bestowed grace; not the path of those who earned Thine anger nor of those who had gone astray.

Non-Muslims are often struck by the range of styles found in the Quran. Passages of impassioned beauty are no less common than vigorous narratives. The sublime "Verse of the Throne" is perhaps one of the most famous:

> God—There is no god but He,
> The Living, the Self-subsisting;
> Slumber seizes Him not, neither sleep;
> To Him belongs all that is
> In the heavens and the earth;
> Who is there that can intercede with Him
> Save by His permission?
> He knows what lies before them
> And what is after them,
> While they encompass nothing of His knowledge
> Except such as He wills;
> His Throne encompasses the heavens and earth;
> And their preservation wearies Him not;
> He is the Most High, the All-Glorious.

Muslims regard the Quran as untranslatable. The language in which it was revealed—Arabic—is inseparable from its message and Muslims everywhere, no matter what their native tongue, must learn Arabic to read the Sacred Book and to perform their worship. Translations of the Quran are, of course, available in many languages. However, these versions are regarded as interpretations rather than translations, partly because the Arabic language, extraordinarily concise and allusive, is impossible to translate in a mechanical, word-for-word way. The inimitability of the Quran has crystallized in the Muslim view of *i'jaz*, or "impossibility," which holds that the style of the Quran, being divine, cannot be imitated.

It must also be remembered that the Quran was originally transmitted orally to the faithful and that the Holy Text is not meant to be read only in silence. From the earliest days, it has always been recited aloud or, more accurately, chanted. As a result, several traditional means of chanting, or intoning, the Quran were found side by side. These methods carefully preserved the elaborate science of reciting the Quran, with all its intonations and its cadence and punctuation. As the exact pronunciation was important, and learning it took years, special schools were founded to be sure that no error would creep in as the traditional chanting methods were handed down. It is largely owing to the existence of these traditional methods of recitation that the text of the Quran was preserved without error. As the script in which the Quran was first written down indicated only the consonantal skeleton of the words, oral recitation was an essential element in the transmission of the text.

Because the circumstances of each revelation were thought necessary to correct interpretation, the community, early in the history of Islam, concluded that it was imperative to gather as many traditions as possible about the life and actions of the Prophet so that the Quran might be more fully understood. These traditions not only provided the historical context for many of the *surahs*—thus contributing to their more exact explication—but also contained a wide variety of subsidiary information on the practice, life and legal rulings of the Prophet and his companions.

This material became the basis for what is called the *sunnah*, or "practice" of the Prophet, his deeds, utterances and *taqrir* (unspoken approval). Together with the Quran, the *sunnah*, as embodied in the canonical collections of traditions, the *hadith*, became the basis for the *shari'ah*, the sacred law of Islam.

Unlike Western legal systems, the *shari'ah* makes no distinction between religious and civil matters. It is the codification of God's Law, and it concerns itself with every aspect of social, political, economic and religious life. Islamic law is thus different from any other legal system; it differs from canon law in that it is not administered by a church hierarchy. In Islam, there is nothing that corresponds to a "church" in the Christian sense. Instead, there is the *ummah*—the community of the believers—whose cohesion is guaranteed by the sacred law. Every action of the pious Muslim, therefore, is determined by the Quran, by precedents set by the Prophet and by the practice of the early community of Islam as enshrined in the *shari'ah*.

No description, however, can fully capture the overwhelming importance of the Quran to Muslims. Objectively, it is the central fact of the Islamic faith, the Word of God, the final and complete revelation, the foundation and framework of Islamic law, and the source of Islamic thought, language and action. To a degree almost incomprehensible in the West, it shapes and colors the thoughts, emotions and values of the devout Muslim from birth to death.

that Muhammad is dead, but whoever worshiped God, let him know that God lives and dies not!"

THE QUESTION OF SUCCESSION

MUHAMMAD HAD MADE NO FORMAL WRITTEN OR VERBAL statement to designate his successor, so it was vital to settle the question of leadership quickly. That evening, the Prophet's followers, closest friends and relatives gathered to discuss the succession. Among them were Abu Bakr, 'Umar ibn al-Khattab, 'Uthman ibn 'Affan of the clan of Umayyah, and the Prophet's son-in-law and cousin 'Ali ibn Abi Talib. All were related to Muhammad either by blood or by marriage, or both, and all had been among the earliest to embrace Islam.

After a lengthy discussion, 'Umar clasped Abu Bakr's hand, signifying that he was his choice for the head of the *ummah*. The others followed suit. The fact that Abu Bakr had taken the Prophet's place as leader of the communal prayers during Muhammad's last illness was a deciding factor in his election.

Abu Bakr was called simply *khalifat rasul Allah,* "successor to the Messenger of God." Anglicized as "caliph," *khalifah* designated the political leader of the *ummah* until the institution of the caliphate was abolished by Mustafa Kamal Ataturk, the President of Turkey, in 1924.

THE UNIFICATION OF ARABIA AND EXPANSION

THE MUSLIMS HAD CONSOLIDATED THEIR POSITION IN MADI-nah and Makkah during Muhammad's lifetime. In the wake of his death, the main danger to the *ummah* came from the tribes. Several tribes had been allies of Quraysh, while others had shown their loyalty to Muhammad. Alliances between nomadic tribes were personal, between leaders, and by custom such agreements terminated on the death of those who had made them. When Muhammad died, a number of important tribes in the Arabian Peninsula revoked their alliances with the Muslims. This is known as the *riddah,* or "apostasy."

'Amr ibn al-'As and Khalid ibn al-Walid led Muslim armies in a brilliant series of campaigns to defeat the most recalcitrant tribes. They made alliances with some, while others voluntarily accepted Islam. In a remarkably short time, just six months, the peninsula was united for the first time in history under a single authority, the successor of the Prophet.

Capitalizing on the peninsula's unification and following the last wishes of the Prophet, Abu Bakr mobilized the tribes under renowned Muslim commanders against the Byzantine and Persian empires. He received news of the first victory over the Byzantines at Ajnadin, about 30 kilometers (18 miles) west of Jerusalem, shortly before his death in 634.

One of Abu Bakr's significant contributions to the legacy of Islam was the compilation of the complete written text of the Quran. This sacred revelation that forms the backbone of the faith had been memorized and kept in the

A calligraphic carving on an Ottoman-built façade in the Sacred Mosque in Makkah commemorates the leadership of Abu Bakr, the first caliph, who demonstrated the viability of a Islamic state to the empires of the Persians and Byzantines.

minds and hearts of the companions of the Prophet, and in some cases written down on whatever materials were at hand. Worried that verses might be lost as those who had memorized them died, Abu Bakr ordered the collection of the text in a written format.

Under Abu Bakr's successor 'Umar, the Byzantine army was annihilated near the Yarmuk River in Palestine. The wealthy towns of Syria surrendered under favorable terms almost without resistance, and in 638 'Umar entered Jerusalem, alone and simply clad, astonishing a populace used to the pomp of the Byzantine emperors. He was welcomed by the Patriarch Sophronios and granted lenient terms to the city, guaranteeing that the Christian churches would not be destroyed or taken over by the Muslims. The pact 'Umar made with the people of Jerusalem became the model for the treatment of populations that peacefully surrendered to the Muslim armies.

While in Palestine, 'Umar organized the administration of the empire. He set up a pension scheme for the conquering warriors and their families and organized taxation of the conquered lands in accordance with the practice of the Prophet. Christians and Jews were allowed freedom of worship and formed protected communities governed under their own laws. 'Umar retained local administrations, and for some years the languages of administration continued to be Greek in former Byzantine provinces, Coptic in Egypt and Pahlavi in former Sasanian provinces.

In the spring of 637, the Muslims won a major victory over the Sasanians at al-Qadisiyah, near Ctesiphon in modern-day Iraq. In 642, a key victory at Nihavand in western Iran added all of Persia to the Muslim empire. The same year, 'Amr ibn al-'As captured Alexandria on the Egyptian coast, the commercial hub and the key to naval control of

The Muslim army captured the ancient city of Ctesiphon, located on the Tigris River, in 637. The victory helped pave the way for expansion into Mesopotamia. The city's vaulted reception hall boasts the largest single span of brickwork in the world.

the Mediterranean. From there, he went on to capture the rest of the country.

'Umar was assassinated by a non-Muslim Persian slave in 644 and an advisory council chose 'Uthman to succeed him. Under 'Uthman, what is now Libya in North Africa and Armenia in Central Asia were added to the growing Islamic state. 'Uthman, through his cousin Mu'awiyah ibn Abi Sufyan, the governor of Syria, established an Arab navy that fought a series of important engagements against the Byzantines.

'Uthman's most enduring legacy was to standardize the text of the Quran as revealed to the Prophet. Realizing that the original message from God might be inadvertently distorted by textual variants as the Muslim state expanded into non-Arabic-speaking territories, he appointed a com-mittee to collect the canonical verses and destroy variant recensions. The result was the text that is accepted to this day throughout the Muslim world.

THE PARTISANS OF 'ALI

THESE SUCCESSES WERE QUALIFIED BY ADMINISTRATIVE WEAK-nesses. 'Uthman was accused of showing favoritism to his own clan of Quraysh—the House of Umayyah. Making use of these allegations, rioters broke into 'Uthman's house and killed him. This opened the first serious rift in the *ummah*, the consequences of which reverberate to this day.

At issue was the legitimacy of the caliphate of 'Ali ibn Abi Talib, the Prophet Muhammad's cousin and son-in-law, and 'Uthman's chosen successor. The House of Umayyah, which included 'Uthman's cousin Mu'awiyah, the powerful Governor of Syria, refused to recognize 'Ali as the legitimate caliph. The conflict came to a head in 657 at Siffin, near the Euphrates River, where 'Ali and his partisans confronted Mu'awiyah and his powerful army. Unwilling to spill the blood of fellow Muslims, 'Ali agreed to submit their differences to arbitration. The arbitration went against him and Mu'awiyah was chosen as caliph.

Later, dissatisfaction among 'Ali's supporters evolved into the idea that 'Ali should have been Muhammad's immediate successor and that he had been unfairly passed over three times in favor of men whom they believed had lesser claims. Thus, the schism of Islam into *Sunni* and *Shi'i* can be dated to Siffin.

The *Sunnis*, or *ahl al-sunnah wa l-jam'ah*, "the people of the Prophet's custom and community," believe the caliph is Muhammad's successor only as head of the community and that those elected caliphs after the death of the Prophet—

Abu Bakr, 'Umar, 'Uthman and 'Ali—were the right selection by the *ummah* at the right time and in the right order. The *Shi'is* (from *shi'at 'Ali*, "partisans of 'Ali") believe the caliphate, which they call the Imamate, is non-elective and that the legitimate head of the Muslim community must be a descendant of Muhammad. They therefore believe that the Imamate, after the death of the Prophet, should have been confined to 'Ali, his children and their progeny. They consider any exception a violation of the divine right given to 'Ali and his descendants.

The *Sunnis* consider the caliph a guardian of the *shari'ah*, the religious law, and his major duty to ensure that society is regulated accordingly. For the *Shi'is*, the imam inherits the Prophet's spiritual knowledge and the ability to interpret the *shari'ah* in its light.

Another faction was born out of the conflict at Siffin: those who refused to recognize either party. They withdrew support from either Mu'awiyah or 'Ali, considering the caliphate to be open to any observant Muslim of sound

The walls of al-Ukhaydir, an Umayyad castle in the Iraqi desert 45 kilometers (28 miles) southwest of Karbala, date to the mid-8th century. They are 21 meters (69 feet) high, and enclose living quarters, a mosque and a bath.

The Umayyad caliphs never lost their nostalgia for life in the desert and spent their leisure hours hunting and hawking as their forefathers had done.

mind and body. They are called Kharijites, from the Arabic word *khawarij,* meaning "those who opt out."

THE UMAYYADS

'ALI HAD MOVED FROM MADINAH TO KUFAH IN IRAQ IN 656 and he was assassinated there by a Kharijite in 661. His death marked the end of the Rightly Guided caliphs. The Kufans proclaimed 'Ali's son Hasan caliph, but Hasan relinquished his rights to Mu'awiyah, who had been proclaimed caliph in Jerusalem the previous year and who now was recognized by most Muslims as the legitimate ruler. Mu'awiyah founded a new dynasty, the Umayyads, named after the clan of Quraysh to which he belonged.

Mu'awiyah moved the capital of the Muslim state from Madinah to Damascus, an event with great symbolic and practical significance. Damascus was a bustling, cosmopolitan city filled with magnificent classical buildings and with a large Christian, Aramaic-speaking population. There, secular affairs and the administration of what, by then, was a large empire began to dominate public life. This was sometimes at the expense of religious concerns, a development that disturbed devout Muslims.

However, Mu'awiyah never forgot his religious duties as leader of the *ummah* or his Arabian origins, and most of his successors followed suit. They built mosques and improved the administrative and judicial systems, while exerting great efforts to expand the Muslim state and spread Islam.

On a more worldly side, the Umayyad rulers established schools, patronized scientists and supported poets. They built magnificent palaces and hunting lodges in the Syrian steppe, where they could escape the crowded cities to hawk, entertain their companions and listen nostalgically to recitations of pre-Islamic poetry. Mu'awiyah himself is credited with editing the famous collection of seven pre-Islamic odes later called the *Mu'allaqat*. This concern with preserving links with the Arabian past while adapting to the urban culture of the late antique world typifies the Umayyad period. In many ways, the Umayyad caliphs ruled like tribal *shaykh*s.

Mu'awiyah maintained the unity of the empire, which by now stretched from Libya to the Oxus River on the northern border of Afghanistan, and established an administration to govern it. But he did not solve the still-simmering discontent of the *Shi'i*s. Nor did he defuse an emerging threat of discontent among the *mawali*, the non-Arab converts to Islam, who felt socially and economically excluded from the privileges enjoyed by Muslims of pure Arab descent. When Mu'awiyah died in 680, at the age of almost 80, after extracting recognition of

The Dome of the Rock in Jerusalem – completed around 691 – stands next to al-Masjid al-Aqsa (the "Farthest Mosque"), Islam's third holiest place and the location from which Prophet Muhammad is believed to have ascended on his nocturnal journey to Heaven. The Dome of the Rock is the earliest surviving example of Islamic architecture.

his son Yazid as heir from his advisory council (*majlis al-shura*), this discontent boiled over.

The *Shi'is* refused to recognize Yazid's legitimacy and urged 'Ali's son Husayn to claim the caliphate by force. On October 10, 680, Yazid's army confronted Husayn and his small band of family members and other followers at Karbala, not far from Kufah. Husayn refused to surrender and made a stand against the Umayyad troops. In the ensuing battle, Husayn met his fate.

The Umayyads had crushed a rebellion. However, they sowed the seeds not only of their own eventual destruction, but also of a distrust of temporal authority among Muslims that persists to this day. The death of the descendants of the Prophet at the hands of a leader of the *ummah* outraged public opinion. Such tragedies would not occur, many devout Muslims reasoned, if the state were ruled in accordance with the teachings of the Prophet.

In 683, the Umayyad army invaded Arabia, sacking Madinah and attacking Makkah, where a rival claimant to the caliphate held out with his supporters. The contender, 'Abd Allah ibn al-Zubayr, was closely related to the Prophet and had played a leading role in the conquests of Egypt and North Africa. Only the death of Yazid saved the city. The bloodshed in the *haram* and the damage to the Ka'bah appalled the Muslim community, increasing opposition to Umayyad rule. The Umayyads also faced an insurrection by the *mawali* who had joined forces led by Mukhtar ibn Abi 'Ubaid, a man who was fighting in the name of another son of 'Ali, and they lost a major battle at the Khazir River near Mosul in 686. Ibn al-Zubayr sent his brother to deal with Mukhtar, who was killed at Kufah in 687.

The Umayyad Caliph 'Abd al-Malik ibn Marwan finally defeated and killed Ibn al-Zubayr in 692 and the long civil war—which had come close to destroying the Arab empire—was brought to a close. Although 'Abd al-Malik did not solve the root problems of such dissent, he restored unity to the empire and implemented several important initiatives. In a notable departure from past practice, he made Arabic the language of administration. He also set up a postal system and reformed the coinage. He replaced coins showing the images of Byzantine and Sasanian rulers with those bearing the name of the Commander of the Faithful and Arabic inscriptions asserting the unity of God. The regime's architecture was one outward sign of its successes. 'Abd al-Malik built the Dome of the Rock in Jerusalem, the oldest surviving work of Islamic architecture.

The end of civil strife meant attention could be turned again to expansion. This second wave of conquests lasted until 751 and took the Arabs into new territory, far from their supply bases in Syria, Egypt and Iraq. On a single day in 711, the Caliph al-Walid ibn 'Abd al-Malik was informed of the conquest of Spain; the conquest of Punjab in India, adding what is now Afghanistan and Pakistan to the empire; and the conquest of Central Asia, an area comprising the

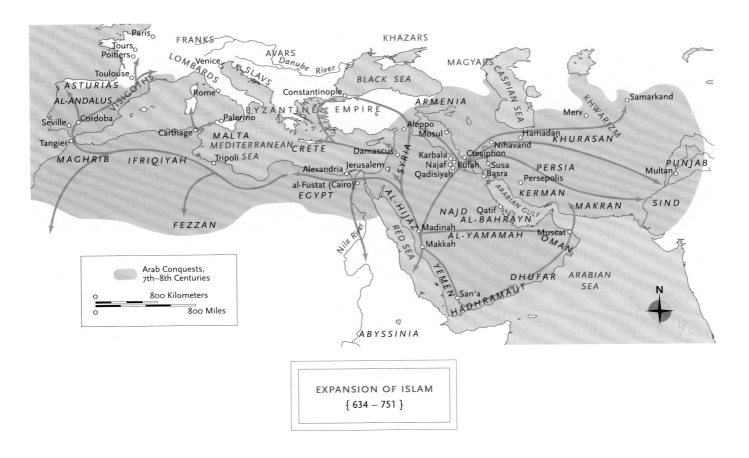

MALTA

EXPANSION OF ISLAM
{ 634 – 751 }

Arab Conquests,
7th–8th Centuries

800 Kilometers

800 Miles

present-day states of Turkmenistan, Uzbekistan, Tajikistan and Kyrgyzstan. The Arab Empire now stretched from the shores of the Atlantic and beyond the Jaxartes River to the borders of China. These territorial acquisitions brought the Arabs into contact with previously unknown ethnic groups who embraced Islam and would later influence the course of Islamic history, particularly the Berbers of North Africa and the Turks in Transoxania (today's southern Kazakhstan and Uzbekistan) in the east.

In spite of their accomplishments, during the 90-year period of their leadership the Umayyads rarely shook off their empire's reputation as *mulk* — that is, a worldly kingdom. In the last years of the dynasty, opponents formed a secret organization devoted to pressing the claims to the caliphate put forward by a descendant of al-'Abbas ibn 'Abd al-Mutallib, an uncle of the Prophet, from which the new dynasty would draw its name. In 750, this group routed the Umayyad army on the banks of the Greater Zab in Iraq.

A single member of the Umayyad clan named 'Abd al-Rahman ibn Mu'awiyah ibn Hisham survived, finally making his way to Spain. There, in al-Andalus, he founded a brilliant continuation of the Umayyad dynasty that ruled for almost 300 years.

The 'Abbasids

THE 'ABBASID REVOLUTION WAS NOT SIMPLY A CASE OF ONE dynasty supplanting another. It represented the triumph

of an idea: the universality of the *ummah*. What had begun as the faith of the Arabic-speaking followers of the Prophet in Makkah and Madinah in the Hijaz was now the common creed of Arab and non-Arab Muslims alike in a huge empire. This empire included a bewildering number of languages, cultures and territories, all with ancient cultural and intellectual traditions. The establishment of a *pax Islamica* resulted in an explosion of creative energy centered in the new capital of the Muslim world — Baghdad.

Baghdad was founded in 763 by Abu Ja'far al-Mansur, the second 'Abbasid caliph, and it remained the political capital of the Islamic world until its destruction by the Mongols in 1258. Built on the banks of the Tigris not far from the former Sasanian capital of Ctesiphon, the city was the hub of overland, river and sea routes to the provinces and to far-flung trading partners.

The cultural unity of the Muslim world in the classical period created an ideal environment for cultivating the sciences. The fact that a single learned language, Arabic, was used throughout the vast 'Abbasid empire and extending beyond its political borders gave Muslim, Christian and Jewish scholars a common medium of communication. As time went on, they developed a commonly accepted set of technical terms and concepts. What Latin was to the learned West in the Middle Ages and Renaissance, Arabic was, and still is, to the Islamic world.

ARABIC WRITING

The Arabs gave to a large part of the world not only a religion – Islam – but also a civilization of which the language and the alphabet were integral parts. The Arabic alphabet has 28 letters and each of the letters may have up to four different forms. All but three of the letters are consonants and, unlike the Latin alphabet used for English and most European languages, Arabic writing goes from right to left.

Another significant difference is that the Arabic script has been used much more extensively for decoration and as a means of artistic expression because it is the language of the Quran. In the countries that use the Arabic alphabet, calligraphy (which means "beautiful writing") has continued to be used not only on important documents but for a variety of other artistic purposes as well. One reason is that the cursive nature of the Arabic script and some of its other peculiarities made its adaptation to printing difficult. The Arab world continued for some centuries after the time of Gutenberg to rely on handwriting for the production of books and other documents. Metal typesetting and typewriters using the Arabic alphabet were introduced in the 18th and 19th centuries, however, and the development of computers has allowed a return to the beauty and simplicity of Arabic writing.

Artistic calligraphy also has a religious calling. Islam prohibits the representation of *dhawat al-arwah* (sentient beings), namely humans or animals. This applies mainly to sculpture, and to a lesser extent drawings and paintings. Islam considers such art an attempt to imitate the highest level of God's creation.

Wherever artistic ornamentation and decoration were required, therefore, Muslim artists directed their attention to calligraphy, or what has since come to be known as "arabesque," that is, design based on geometrical forms or patterns of leaves and flowers. Arabic calligraphy came to be used not only in producing copies of the Quran (its first and for many centuries its most important use), but also for all kinds of other artistic purposes. It figured on porcelain and metalwork, for carpets and other textiles, on coins and as architectural ornament.

Thuluth

Farisi

Diwani

Naskhi

Ruq'ah

Kufic

Renderings of the opening line of the first surah of the Quran—"In the name of God, the Merciful, the Compassionate"—range from the flowing farisi to the ornate kufic.

At the start of the Islamic era, two types of script seem to have been in use – both derived from different forms of the Nabataean alphabet. One was square and angular and known as *kufic*, after the town of Kufah in Iraq. The other, called *naskhi*, was more rounded and cursive and was used for letters, business documents and whenever speed rather than elaborate formalism was needed. *Kufic* was obsolete as an everyday script by the 12th century, although elaborate artistic forms of it are still used in the Arab and Muslim worlds today, and in northwest Africa, where it evolved into the *maghribi* style of writing. *Naskhi*, on the other hand, remained in use and most of the later styles of Arabic calligraphy have been developed from it.

Calligraphy flourished during the Umayyad era in Damascus. During this period, scribes began modifying the original thick and heavy *kufic* script into the form employed today for decorative purposes. It was under the 'Abbasids, however, that calligraphy first began to be systematized. In the first half of the 10th century, the 'Abbasid Vizier Ibn Muqlah completed the development of *kufic* and established some of the rules of shape and proportion followed by calligraphers to this day.

Ibn Muqlah was also the first to develop what became the traditional classification of Arabic writing into the "six styles" of cursive script: *naskhi* (from which most present-day printing types are derived); *thuluth* (a more cursive outgrowth of *naskhi*); *rayhani* (a more ornate version of *thuluth*); *muhaqqaq* (a bold script with sweeping diagonal flourishes); *tawqi'* (a somewhat compressed variety of *thuluth* in which all the letters are sometimes joined to each other); and *ruq'ah* (the style commonly used today for ordinary handwriting in most of the Arab world).

From these six, and from *kufic*, later calligraphers developed other scripts. In Iran, for example, a particularly graceful and delicate *farisi* or *ta'liq* came into use. In Ottoman Turkey, an important addition was the highly artistic script called *diwani*, which means "of the court."

QASR 'AMRA

The first concerted efforts to incorporate Greek scientific thought into an Islamic context began in the Umayyad period and flowered with the establishment of the 'Abassid dynasty in the mid-8th century. At Qasr 'Amra, built between 712 and 715 in Jordan, Umayyad princes bathed in splendor. The little palace contains a fresco of the zodiac on a domed ceiling, shown here, made on what appears to be a stereographic projection as described by Ptolemy. The figure in the foreground holding the bow represents Sagittarius, "The Archer." The room also has paintings of personifications of History, Philosophy and Poetry, with each figure labeled in Greek. In addition, Qasr 'Amra contains portraits of the rulers of the earth, hunting scenes and even workmen engaged in building the palace itself.

(Facing page) The science of optics was first put on a rational basis by Ibn al-Haytham (965-1039) in his Kitab al-Manazir (Book of Optics), a work which had a profound influence on European science. This page is from a 13th-century manuscript of that work.

THE PRESERVATION, ELABORATION AND TRANSMISSION OF THE scientific tradition of late antiquity, in particular that of Greece, comprised one of the greatest achievements of classical Islamic civilization. The overwhelming majority of the effort of translating and assimilating Greek, Indian and Persian scientific works took place in Baghdad between the 8th and the 10th centuries.

Here, too, Islamic culture took definitive form and *Sunni* orthodoxy was first defined. Hand in hand with scientific investigations went the study of the Arabic language and the formulation of the *shari'ah*, the system of divine law that regulates the lives of Muslims.

The Caliph al-Mansur (755–75) sent embassies to the Byzantine emperor seeking Greek mathematical texts, in particular the *Elements* of Euclid. His son Harun al-Rashid acquired a number of other Greek texts in raids on Byzantine territory. Manuscript copies of secular texts were exceedingly rare in Byzantine times, as the works of the pagan philosophers were regarded with deep suspicion by Byzantine orthodoxy. The fact that the Arabic annals often mention diplomatic embassies sent to find specific works indicates how rare they were. It is little short of a miracle that under the early 'Abbasid caliphs almost the complete works of Aristotle, Plato, Galen, Archimedes, Ptolemy and many more classical authors were collected and translated. The works of the ancient Greek poets and playwrights were neglected, and it was only the philosophical and scientific legacy of Greece that passed into Arabic.

These Arabic translations of Greek scientific and philosophical works became the patrimony of Muslims and non-Muslims alike throughout the Islamic world. Studied, abridged and reworked by generations of scholars from Morocco to Yemen, they established the framework within which new ideas were debated and the departure point for original research. Contact with the works of the Greek philosophers Aristotle and Plato generated debate about the relationship between reason and revelation that persists to this day. These texts, embedded in their Arabic commentaries, were translated into Latin and transmitted to Europe beginning in the 11th century, and formed the basis of the pre-modern Western scientific and philosophical tradition. They only finally lost their relevance with the recovery of their Greek originals in the Renaissance and the birth of modern science with the discoveries of Copernicus, Galileo and Newton.

It was the Caliph Harun al-Rashid (786–809) who took the first steps toward systematically preserving these rich sources of knowledge when he established the research institute that under his son al-Mamun became known as *Bayt al-Hikmah*, the "House of Wisdom." As the Arab chronicles put it, Harun al-Rashid ruled when the world was young, a felicitous description of what in later years has come to be called the Golden Age of Islam.

The Golden Age was a period of unrivaled intellectual activity in all fields: science, technology and literature—

لـدد سمىهـا ... الـعشيمها بقـل لهـا الـيوما نيه اقـفيـقـفـفـوـن راى الطـلـحم من ابها
قـه اخرى لا تـعشـيمها بقـل لهـا الـيوما نيه اقـفيـقـفـفـوـن راى الطـلـحم من ابها
شـا يلـتـحم حول الطـبقـه القـرنيـه ودتـعـنيـبها جما تـعشـى سـايـر الطـبـقـات لـعـضـها
عضـها بعـضـا لانـه لـوغـشـاه كـلـه لمـنـع الـبصـر مـن ان يـنـفـ ـلـه

وهـو عـلـى هـذا المـثـال

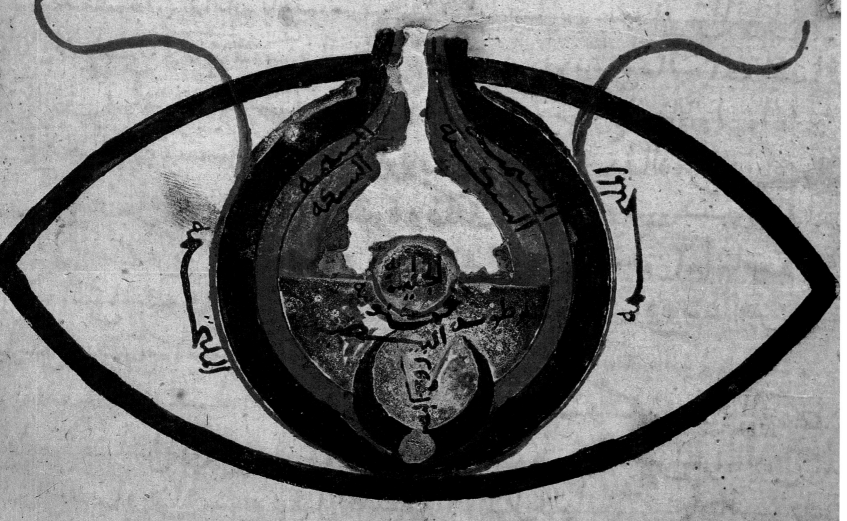

وانـا مـبـتـدى بـالاخـبـار عـن مـنـافـع كـل واحـد مـن الـرطـوبـات والـطـبـقـات الـتى وصـفـنـا
ابـتـدا اشـانـهـا وكـونـهـا ومـنـتـهـا ومـواضـعـهـا وذكـرت تـقـدمـت فـى اخـبـارك
ان الـرطـوبـه الـجـلـيـديـه فـى وسـط الـعـبـز وان خـلـفـهـا رطـوبـه واحـده وثـلـث طـبـق
وقـدامـهـا رطـوبـه واحـد وثـلـث طـبـقـات فـنـبـتـدى بـعـون اللـه بـالـخـبـ
عـن مـنـفـعـه الـرطـوبـه الـتـى خـلـف الـجـلـيـديـه وهـو الـزجـاجـيـه وعـن الـثـ
طـبـقـات الـتـى ذكـرنـا بـا خـلـفـا فـنـقـول ان كـل عـضـو مـن اعـضـا الـبـدن لا بـد لـه مـن عـ

particularly biography, history and linguistics. During this era, Muslim scholars also made important and original contributions in mathematics, astronomy, medicine and chemistry. They collected and corrected previous astronomical data, built the world's first observatory and developed the astrolabe, an instrument that was once called "a mathematical jewel."

Important advances in agriculture were also made in the Golden Age. The 'Abbasids preserved and improved the ancient network of wells, underground canals and waterwheels, introduced new breeds of livestock and, from the Chinese, learned the art of papermaking, a key to the revival of learning in Europe in the Middle Ages.

Al-Mamun staffed *Bayt al-Hikmah* with Muslim, Christian and Jewish scholars who dedicated themselves to the translation of Greek scientific works into Arabic. Some 57 scholars including Hunayn ibn Ishaq and Qusta ibn Luqa were associated with the House of Wisdom, and the costs to operate it ran to 500 gold dinars a month—about half the salary of the *wazir* (anglicized as "vizier"), the most important state official. Christian scholars first translated the Greek into Syriac, a written form of Aramaic. These versions were then rendered into Arabic by Muslim scholars working with their Christian colleagues.

Original works underwent continual revision as new texts were translated. In the process, the procedures of modern scholarship were developed, from collating a number of manuscripts to establish a critical text, to drafting glossaries of technical terms and marginal commentaries.

How Islamic Science Reached Europe

Many scientific works produced by the *Bayt al-Hikmah* and the succeeding generations of Muslim thinkers were translated into Latin and gave birth to medieval European science and philosophy. Four European centers—Salerno in Italy, Palermo in Sicily and Toledo and Seville in Spain—diffused these works through translations.

When the Christian ruler Alfonso VII conquered Toledo in 1085, he did not expel the Muslim and Jewish communities and he kept the mosque library intact, allowing firsthand contact among Christian, Jewish and Muslim scholars. Men keen to learn flocked to Toledo, where Arabic works were translated into Hebrew and then into Latin. Some Christian scholars even learned Arabic to read the works of Muslim scientists and philosophers in the original. At this time, Aristotle's works were still virtually unknown in Europe. They first became widely known through their Arabic versions and commentaries by Muslim scholars in places like Toledo.

One of the most prolific translators associated with Toledo was the Italian Gerard of Cremona. Before his death in 1187, Gerard had produced 80 translations of Arabic works, almost single-handedly transferring Arabic learning to Europe. He translated Hunayn ibn Ishaq's translations of Galen and Hippocrates, the *Canon of Medicine* of Ibn Sina and Abu al-Qasim al-Zahrawi's famous work on surgery, as well as philosophical works by al-Farabi and al-Kindi.

It was in Spain, too, that the

The De Materia Medica, *a guide to the medicinal properties of plants by the 1st-century Greek botanist Pedanius Dioscorides, was among the earliest Greek texts to be translated into Arabic, first in Baghdad in the early 9th century and again in Cordoba in Spain in the 10th century. This version, translated into Hebrew and Latin, became the pharmacists' reference manual and was still being studied in European universities in the 17th century. Here, in a 13th-century Arabic version, Dioscorides and a disciple hold a mandrake.*

church first made an attempt to understand Islam. Peter the Venerable, the head of the Cluniac order, sponsored a team of translators to produce Latin versions of key Islamic texts. Under his supervision, the Englishman Robert of Ketton produced a literal Latin version of the Quran in 1143.

The transmission of knowledge surged after the Normans conquered Muslim Sicily in 1091. Arabic, Greek, Latin, Italian and Hebrew were spoken on the island, and its rulers from Roger I (1091-1101) to Frederick II (1215-50) actively encouraged the translation of Arabic scientific works into Latin.

Another intense period of translation and adaptation followed Fernando III's conquest of Seville in 1248. Works by Muslim agronomists like Ibn al-Awwam were translated and were still being consulted in the 16th century.

Fernando III's son and successor, Alfonso IX, "The Wise," sponsored translations not only of Arabic scientific works, but also *Kalilah wa Dimnah*, the charming animal fables of Ibn al-Muqaffaʻ that were originally penned in 8th-century Damascus. Alfonso set his own religious poetry to the tunes of popular Arabic songs.

Scholars working at *Bayt al-Hikmah* had access through translation to the Greek and Indian mathematical traditions. Although Greek material was by far the richest, the development of mathematics by Muslim scholars would not have been possible without a key Indian contribution, the decimal place-value system of enumeration. Any number can be indicated by using nine signs, with zero (Arabic *sifr*, anglicized as "cipher") as a placeholder. This vastly simplified arithmetic calculation and virtually eliminated the errors intrinsic to previous cumbersome systems such as Roman numerals.

The work of these scholars and its diffusion was greatly facilitated by a Chinese technique that reached the Islamic world shortly before the foundation of Baghdad. In 751, the Muslim armies defeated a Chinese expeditionary force in Central Asia, in present-day Uzbekistan. Among the prisoners were some Chinese papermakers, who set up a paper factory, first in Samarkand and later in Baghdad itself. Paper quickly replaced papyrus and very expensive parchment, until then the only available writing materials. Papermaking technology was slow to reach the Latin West and was not commonly used as a writing material there until the 15th century.

While al-Mamun's caliphate saw the flowering of science, literature and trade, politically the signs of decay had already become evident, as distant provinces fell away and generals asserted their independence, even in Baghdad itself. After he died in 833, the symptoms of decline grew steadily worse. As al-Mamun's successor, his brother al-Mu'tasim could no longer rely on the loyalty of his military, he recruited an army of Turks from Transoxania and Turkistan. The outcome was the domination of the caliphate by its own praetorian guard. In the years after 861, the Turks made and unmade rulers at will. Although the religious authority of the 'Abbasid caliphate remained unchallenged, the next four centuries saw political power dispersed among many independent states: Taharids, Saffarids, Samanids, Buwayhids, Ziyarids and Ghaznavids in the east; Hamdanids in Syria and northern Mesopotamia; and Tulunids, Ikhshidids and Fatimids in Egypt.

In 1258, a Mongol army under Hülagü Khan, the grandson of Genghis Khan, invaded Baghdad and put an end to the once-glorious 'Abbasid Empire.

This miniature from a 13th-century Arabic translation of Dioscorides shows a method of refining lead.

ARABIC NUMERALS

The system of numeration employed throughout the greater part of the world today probably has its roots in India, but because the Arabs developed its numbers and transmitted this system to the West the numerals it uses have come to be called Arabic.

After extending Islam throughout the Middle East, the Arabs and the people of the societies that became part of the Muslim state started a long and impressive process of adaptation, assimilation and cultural exchange. One of the great centers of learning was Baghdad, where Arab, Greek, Persian, Jewish and other scholars pooled their cultural heritages and where in 771 an Indian scholar appeared, bringing with him a treatise on astronomy using the Indian numerical system.

Until that time the Egyptian, Greek and other cultures used their own numerals in a manner similar to that of the Romans. Thus the number 323 was expressed like this:

EGYPTIAN	999	∩∩	III
GREEK	HHH	△△	III
ROMAN	CCC	XX	III

The Egyptians actually wrote them from right to left, but they are set down above from left to right to call attention to the similarities of the systems.

The Indian contribution was to substitute a single sign (in this case meaning "3" and meaning "2") indicating the number of signs in each cluster of similar signs. In this manner, the Indians would render Roman CCC XX III as: **3   2   3**
(CCC) (XX) (III)

This new way of writing numbers was economical but not flawless. The Roman numeral CCC II, for instance, presented a problem. If a 3 and a 2, respectively, were substituted for the Roman clusters CCC and II, the written result was 32, when the correct value was 302. The Arab scholars perceived that a sign representing "nothing" or "naught" was required because the place of a sign gave as much information as its unitary value did. The place had to be shown even if the sign showing it indicated a unitary value of "nothing." It is uncertain whether the Arabs or the Indians filled this need by inventing the zero, but in any case the problem was solved: now the new system could show neatly the difference between XXX II (32) and CCC II (302).

If the origin of this new method was Indian, it is not at all certain that the original shapes of the Arabic numerals also were Indian.

There are several theories on the subject. In fact, it seems quite possible that the Arab scholars used their own numerals — which are of Nabataean origin — but manipulated them in the Indian way. It had the advantage of using much smaller clusters of symbols and greatly simplifying written computations. The modern forms of the individual numbers in both eastern Arabic and western Arabic (or European) appear to have evolved from letters of the Arabic alphabet.

The most prominent theory about the origin of the numerical systems used in the Arab world posits that the eastern Arabian

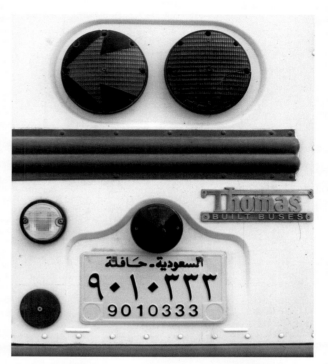

The similarity between Arabic and European numerals is readily apparent in this license plate from Saudi Arabia. Arabic numbers may be written and read from left to right, just like Western numbers; they may also be written and read from right to left.

numerals were obviously of Indian origin and were adapted, developed and assimilated by the Arabs, particularly those from Egypt going east. The western Arabic numerals were developed by Arab mathematicians to give each number a shape reflecting its actual value (in this case, the number of angles in each separate figure conformed to its numerical value).

The Semites and Greeks traditionally assigned numerical values to their letters and used them as numerals. This alphabetical system is still used by the Arabs, much as Roman numerals are used in the West for formal outlines and for enumerating kings, emperors and popes.

The new mathematical principle on which the Arabic numerals were based greatly simplified arithmetic. Their adoption in Europe began in the 10th century after an Arabic mathematical treatise was translated by a scholar in Spain and spread throughout the West.

	1	2	3	4	5	6	7	8	9	10
MODERN ARABIC (western)	1	2	3	4	5	6	7	8	9	10
EARLY ARABIC (western)	1	2	3	૪	୯	6	6	7	8	9	0
ARABIC LETTERS USED AS NUMERALS	ا	ب	ج	د	ه	و	ز	ح	ط	ي
MODERN ARABIC (eastern)	١	٢	٣	٤	٥	٦	٧	٨	٩	٠
EARLY ARABIC (eastern)	١	٢	٣	٤	٥	٦	٧	٨	٩	٠
EARLY DEVANAGARI (Indian)		૨	૩	♃	Ⴑ	७	؏	৮	૪	♂
LATER DEVANAGARI (10th-century Sanskrit)	१	२	३	४	५	६	७	८	९	०

The annual fair of 'Ukaz, southeast of Makkah and astride the old spice route north from Yemen, was held in the month of Dhu al-Qa'dah. It was an occasion for tribal poets to declaim their latest works, for peace treaties to be concluded between warring tribes, and for buying and selling.

THE ARABIC LANGUAGE

Of all the Semitic languages, ancient and modern, Arabic is the most fully developed and has the most extensive literature. A characteristic present in all Semitic languages, but most clearly seen in classical Arabic, is the almost mathematical way in which words can be formed from a root concept. Grammarians working in Kufah and Basra in Iraq in the 8th and early 9th centuries identified these roots as the building blocks of the language. They showed how verbal and nominal forms could be generated by inserting additional consonants as well as short and long vowels before, after or between the root consonants according to fixed patterns.

The grammarians of Kufah and Basra and their successors not only described the Arabic language, but normalized it. The tribes of the Arabian Peninsula spoke many different dialects, and there was a linguistic cleavage between northern and southern tribes. In pre-Islamic times, however, there appears to have been an agreed common poetic language that was understood by all. It was this language, in particular the form used by the poets of central Arabia, that together with the language of the Quran was used as the touchstone of correct usage.

The eventual result was a written language with fixed rules and orthography: classical Arabic. No matter what form of the language is spoken in the home—and spoken Arabic dialects differ widely—the classical language, written and spoken, is the same throughout the Arabic-speaking world. Classical Arabic, *al-lughah al-fus-ha,* "the eloquent language," is the shared language of the *ummah,* the vehicle of scholarly discourse, government and literature.

The earliest descriptive grammar of Arabic, and by far the most important, was written by a Persian named Sibawayh in the 8th century. It was called simply *al-Kitab* (*The Book*) and is still considered the final word on Arabic grammar.

Sibawayh's early training appears to have been in law, for a number of the technical terms he uses have been transferred from the legal to the linguistic domain. This transference of technical terminology from one discipline to another is characteristic of Islamic scholarship, creating a sense of the unity of human knowledge. It also reflects the multiple interests of scholars, who moved seamlessly from one discipline to another, often producing works on a wide variety of topics.

To understand the grammar and lexicon of the Quran better, the scholars of Basra and Kufah collected the oral poetry of the tribes of Arabia, particularly those of central Arabia, and subjected it to linguistic analysis. What began as a purely linguistic endeavor led to an appreciation of this poetry for its own sake, and the beginnings of literary criticism and the science of metrics.

ARABIC LITERATURE

Arabic literature dates to the pre-Islamic era, but it is the Quran, its style at once vigorous, allusive and concise, that most deeply influenced later compositions in Arabic. Today, it continues to color the mode of expression of native speakers of Arabic, Christian as well as Muslim, in both writing and speech.

Arabic prose came into being basically to serve the religious and practical needs of the Muslim community more than 14 centuries ago. The sayings and actions of the Prophet Muhammad and his companions were collected and preserved in written form, known collectively as the *hadith*, by such dedicated scholars as al-Bukhari and Muslim in the 9th century. Each *hadith* is a first-person narrative, usually by an eyewitness to the event described.

In Umayyad times, a number of historians wrote monographs on specific historical, legal and religious questions and in each case they seem to have adhered to the *hadith* method of referenced composition. Although few of these monographs have survived in entirety, enough has been preserved by later incorporation in such vast works as the *Annals* of al-Tabari to provide an idea of the writers' method of composition and their wide-ranging interests.

The practice of prefacing a chain of authorities to each *hadith* led to the compilation of vast biographic dictionaries, like the *Book of Superior Classes* of the early 9th-century author Ibn Sa'd, which includes a biography of the Prophet and a great deal of information on notable personalities in Makkah and Madinah during the author's lifetime. Works like this allowed readers to identify and judge the veracity of transmitters of *hadith*. Later, biographical dictionaries were broadened to include poets, writers, eminent reciters of the Quran and scientists, resulting in lively reading and a wealth of information about early Islamic social and political circumstances.

By the 9th century, the method of compiling history following the *hadith* methodology was abandoned, replaced by new, more "literary" historical writing. This style reached its apogee in the 10th century in al-Mas'udi's brilliant and entertaining *Meadows of Gold and Mines of Gems,* a comprehensive encyclopedia of history, geography and literature.

The Quran and *hadith* apart, poetry has always been the highest expression of literary art among the Arabs. Long before Islam, Arab poets had perfected various forms. The Muslim conquests of the 7th and 8th centuries radically changed the social circumstances that had produced the preeminent pre-

Islamic verse form, the *qasidah* (a poem or an ode). The expansion of Islam put the Arabs in direct contact with the other civilizations in western Asia, producing not the heroic poetry that might have been expected, but a sudden and brilliant explosion of lyric poetry and song.

Already in early Umayyad times, a school of lyric poetry flourishing in Makkah and Madinah had broken with tradition to produce urbane love songs in the poetic form known as the *ghazal*. In various styles, this has lasted to the present day as the principal lyrical form in Arabic, Persian, Turkish and Urdu. The 'Udhri poets, named after the 'Udhrah tribe in northwestern Hijaz, exemplify this genre. They sang of unrequited devotion and individuals withering from lovesickness. These conventions of romantic love, now so familiar in European and Asian lyric poetry, first appeared in world literature in the Hijaz. Love songs and anecdotes are preserved in *Kitab al-Aghani* (*The Book of Songs*), a vast 10th-century anthology by Abu al-Faraj al-Isfahani. It is a rich source of court poetry of the time and of the social history of the Umayyad era (661-750) when the caliphs patronized poets and musicians.

The jackal Kalilah tries to dissuade the lion from attacking the beasts of the jungle and devote himself to pious acts. This miniature adorns an early 15th-century Persian translation of Kalilah wa Dimnah, *a landmark of early Arabic prose, based on a Sanskrit original composed around the year 300.*

The first work of secular Arabic prose, *Kalilah wa Dimnah,* was produced in late Umayyad times and is still considered a model of Arabic style. A translation of the *Panchatantra,* an Indian book of advice for princes cast in the form of animal fables, it takes its title from the names of the two principal characters. 'Abd Allah ibn al-Muqaffa', of Iranian origin, translated *Kalilah wa Dimnah* from Pahlavi, the language of Sasanid Iran.

The works of Ibn al-Muqaffa' fall into a uniquely Arabic literary genre called *adab,* usually translated as "belles-lettres," which

is slightly misleading. *Adab* originated to educate the growing class of government ministers, often of non-Arab origin, in the Arabic language, manners and deportment, history and statecraft. Works of *adab* were among the most attractive and accessible products of Arabic literature and continued to be produced throughout the classical period, beginning in the 9th century.

By that time, the various literary genres had been defined—*adab*, history, geography, biography, poetry, satire and many more. What is striking about Arabic literature is its mixing of genres—a feature calculated to surprise and entertain the reader. Al-Jahiz, a Basra native, carried the technique to high art form and was the greatest stylist of his age. He wrote more than 200 books, the most famous of which is the seven-volume *Kitab al-Hayawan* (*Book of Animals*).

The 10th century witnessed the creation of another new genre in Arabic literature, the *maqamat*. Al-Hamadhani and al-Hariri were the most famous writers of this form. Al-Hariri's *Maqamat* (*Sessions*) is a series of episodes written in rhymed prose and verse with intricate wordplays, puns, literary allusions and rhetorical flourishes. Grounded in the daily reality of city life, it is regarded as a literary masterpiece. This form may have influenced the picaresque novels of 16th-century Spain, even Cervantes' *Don Quixote*.

This lively scene from al-Hariri's Maqamat *was illuminated by al-Wasiti, a famous artist from Baghdad, for a manuscript completed in 1237. It shows the main character of the* Maqamat, *Abu Zayd, and his companion al-Harith asking directions of villagers.*

Two new departures in Arabic poetry, the *muwashshah* (the ornamented) and the *zajal* (melody) developed in al-Andalus, or Arab Spain. These were rhymed stanzaic poems, ending in a couplet. The *muwashshah* was commonly written in classical Arabic, but the final couplet was sometimes written in colloquial Arabic or even in Spanish, transliterated in the Arabic alphabet. The *zajal*, also a light form of poetry, was often written in colloquial Arabic. Both forms were set to music and, like pop songs today, were overwhelmingly love lyrics. The two types predate the earliest Provençal poetry, which they uncannily resemble in both form and subject matter.

Al-Mutanabbi, born in Kufah in 915, stands out as the most important representative of the panegyric poetic style. He occu-

pies a position in Arabic literature comparable to that of Shakespeare in English. One of his *qasidah*s describes a journey from Egypt to Iraq across northern Arabia where, remarkably, almost all the place names he describes survive today. Al-Ma'arri, a blind, 11th-century Syrian poet, also employed the rhymed prose so characteristic of the *maqamat* genre in his famous *Risalat al-Ghufran* (*Message of Forgiveness*). It is cast in the form of a journey to the other world, where the narrator questions the spirits of famous poets and scholars of the past about their lives and works. The book is an extended critique of literature and philology and is a high point of classical Arabic literature.

The 500 years that followed the Mongol destruction of Baghdad in 1258 was an extended period of literary and political decline for the Arabs. Nevertheless, it was an age of encyclopedias, commentaries, compilations and lexicons — many of which preserve important material that would otherwise have been lost forever. The period also saw the rise of great scholars such as Ibn Khaldun in North Africa, the 14th-century historian and philosopher whose theories are expressed in a style and vocabulary unlike anything before his time.

Epics or heroic romances blossomed in the post-classical period. They included the *Romance of Antar*, based on the life of the famous pre-Islamic poet 'Antarah ibn Shaddad al-'Absi, commonly known as 'Antar; *Dhu Yazan*, about a pre-Islamic king of Yemen; *The Two-Horned Iskander*, about Alexander the Great; and *Abu Zayd al-Hilali*, which chronicles the expansion of Arabian tribes into North Africa in the 11th century. The famous *Thousand and One Nights* (known commonly in the West as the *Arabian Nights*) took form in the 15th century, although two key tales, *Ali Baba and the Forty Thieves* and *Aladdin and the Magic Lamp*, were not added until the 18th century. The core of the collection dates back to pre-Islamic Iran. All of these works of popular literature were designed for oral recitation and, until quite recently, could be heard in coffeehouses from Marrakech to Damascus.

The rebirth of Arabic literature began in the 19th century when Arabic-speaking countries began to assert their independence from Ottoman rule. Muhammad 'Ali, the modernizing ruler of Egypt between 1805 and 1848, encouraged the use of Arabic in schools and government. The printing press at Bulaq, near Cairo, produced a variety of scientific and literary publications that had a profound impact on intellectuals across the Arab world.

One of the leaders of the Arabic literary renaissance was the Lebanese writer and scholar Butrus al-Bustani, whose dictionary and encyclopedia awakened great interest in the problems of expressing modern Western ideas in the Arabic language. Other writers, such as the Egyptian Mustafa al-Manfaluti, adapted French romantic novels to the tastes of the Arab public. The first Arabic novel that can rank with European productions is Muhammad Husayn Haykal's *Zaynab*, set in Egypt and dealing with local problems.

One of the greatest figures in modern Arabic literature is Taha Husayn (1889-1973). Blind from an early age, he wrote movingly of his life and beloved Egypt in his autobiography, *al-Ayyam* (*The Days*). His voluminous writings on Arabic literature contributed a new critique of this vast subject. It was his near-contemporary compatriot Naguib Mahfouz, however, who placed modern Arabic works firmly on the world literary stage by winning the 1988 Nobel Prize for Literature.

The novel and the short story were not the only new forms introduced to the Arabic-reading public. The drama, first in the form of translations of Western works, then of original compositions, was pioneered by Ahmad Shawqi, who was also a talented poet, and came to maturity in the hands of fellow Egyptian Tawfiq al-Hakim. Al-Hakim's long career and devotion to the theater did much to make this one of the liveliest arts of the Middle East.

The history of modern Arab poetry, with its many schools and contending styles, is almost impossible to summarize. Traditional forms and subjects were challenged by 'Abbas Mahmud al-'Aqqad, Mahmud Shukri and Ibrahim al-Mazini from Egypt, who strove to introduce 19th-century European themes and techniques into Arabic, not always with success. Lebanese poets were in the forefront of modernist verse, and one of them, Gibran Khalil Gibran, proved very popular in the West.

In the Arabian Peninsula in general and in Saudi Arabia in particular, it was not until well into the 20th century that literary movements in neighboring lands made themselves felt. Some modern writers, such as 'Abd Allah ibn Khamis, have held strictly to classical forms and serious subject matter. Others have adopted new techniques and content. Hasan al-Qurashi, Tahir Zamakhshari, Muhammad Hasan Faqi, Ghazi al-Gosaibi and 'Abd Allah al-Faysal, to name a few, have won renown for their poetry throughout the Arab world. Moreover, the long tradition of Bedouin folk poetry, known as *nabati*, still flourishes today and has been adopted in new compositions.

Novels and short story genres are exemplified by, among others, the early works of Hamid al-Damanhuri, Khalil al-Fuzay' and 'Abd al-'Aziz al-Mishri, and the more recent writing of Ghazi al-Gosaibi, Turki al-Hamad and 'Abduh Khal. Other Saudi writers have gained high reputations in journalistic and scholarly pursuits. Such offerings include the lively and sometimes controversial literary criticism of 'Abd Allah al-Ghudhami, the wide-ranging writings of 'Aziz Diya and 'Abd Allah Jifri, and the many volumes of Saudi ethnographic and geographic lore by national prizewinner Hamad al-Jasir.

Women's contributions to Arabic literature in both theory and practice have long been an inspiration and instrumental in bringing about a revitalizing change. Tumadir bint 'Amr, better known as *al-Khansa*, the dauntless poetess of the 7th century, and Walladah bint al-Mustakfi, a famed beauty and daughter of the ruler of Cordoba in Muslim Andalusia in the 11th century, are but two bright examples.

Starting with the 10th century, however, in the face of growing political, social and religious conflict, the role of women in literature subsided. Perhaps the only woman to gain fame during that period was the fictional character Shaharazad, heroine of the *Thousand and One Nights*.

At the beginning of the 20th century, however, a revival in all aspects of life took root in the region. With it came very active and ambitious literary and intellectual movements that included women as well as men. In Saudi Arabia in particular, the last 40 years have witnessed the notable participation of women in literary and intellectual life. Talented writers such as Khayriyah al-Saqqaf, Qumashah al-'Ulayyan and Sultanah al-Sudayri, poets Thuraya al-'Arrayed and Fouziyah Abu Khalid, columnist 'Azizah al-Mani', short-story writer Sharifah al-Shamlan, novelist Layla al-Juhani, and scholars Fatimah al-Wuhaybi and Su'ad al-Mani, to name just a few, are among the most prominent women in the literary, cultural and intellectual movement in Saudi Arabia.

Literary periodicals are quite common today in Saudi Arabia, almost every newspaper and magazine contains a literary section, and literary clubs have spread throughout the country's regions, with handsome support from the government. Overall, the increasing number of high-quality works by Saudi men and women bodes well for the future of literary development in the Kingdom.

Tadmor   Arabia

Zues   Batoch   deserta

Fara   Anna

Betani

Sicabo   **AYAMAN**   Adari

Mo tui   Conga   Catiffa

PERSICUS

Medina talnabi.   Carnon

Janbut   Elcatif.   Luna

Dacatu   Tacine   Lacoch   Catura

Satan   Elach   Leme. ue

Cassir   Farsi   Gacha   desertum   Tumisa   Mascalat

Rabon

Cor   Mecha   Antax   Caburz

Zibid   Ziden

Carna   Siler   Vodora

Buge   **ARABIA**

Jusama   Nalober   Elsergiech.

Saira   Core

Sacola   Fasaf   Siangar   Cibelrian   **Amasir**

LIX.   Sara   **ifdin.**

Mensuria   Abrolho   **Irmin**

Mugora   Sarunbum

Santer   Ahgue

Giabel   Agoada   **Zibit.**   P.Furada

Homara   Xael

Alhor   Zibit   Borurna

Ercoco   Zeibam   Bandel dazebi

Camara   Dancar

Mazua   As Portass

Dalacea   Pedes Antonio

Aden

Milliaria German

AFRICAE PARS

Mare Rubrum

الذى فيه قبر محمد فى المدينة

Madinah is the final resting place of the Prophet Muhammad and the first three Rightly Guided caliphs. This is an 18th-century European artist's conception of the Prophet's Mosque in Madinah.

THE HEARTLAND

MADINAH WAS THE FIRST CAPITAL OF ISLAM AND THE FOUR Rightly Guided caliphs—Abu Bakr, 'Umar, 'Uthman and 'Ali—ruled here from 632 to 656. Although Arabia's political importance was eclipsed by the transfer of the capital to Damascus under the Umayyad caliphate (661-750), and then to Baghdad under the 'Abbasids (750-1258), it remained the spiritual center of the ever-expanding Muslim world.

Umayyad and early 'Abbasid caliphs devoted great energy and treasure to providing amenities along the pilgrimage routes that led to Makkah. They also improved and embellished the Sacred Mosque at Makkah and the Mosque of the Prophet in Madinah, where the Prophet Muhammad, Abu Bakr and 'Umar are buried. The pilgrimage continued even as 'Abbasid political authority began to weaken in the mid-10th century and new dynasties arose. Indeed, as the *ummah* grew, more and more pilgrims made their way to the Holy Cities in the Hijaz.

In Umayyad times, Madinah and Makkah became the preferred places of retirement for men who had taken part in the stirring events accompanying the expansion of the Islamic state. The sons of the fourth caliph, 'Ali, both settled in Madinah with their families and supporters. Hasan died there in 669, and when Husayn was killed at Karbala in 680 his surviving relatives and some of their supporters also settled in Madinah.

It is not surprising then that Madinah saw the first attempts to gather together the *hadith*, or reports of the deeds and sayings of the Prophet, and to elaborate the *sunnah*, or practices of the Prophet. In early Umayyad times, there were still men and women alive who had seen and spoken with the Prophet.

Previous spread: (Left) This map of the Arabian Peninsula, drawn by Dutch cartographer Pieter Bertius in 1616, shows reasonably accurate contour and coastal features, because Western mariners knew them from experience. But interior towns and landforms, knowledge of which came secondhand, are approximate and often fanciful. (Right) This miniature painting depicts a lateen-sailed ship that made sailors from the Arabian Peninsula masters of the sea.

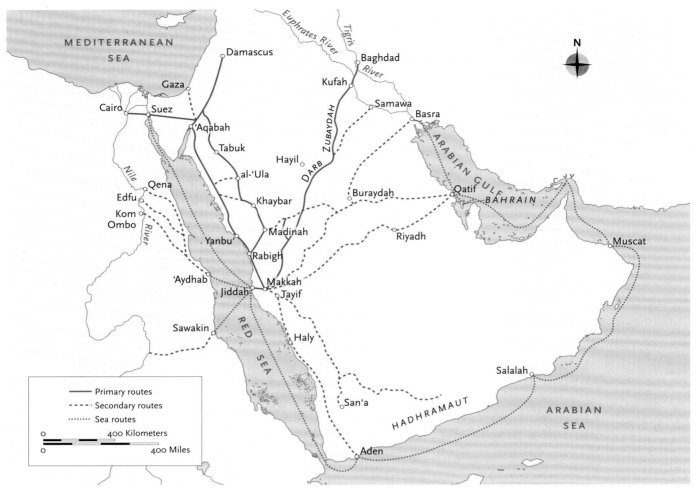

These land and sea routes to the Holy Cities were the locus of a network reaching to the far corners of the Muslim world.

MAJOR PILGRIMAGE
ROUTES OF ARABIA IN
PRE-MODERN TIMES

These "companions" were the source of the *hadith* which, along with the Quran, formed the basis of Islamic law.

Madinah was famous as the home of "The Seven Jurists of Madinah," a group of men who were among the first to formulate Islamic law. The most prominent of them was 'Urwah ibn al-Zubayr (643-712), whose mother was the daughter of the Caliph Abu Bakr and the sister of the Prophet's wife 'Aishah.

Because of his wisdom and blood relationship to men and women who were closely related to the Prophet, 'Urwah was the ideal transmitter of authentic traditions. He is credited with the first attempt to create an Islamic code of law based on the *sunnah* and the Quran. He is responsible for some 2,000 historical and legal *hadith*s, two-thirds of which go back to 'Aishah. Much of what later historians knew of the early history of Islam came from 'Urwah, who is thus considered the father of Islamic history. His devotion to history was continued by his student, Muhammad ibn Shi-

hab al-Zuhri, who died in 742. The historical traditions collected and transmitted by these two early scholars of Madinah constitute the most authentic information on the rise and progress of the early Islamic community.

The earliest surviving code of Islamic law was composed in Madinah by Malik ibn Anas (715–95), founder of the Maliki school of Islamic jurisprudence. He used the consensus of the Muslim community of Madinah, the city of the Prophet, as a guide to situations on which the Quran and *sunnah* were silent. There are three other major S*unni* schools of jurisprudence: Hanafi, Shafi'i and Hanbali. Each takes its name from its founder. All schools of thought agree on fundamentals, differing only in emphasis and minor details.

Most *Shi'i* Muslims follow the Ja'fari school. It has conceptual and procedural differences from the main schools of thought of the *Sunni*s.

In Makkah, great physical changes were engineered by the Umayyad caliphs, beginning with Mu'awiyah. The

THE DEVELOPMENT OF ISLAMIC LAW

The *shari'ah*, or Islamic law, was elaborated on the basis of the Quran and the practice of the Prophet, beginning in Madinah in the 7th century and reaching its full flowering in Iraq in the early 9th century.

The Quran contains the essence of the *shari'ah*, covering subjects as diverse as questions of inheritance and dietary prohibitions. On other areas of concern it is silent, so legal scholars turned to the deeds and sayings of the Prophet. These were preserved in the *hadith*. These reports, kept safe by men and women who were in direct contact with the Prophet, were passed down orally to later generations. Great attention was paid to transmitting the exact wording of the original *hadith*, and only *hadith* transmitted by established authorities were considered acceptable. Since the Prophet was the chosen instrument of revelation, it followed that his speech and acts were in accordance with God's will. Every Muslim thus tries to emulate his example.

The *shari'ah* is an ideal system covering all aspects of Muslim life, including prayer, manners, deportment, dress, diet, marriage, hygiene, commercial transactions and a host of other topics not covered by Western legal codes. It is concerned with everyday life, and how a Muslim should behave in order to conform to God's will. The basic principles of the *shari'ah* are justice, equality, consultation, the public interest and "enjoining good and forbidding evil."

Importantly for the expanding Muslim empire, the *shari'ah* also formulated a legal definition of the position of the *ahl al-kitab*, "the people of the book," within the *ummah*. Islamic law, following the Quran, recognizes the validity of the scriptural traditions of Judaism and Christianity. The Torah and the Gospels are seen as inspired but partial revelations, completed by the final revelation, the Quran. Jews and Christians were subject to the *jizyah*, a poll tax levied on adult males, which served to indicate a subordinate status. At the same time they were exempted from certain duties incumbent on Muslims, for example, military service.

The economic and social position of the Christians and Jews living under Muslim domination varied widely over time and place. As far as is known, neither community was ghettoized in Islamic lands, although there was a natural tendency to live in quarters with coreligionists for practical reasons.

All of the *hadith* constitute the *sunnah*, a word meaning "path" or "way," that is, the way of the Prophet. Each *hadith* consists of two parts, the report itself, called the *matn*, and the chain of transmission, the *isnad*. The *isnad* gives the names of the transmitters, beginning with the most recent and ending with the eyewitness who originated the *hadith*. For the *hadith* to be acceptable, each link in the chain had to be a known individual of proven probity and reliability.

The methods of deriving legal rulings from the Quran and the *hadith* were most clearly formulated by al-Shafi'i, who died in 820. He distinguished four sources of *shari'ah*: the Quran, the practice of the Prophet (*sunnah*), the consensus of the Muslim community (*ijma'*) and reasoning by analogy (*qiyas*).

Consensus, whether of the Muslim community at large or, more narrowly, of qualified legal experts, was extremely important in cases where both the Quran and the *sunnah* were silent. A famous *hadith* stated: "My community cannot agree upon an error." In other words, a commonly accepted practice that had not attracted censure from those versed in the *shari'ah* must be considered in conformity with divine law.

Qiyas, reasoning by analogy, gave the system great flexibility. When a case arose involving a situation not addressed by the Quran or the *sunnah*, or for which there was no legal precedent, a similar case with a common element could provide the point of departure for a ruling. In the modern world, great ingenuity is sometimes required to find such a common link in a precedent. Are satellite television channels permitted? *Qiyas*, in the hands of an accomplished legal scholar, can provide the answer.

Qiyas is intimately linked with the concept of *ijtihad*. It means "striving," but is used in the sense of "independent judgment." In the 10th century, some leading jurists concurred that the sources of Islamic law were now fully available to all and had been thoroughly studied, and that *ijtihad* was no longer necessary. This meant that precedent should be followed, although *qiyas* was still a legitimate tool. In modern times, *ijtihad* is once more a common juristic tool, as Islam faces the challenges of modernism.

Islam is a religion without clergy and authority rests in the *shari'ah*. Its custodians are scholars (*faqih*s) with a deep knowledge of the sources of the law. It is administered by *qadi*s, or judges appointed by political authorities. Traditionally, a chief judge (*qadi al-qudat*) appointed by the government resided in the capital and dealt with difficult cases referred by provincial *qadi*s and the rulers themselves. There are numerous cases in Islamic history of jurists who refused the post of *qadi*, either from fear of damnation for making the wrong ruling, or from an unwillingness to be forced to compromise their principles when serving an unjust ruler.

Twelfth-century philosopher and jurist Ibn Rushd (known as Averroes in the West) is celebrated with a statue in his native Cordoba in southern Spain.

The Darb Zubaydah *(the "Road of Zubaydah") connected the 'Abbasid capital of Baghdad, via Kufah, to Makkah. It is named after the wife of the Caliph Harun al-Rashid, who endowed it with amenities for pilgrims.*

Sacred Mosque was built around the Holy Ka'bah in the *bat-ha*, a low depression in a dry *wadi* bed with no outlet, and the area was subject to flooding. Even in the time of the Rightly Guided caliphs, steps had been taken to protect the Ka'bah and surrounding buildings by constructing dikes and embankments. Mu'awiyah had a channel cut to carry off floodwater; at the same time, dams were built and wells were dug to ensure adequate supplies of water year-round. New buildings were constructed, and those immediately adjoining the Ka'bah removed. This created a space surrounding the Ka'bah that under the Caliph al-Walid (705-15) was enclosed in the vast galleries that remain such a distinctive feature of the Sacred Mosque.

The contrast between the simplicity of life in Makkah and Madinah at the time of the Prophet and the Rightly Guided caliphs and the wealth and luxury they now reflected could not have been more striking. It is paralleled in modern times only by the rapid development of the cities of the Kingdom of Saudi Arabia after the discovery of oil.

Arabia in 'Abbasid Times

The reign of the Caliph Harun al-Rashid in the late 8th and early 9th centuries was a Golden Age for Makkah and Madinah. He personally led nine pilgrimage caravans from Baghdad to Makkah, scattering largess on the Holy Cites. His beloved wife Zubaydah spent more than 3 million dinars to improve the water supply of Makkah, building an aqueduct that brought water to the city from a well 20 kilometers (12 miles) away. The main pilgrimage route stretching some 1,300 kilometers (800 miles) from Kufah in

This pool, called Birkat al-'Aqiq, is 130 kilometers (80 miles) northeast of Makkah. It was a welcome resting place for pilgrims on the Darb Zubaydah.

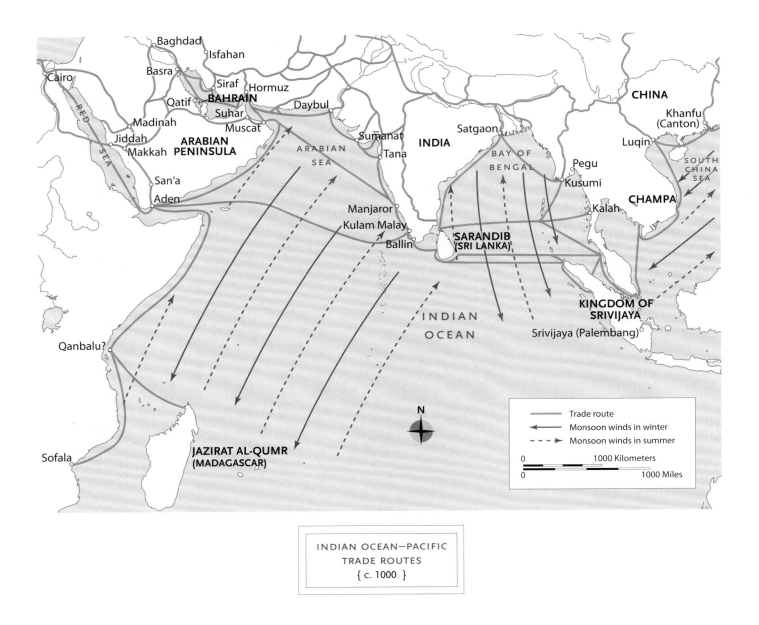

Iraq is named *Darb Zubaydah* (the "Road of Zubaydah") in her honor, for she supplied it with wells and rest houses for its entire length. In fact, clear remnants of her handiwork remain even in the 21st century.

Arabia's distance from the center of power in Baghdad made it an ideal refuge for dissidents. Almost all such movements in early Islam arose over the question of the caliphate.

The Kharijites were the earliest and most radical group (see page 73). More long-lasting was the threat from various groups that supported the claims of the descendants of 'Ali to the caliphate. They included the Qarmatians, a militant offshoot of the Isma'ilis—a *Shi'i* movement that evolved into the Fatimid dynasty—who found safe haven in al-Hasa. In 915, they began attacking pilgrim caravans and the number of pilgrims reaching Makkah slowed to a trickle. In 930, they attacked Makkah itself during the pilgrimage and carried off the Black Stone from the Ka'bah. They kept the stone, said to have been placed in the corner of the Ka'bah by the Patriarch Abraham, in al-Hasa until 950, when it was returned under Fatimid pressure. The Qarmatians held out in al-Hasa—making forays as far west as Egypt—until they were finally crushed in the 11th century.

The Isma'ilis were prominent in the 900s in southern and southwestern Arabia. They produced a number of small dynasties, and there are still small Isma'ili communities in Najran and Yemen. The Zaydis, yet another *Shi'i* group, were numerically and politically more important there. They take their name from Zayd, a grandson of Husayn ibn 'Ali. The first Zaydi *imam* appeared in Yemen in 860, and the Zaydis continue to play an important role in the country.

Maritime trade with India, southeastern Asia and China through the Gulf was highly developed in 'Abbasid times. Chinese goods, particularly silk, had flowed overland into western Asia since late Roman times, but the Romans, like the Greeks before them, never succeeded in making direct contact with China. The first Westerners to do so were probably Persian merchants in the 6th century, during Sasanid times, on the eve of the rise of Islam. During early

'Abbasid times, Muslim merchants began to trade directly and regularly with China by sea and to establish colonies in the South China ports.

The development and exploitation of a direct sea route to China by Muslim merchants and sailors was as significant as the Portuguese discovery of the sea route to India would be in 1498. It was not simply that the two major world economies of the time, China and the 'Abbasid Empire, had made contact. The western hub of the system was dominated by the Arabian Peninsula and its ports, just as the men who manned the ships were overwhelmingly of Arabian origin. The complex network of trade into which they fitted linked the 'Abbasid Empire with the emerging economies of the Indian Ocean, in particular the Kingdom of Srivijaya in Sumatra, and India, Ceylon, Malaya, East Africa and Madagascar.

In 'Abbasid times, the major Gulf ports were Siraf on the Persian side, and Suhar in Oman and Basra. Qatif and Bahrain played lesser, but still important trade roles as secondary ports. The Gulf's control of this lucrative trade with the East would not go unchallenged, however.

ARABIA IN FATIMID TIMES

THE FATIMID DYNASTY APPEARED IN NORTH AFRICA IN 909, deploying a powerful navy to establish control of the Mediterranean, including the important islands of Sicily, Corsica, Malta and the Balearics. In 958, Fatimid ships even entered the Atlantic, sending Atlantic fish preserved in jars back to their caliph in what is now Tunisia to prove they had done so. The Fatimid dynasty was *Shi'i* and took its name from Fatimah, the daughter of the Prophet Muhammad, who was married to 'Ali, the Prophet's cousin.

After conquering Egypt in 969, the Fatimid General Jawhar as-Siqilli began laying out the ground plan of a new capital, Cairo. In 972, he founded al-Azhar, the world's oldest university and the leading center of Islamic studies in the Arabic-speaking world. The next year, the Fatimid caliph took up residence in Cairo. His authority was acknowledged in the Hijaz and Yemen and even in Syria, as well as throughout North Africa.

The Fatimids did not go unopposed. In 971, the Qarmatians attacked Cairo and were only driven back at the last minute. They attacked again in 974, and once again were defeated by the Fatimids. Four years later, in 978, the Fatimids finally crushed them at al-Ramlah in Palestine. Two tribes that had been the main allies of the Qarmatians, Bani Sulaym from the Hijaz and Bani Hilal from Najd, were sent to Upper Egypt.

The Fatimids moved quickly to shift Indian Ocean trade from the Gulf to the Red Sea to increase their revenues and undermine the economy of their rivals in Baghdad, the Buwayhids, who had seized political power there in 945. Aden, Jiddah and Makkah itself became major entrepôts for the Indian Ocean trade. Some cargoes were off-loaded in Arabian ports and carried overland to northern markets;

Umayyad	'Abbasid
{ 696 }	{ 760 }
Seljuq	Fatimid
{ 1056 }	{ 1072 }
Ayyubid	Mamluk
{ c. 1250 }	{ 1268 }

THE DINAR

In the Middle Ages, the dinar circulated throughout the Muslim world and its peripheries, as well as in many regions of Europe. Today, it is still the name of the official currency of 11 countries, second only to the euro. The first gold dinar was issued under the Umayyads in their capital of Damascus in 691. The coin was at first an imitation of the Byzantine *denarius*, both in its name and in its weight, 4.55 grams (1/6 ounce). The decoration on the coin was purely calligraphic, almost always a Quranic passage asserting the Unity of God. In later 'Abbasid times, the inscription around the rim gave the date and often the name of the mint and sometimes the name of the official who oversaw the minting, as well as the name of the reigning caliph. Dinars were imitated in weight and design as far away as Anglo-Saxon England. Notably, the Spanish word for money is *dinero*, a reflection of Spain's Muslim heritage.

AL-MUQADDASI

Al-Muqaddasi, commonly known in Arabic as al-Maqdisi, was one of the great travelers and geographers of the early Islamic period. Originally from Jerusalem, he made pilgrimages to Makkah in 966 and 977 and again in 987, the year before completing the final version of his comprehensive geography of Islamic lands, *Ahsan al-Taqasim fi Ma'rifat al-Aqalim* (*The Best Divisions for Knowledge of the Regions*).

Al-Muqaddasi's notes on what is now the Eastern Province, a region that received less attention in the literary sources than the Hijaz and the Holy Cities, are particularly valuable. He probably did not visit the places he discussed, relying instead on the reports of others. He described al-Hasa, the capital, as "abounding in date palms, flourishing and populous" and called the nearby Gulf a "cornucopia of merchandise." He mentioned the pearl beds of Bahrain and Kharg Island off Persia, where the famous "Unique Pearl"—sold to the 'Abbasid Caliph Harun al-Rashid for 70,000 dinars in the late 8th century—was found.

Jiddah was the major port on the western side of Arabia. Al-Muqaddasi called it "the granary of Makkah, the entrepôt of Yemen and Egypt ... [whose] inhabitants are well-to-do merchants."

Many of the places he describes—Makkah, Madinah, Jiddah, Tayif, Yanbu' and al-Hasa—are still flourishing. By al-Muqaddasi's time, Aden was the main south Arabian port. He called it the "corridor to China." Goods imported from the Indian Ocean trading area and China were transshipped to Jiddah or carried overland to Makkah, where they percolated into the regional markets of the Hijaz and central Arabia, or were carried north by caravan to Egypt, Syria and Iraq.

Although the Gulf was beginning to lose ground to the Red Sea as the principal maritime route to the east, it was still important in al-Muqaddasi's time. Suhar in Oman remained the main port of entry for the India trade on the southeastern coast of Arabia. Its principal imports included all kinds of drugs, scents, saffron, teak, brazilwood (used in dyeing), ivory, pearls, silk brocade, precious stones, coconuts, camphor (used liberally in cooking and medicine), sandarac resin (used in varnish) and aloe, as well as iron, lead, bamboo, porcelain, sandalwood, glass and pepper.

Among the exports from Arabia were horses, camels, the prized white riding donkeys of al-Hasa and Qatif, and a large variety of dates from Qatif and al-Hasa, Wadi al-Qura in the Hijaz and other oases. Leather came from the Hijaz and Yemen, ambergris (a perfume fixative made from a substance discharged from whales) from Tihamah's shores, and linen textiles and indigo from Yemen. Gold came from the Hijaz and Najd and pearls from Bahrain. Frankincense was exported from the Mahrah area of south Arabia.

Millet, sorghum and wheat were grown in the oases and, when times were good, exported to cities like Makkah and Madinah. Domestic supplies were rarely sufficient, however, particularly during the pilgrimage season, when the population of Makkah would increase 10-fold or more.

NASIR-I KHUSRAW

The Persian traveler Nasir-i Khusraw journeyed to Makkah several times, beginning with the *hajj* in 1048 when there were very few pilgrims because of famine in the region. In 1050, he traveled again to the Hijaz, and later to al-Hasa in the east. "Jiddah is a large town on the coast, surrounded by a stout wall," he wrote. It has "some 5,000 male residents ...."

He put the male population of Makkah at just 2,000, with another 500 foreigners dwelling there as "temporary residents." It was the custom of scholars from other lands to take up residence in the Holy City out of piety and to pursue their studies in the quiet and calm of the city.

Nasir-i Khusraw visited Arabia's interior in 1051, traveling to Basra via Najd and al-Hasa. His description of the journey is virtually the only eyewitness account of conditions in the interior before modern times. Ibn Battutah, who made the same journey in the opposite direction in 1330, briefly mentions only Qatif on the coast and al-Yamamah, not far from present-day Riyadh.

Nasir-i Khusraw first visited Tayif in the Hijaz. He described it as "a little town defended by a well-fortified castle," with "many streams of running water and a great number of fig and pomegranate trees." Journeying inland by camel, he stopped at Jaz', about 240 kilometers (150 miles) due east, where he waited 15 days to secure a *khafir*, or protector, to pass safely through the tribal territories. "Everywhere there were independent lords and chiefs," he wrote.

Finally reaching the Tuwayq Escarpment in central Arabia, he crossed to the district of al-Aflaj, named after the system of underground water channels that fed its crops. "It is a large area, completely ruined by tribal wars," he noted. "At the time we were there, only an area half a *farsakh* long and wide (2.5 kilometers, or 1.5 miles) was cultivated and inhabited."

Four months later, he reached al-Yamamah, in the region of al-Kharj. In early 'Abbasid times, al-Yamamah was famous for the excellent quality of its wheat, which was exported to Baghdad. The area was irrigated by *aflaj* and produced abundant dates.

Nasir-i Khusraw arrived next in al-Hasa, 195 kilometers (120 miles) to the northeast. "The term al-Hasa indicates at one and the same time a town, a region, a suburb and a castle," he wrote. "Four strong, solidly built concentric walls, each separated from the next by the space of a *farsakh*, surround the town. Al-Hasa has many natural springs, each sufficient to turn five millstones .... Inside the walls is a handsome town [with] more than 20,000 inhabitants capable of bearing arms."

The town of al-Hasa lay on or near the site of modern Hofuf, the largest city of the oasis. Agriculture was the economic mainstay of the oasis. There were state-owned mills which ground grain free of charge, interest-free loans for craftsmen and no taxes. Aside from dates and white riding donkeys, the principal export was finely woven turban lengths for the Basra market.

A 1930s view of the Makkah Gate in Jiddah, through which pilgrims departed on the pilgrimage to the Holy City.

others were taken to the Egyptian port of 'Aydhab, carried overland to the Nile and shipped downstream to Alexandria, the major port in the eastern Mediterranean. This new trade paradigm set the stage to link the highly developed economies of Islamic lands and the Indian Ocean trading network with the infant economies of the western Mediterranean. A major consequence of Fatimid success in shifting trade from the Gulf to the Red Sea was the rise of Venice, which would become the main engine of European commercial growth.

Around 965, shortly before the Fatimid conquest of Egypt, a descendent of the Prophet's grandson Hasan named Ja'far arrived in Makkah with the pilgrimage caravan from Egypt and took power in the Holy City. Members of this dynasty were entitled to the title of *sharif*, or "noble," because of their descent from the Prophet. Another family of *sharif*s, descended from Hasan's brother Husayn, took power in Madinah at about the same time.

The new rulers of Makkah may have come to power with Fatimid encouragement, but they soon sought independence from Egypt. The Buwayhid ruler in Baghdad built the first wall around the inner city of Madinah in 974, perhaps to defend it from Fatimid attack. In 976,

the *sharif* of Makkah withdrew allegiance to the Fatimid Caliph al-Mu'izz, who retaliated by halting grain shipments to the Hijaz.

This situation continued intermittently throughout the rest of the century. In 1011, the *sharif* of Makkah, Abu al-Futuh Hasan, briefly declared himself caliph, but was unable to gain recognition from the *ummah* and abandoned his claim.

ARABIA IN AYYUBID TIMES

IN 1055, THE SELJUK TURKS TOOK CONTROL OF BAGHDAD, AN event that had far-reaching consequences for Arabia and its neighbors. Not long after they came to power, the era of the Crusades began, and Islamic unity was vital to oppose this threat from overseas. The Seljuks and the Ayyubid dynasty of Salah al-Din (Saladin), which replaced the Fatimids in Egypt in 1171, were in the forefront of the battle against the Crusaders in Syria and Palestine.

The struggle extended as far south as the Red Sea, where in 1182-83 raiders sent by Reynaud of Châtillon attacked shipping on the African side. They burned 16 vessels en route to 'Aydhab, where they captured and sank a loaded pilgrim ship

100

returning from Jiddah. Chased by an Ayyubid fleet, they were run aground on the Hijaz coast near Rabigh. In Alexandria on his way to Makkah in 1183, the Andalusian traveler and writer Ibn Jubayr saw some of the captives being led through the streets on the backs of camels. He reported they were within a day's march of Makkah when they surrendered.

Although the attacks were undoubtedly pirate raids rather than the start of a long-term campaign to take control of Red Sea commerce, it is easy to see why the response to the incursion was swift. The Egyptian port of Alexandria was supplying all of Europe with spices from India and the Far East, and this lucrative trade passed through the Red Sea. Its major European trading partner was Venice.

THE KARIMI MERCHANTS

A GROUP OF SOME 200 WEALTHY *SUNNI* MERCHANTS CALLED the Karim handled the Red Sea spice trade in Fatimid times, and they were very rich indeed. They operated in Egypt, North Africa, and Red Sea and Indian Ocean ports with their own ships and caravans, continuing to play a vital economic role in the region until the 15th century.

After Salah al-Din ousted the Fatimids, he imposed high taxes on the Karim, presumably in return for government protection. A delegation of Karimi merchants that came to Cairo from Aden in 1181 was asked to pay four years of taxes in advance.

Until the rise of the Karim, the India trade had largely been in the hands of *dhimmi*s, Copts and Jews, or sectarians like the Isma'ilis and Ibadhis of Oman. From Ayyubid times on, however, the Karimi merchants played the major role, building trading networks that linked Egypt and Aden with East Africa, India, Indonesia, Ceylon, the Moluccas and China. This system reached its fullest development under the Mamluks, who succeeded the Ayyubids in Egypt in 1250.

This illustration from al-Hariri's Maqamat *shows the character Abu Zayd meeting two merchants mounting their camels. It was executed by al-Wasiti in Baghdad in 1237.*

101

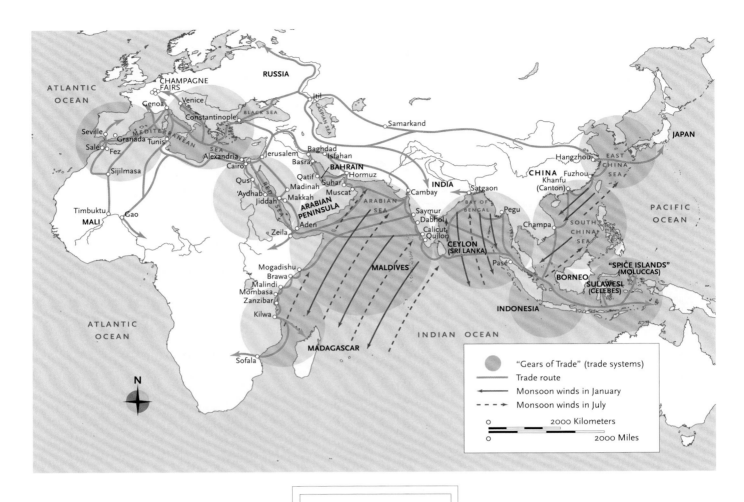

ARABIA IN MAMLUK TIMES

IN 1256, A SERIES OF SEVERE EARTHQUAKES STRUCK THE HIJAZ, accompanied by a volcanic eruption near Madinah that came close to engulfing the city with lava. Four years later, al-Zahir Baybars of Egypt vanquished the Mongol army under Hül-agü Khan at 'Ayn Jalut in Palestine. The Mongols had already conquered China and Russia, devastated the great cities of Central Asia and Iran, and destroyed Baghdad. Thanks to Baybars, the founder of the Mamluk dynasty, Egypt, Arabia, North Africa and Islamic Spain escaped attack.

By 1260, maritime domination of the Mediterranean had long since passed from Muslim hands to the Venetians and Genoese. But the revived European economy, stimulated by the maritime trade with the east, was linked to the Indian Ocean and Pacific trading network controlled by the Muslim merchants whose hub was in Egypt. Like a system of interlocking gears, the commercial fairs of Northern Europe were tied to the arrival of the annual Venetian fleet from Alexandria, which in turn depended on the arrival of ships from the Indian Ocean, driven by the predictable

monsoon winds. At the heart of this global trading system was the Arabian Peninsula, whose ports, sailors and merchants dominated the western Indian Ocean.

Taxes on pepper and other spices imported from the east by the Karimi mechants provided a major source of revenue to the Mamluk regime. As in past times, Aden and Jiddah were the coastal linchpins for goods destined for shipment overland, or across the Red Sea to 'Aydhab and down the Nile. Protection of the route was vital to the Mamluk state, and the Mamluks even established a small navy to protect Red Sea merchant ships from pirates.

The most lucrative commodity traded by the Karimi merchants was pepper, for which there was an unlimited demand in Europe. As pepper made its long journey from the groves of the Malabar coast of India to European markets, its value increased a thousand times, through tolls, levies, taxes and carriage charges, generating income for all who handled it along the way. In the 14th and 15th centuries, Jiddah and Makkah were major pepper markets.

In 1429, the Mamluk ruler Barsbay dealt the Karimi merchants a death blow by instituting [CONTINUED ON PAGE 109]

A miniature from the Maqamat of al-Hariri, done in Baghdad in 1337, depicts an East African trading vessel in the Arabian Gulf.

104

Zheng He and the Ming Voyages

On June 21, 1432, the Mamluk chronicler Ibn Taghribirdi told Sultan Barsbay in Cairo that two Chinese junks had arrived in the Red Sea port of Aden and requested permission to visit Jiddah.

A number of junks — part of a larger Chinese expedition to the seaports of India — had anchored in Aden, but their cargoes of chinaware, silk and musk could not be sold because of disorder in Yemen. The captains of two junks wrote to the *amir* of Makkah and to the governor of Jiddah, asking to land in Jiddah. They, in turn, wrote to the sultan, emphasizing the profit to be made by welcoming the Chinese. "The sultan wrote ... to let them come to Jiddah, and to show them honor," noted Ibn Taghribirdi.

This is one of the few references in the contemporary Arabic chronicles to a remarkable series of Chinese naval expeditions to Southeast Asia, the Indian Ocean and — ultimately — the Arabian Peninsula during the first three decades of the 15th century.

The Ming Emperor Zhu Di undertook the missions after Tamerlane disrupted the overland trade route to China in the late 14th century and was poised to attack China itself. Zhu Di's aim seems to have been to establish contact with the rulers of western regions, overawe them with Chinese power, bring back exotic products and gather useful information on western kingdoms, the extent of their strength and their principal exports.

The first expedition set out from Nanking in 1405. The 317-vessel fleet included 62 "treasure ships" designed to bring back the riches of the fabled West. It was led by huge, nine-masted junks and had a complement of 27,870 men, ranging from common seamen to marines, doctors, scribes, scholars, bookkeepers and high-ranking government officials.

The ships were commanded by Admiral Zheng He, a Muslim court official who organized and led seven major expeditions between 1405 and 1433. The fleets were the largest seen in the waters of the Indian Ocean until the Allied armadas of World War II.

The first three expeditions, in 1405-07, 1407-09 and 1409-11, did not reach beyond the west coast of India. They called at Champa in Southeast Asia, Java, Sumatra, Aceh, Ceylon, Malacca, Quilon, Calicut, Cochin and many other places. A fourth expedition, in 1413-15, reached Arabian waters, calling at Hormuz at the southern end of the Arabian Gulf. This armada was accompanied by Ma Huan, a convert to Islam whose book about this and other voyages under Zheng is a precious source of information about Arabia and its trading partners in the Indian Ocean before the coming of the Portuguese in the late 15th century.

Ma Huan was born in 1380 in Zhejiang Province, near Hangzhou Bay, the main port of Ming China. He embraced Islam as a young man and devoted himself to the study of Arabic and Persian. Appointed to Zheng He's staff in 1412, he joined the expedition of 63 ships and 28,560 men in 1413 as an interpreter. Ma Huan took copious notes when the fleet visited Hormuz, and on short visits to neighboring places.

On his return to China in 1415, Ma Huan set down his notes "about the appearance of the people in each country, the variations of the local customs, the differences in the natural products and the boundary limits" in a book entitled *The Overall Survey of the Ocean's Shore (Ying-yai sheng-lan chiao-chu)*.

Ma Huan did not accompany Zheng He on the next expedition, 1417-19, but he signed up again for the sixth trip in 1421. This time he visited Dhufar in Oman and Aden, while a detachment of 41 other ships visited Mogadishu and Brawa on the East African coast.

The Chinese Emperor Zhu Gaozhi forbade further expeditions in 1424, but his edict was revoked six years later by his successor Zhu Zhanji, who ordered the seventh and last Ming expedition. It embarked in 1431.

Thanks to Ma Huan, this was the best documented voyage of all. The armada of 100 large ships visited Southeast Asia, Bengal, southern India, the Arabian Gulf, Aden, Jiddah and the ports of East Africa. Ma Huan accompanied the main fleet to Bengal, then to Calicut.

From there, he was sent with six Muslim emissaries to Aden, Jiddah and Makkah. The letter received by the Sultan Barsbay in Cairo in 1432 was sent while Ma Huan's ship was anchored in Aden harbor.

When granted permission to sail to Jiddah, Ma Huan disembarked in that port (which he calls *Chih-ta*) and made his way to Makkah (*Mo-ch'ieh*), "the city of the Heavenly Square," a reference to the Ka'bah. He spent three months in Makkah and describes the "Heavenly Hall" mosque, the Ka'bah and some of the rites of the pilgrimage.

"The people of this country are stalwart and fine-looking, and their limbs and faces are of a very dark purple color," he wrote.

"The menfolk bind up their heads; they wear long garments; on their feet they put leather shoes. The women all wear a covering over their heads, and you cannot see their faces. They speak the *A-la-pi* (Arabic) language. The law of the country prohibits wine-drinking. The customs of the people are pacific and admirable. There are no poverty-stricken families. They all observe the precepts of their religion, and law-breakers are few. It is in truth a most happy country."

Zheng He's last expedition ended China's attempt to establish a presence in the "Far West." The expense of such naval expeditions was enormous and the returns, at least in economic terms, were slight. China withdrew into itself, confining overseas trade to a few chosen ports.

By the end of the century, the Ming armadas were but a faint memory and the Portuguese had found their way to Calicut and all the spices of the East. Much of the information gathered by Ma Huan and others found its way into the Ming encyclopedias, frozen in time. The Arabian ports that had traded directly and indirectly with China since the early 8th century had finally received return visits from their distant trading partner, a historic encounter overshadowed by the arrival of the Portuguese fleets.

AHMAD IBN MAJID

Shihab al-Din Ahmad ibn Majid, whose family came from Najd, was the foremost Arab navigator of the mid- to late 1500s. With justifiable pride, he called himself "the lion of the raging sea." Ibn Majid, who lived in Oman, wrote more than 40 works in both prose and verse on navigating the Indian Ocean, Arabian Gulf and Red Sea. Well into the 19th century he was remembered by Arabian pilots and sailors as "Al-Shaykh ibn Majid," an almost legendary figure. Although Ibn Majid did not invent the compass, as many of the men who sailed the Indian Ocean believed, he was the first to affix the needle to the compass card, creating the forerunner of the modern mariner's compass.

Both Ibn Majid's father and grandfather had been skilled navigators and pilots as familiar with the treacherous reefs of the Red Sea as they were with the coasts of Malabar and East Africa. He inherited the accumulated lore of his ancestors, organized it and wrote the navigational manuals that earned him his reputation. The exact dates of his birth and death are unknown, but internal evidence in his works suggests that he was born around 1432,

about the time ships from Zheng He's last expedition reached Aden and Jiddah (see pages 104–105). He probably died soon after 1501, having lived to witness the coming of the Portuguese to the Indian Ocean in 1498.

Ibn Majid was the first Arab author to attempt to systematize the navigational techniques of Arabian seamen. His two major prose works, the *Hawiyat al-Ikhtisar fi Usul 'Ilm al-Bihar* (*A Short Comprehensive Account of the Principles of Navigation*), written in 1462, and the *Kitab al-Fawa'id fi Usul 'Ilm al Bahr wa-l-Qawa'id* (*The Book of Useful Information on the Principles and Rules of Navigation*), written in 1490, are encyclopedic works that cover both theoretical and practical navigation. *Kitab al-Fawa'id* covers topics such as the 28 lunar mansions and the principles of stellar navigation, including the names of the stars corresponding to the 32 rhumbs, or points, of the Indian Ocean compass.

Latitude was found by measuring the height of the Pole Star above the horizon in "fingers," the width of the finger of the outstretched hand serving as the basic unit of measurement. This was the same system used by the Muslim Chinese pilots who accompanied the Ming voyages of Zheng He, and is undoubtedly very ancient.

The calculation of longitude was, of course, impossible before the invention of accurate marine chronometers, which did not happen until well into the 18th century. Nevertheless, Ahmad ibn Majid showed how it could be estimated by average running times along a meridian, and there is no doubt that this simple and practical method was effective in the hands of an experienced navigator.

He gives the latitudes of all the major harbors of the Indian Ocean (including the islands of the Indonesian archipelago and Madagascar), all in terms of the height of the Pole Star and other fixed stars observed from that locality, rather than in the astronomically observed stellar coordinates of mathematically based cartographers like al-Idrisi and other followers of Ptolemy. In other words, Ahmad ibn Majid was writing to instruct fellow mariners, using the system of stellar navigation that had been used in Arabia on both land and sea for centuries.

He pays great attention to navigating by landmarks and seamarks—changes in the color of the water, presence or absence of certain kinds of seaweed, direction of flight of land and seabirds, wave patterns and even the presence of sea snakes. He gives detailed descriptions of the coasts of the major islands—Arabia itself (always referred to as "The Island of the Arabs"), Socotra, Bahrain, Ceylon, Java, Sumatra, Taiwan and Zanzibar. He provides a detailed coastal survey of Asia and East Africa, describes the monsoon wind system and gives a detailed description of how to navigate the lower reaches of the Red Sea, from Jiddah to Aden.

Most interestingly of all, both the *Kitab al-Fawa'id* and the earlier *Hawiyat al-Ikhtisar* contain brief passages describing the possibility of circumnavigating Africa from east to west. Both books were written before Vasco da Gama's epoch-making voyage—from the opposite direction—at the end of the 15th century.

Ahmad ibn Majid has another claim to fame, of a more controversial sort. In 1573, Makkan author Qutb al-Din al-Nahrawali, who wrote a history of Mamluk and Ottoman incursions into Arabia in the 16th century, including their efforts against the Portuguese, stated that Ahmad ibn Majid had guided Vasco da Gama from the East African port of Malindi across the Indian Ocean to the port of Calicut in southwestern India. The Portuguese sources do refer to such a pilot, but always as coming from Gujerat in northwestern India, not as an Arab. In any case, by the time Vasco da Gama arrived in Malindi, Ahmad ibn Majid was more than 70 years old and very eminent. It is extremely unlikely that he would have been available as a pilot in Malindi. His last known work, *Kitab al-Sufaliya* (*The Book of Sofala*), written about 1501, refers to the Portuguese arrival in the Indian Ocean as an unmitigated disaster.

The Portuguese used Arab mariners' charts, apparently constructed on a grid pattern, as the basis of their own early maps of the Indian Ocean. This is specifically mentioned in Portuguese chronicles and can be deduced from the forms of the place names. None of these Arab charts, unfortunately, has survived.

The simultaneous Chinese, Arab and Portuguese interest in navigational techniques and marine charting is striking and still not adequately explained. What is clear from the works of Ahmad ibn Majid and the accounts of the early Portuguese navigators is that Arabian seamen were able to find their way unerringly from Arabian ports as far as the Moluccas and Timor. The Muslim Chinese Admiral Zheng He used the same techniques to safely navigate from China to Arabia and back. Thanks to Ahmad ibn Majid, we know how this was done.

Dhows of the type Ibn Majid sailed coast through the water off the Arabian Peninsula.

"THEY HAVE TO ACKNOWLEDGE THAT WE KNOW BEST"

We use 32 rhumbs, and we have tirfa, *and* zam *and* qiyas *(measurements of star altitude), but they are not able to do these things nor can they understand the things which we do, although we can understand what they do and we can use their knowledge and can travel in their ships....*

We can easily travel in their ships and upon their sea, so some of them have magnified us in this business and look up to us for it. They acknowledge that we have a better knowledge of the sea and its sciences and the wisdom of the stars in the high roads of the sea, and the knowledge of the division of the ship in length and breadth.

For we divide the ship in length and breadth according to the compass rose and we have measurements of star altitudes. They have no similar division or any way of dividing from the prow of the ship to guide themselves. Neither do they use star altitude measurements to guide them when they turn to the right or left. Hence they have to acknowledge that we know best in that.

—From Ibn Majid's *Kitab al-Fawa'id* (translated by G.R. Tibbetts), written before the Europeans rounded the Cape of Good Hope and entered the Indian Ocean in 1498, and well after the navigators of the Arabian Peninsula had perfected the art of long-distance sailing and reached distant waters.

The coffee bean, grown for centuries in the highlands of Yemen, was exported from Mocha—a name that has stuck for the most flavorful bean of all.

ARABIAN COFFEE TAKES OVER THE WORLD

Legend has it that sometime in the 14th century a goatherd in the Ethiopian highlands noticed that his goats became noticeably livelier after eating the berries of a certain plant. Thus was coffee discovered. At first, the drink was limited to circles of mystics in Yemen. The coffee bush was transplanted from Ethiopia to the Yemeni highlands. By the end of the 15th century, the new drink began to spread throughout the Ottoman Empire, exported from Mocha, which gave its name to the earliest and best form of the bean.

The earliest documents mentioning coffee (*qahwah* in Arabic) have been recovered by Japanese archeologists working on the sites of al-Tur and Raya in Sinai, both Red Sea ports and caravan stages for the pilgrimage. The oldest document dates to 1497, the year before the Portuguese discovered the sea route to India.

Although it is now difficult to imagine a world without coffee, it took some time to spread, not really becoming common in Europe until the 17th and 18th centuries. At first opposed by religious authorities of the Ottoman Empire, coffee gradually gained widespread acceptance. By the 16th century, every town in the Ottoman Empire had its coffee shop. In Arabia, it was enthusiastically adopted by both townsmen and Bedouin and became an essential part of life and custom. Here, coffee is made both of the husk of the bean (*qishr*) and of the roasted bean itself (*bunn*). Tribal hospitality is synonymous with the ringing of the brass pestle crushing the bean in the mortar, a sound that is an open invitation to guests.

Until the advent of coffee, the main commodity in the Red Sea trade was pepper. Around 1600, despite the recovery of the spice trade, the price of pepper in Jiddah and Cairo began to rise. The Dutch and English were now replacing the Portuguese as the major European traders in the Indian Ocean, and were shipping the bulk of the pepper production from Malabar, on the west coast of India, directly to Europe via the Cape of Good Hope. In Cairo, the price of pepper doubled between 1580 and 1600. Merchants consequently began investing in coffee, which was cheaper.

Mocha, Jiddah and Makkah became centers of the trade and, as coffee-drinking spread into the interior of Arabia, tribes that had formerly used barter as a means of exchange increasingly began to join the money economy. The Arabian coffee trade only began to decline in the 18th century, when the English succeeded in transplanting cuttings of the coffee bush to the Malabar coast of India and then to other suitable sites, shattering the Arabian monopoly.

[CONTINUED FROM PAGE 102] a state monopoly of the pepper trade. At the very time this policy was being carried out, the ruler of Yemen, an-Nasir Ahmad, began attacking the Karimi merchants in Aden and attempting to extend his power to the Hijaz. Many of the Karim fled to Jiddah, while others left for India. This disruption of the trade network resonated as far away as China; the Ming emperor sent an envoy to Aden with a note of protest in 1431.

Increased Mamluk taxes on the Karimi merchants caused further emigration. The last two mentioned by name in the historical sources died in 1492, on the eve of the establishment of a global trading network that would have surpassed even their wildest dreams.

The Gulf port of Siraf, on the Persian shore, had declined in the late 10th century, when a series of earthquakes devastated the town. Around the year 1000, an Arab tribe, the Bani Qaysar, captured the island of Qays. This became the main Gulf port for the India and China trade until 1229 when it was captured by the ruler of Hormuz, an ancient port on the Persian mainland. In 1300, because of the raids of Turkic tribes, Hormuz was moved offshore to the island of Jarun. This "new" Hormuz became the principal emporium for the eastern trade until 1622. During its heyday, it was one of the wealthiest trade centers in the world. It was the principal port for the lucrative export of Arabian horses to India.

THE COMING OF THE PORTUGUESE

WHEN VASCO DA GAMA ROUNDED THE CAPE OF GOOD HOPE in 1498, sailing with the monsoon winds to the Malabar coast of India and anchoring off Calicut, he initiated a chain of events that eventually enabled Europe to dominate the eastern markets. This opened a new chapter in East-West affairs. The Portuguese established themselves by force or treaty in the major ports of western India and along the coast of East Africa. Portuguese ships with their iron cannon quickly dominated the unarmed shipping of the Indian Ocean, and their admirals took control of the spice and textile trade from India to Arabian ports. The effect on Arabia and Egypt was almost immediate.

In 1498, Venetian merchants in Alexandria had insufficient funds to purchase the wealth of spices on offer. Four years later, in 1502, there were no spices to load: The Portuguese were already shipping their cargoes to Lisbon around the Cape and selling directly to European markets — at a 500 percent markup. In 1507, the Mamluk Sultan Qansawh al-Ghawri responded by sending a fleet of 12 ships from Suez under the command of Husayn al-Kurdi. He anchored at Jiddah, an obvious Portuguese target, and fortified the city, raising new walls on the landward side and constructing six towers that commanded the port with cannon. The fleet then sailed for India, where after two successful engagements against the Portuguese, it was defeated.

Portugal's formidable Afonso de Albuquerque, learning that another Mamluk fleet was under construction, decided

Vasco da Gama, from Portugal, rounded the southern tip of Africa in 1498, pioneering a route to India and dramatically affecting East-West relations.

to strike at Aden and the Red Sea ports of Arabia. He attacked Aden in 1513, but was repelled by brave defenders and retired to the Kamaran Islands at the mouth of the Red Sea. From here, he raided ports and shipping and gathered information about the region, even contemplating a raid against Makkah. In 1514, he sailed to the other side of the peninsula and captured Hormuz, whose ruler also controlled Bahrain. Now both islands belonged to the Portuguese, effectively giving them control of the entire Gulf trade.

In the meantime, the Mamluks had built a new fleet, with the help of the Ottoman Turks to the northeast. A Mamluk fleet of 20 ships and 6,000 men set sail from Egypt in 1515, the year Albuquerque died, to drive the Portuguese from the Red Sea and Indian Ocean. But unrest in Yemen caused a change in plans. By the time Yemen was pacified in 1517, the Ottoman Turks had invaded Egypt, killing the last Mamluk sultan. The Ottomans thereby inherited the Mamluk foothold in Yemen, along with the tasks of opposing Portuguese expansion and guaranteeing the safety of the Holy Cities.

The Ottomans were descended from Turkish tribes who had been driven from their homeland in the steppes of Central Asia by the Mongols. They had embraced Islam (as had the Mongols themselves) and settled in Anatolia where they formed the Ottoman confederation. They were called *ghazi*s,

109

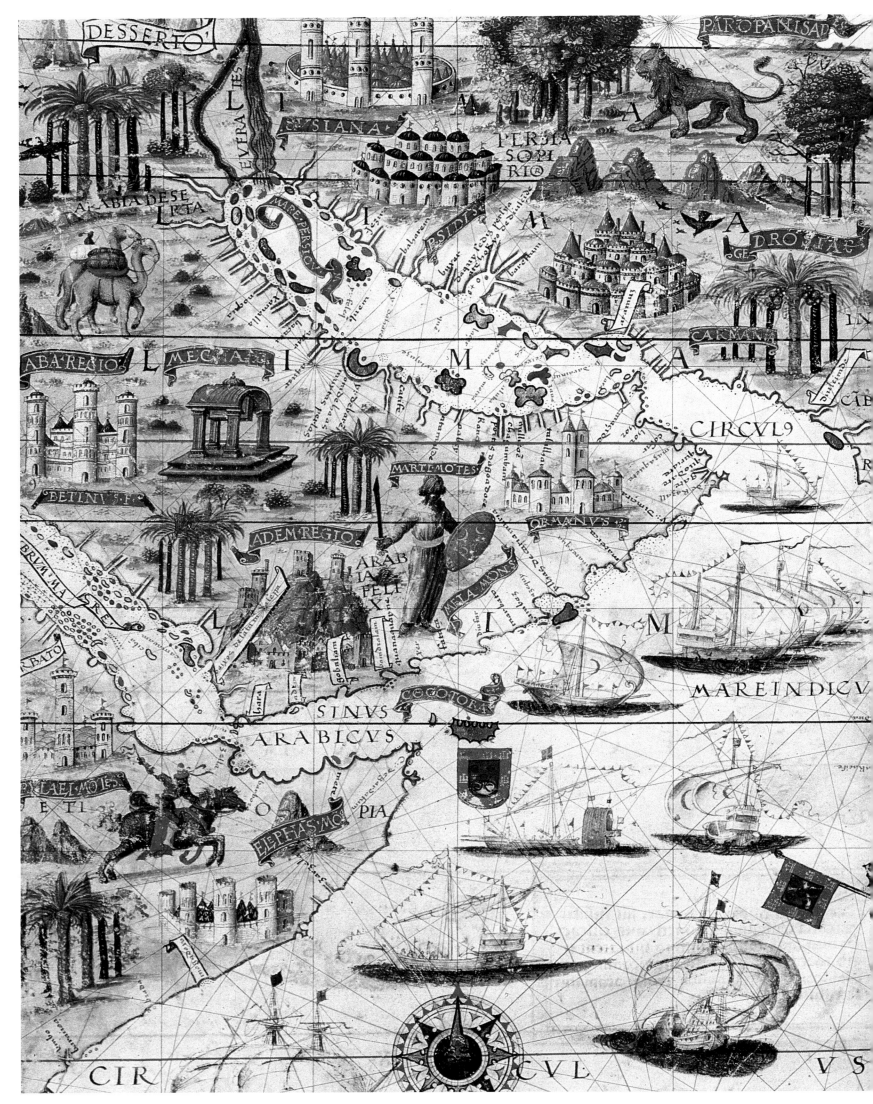

This remarkable map of the Indian Ocean was produced by Pedro Reinal in 1519, soon after the voyages of Vasco da Gama and other Portuguese mariners into the region. Medieval conceptions jostle with new discoveries in scenes in the Arabian Peninsula and elsewhere.

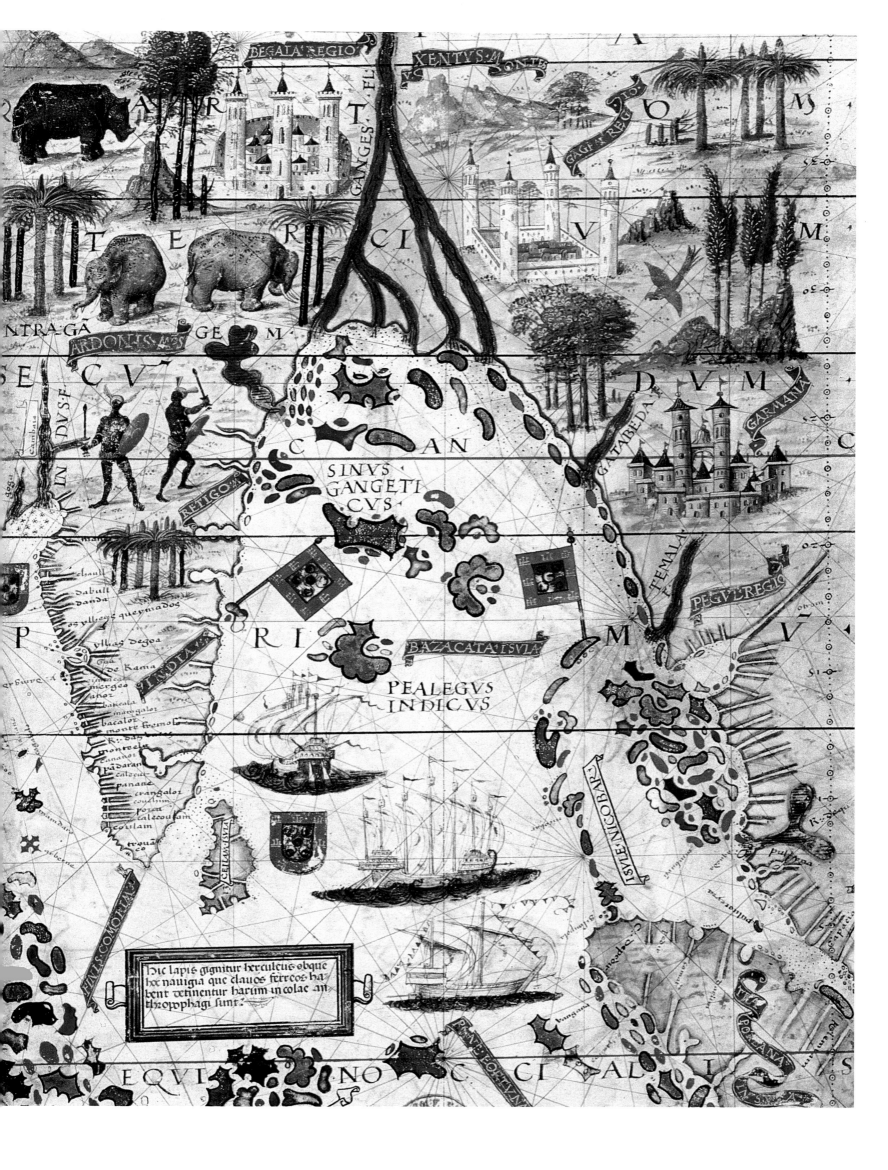

BEGALA REGIO

XENTVS MONTE

GANGES FL

GAGIA REGIO

EQVIR

T

O

M

TER

CI

V

M

NTRA GA

GE M

ARDONIS ASS

SE CV

IN DVSE

D

V M

GARMANA

C

AN

GATABEDA

SINVS GANGETI CVS

RETIGO

TEMALA

F

PEGV REGIO

P

RI

INDIA

BAZACATA ISVLA

M

V

PEALEGVS INDICVS

ISVLE NICOBAR

CELA ISVLA

FINIS COMORIN

Hic lapis gignitur herculeus obque hoc nauigia que clauos ferreos habent detinentur harum incolae an thropphagi sunt?

EQVIR

NO

C CI AL

S

Marco Polo is shown arriving in Hormuz in 1292, accompanied by a small menagerie, in this miniature from the 14th-century Livre de Merveilles.

WESTERN KNOWLEDGE OF ISLAMIC LANDS

Western knowledge of eastern lands was almost nonexistent before the First Crusade of 1096-99. Although pilgrims had always made their way to Jerusalem, early medieval pilgrimage accounts scarcely mention anything but sacred sites. In the 11th century, Venetian and Genoese merchants began trading in the eastern Mediterranean ports and Black Sea region and slowly a more accurate image of these regions began to circulate. The Quran was translated several times into Latin in the Middle Ages, but knowledge of Islam and the Islamic world remained very limited.

Marco Polo's description of his journeys through the Middle East to China in the late 13th century was enormously popular, judging by the large number of surviving manuscripts. His *Travels* contains a great deal of fact, mixed with some fable, but his medieval readers regarded the book as entertainment and it was only much later that the essential truth of his account was recognized.

Common geographical misconceptions were only gradually corrected. Beginning in the 13th century, mariners' charts of the eastern Mediterranean and North Africa show great familiarity even with obscure ports and some inland cites, as European countries were entering into trade agreements with Muslim rulers, particularly with the Mamluks in Egypt. The fall of Constantinople to the Ottoman Turks in 1453 and the arrival in Europe of educated Byzantine refugees vastly increased European knowledge of the East, although this knowledge did not reach the common man. Vasco da Gama's discovery of the ocean route to India in 1498 and the Portuguese naval presence in the Indian Ocean and Red Sea that followed led to the first accurate maps of the shape of the Arabian Peninsula and its coasts.

By the end of the 17th century, travelers had visited most Muslim lands and there was enough reliable information available to produce relatively accurate maps. The interior of the Arabian Peninsula was the last region to succumb to Western curiosity, beginning in the 18th century with the Danish traveler Carsten Niebuhr's careful observations and perhaps concluding with the work of oil exploration parties, supported by aerial surveys, beginning in the 1930s.

warriors for the faith, and their ambition was to die in battle for their adopted religion. The Ottoman Empire, governed from Constantinople (today's Istanbul) after 1453, by the 16th century encompassed the east and west coasts of the Arabian Peninsula, Egypt and North Africa and stretched from Persia almost to the gates of Vienna.

ARABIA IN OTTOMAN TIMES

THE OTTOMAN CONQUEROR OF EGYPT, SELIM I, ASSUMED THE title of Servant of the Holy Cities. The *sharif*s of Makkah acknowledged his suzerainty and, with Ottoman support, extended their authority as far north as Khaybar and as far south as Haly on the Tihamah coast. The Ottoman sultans did their best to protect the major pilgrim routes to Makkah, building fortresses at the wells along the way and garrisoning troops to protect pilgrims from Bedouin attack.

Suleiman the Magnificent (1520-66) fortified Madinah, surrounding the city with a 12-meter high (40-foot) basalt and granite wall and building a covered aqueduct to bring it water. Distances in Arabia were so vast, however, that small garrisons of Ottoman troops were for the most part ineffective in protecting pilgrim caravans. In the long run, it proved easier and cheaper to pay subsidies to the tribes to refrain from attacks.

When the Portuguese attacked Bahrain during Suleiman's rule, he responded by installing a governor in al-Hasa. The Ottomans remained in power there until they were expelled by the Bani Khalid tribe in 1663. The grazing lands and oases of what is now the Eastern Province stayed in the hands of the Bani Khalid until the establishment of the First Saudi State in the late 18th and early 19th centuries.

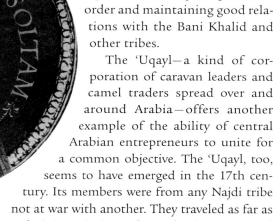

Suleiman made a determined effort to establish Ottoman naval control of the Red Sea and oust the Portuguese from India, in 1538 sending a fleet of 100 ships and 20,000 men to the Indian Ocean. The expeditions did not succeed in driving the Portuguese out of the Indian Ocean, but they did clear them from the Red Sea and the waterway recovered its former importance as the main route for the spice trade. By 1550, business was booming at the same level as before the Portuguese discovery of the Cape route to India.

In 1564, twenty-three ships unloaded cargoes of spices at Jiddah. The following year, 20,000 quintals (nearly 2 million kilograms, or 4.4 million pounds) of pepper, ginger, benzoin, cinnamon, silk, sandalwood, camphor, gold and sulfur were unloaded there, more than was reaching Lisbon.

To the east, in 1622, Shah Abbas of Iran prevailed upon the English East India Company to help him expel the Por-

Suleiman the Magnificent

tuguese from Hormuz. Shah Abbas founded a new port, Bandar Abbas, and Hormuz sank into oblivion. In the Hijaz, the *sharif*s of Makkah continued to control the Holy Cities and their hinterlands, under the suzerainty of the Ottoman sultans.

TRIBAL ACTIVITY

THROUGHOUT THE 1600S, THE TRIBES OF THE HIJAZ AND NAJD were on the move. This may have been part of a wider tribal movement, for at the same time large areas of Syria and Iraq were occupied by Bedouin tribes as Ottoman power waned.

An alliance of the tribes known as the 'Utub began to migrate from Najd to the east. They were led by three clans of 'Anazah—the Al Khalifa, now the ruling family of Bahrain; the Al Sabah, rulers of Kuwait; and the Jalahimah. They seem to have left their homeland around al-Aflaj in central Arabia in 1674 because of famine. The 'Utub set sail in 150 boats for Basra, then moved to Kuwait, where they settled with the permission of the *shaykh* of Bani Khalid, who controlled eastern Arabia. Gradually, the three leading clans specialized, the Al Khalifah in pearling and trade, and the Jalahimah in ships and naval defense, while the Al Sabah were responsible for imposing law and order and maintaining good relations with the Bani Khalid and other tribes.

The 'Uqayl—a kind of corporation of caravan leaders and camel traders spread over and around Arabia—offers another example of the ability of central Arabian entrepreneurs to unite for a common objective. The 'Uqayl, too, seems to have emerged in the 17th century. Its members were from any Najdi tribe not at war with another. They traveled as far as today's Iraq, Syria, Jordan, Palestine, Egypt and even Sudan.

They bought camels and horses from Bedouin tribes, paying for them with manufactured goods from the cities. The town of Buraydah, now capital of the Qasim district of Saudi Arabia, was one of their centers of operation. Their trading corporation was vital in servicing central Arabia and exporting its products during the period immediately preceding the event that ushered in the modern era in Arab lands: the alliance between Muhammad ibn Sa'ud, the ruler of al-Dir'iyah, and the religious reformer Muhammad ibn 'Abd al-Wahhab. This pact would lay the foundations of the modern Saudi state, launch its first successful movement against Ottoman rule, and focus the eyes of the world once more on Arabia.

113

The northern part of Riyadh, the capital of the Kingdom, now stretches within sight of the mud-walled ruins of al-Dir'iyah (foreground), fountainhead of the First Saudi State in the 1700s.

A Historic Meeting

ONE DAY IN 1744, AN ARDENT AND ELOQUENT PREACHER named Shaykh Muhammad ibn 'Abd al-Wahhab arrived at the oasis of al-Dir'iyah, on the Wadi Hanifah just northwest of Riyadh. He came on foot, seeking sanctuary from his hometown of al-'Uyaynah, 40 kilometers (25 miles) to the north—where unrest resulting from his reforms had caused its ruler to expel him.

The lord of al-Dir'iyah, Muhammad ibn Sa'ud, had heard about the *shaykh* and his call to purify Islam by imploring the people to adhere to the true teachings of the Quran and the *sunnah*. He welcomed Shaykh Muhammad warmly and committed himself to his support and protection. Indeed, Muhammad ibn Sa'ud called on Shaykh Muhammad, thus elevating the teacher in the eyes of the townspeople.

Muhammad ibn Sa'ud greeted Shaykh Muhammad with the words, "I bring you tidings of a home that is better than your native home." And the teacher replied, "I bring you tidings of glory and power; whoever holds fast to this word of unity will by means of it rule lands and men."

This exchange ushered in a new era in the history of Arabia. The two men—one an astute chieftain and the other an idealistic reformer bent on bringing the Islamic community back to the purity of its origins—formed an immediate warm regard for one another. The pact agreed upon that day inspired the rapid rise of the First Saudi State (1744–1818), propelling Najd and the House of Sa'ud into

Previous spread: (Left) Bearing an early version of Saudi Arabia's national flag, a contingent of 'Abd al-'Aziz Al Sa'ud's troops rides across the scrub desert near Thaj in March 1911 as part of his campaign to unify the tribes of the region within a single state. (Right) The Saudi Arabian flag today reflects the origins of the state in the 18th century. The Muslim profession of faith, "There is no god but Allah; Muhammad is the Messenger of Allah," appears above a drawn sword over a green background, thus reflecting faith and prosperity, and the power protecting both.

117

Riyadh's old city walls: "A good ruler protects his people."

TRIBAL SETTLERS AND NOMADS

The Najdi town was ruled by a *shaykh* or *amir*. The ruler was usually drawn from the town's chief tribal family, but sometimes a man whose impartiality in arbitration between rival sections was respected by all sides might be chosen from a lesser clan. Succession, though it could pass from father to son, was never clear-cut because it was felt that leadership should go to the kinsman deemed best suited for the job by the ruling family. Bitter family feuds could therefore erupt among rival claimants and their factions.

The power of the ruling group was usually rooted in a strong leader and augmented by property ownership. For his part, the ruler was expected to protect his people against internal strife, external raids and robbery, to maintain loyalty through open-handedness, and to arbitrate in disputes, increasingly with the aid of a judge versed in *shari'ah* law.

The nomadic tribes controlled the vast expanses of steppe and desert separating settlements. They depended on the settlements as markets for their animal products, which they exchanged for foodstuffs from farms and trade goods from outside. Thus, tribal settlers and nomads were linked not only by kinship, but also by economic interdependence. Nomads maintained relations with particular oases, dominating weak ones or owing allegiance to the rulers of strong ones.

prominence for the first time in Arabian affairs. Indeed, the reasons why the American oilmen in 1933 found a unified Kingdom of Saudi Arabia, with its capital at Riyadh, can be traced back to the First Saudi State, with its capital at al-Dir'iyah.

Al-Dir'iyah's foundation is traditionally ascribed to 1446, when the chief of the Dir' clan invited kinsmen from another Dir'iyah near Qatif on the Arabian Gulf to settle in his territory. This clan, al-Murayd, named their new settlement after their old home. It grew rapidly, but dispute over succession in the 17th century meant that it was outshone by a rival, the town of al-'Uyaynah.

By the end of the century, al-'Uyaynah's ruling family, Al Mu'ammar, had extended its territorial sway. In the process, it had acquired a potent ally, the Bani Khalid tribe of al-Hasa (today's Eastern Province). Bani Khalid had ended Ottoman rule in al-Hasa in 1670, and the tribe was seeking to expand its power into Najd. Al-'Uyaynah was an obvious ally.

Al-'Uyaynah's rulers welcomed Bani Khalid support, and the two allies dominated the region. The *amir*s of al-Dir'iyah occasionally contested the arrangement, but found opposition unprofitable.

Around 1720, Sa'ud ibn Muhammad, of the Muqrin branch of the al-Murayd clan, became lord of al-Dir'iyah. He did not rule for long, and his son Muhammad ibn Sa'ud took his place at the helm.

THE REFORM MOVEMENT AND THE *MUWAHHIDUN*

WHEN SHAYKH MUHAMMAD IBN 'ABD AL-WAHHAB ARRIVED in al-Dir'iyah, there was much in local customs to offend any devout Muslim, let alone a scholar of *shari'ah*. People venerated tombs, certain trees featured in a fertility cult, a sacred cave was frequented and a blind "holy man" was revered as a miracle-worker.

Such practices were not uncommon in the Muslim world at large. But they had been denounced by Ahmad ibn Hanbal, the 9th-century founder of one of the most prominent *Sunni* schools of theology and law, and his followers, who included the Najdi *'ulama*, or religious scholars.

Shaykh Muhammad had sat at the feet of many learned scholars in Makkah, Madinah, Basra and al-Hasa, and he now had firm opinions. In 1740, he set about propagating his views openly. He published his famous work, *Kitab al-Tawhid* (*The Book of the Oneness of God*), and vehemently denounced the heresies he perceived all around. Some applauded his views, but his denunciations naturally provoked antagonism, too.

Shaykh Muhammad and his followers referred to themselves simply as Muslims, or else as *muwahhidun*, or "Unitarians": upholders of *tawhid*. Shaykh Muhammad would have objected to the name Wahhabism, which was coined by outsiders for his movement, because it would imply

The palace of Sa'd ibn Sa'ud was the first major building at al-Dir'iyah to be restored, in the early 1980s. The original palace was built at the start of the 19th century, during the heyday of the city.

that he was a founder of a new sect. He was a *salafi*, a traditionalist, and movements such as his hearken back to the origins of Islam.

THE FIRST SAUDI STATE, 1744–1818

AFTER SHAYKH MUHAMMAD WAS INSTALLED AT AL-DIR'IYAH, he and Muhammad ibn Sa'ud set about creating a godly community and propagating the call to reform. Commitment to the correct form of all practices sanctioned by *shari'ah* was at the heart of this idea of the state.

Henceforth, the Saudi ruler was known by the religio-political title of *imam,* or leader of the community. The rapid rise of al-Dir'iyah exemplifies the great unifying power of a religious ideal.

In the mid-18th century, al-Dir'iyah was a modest settlement, and the beginnings of the reform movement were small. By the time of Muhammad ibn Sa'ud's death in 1765, however, al-Dir'iyah's writ ran in several of the towns of central Najd, with opposition centered in the neighboring town of Riyadh. Imam Muhammad was succeeded by his son 'Abd al-'Aziz, under whom expansion escalated. In 1773—three years before the American Declaration of Inde-

pendence—he captured Riyadh, and within a dozen years he controlled all of Najd.

When 'Abd al-'Aziz's warriors entered Riyadh, it was a ghost town: Its leader had fled south with almost all its inhabitants. The town and all its property were expropriated by the *Bayt al-Mal,* or Public Treasury, and its people were invited to return.

The First Saudi State was a remarkable example of Arabian state formation, combining ancient kinship traditions with Islamic ideals. It brought settlers and nomads together under the influence of a religious idea into a centralized entity that harnessed tribal energies without obliterating tribal affiliations. The state was founded on the principle of equal partnership between ruler and religious advisors. When Shaykh Muhammad died in 1792, his position as an advisor to the *imam* was passed to his four sons.

By 1785, al-Dir'iyah had consolidated its hold on all of Najd and could look beyond central Arabia. With unity in Najd, larger armies could be levied and revenues increased. The Imam 'Abd al-'Aziz and his son Sa'ud were gifted leaders and field commanders.

'Abd al-'Aziz was legendarily devout. He wore only woollen clothes and bore undecorated weapons. He ate simple food, off wooden dishes. Devoid of pomp, he used to sit on the ground, saying, "One must be humble as dignity is for God alone."

One of the great attractions of the reform movement to a previously insecure society was the universal law and order it established in both oasis and desert. Theft and banditry were eradicated, people could travel in safety and it was said that livestock could be left grazing with no one to tend it. If anybody found a stray camel, he would bring it to al-Dir'iyah for the owner to claim.

Al-Dir'iyah then moved against al-Hasa. A series of campaigns up to 1795, marked by a famous battle at the hill of Ghuraymil just southwest of present-day Abqaiq in the winter of 1789–90, ensured the submission of its Bani Khalid masters. But raids north toward Iraq alarmed the Ottoman authorities in Baghdad.

The Ottoman sultan, roused also by raids on the Hijaz borderlands to the west, urged the Sharif Ghalib of Makkah to take action. All attempts to curb Unitarian gains were repulsed. In 1801, their forces struck inside Iraq and destroyed the mausoleums built on the tombs of the saints at Karbala.

In 1802, a Unitarian force took Tayif in the Hijaz. Sa'ud then laid siege to Makkah, whose people held out for several months before the Sharif Ghalib abandoned it for Jiddah. In April 1803, al-Dir'iyah's warriors, led by Sa'ud, donned pilgrim garb and entered the city in peace.

They performed the *'umrah*, the "little pilgrimage," and then demolished shrines and memorials in Makkah that offended their beliefs. Sa'ud then marched on Jiddah but failed to take it and withdrew to Najd. The Sharif Ghalib returned to Makkah, taking care to maintain an outward adherence to Unitarian doctrines.

In late 1803, the Imam 'Abd al-'Aziz was killed in the mosque at al-Dir'iyah by an assassin avenging the attack on Karbala. Sa'ud succeeded him, ruling till his death in 1814. Sa'ud's reign marks the widest extent of the First

The old buildings of Yanbu', like those of Jiddah, are fine examples of traditional Red Sea architecture. Yanbu' enjoyed a role as trade and pilgrim port for Madinah, just as Jiddah did for Makkah. It was also the most convenient point of entry into the Hijaz for Muhammad 'Ali Pasha's expeditionary forces from Egypt in 1816.

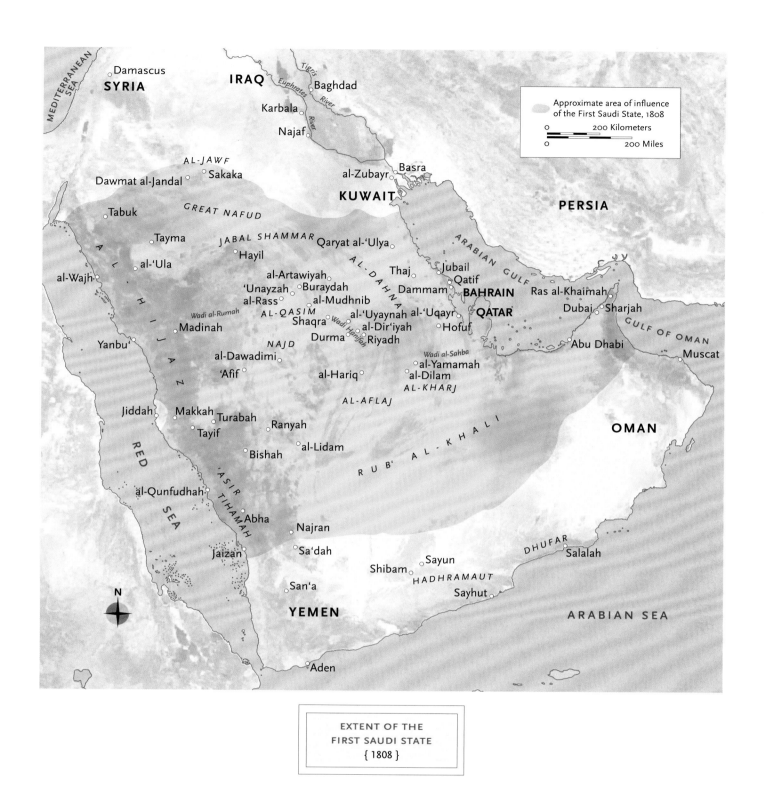

MEDITERRANEAN SEA

SYRIA

o Damascus

IRAQ

Tigris
Euphrates River

o Baghdad

o Karbala

o Najaf

o Basra

AL-JAWF

Dawmat al-Jandal o

o Sakaka

o al-Zubayr

KUWAIT

PERSIA

o Tabuk

GREAT NAFUD

o Tayma

JABAL SHAMMAR

o Qaryat al-'Ulya

AL-DAHNA

ARABIAN GULF

o al-'Ula

o Hayil

o Thaj

o Jubail

o Qatif

o al-Wajh

al-Artawiyah o

'Unayzah o Buraydah o
al-Rass o

Dammam o

BAHRAIN

Ras al-Khaimah o

o al-Mudhnib

AL-QASIM

Wadi al-Rumah

o Shaqra

al-'Uyaynah o al-'Uqayr o

QATAR

Dubai o Sharjah

Wadi Hanifah

al-Dir'iyah o

o Hofuf

GULF OF OMAN

o Madinah

Durma o Riyadh

Abu Dhabi

Yanbu' o

NAJD

Wadi al-Sahba

o al-Yamamah

o Muscat

o al-Dawadimi

o al-Dilam

'Afif o

o al-Hariq

AL-KHARJ

AL-AFLAJ

OMAN

Jiddah o

Makkah o

o Turabah

RUB' AL-KHALI

Tayif o

o Ranyah

o al-Lidam

o Bishah

RED SEA

'ASIR

al-Qunfudhah o

TIHAMAH

o Abha

o Najran

DHUFAR

Salalah o

Jaizan o

o Sa'dah

Shibam o

o Sayun

HADHRAMAUT

N

o San'a

Sayhut o

YEMEN

ARABIAN SEA

o Aden

Approximate area of influence
of the First Saudi State, 1808

0   200 Kilometers

0   200 Miles

EXTENT OF THE
FIRST SAUDI STATE
{ 1808 }

Saudi State. In 1804, his forces took Madinah and Yanbu'. 'Asir was added to the domain, raids were made into Syria, and in 1811 a campaign against Baghdad was contemplated. By then, the territory controlled by the House of Sa'ud was so vast that the peninsula was divided into 20 provinces, each with a loyal Unitarian as governor and a *qadi* in charge of religious affairs and education. Part of the revenue of each district was consigned to the construction of forts and mosques.

The Siege and Fall of al-Dir'iyah

WITH THE LOSS OF THE HOLY CITIES IN 1803-04, THE OTToman sultan became more anxious than ever to suppress the reform movement in Najd. He ordered Muhammad 'Ali Pasha, the Ottoman governor of Egypt, to undertake a punitive expedition against the Saudis and reestablish Ottoman authority over the Holy Cities. In 1811, Muhammad 'Ali sent his son Tusun to recover the Hijaz. Then, exasperated

EARLY EUROPEAN VISITORS TO THE HIJAZ

For centuries, Arabia remained a land of mystery to non-Muslim nations. Only a handful of accounts of early European travelers to Makkah and Madinah have survived, such as those of Ludovico di Varthema (1503), Johann Wild (1606) and Joseph Pitts (c. 1685).

Things changed in the 18th century with the European Enlightenment, which ushered in the age of exploration. The first scientific expedition to Arabia was that of the Dane Carsten Niebuhr (1733–1815) and his companions. Most of the work was done in Yemen, but on the voyage there in 1762 the expedition spent six weeks in Jiddah. Niebuhr wrote the fullest description yet of Jiddah and its trade and produced the first measured plan of the city. News of the reform movement in Najd came to his ears and he was the first to report on it for European readers, noting its adherence to the fundamentals of Islam. But neither Niebuhr nor the seamen of the English East India Company, who were by now frequenting Jiddah, were able to penetrate inland.

The next important traveler to the Hijaz was the mysterious Catalan 'Ali Bey al-'Abbasi (c. 1766–1818), whose real name was Domingo Badia y Leblich. Thought to have been an agent in the pay of Napoleon, 'Ali Bey arrived in the Hijaz in 1807 when Makkah and Madinah were under the control of the First Saudi State. Traveling in the grand manner with a retinue and plenty of money, he passed for a Muslim and attended the pilgrimage. He was the first to give the West a systematic account of Makkah, then much reduced by the war with al-Dir'iyah. He was the first since Pitts to witness the pilgrimage. When he tried to reach Madinah, he was turned back by the Unitarians, who condemned visits to the Prophet's tomb as saint worship.

Shortly after 'Ali Bey, the Hijaz received one of the most remarkable of all explorers, the Anglo-Swiss traveller Johann Ludwig Burckhardt (1784–1817), who also visited Egypt, Nubia and Syria. He was the first Western explorer to see Petra in today's Jordan. Traveling as a Muslim, "Shaykh Ibrahim" arrived in Jiddah in 1814, and spent almost a year in the Hijaz when Muhammad 'Ali of Egypt was personally conducting the campaign to recover it from Unitarian control. His descriptions of Jiddah and Makkah were not surpassed until the 1880s. His two books, *Travels in Arabia* and *Notes on the Bedouins and Wahabys*, are his lasting memorial. In the latter, he notes: "The doctrines of Abd el Wahab were not those of a new religion; his efforts were directed only to reform abuses in the followers of Islam."

Burckhardt's account of his sojourn in the Hijaz became standard reading for those who followed him. The most famous of his successors, Richard Burton (1821-90), contributed greatly to the world's knowledge of Madinah, but conceded that Burckhardt's description of Makkah was so accurate that he had little to add.

(Clockwise from top left) Carsten Niebuhr, depicted in the costume given him by the imam of the Yemen. Johann Ludwig Burckhardt, sketched in the costume he wore in the Hijaz as "Shaykh Ibrahim." The mysterious Domingo Badia y Leblich traveled in the Muslim world under the name 'Ali Bey al-'Abbasi.

by Tusun's considerable losses of men, in 1813 he went to Arabia and took charge himself.

As long as Sa'ud was alive, the Egyptians met with mixed success, although they managed to reoccupy Madinah and Makkah. When Sa'ud died in 1814, he was succeeded by his son 'Abd Allah. A heavy defeat at Basal, near Tayif, in January 1815 put the Saudis on the defensive.

Forced to return to Egypt for political reasons, in 1816 Muhammad 'Ali sent his second son Ibrahim Pasha across the Red Sea at the head of a more powerful army to invade Najd and destroy al-Dir'iyah. With Ibrahim's arrival in Najd, Imam 'Abd Allah called up all the loyal towns and tribes of Najd and withdrew to his capital, which he set about fortifying. By March 1818, Ibrahim was ready to march on al-Dir'iyah.

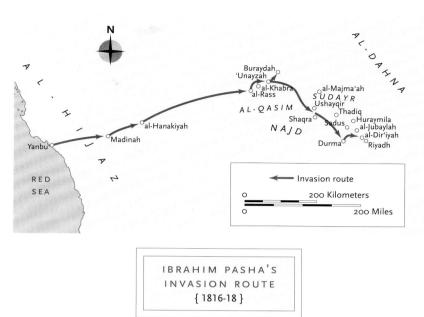

Following a six-month siege through Najd's intensely hot summer, al-Dir'iyah finally fell. Ibrahim captured 'Abd Allah and many other members of the House of Sa'ud. 'Abd Allah faced his fate with dignified resignation and reportedly said:

> "You are a brave man, ya Ibrahim Pasha, your father is greater than you, and Sultan Mahmoud is greater still than your father. But God is much greater than all of you, and if it is not destined that I should lose my head, nothing will be able to remove it from my shoulders."

'Abd Allah was sent to prison in Cairo, and then to the Ottoman capital Constantinople. There, Turkish 'ulama tried to convince him of the error of his creed, but he clung to his Unitarian principles. In late November 1818, he was executed. Ibrahim Pasha leveled al-Dir'iyah, destroyed local forts and other defense works, and encouraged local rivalries. In 1819, believing he had destroyed Al Sa'ud forever, he returned to the Hijaz and then to Egypt.

THE SECOND SAUDI STATE, 1824–91

VARIOUS CLAIMANTS ATTEMPTED TO REVIVE a Saudi state at al-Dir'iyah, and Ottoman occupation of Najd was briefly renewed in 1820. In 1824, Turki ibn 'Abd Allah, a close relative (though not the son) of the dead 'Abd Allah, established himself in Riyadh and evicted the occupiers. Riyadh has remained the capital of the Saudi dynasty ever since, with a short break from 1891 to 1902.

Turki, a nephew of Sa'ud, ruled until his assassination in 1834, masterminding the rise of the Second Saudi State. He and his son Faysal, who ruled 1834-37 and 1843-65,

Muhammad 'Ali Pasha, Ottoman governor of Egypt, twice invaded the Hijaz and Najd to suppress the reform movement on behalf of his overlord the Ottoman sultan in Constantinople.

upheld the values of Unitarianism. When Turki recovered a region, he closely monitored the performance of the five daily prayers, ordered all to follow the precepts of Islam meticulously and exhorted his people to fear God, to pray and to pay the zakah. He also stressed the responsibility of the individual not only for his own behavior, but for that of the community, and urged avoidance of usury—always regarded as contrary to the teaching of Islam. In a letter setting out his views, he instructed his district governors to standardize all weights and measures to prevent cheating and misunderstandings. He stated that any bargain once made was inviolable.

The Second Saudi State differed from its predecessor in two important ways. First, there was a shift in the balance between ruler and 'ulama toward greater authority on the ruler's part, and this continued to be the case throughout the 19th century.

The Second Saudi State was also less ambitious in territorial scope than its parent, and—no doubt because of the trauma of al-Dir'iyah's destruction—more conscious of the dangers from outside. Turki showed circumspection in dealing with foreign powers: He paid a nominal tribute to the Ottoman Government, did not threaten the Hijaz and 'Asir, and established friendly relations with the British, who had begun to impose a series of treaties on the coastal rulers with a view to establishing peace in the Gulf.

In 1830, Turki brought al-Hasa and its coast once again under Saudi rule. By 1833, he had made Bahrain, the Trucial Shaykhdoms (today's United Arab Emirates) and Muscat tributary to Riyadh, bringing his

Al-Dir'iyah was abandoned following the siege in 1818 and the town was never fully repopulated, as the new Saudi capital was founded at Riyadh in 1824. What remains after nearly two centuries is testament to the quality of the sun-dried mud used by its builders. Parts of the site are now being restored.

RULERS OF THE HOUSE OF SA'UD

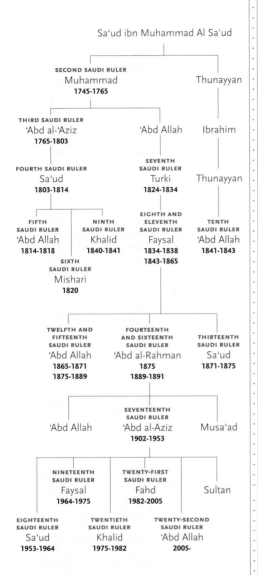

Sa'ud ibn Muhammad Al Sa'ud

SECOND SAUDI RULER
Muhammad
1745-1765

Thunayyan

THIRD SAUDI RULER
'Abd al-'Aziz
1765-1803

'Abd Allah

Ibrahim

FOURTH SAUDI RULER
Sa'ud
1803-1814

SEVENTH SAUDI RULER
Turki
1824-1834

Thunayyan

FIFTH SAUDI RULER
'Abd Allah
1814-1818

NINTH SAUDI RULER
Khalid
1840-1841

EIGHTH AND ELEVENTH SAUDI RULER
Faysal
1834-1838
1843-1865

TENTH SAUDI RULER
'Abd Allah
1841-1843

SIXTH SAUDI RULER
Mishari
1820

TWELFTH AND FIFTEENTH SAUDI RULER
'Abd Allah
1865-1871
1875-1889

FOURTEENTH AND SIXTEENTH SAUDI RULER
'Abd al-Rahman
1875
1889-1891

THIRTEENTH SAUDI RULER
Sa'ud
1871-1875

SEVENTEENTH SAUDI RULER
'Abd Allah

'Abd al-Aziz
1902-1953

Musa'ad

NINETEENTH SAUDI RULER
Faysal
1964-1975

TWENTY-FIRST SAUDI RULER
Fahd
1982-2005

Sultan

EIGHTEENTH SAUDI RULER
Sa'ud
1953-1964

TWENTIETH SAUDI RULER
Khalid
1975-1982

TWENTY-SECOND SAUDI RULER
'Abd Allah
2005-

Sa'ud ibn Muhammad Al Muqrin is regarded as the founder of the House of Sa'ud, and it is from him that it takes its name. However, he came from a long line of *amir*s of al-Dir'iyah, drawn from two chief clans, Al Muqrin and Al Watban, both descended from Mani' al-Muraydi, whom tradition names as the founder of al-Dir'iyah in 1446.

realm into contact with British protectorates. But he did so without provoking a hostile response from the British, whose policy was to avoid becoming involved in land-based hostilities against any Arabian potentate. Furthermore, from this time on, many British officials regarded Saudi rule with a benevolent eye, as an essentially civilizing force in a region of otherwise chaotic tribal rivalries.

In 1834, Turki was succeeded by his son Faysal, who had been captured and then had escaped from the Egyptians. Significantly, in the 1830s Faysal acted to settle the affairs of northern Najd by helping to install the Al Rashid, the ruling clan of the Shammar tribe, at Hayil. Then he was faced with yet another Egyptian campaign to conquer Najd.

In 1838, Faysal was captured again, giving himself up rather than see his loyal followers slaughtered, and for the second time was taken off to exile in Cairo. During his exile, the Egyptians placed a relative of Al Sa'ud in Riyadh to rule on their behalf. In 1840, however, Egypt's ruler abandoned his dream of empire in central and eastern Arabia and his forces retreated to their province of the Hijaz.

Faysal escaped from Cairo once more in 1843 and reestablished himself in Riyadh. His second reign, which lasted 22 years, marked the high point of the Second Saudi State, which maintained itself in all of Najd and al-Hasa until his death. Faysal was both a scholar and a stern *imam* who was generous to the poor.

Colonel Lewis Pelly, the British Resident in the Gulf who visited Riyadh in 1865, noted Faysal's concern about the

A 19th-century European artist depicted (left) a Bedouin in the Al Sa'ud camp with a more ornately dressed member of the 'Awazim tribe.

A groom leads horses of the royal stud from their stables in the Kut quarter of Hofuf in the Eastern Province in the mid-20th century. For much of the 19th century and before, fine Arabian horses were a lucrative export from Najd, especially to India, and powerful rulers, such as the imams of al-Dir'iyah, maintained hundreds of horses.

economic problems of Arabia. Pelly wrote that he spoke "very sensibly on the physical and political position of Arabia, explaining its great want to be that of rain. If only rain would fall, agriculture would be possible, and the tribes might then be rendered sedentary." This idea that the Bedouin might be turned toward agriculture and trade foreshadowed the settlement of nomadic tribes in the early 20th century by Faysal's grandson King 'Abd al-'Aziz. Pelly also records Faysal as saying:

> "... be Arabia what it may, it is ours. We dare say you wonder how we can remain here cut off from the rest of the world. Yet we are content. We are princes according to our degree. We feel ourselves a king every inch." He said he could manage his own Arabs; and that his plan was to come down

severely on his chiefs of tribes, when their followers plundered or committed other crimes ... "Yes, we are very severe; but we are just."

Both agriculture and trade were limited in the Saudi domain in the 19th century, but during Faysal's rule a market for Arabian horses developed in British India. While Najd had bred fine horses for centuries, in the 1860s demand picked up and exports soared. Horses bred by the Shammar tribe were exported through Kuwait and such Saudi ports as Qatif. An estimated 600 horses were exported through Kuwait in 1863 alone, helping Hayil grow into an important town. The only other exports of consequence were dates and pearls from the al-Hasa region. In return, imports grew and

EARLY TRAVELERS TO RIYADH

Najd, remote and inaccessible, remained unknown to the outside world for longer than the Hijaz and the east coast of Arabia. Before Ibrahim Pasha invaded from Egypt in 1816-19, only a single European is known to have reached al-Dir'iyah. That was John Lewis Reinaud, who was sent from Kuwait between 1793 and 1795, by the English East India Company, to prevail upon the Imam 'Abd al-'Aziz ibn Muhammad, the second leader of the First Saudi State, to desist from interfering with the desert mail to Aleppo, Syria. Sadly, Reinaud left no extended account of his visit.

That changed with Ibrahim Pasha's invasion, on which several French and Italian mercenaries and doctors served. Some later reported their experiences to the eminent French geographer E. F. Jomard, whose work became the basis of outside knowledge of Najd for several decades to come.

Ibrahim Pasha's campaign caught the attention of the British in India and the Gulf. Assuming he was set on colonizing central and eastern Arabia, they sent George Forster Sadleir, an Indian Army officer, to meet him. In fact, when Sadleir set out in 1819, Ibrahim was in the process of evacuating al-Hasa and Najd, and his dogged pursuit of Ibrahim Pasha through Riyadh, al-Dir'iyah and al-Qasim to Madinah inadvertently made him the first European to cross the Arabian Peninsula via Lower Najd. This feat was not to be repeated for nearly 100 years, when Harry St. John B. Philby of England made his crossing in 1917.

Al-Qasim and points north received several visitors during the 19th century, the most notable of whom were Georg Wallin in the 1840s, Carlo Guarmani in the 1860s, Charles Doughty and Wilfred and Lady Anne Blunt in the 1870s, and Charles Huber and Julius Euting in the 1880s. Doughty's *Travels in Arabia Deserta* is a towering literary masterpiece. But only two foreigners visited Riyadh: William Gifford Palgrave and Colonel Lewis Pelly.

Palgrave, though British, came in 1862 as an agent of the French and disguised as a Syrian doctor.

William Gifford Palgrave (top) and Colonel Lewis Pelly (above) were the only two Westerners to visit Riyadh in the latter half of the 19th century.

His vivid account of his six weeks in Riyadh appears in his best-seller, *Narrative of a Year's Journey Through Central and Eastern Arabia*.

Pelly, who came to Riyadh in 1865 for meetings with the Imam Faysal, was in many ways Palgrave's opposite. Pelly was British Resident in the Gulf. Eschewing disguise, he traveled in his uniform. His motives were part political, part geographical: He wanted to see if Palgrave's visit had damaged British interests (it had not) and discover more about the topography of central Arabia. He was the first to fix the latitude and longitude of Riyadh. He left a graphic description of his meetings with the blind *imam*, then in the last year of his life.

Almost 50 years passed before the next visitors. Then, in 1912, in the run-up to World War I, two came in rapid succession: the Dane Barclay Raunkiaer and the Englishman Gerard Leachman. Raunkiaer has been suspected of being an agent of Turco-German interests. Leachman, an army officer who could pass himself off as an Arab of the desert, was a specialist in desert intelligence who became something of a legend among the tribes of northeast Arabia and Iraq. He has the distinction of being the first person to photograph Riyadh.

Such early travelers to Riyadh and other places in the land that became Saudi Arabia in 1932 would be astonished by developments since they made their trips—especially the air and highway systems that carry visitors near and far. In April 2000, Saudi Arabia's Council of Ministers acted to encourage national and international tourism in the Kingdom by establishing the Riyadh-based Supreme Commission for Tourism, headed by Prince Sultan ibn Salman ibn 'Abd al-'Aziz, and charging it to expand opportunities for domestic investment and job creation in the field.

Since then, the commission has worked to build an inventory of archeological, historical and cultural sites throughout the Kingdom, and cooperated with travel organizations and educational institutions to promote tourism.

the first manufactured goods began to make their way into the markets of eastern and central Arabia.

The trade of the period, although limited, required some form of currency, and several were available: coins minted by the Ottomans, the British, the Indians and the common currency—the Maria Theresa *thaler* from Austria. There was also a coin called *tawilah* ("long one"), minted in al-Hasa, Persia and perhaps other Gulf areas. Made of silver, copper or lead, it consisted of a strip of metal folded in half to make what looked like a cotter pin and was stamped on the side with an Arabic inscription in *kufic* script. At one time the *tawilah*—called *larin* outside Arabia—was accepted as legal tender from the Gulf to Ceylon.

Faysal's death in 1865 was followed by dynastic strife and gradual loss of allegiance to the Al Saʿud. This led to Riyadh's eclipse by the rising power of Hayil under Muhammad ibn Rashid. A struggle between Faysal's sons ʿAbd Allah and Saʿud enabled the Ottomans to occupy much of the eastern seaboard and the oasis of al-Hasa. Landing in 1871 at Ras Tanura, today the site of a major Saudi Aramco refinery and shipping terminal, they marched 160 kilometers (100 miles) to Hofuf, the main town of al-Hasa, overcame stubborn resistance by the Saudi governor and occupied the fortress. The Ottomans incorporated the province into the imperial administration—where it would remain until 1913.

By the time Saʿud died in Riyadh in 1875, ten years of civil war had reduced the city's influence to a shadow of what it had been under the Imam Faysal. Imam ʿAbd Allah lived out his last years facing rivalry from the sons of Saʿud. In 1887, Ibn Rashid intervened on ʿAbd Allah's side to rescue Riyadh from Saʿud's sons, but then took the ailing *imam* off to Hayil and installed a Rashidi governor in the city. When ʿAbd Allah died in 1889, his brother ʿAbd al-Rahman tried to revive Saudi fortunes.

In 1890, ʿAbd al-Rahman, appointed governor of Riyadh by Ibn Rashid, took the Rashidi garrison prisoner. Muhammad ibn Rashid then marched on the town and besieged it. He cut down a large number of date palms on which the residents depended for sustenance, a common practice in Arabian warfare at the time. After 40 days, Ibn Rashid proposed negotiations. In the Saudi delegation was the boy and future king, ʿAbd al-ʿAziz, making his debut on the stage of history.

The truce signed that day was short-lived. Ibn Rashid soon led his men to the area of al-Qasim in northern Najd. There, on January 21, 1891, Hayil inflicted a crushing defeat on a coalition of Riyadh and its allies at the Battle of al-Mulaydah.

Exile, 1891–1902

Isolated and bereft of allies, ʿAbd al-Rahman abandoned Riyadh. He sent his women and children to seek refuge in Bahrain, while with his son ʿAbd al-ʿAziz, aged about 15, he took to the southern deserts where he had friends among the Al Murrah tribe. Here, ʿAbd al-ʿAziz learned much about survival in desert conditions. For a time, they

The Maria Theresa thaler is still prized by silversmiths throughout the Middle East and North Africa. The coins are often incorporated into jewelry, such as this Saudi Bedouin necklace.

THE MARIA THERESA *THALER*

One of the most distinctive coins ever minted, the Maria Theresa *thaler* (the origin of the word "dollar") was first struck in 1741 by the Hapsburg Empress Maria Theresa of Austria. As a trade coin, it rapidly established itself as the favored currency throughout the Levant, the Red Sea, much of Arabia and the Horn of Africa. It also circulated in the Americas and as far east as China, and some historians consider it to be the first truly international currency. The Empress Maria Theresa died in 1780, but the coins had achieved such prestige by then that they continued to be minted with the date 1780 and used for another two centuries. Though they have not been an official state currency for a long time, they are still a familiar sight in the *suqs* of the Arabian Peninsula.

In 1896, 'Abd al-Rahman Al Sa'ud took refuge with his family, including the young future King 'Abd al-'Aziz, in Kuwait, then a bustling port. Their host Shaykh Mubarak Al Sabah was proving to be an astute manipulator of the Ottomans and the European powers then competing for influence at the head of the Gulf, and by attending Mubarak's court 'Abd al-'Aziz sharpened his statecraft skills.

roamed the fringes of the Rub' al-Khali, but later moved on to Qatar and then Bahrain. Finally, in 1896, 'Abd al-Rahman and his family took refuge with Shaykh Mubarak Al Sabah of Kuwait.

Visitors to Shaykh Mubarak's court could hardly have failed to notice the exceptionally tall young man among the guests from the House of Sa'ud. 'Abd al-'Aziz, then about 20 years old, was a strapping 1.9 meters (six feet, three inches) tall. The years the Al Sa'ud spent in Kuwait as guests of Mubarak proved formative for 'Abd al-'Aziz, providing valuable insights into the conduct of international relations.

The 19th century had seen the rapid spread of European empires around the globe. Mubarak was a nimble politi-

cian trying to maintain Kuwait's autonomy in an arena of imperial rivalry. The tiny principality, strategically placed at the northwestern tip of the Gulf, was being courted by Germany and the Ottomans, Russia, France and Britain.

The British project to secure communications between Britain and India had led to a series of protectorate treaties with Muscat, the Trucial Shaykhdoms and Bahrain, and to Britain's occupation of Aden. The Ottomans had tightened their grip on the Hijaz, 'Asir and Yemen outside Aden; al-Hasa had been an Ottoman province since 1871. The Ottomans even claimed Kuwait, where Shaykh Mubarak had acknowledged the suzerainty of the Ottoman sultan to keep the Turks at arm's length.

early 1901 failed, and for his second late that year the Saudis could muster just 40 men. Toward the end of the year, 'Abd al-'Aziz and his men set off for Najd in the first phase of a campaign to recover his patrimony and rebuild the fortunes of the House of Sa'ud.

Riyadh Recovered, January 1902

The Saudis did not march straight on Riyadh. Instead, they spent several months on the northern fringes of the Rub' al-Khali, hoping to win reinforcements from the tribes camped near the wells of Yabrin and Haradh. 'Abd al-'Aziz was able to recruit about 20 more warriors and, reluctant to wait any longer, he decided to attack Riyadh. He set off via the wells of Abu Jifan, 100 kilometers (65 miles) east of the town.

One and a half hour's march from Riyadh, 'Abd al-'Aziz left one-third of his force with the camels, instructing them to return to Kuwait if no message was received from him within 24 hours. Then, with the rest of his men, he advanced on foot—to be less conspicuous—until he reached the outskirts of the city. There they waited for night to fall.

At last it was time. 'Abd al-'Aziz stationed his brother Muhammad in the palm groves with 33 men to act as a backup force and quietly scaled the city's adobe walls with the others. Once in the town, they knocked on the door of the house of a cattle-dealer, who fled. His daughters, recognizing 'Abd al-'Aziz, were gagged and locked up. Next, 'Abd al-'Aziz sent a messenger back to tell Muhammad, waiting outside the walls, to advance with all possible stealth into the city. Finally, by standing on one another's shoulders, 'Abd al-'Aziz and his men entered the house of 'Ajlan, Ibn Rashid's governor, silenced the servants and searched the house. Learning that 'Ajlan had the habit of spending his nights in the garrison fortress of al-Masmak, just across the open space in front of the house, they decided to watch and wait till morning when the gates of the fortress would be opened.

Waiting proved difficult. As 'Abd al-'Aziz recalled in later years, they "slept a little while ... prayed the morning prayer and sat thinking about what we should do." At last the dark desert sky lightened and they got set for action.

Originally, they had planned to take 'Ajlan prisoner as soon as he had left the fort and entered the house. But as the sun rose and the gate of the fort swung open, they saw that 'Ajlan was not alone: He walked out of the gate accompanied by 10 bodyguards. Instantly 'Abd al-'Aziz and his men sprang to the attack, leaving four men in the house to cover them with rifles.

At the sudden appearance of 'Abd al-'Aziz, 'Ajlan's bodyguard bolted, leaving the governor to face the Saudi onslaught alone, with only his sword. Darting forward, 'Abd Allah ibn Jiluwi, a cousin of 'Abd al-'Aziz, threw a spear at 'Ajlan but missed; the spear lodged in the gate of the fort.

International politics thus impinged upon Arabia much more strongly than it had in the days of the First Saudi State. As 'Abd al-'Aziz observed Mubarak's dextrous international footwork, he also kept an eye on the Rashids of Hayil, now allied with the Ottomans. The House of Rashid was led by a nephew of Muhammad ibn Rashid. His name was also 'Abd al-'Aziz and he had a reputation for being weaker and more impetuous than his formidable uncle.

This Ibn Rashid had designs of his own on Kuwait. So when 'Abd al-'Aziz decided it was time for the House of Sa'ud to win back the lands wrested from it by Hayil, he found a ready supporter in Shaykh Mubarak. His first attempt in

No coward, 'Ajlan lunged at 'Abd al-'Aziz, who later reminisced:

> He made at me with his sword, but its edge was not good. I covered my face and shot at him with my gun. I heard the crash of the sword upon the ground and knew that the shot had hit 'Ajlan, but had not killed him. He started to go through the postern gate, but I caught hold of his legs. The men inside caught hold of his arms while I still held his legs. His company were shooting their firearms at us and throwing stones upon us. 'Ajlan gave me a powerful kick in the side so that I was about to faint. I let go of his legs and he got inside. I wished to enter, but my men would not let me. Then 'Abd Allah Jiluwi entered with the bullets falling about him. After him, 10 others entered. We flung the gate wide open and our company ran up to reinforce us. We were 40 and there before us were 80. We killed half of them. Then four fell from the wall and were crushed. The rest were trapped in a tower; we granted safe-conduct to them and they descended. As for 'Ajlan, Ibn Jiluwi slew him.

Such is the epic story of how Riyadh was recovered on January 16, 1902, as the sun was rising over the desert and the city was just coming to life. The capture of Riyadh marked the dawn of a new era in the history of Arabia and a turning point in the fortunes of the House of Sa'ud.

In later years, King 'Abd al-'Aziz regaled his listeners over and over again with this story. In a real sense it has become the creation story of the state. The national celebrations in 1999 to mark the first hundred *Hijri* years (1319–1419 AH) of the Kingdom used this date as its point of origin, rather than the "official" inauguration of the Kingdom of Saudi Arabia in September 1932.

Naturally enough, the celebrations focused on the personality of King 'Abd al-'Aziz and his great achievement in forging a new country out of his series of campaigns between 1902 and 1930. The contrast between the tiny beginning—a fortress falling to a heroic handful of men— and its towering consequences has always captured the public imagination, and the story of *tawhid al-mamlakah*, the "unification of the Kingdom," is one that all Saudi schoolchildren learn.

By any measure, King 'Abd al-'Aziz was one of the great men of the first half of the 20th century. Modern Saudi Arabia owes its creation to his vision, charisma and leadership. It is also true that the character of what he created—in effect the Third Saudi State, though it is not conventional to refer to it by that name—owed a great deal to its forerunners, the First and Second Saudi States. He himself was keenly aware that unification was achieved not just by military means, but by rekindling trends and ideas that had developed in Najd over the previous two centuries. To this heritage he brought vital extra ingredients: political realism, a grasp of international affairs and a willingness to try to conciliate his enemies before resorting to force.

Schoolchildren romp in front of the entrance to the Masmak fort in Riyadh, which the young 'Abd al-'Aziz Al Sa'ud captured in 1902 as his first step toward unifying the country and establishing the Kingdom of Saudi Arabia.

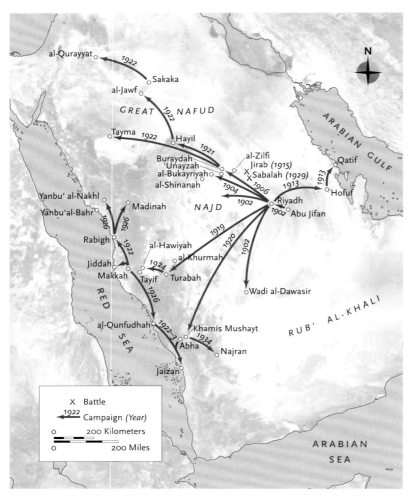

**UNIFICATION
OF SAUDI ARABIA
{ 1902-34 }**

The unification of the Kingdom, 1902–27

Riyadh awoke to the new order as the proclamation rang out from one of the towers of the Masmak fort: "To God the sovereignty, to 'Abd al-'Aziz ibn 'Abd al-Rahman Al Faysal Al Sa'ud the rule!" The news spread swiftly through the little mud-built town, and its people welcomed the new ruler.

'Abd al-'Aziz quickly set about repairing Riyadh's walls against the expected counterattack. That did not materialize, however, and during the next six months he completed his defenses and sent for his father in Kuwait. Imam 'Abd al-Rahman renounced his rights of rule in favor of his son, presenting him with the sword of Imam Sa'ud ibn 'Abd al-'Aziz, the symbol of Saudi leadership. 'Abd al-Rahman retained the title of *imam* until his death in June 1928.

'Abd al-'Aziz soon began to prepare for a large-scale offensive against the Rashids. He knew that his situation was still precarious and that he faced a long, arduous campaign against Hayil and its Ottoman allies. He had demonstrated

his daring with the recovery of Riyadh. Now, and for the next quarter of a century, he would demonstrate the rarer qualities of knowing when to advance and when to retreat, when to conciliate and when to punish, and how to apply the lessons of previous Saudi rule.

The Battle of al-Dilam, 1902

When he heard of 'Abd al-'Aziz's coup at Riyadh, Ibn Rashid was engaged in the far north planning a move against Kuwait, so he delayed his response to the threat from the south. In the fall of 1902, Ibn Rashid finally headed south. Bypassing Riyadh, which was now strongly fortified, he made a raid into al-Kharj some 80 kilometers (50 miles) southeast, hoping to subdue the district before 'Abd al-'Aziz had prepared its defense.

Again, he miscalculated. By means of a forced night march, 'Abd al-'Aziz had reached the village and date groves of al-Dilam and prepared an ambush. A withering fusillade caught Ibn Rashid's men by surprise and fierce fighting won the day for the Saudis. It was another bold stroke. 'Abd al-'Aziz's reputation soared, the enemy was forced to retreat all the way north and the young *amir* of Riyadh found himself master of all southern Najd.

Al-Qasim, 1904–06

Ibn Rashid, however, did not intend to let Najd slip from his grasp. The fertile district of al-Qasim in central Najd, with its two prosperous towns of 'Unayzah and Buraydah, lay between Riyadh and Hayil, and it was natural that it should become the next arena of confrontation. First, 'Abd al-'Aziz brought over the towns of al-Washm and then, in spring of 1904, 'Unayzah fell to him. But Ibn Rashid had a big advantage at this stage: He had an alliance with an outside power, the Ottoman Turks, and he now appealed to them for help.

Late that summer, the Turks responded with eight battalions of infantry with field artillery. The Saudi forces met the combined troops of Ibn Rashid and the Turks at al-Bukayriyah west of Buraydah. The battle was a confused, long-running skirmish, its outcome neither victory nor defeat. 'Abd al-'Aziz was wounded by shrapnel from a Turkish field gun, but remained in command. By the time he had recovered and returned to the fray, the fierce Arabian summer had taken its toll on the Ottoman troops.

The next encounter was at al-Shinanah near al-Rass, where 'Abd al-'Aziz, seeing some of his men waver, personally led an attack on the Turkish guns. The Turks gave ground, Ibn Rashid's forces broke, the retreat became a rout and the Saudis took possession of copious amounts of equipment, artillery and Turkish gold.

The lesson of outside support was not lost on 'Abd al-'Aziz and he did not glory in his triumph. Instead, he offered his nominal submission to the sultan, hoping to make the Ottoman Government reconsider its support for Ibn Rashid in Najd. This plan succeeded only partially, because the Ottomans wanted neither side to prevail there.

'Abd al-'Aziz had to settle for allowing the towns of al-Qasim to be garrisoned by Ottoman troops, but he did manage to extract the concession that Ibn Rashid should be kept out of that district. The Ottomans garrisoned Buraydah and 'Unayzah in April 1905 and declared al-Qasim and southern Najd to be districts of the Ottoman province of Basra. 'Abd al-'Aziz waited. By late 1906, the Ottoman garrisons had been decimated by starvation, disease, attacks by the local people and desertions, and abandoned central Arabia for good.

In 1905, 'Abd al-'Aziz had enlisted tribal support in Ottoman-occupied al-Hasa and probed as far as the base of the Qatar peninsula. When Ibn Rashid tried to reassert his authority in al-Qasim in the spring of 1906, 'Abd al-'Aziz

met him at the wells of Rawdhat Muhanna east of Buraydah. Ibn Rashid was caught by surprise and lost his life. The threat from Hayil was over for the time being. Ibn Rashid's death ushered in a series of assassinations among the ruling family of Hayil, and 'Abd al-'Aziz turned his attention to consolidating his gains.

CONSOLIDATION, 1906–12

THE NOMADIC TRIBES LOYAL TO IBN RASHID EXPECTED TO return to independence and take control of their own affairs after his death. They were not anxious to give up that freedom. Riyadh's difficulties with both tribes and towns took the usual form: refusal to pay taxes, to send levies or to receive emissaries and governors appointed from Riyadh. 'Abd al-'Aziz's response, however, was generally to be forbearing and lenient rather than punitive. It was also marked by great energy and swiftness. By 1911, the problems had been mostly solved.

These years were also marked by the start of the conflict with the rulers of the Hijaz which would rumble on through

'Abd al-'Aziz Al Sa'ud maintained good relations with Shaykh Mubarak of Kuwait and continued to visit him while extending his authority through central and eastern Arabia. He is pictured (left) with the Kuwaiti ruler in March 1910 in Kuwait.

World War I and after. In 1908, the Sharif Husayn ibn 'Ali was appointed by the Ottoman Government as *sharif* of Makkah and *amir* of the Hijaz. Although he was born in Makkah, Husayn had spent most of his life in Constantinople and was nearly 60 years old. He was a man of great culture, charm and integrity, but also extremely ambitious and committed to the preservation of the Hijaz as a fief of his family. The family is known as the Hashimites because, like all sharifian families, it traced its descent from Hashim ibn 'Abd Manaf, founder of the Bani Hashim clan of Quraysh at Makkah and great-grandfather of the Prophet Muhammad.

The *sharif*'s position was bolstered by the rise in pilgrim traffic to the Holy Cities that had taken place with the coming of steam power, for the pilgrimage—often requiring long-distance travel—was his main source of income. In 1908, the Turks completed the Hijaz Railway linking Damascus to Madinah. Pilgrim traffic increased from a maximum of around 200,000 per year in the 19th century to nearly 250,000 in 1908 and 360,000 in 1913. But the railway was a mixed blessing, since it meant that the Turks could move troops expeditiously toward the very heart of Arabia if need be.

In late 1910, Husayn mounted an expedition into the domain of the 'Utaybah tribe in the Hijaz-Najd borderlands. There, he captured 'Abd al-'Aziz's brother Sa'd. Husayn demanded a ransom for his release, as well as 'Abd al-'Aziz's recognition of Ottoman sovereignty over the Najd borderlands. The ransom was paid, but once Sa'd was released Abd al-'Aziz withdrew his recognition of Turkish sovereignty on the grounds that it had been extracted under duress.

THE *IKHWAN*: HARNESSING THE NOMADIC TRIBES

THESE YEARS TURNED 'ABD AL-'AZIZ'S THOUGHTS TO A MORE permanent way of unifying the tribes, whose constant feuds and shifting allegiances made state-building impracticable. Pondering this problem, 'Abd al-'Aziz recognized that the tribesman's genuine loyalty could be pressed no farther without some fundamental change in his outlook. Until order had been established among the tribes in Najd, his vision of uniting the provinces of Arabia into a single state was doomed.

To set this profound change in motion, he drew on the experience of the First Saudi State and his grandfather Imam Faysal's ideas. After long consultation with his family and religious advisors, he set about harnessing tribal loyalty to a greater one: to a creed and, by extension, to the central government in Riyadh. Its implementation involved settling the Bedouin in agricultural communities while preserving their fighting qualities and inculcating into them the tenets of Shaykh Muhammad ibn 'Abd al-Wahhab. Settlement would render the Bedouin accessible to the beneficial effects of religious instruction, education and commerce.

The scheme took hold in an astonishingly short time. This was due largely to the efforts in Riyadh of the religious leader and scholar 'Abd Allah ibn Muhammad ibn 'Abd al-Latif, who developed the theory of the settlements in his writings and promoted his message vigorously by distributing tracts among the tribes. Many religious instructors were trained in the houses of the *'ulama* in Riyadh. Then they were sent out to the settlements in a ratio of about one to 50 tribesmen. The instructors were overwhelmingly drawn from the settled, non-tribal families of the oases. They owed total allegiance to 'Abd al-'Aziz and his father the Imam 'Abd al-Rahman.

In the winter of 1912–13, the first *hijrah*, or settlement, was established by the Mutayr tribe at the wells of al-Artawiyah, some 70 kilometers (45 miles) north of al-Majma'ah, in Sudayr. In just 10 years, al-Artawiyah grew into a town of some 10,000 people—almost as large as Riyadh. It was soon followed by many others, some large, some small, some long-lived and some soon abandoned. By 1917, there were over 200 settlements, and they drew in the majority of the tribespeople of Najd. Settlers received land, farming tools, seeds, money and weapons.

A warrior of the Ikhwan *tribesmen settled by 'Abd al-'Aziz Al Sa'ud is pictured in the Eastern Province in 1923-24.*

The Kut, the inner fortified enclosure of Hofuf, in 1950 still dominated the marketplace, just as it did when 'Abd al-'Aziz Al Sa'ud and his men captured it from the Ottoman garrison in 1913.

After his capture of al-Hasa and the outbreak of World War I in 1914, 'Abd al-'Aziz was courted by the British as a possible ally against the Turks, and an Anglo-Saudi treaty was concluded in December 1915. In November 1916, he met the English in Basra, where he is pictured with Sir Percy Cox, Britain's chief political officer for Mesopotamia, and his aide, Gertrude Bell. (Photograph © University of Newcastle-upon-Tyne)

These tribal settlers were known as the *Ikhwan* ("brethren"). Within a few years, they formed the backbone of Riyadh's forces. While the Saudi state was expanding, it suited 'Abd al-'Aziz to allow them freedom to spread their ideals. After the conquest of the Hijaz in 1926, however, their inability to grasp political and social realities would make them a liability for the emerging state.

EXPANSION INTO AL-HASA, 1913

'ABD AL-'AZIZ NOW TURNED HIS ATTENTION TO EASTERN ARABia where the Turks, who had occupied the region in 1871, remained in control. It was a propitious moment. The Young Turks had replaced the sultan and taken power, and the Balkan provinces were in revolt. 'Abd al-'Aziz struck out on a moonless night in April 1913 with a newly formed corps of *Ikhwan*. Leading 600 men, he crept up to the fortifications of Hofuf, the Turkish headquarters in al-Hasa, scaled the walls on ropes and palm trunks and, before the sleeping garrison could gather its wits, captured the inner fortress and accepted the Turkish governor's surrender. To press his advantage, 'Abd al-'Aziz moved quickly on other Turkish garrisons in al-'Uqayr and Qatif on the coast, allow-

ing the Turks to depart unharmed and without surrendering their weapons. He was now master of the al-Hasa region and its two fertile oases. He had doubled his tax revenues at a stroke and had acquired a coastline on the Gulf, with all its implications for relations with the British.

'Abd al-'Aziz's first act on taking al-Hasa was to enter into negotiations with the Turks to regularize his position there vis-à-vis the Ottoman Empire. The agreement reached in May 1914 provided for 'Abd al-'Aziz to be Ottoman "Wali (Governor) and Commandant of Najd," obliged to allow Ottoman troops into his territory and not to enter into relations with other powers.

The Turks, while negotiating with 'Abd al-'Aziz, made an agreement to deliver arms to the supporters of the House of Rashid, who were still hostile. 'Abd al-'Aziz, therefore, laid the groundwork for an understanding with the British, and in 1913-14 met with Captain William Shakespear, the British political agent in Kuwait, at al-'Uqayr and Riyadh. Their discussions established the basis of the Anglo-Saudi Treaty of December 1915 whereby Britain recognized 'Abd al-'Aziz as hereditary ruler of Najd, al-Hasa, Qatif, Jubail and their dependencies in return for support in World War I.

WORLD WAR I, 1914–18

WHEN THE WAR BROKE OUT, CONTROL OF THE MIDDLE EAST was divided between Great Britain and the Ottoman Empire, two of the greatest colonial powers in the world. The Ottomans still exerted a form of authority over most of the Red Sea coast as far south as Yemen, and still actively ruled Palestine, Syria and Mesopotamia. The British controlled Egypt and the Suez Canal, their lifeline to India, as well as Aden. They considered the Arabian Gulf within their sphere of influence and had announced, in 1903, that the establishment of a naval base or fortified port by any other power would be regarded as "a very grave menace" that Britain would resist by all the means at its disposal.

Britain's first objective after the outbreak of war was to wrest control of Mesopotamia—now Iraq—from the Turks. As part of their campaign they sought Saudi help against the House of Rashid, an ally of the Ottomans, while at the same time encouraging the Sharif Husayn to expel the Turks from the Hijaz.

In the Anglo-Saudi Treaty of 1915, Britain committed itself to aiding Ibn Sa'ud (as 'Abd al-'Aziz was known in the West) in the event of foreign aggression. Ibn Sa'ud pledged not to enter into relations with foreign powers and not to act against any of the Gulf principalities with which Britain had treaties. In return, he received a loan of £20,000 (approximately $100,000) along with firearms and ammunition. Later, a monthly subsidy of £5,000 was agreed on, effectively doubling his income again. 'Abd al-'Aziz was now on equal terms with his enemies in Arabia: He had achieved the recognition and support of his emerging state by a foreign power, and money that would help him maintain his power base.

'Abd al-'Aziz did not take a decisive part in World War I. He had domestic troubles enough: first, as always, with the House of Rashid, and second with a rebellion by the tribe of 'Ujman during which he was twice severely wounded and lost his beloved brother Sa'd in battle. His border dispute with the Hijaz simmered on, but he was restrained from acting against the Sharif Husayn by their shared status as allies of the British.

By 1915, the Sharif Husayn was reconsidering his allegiance to the Ottomans and deciding to enlist Britain's help in fighting for Arab independence. In June 1916, he finally proclaimed the Arab Revolt against the Turks with full British backing. In 1917, British officials in the Gulf got the go-ahead to support 'Abd al-'Aziz in his continuing struggle against the House of Rashid.

The Arab attacks against the Turks during 1916-18 contributed to the downfall of the Ottoman Empire and also made a celebrity of T. E. Lawrence, assigned as political officer to the Sharif Husayn's son Faysal. But after the capture of Damascus in 1918 by British and Hijazi forces, Britain withdrew its support from 'Abd al-'Aziz's campaign against the Al Rashids in Hayil. 'Abd al-'Aziz was furious.

Ibn Sa'ud had strong reasons for resenting British power during and after the war. London supported and subsidized

CAPTAIN WILLIAM SHAKESPEAR

Captain William Shakespear, Britain's political agent at Kuwait, first met 'Abd al-'Aziz Al Sa'ud at Kuwait in 1910. By then he had already taken the first two of his annual journeys into the interior which were to make him the foremost scientific Western explorer of inner Arabia of the time.

In his travels in Arabia, Shakespear built up a friendship with the Saudi leader based on integrity and courage, and became a champion of 'Abd al-'Aziz's claim to greater recognition by British policy-makers. In early 1914 he fulfilled his main ambition, to traverse Arabia crossing the routes of his predecessors in Arabian exploration, visiting Riyadh en route.

In mid-1914, after leave in London, Shakespear returned to Kuwait. The imminence of war with Turkey and 'Abd al-'Aziz's recovery of al-Hasa from the Ottomans combined to force Britain to reconsider its relations with Riyadh, and Shakespear was deputed as special envoy to 'Abd al-'Aziz to formulate a treaty. But he was killed in January 1915 while fighting on 'Abd al-'Aziz's side against Ibn Rashid at the Battle of Jirab in al-Qasim, while negotiations were in progress. Later, when asked to name the most remarkable non-Muslim he knew, 'Abd al-'Aziz replied without hesitation: "Shakespear."

the *sharif* of Makkah. In addition, Britain maintained an equivocal position on Palestine, in whose freedom from Zionist domination Ibn Sa'ud passionately believed. The Balfour Declaration of November 1917 had pledged British support for a "national home" for the Jews in Palestine—a promise that Arabs saw as flatly contradicting the British pledges of Arab sovereignty that lay behind the Arab Revolt.

THE KHURMAH DISPUTE, 1919

IF DISAPPOINTED BY THE ALLIES' BETRAYAL, HUSAYN WAS STILL determined to retain the Hijaz and launched attacks on the oasis of al-Khurmah, strategically located on the route between the Hijaz and Najd. Initially, al-Khurmah held its own, but as the situation became desperate it appealed to 'Abd al-'Aziz for help. 'Abd al-'Aziz warned Husayn to desist. But when the *sharif* sent in 5,000 men armed with machine guns and artillery, 'Abd al-'Aziz sent the *Ikhwan* into action. In May 1919, they inflicted a crushing defeat upon Husayn's expedition at the nearby town of Turabah.

'Abd al-'Aziz could easily have marched into the Hijaz and unseated the Sharif Husayn and his family, but he stayed his hand. He could see that the British were still closely involved with Husayn, and that the Muslim world was not ready to accept a new power controlling the holy places. He was also certain that Husayn's days were numbered.

'ASIR, HAYIL AND THE NORTHERN BORDER, 1919–22

THE *IKHWAN* PLAYED A CRUCIAL ROLE ELSEWHERE, AS WELL. IN 1919 and 1920, *Ikhwan* of the al-Mutayr tribe threatened Kuwaiti territory and raided over the as-yet-undefined border into British-controlled Iraq. In both cases, the British military moved to deter them. 'Abd al-'Aziz, who had not authorized the raids, was content to accept these limits to expansion in the north.

Instead, he turned to 'Asir, the way to which was now open. In 1920, the *Ikhwan* captured Abha, the capital of highland 'Asir. Two years later 'Abd al-'Aziz's son Faysal led an army to 'Asir to suppress a rebellion, in the process adding lowland Tihamah to the Saudi domain.

In November 1921, 'Abd al-'Aziz took personal charge of the final campaign against the Al Rashid of Hayil. A deal was reached by which its gates were opened and its people spared. Hayil's days as a political force were over. In a spirit of reconciliation, 'Abd al-'Aziz showed clemency to the Rashid family, whose members were taken to Riyadh as honored guests.

That same year, the *Ikhwan* staged a raid into Transjordan, suffering heavy losses to British airplanes. In 1922, 'Abd al-'Aziz extended the Saudi domain farther north by absorbing the oasis of al-Jawf and the Wadi al-Sirhan. At the same time, he annexed the oases of Tayma and Khaybar.

'Abd al-'Aziz recognized it was time to establish formal boundaries with his neighbors to the north. He concluded a treaty with the British at al-'Uqayr on the Gulf coast in 1922 that settled the Iraq and Kuwait frontiers with Saudi

territory. This marked the first time that fixed international borders, rather than vague spheres of influence, had been formally agreed by a Saudi state with a foreign power.

It was also the first time that oil entered into political calculations. Present at the 'Uqayr Conference, called by Sir Percy Cox, was Major Frank Holmes. Although Cox prevented the New Zealand mining engineer from obtaining an oil concession in al-Hasa from Ibn Sa'ud at that time, Holmes managed to clinch a deal in 1923. But his Eastern and General Syndicate failed to interest any prospectors, and the concession lapsed in 1927.

ANNEXATION OF THE HIJAZ AND INTERNATIONAL RECOGNITION, 1924–27

EVENTS WERE MOVING TOWARD A CLIMAX ON THE OTHER SIDE OF the peninsula. 'Abd al-'Aziz convened a gathering in Riyadh in June 1924, at which the main *Ikhwan* chiefs and the *'ulama* supported his decision to move on the Hijaz. In September, a detachment of the *Ikhwan* appeared before Tayif in the highlands above Makkah. Panic took hold of the town as the Sharif Husayn's eldest son 'Ali abandoned the town with his troops. The defenseless town surrendered to 'Abd al-'Aziz's forces.

When the gates were opened, however, the *Ikhwan* were reported fired upon. Believing themselves betrayed, they

The mud-built city of Hayil was the political center of northern Najd until absorbed into the Saudi domain in 1921. Its main square is shown here in 1914.

attacked and a massacre of civilians ensued. This was the only time during the Hijaz campaign that the Saudi forces lost their heads; normally, they kept strict discipline.

With the Saudis in Tayif, the days of the Sharif Husayn were obviously numbered, and prominent citizens of the Hijaz began to bring pressure on him to abdicate in favor of his son 'Ali. For a long time the aged ruler refused, but in October 1924 he boarded a ship in Jiddah and sought refuge in Transjordan, from which the British removed him to Cyprus, where he spent his last years. The *Ikhwan* entered Makkah that same month to find most of its people had fled.

When 'Abd al-'Aziz arrived in the Holy City in early December, he came not as a conqueror but as a pilgrim wearing humble garb, a reminder of the entry into the city by his forebears in 1803. He knew that the eyes of the Muslim world were upon him and he was keenly aware of the importance of a peaceful takeover. He wished to provide assurance that the new custodianship of the holy places would be an improvement on the insecurity of the Sharif Husayn's years, and that the pilgrimage would be safe and well organized. This has remained a major preoccupation of the Saudi Government ever since. His first act was to invite representatives from the entire Muslim world to Makkah to discuss the future governance of the holy places.

For Husayn's son King 'Ali, coralled in Jiddah, the end was in sight. During 1925, the port city was subjected to a desultory yearlong siege before surrendering bloodlessly to the Saudis. Madinah and the port of Yanbu' soon followed. 'Ali sailed for Transjordan and then Iraq, where his brother Faysal was king. On January 8, 1926, the leading Hijazi notables pledged allegiance to 'Abd al-'Aziz as King of the Hijaz and Sultan of Najd and its Dependencies. Soon after that, in the Sacred Mosque of Makkah, the new King swore that he would rule his new domains in accordance with the *shari'ah*, the sacred law of Islam.

Britain accepted the Saudi takeover as a fait accompli. It was time to demarcate northern frontiers once again, this time with Transjordan. During 1925 and 1926, this border was negotiated and outstanding matters with Iraq were settled.

Demarcation of southern frontiers with Yemen, Oman and other Gulf states would wait for several decades. But essentially the expansion of the revived Saudi state was now complete, except for Wadi Najran—which would be added in 1934 as a result of a war with Yemen. During 1926, 'Abd al-'Aziz received recognition from the Soviet Union, Britain, France and the Netherlands, all powers with substantial Muslim populations in their dominions. In January 1927, 'Abd

141

King 'Abd al-'Aziz dances the 'ardah, or sword dance, in the palace square, Riyadh, in the 1930s.

al-'Aziz was officially proclaimed King of Hijaz and Najd and its Dependencies, with Riyadh and Makkah as its two capitals. In May, the Treaty of Jiddah with Britain ratified the new northern frontier and recognized the King's status as a completely independent and sovereign ruler, superseding the Anglo-Saudi Treaty of 1915.

CRISIS AND FINAL TRIUMPH

IN 1928, AS 'ABD AL-'AZIZ WAS STILL ORGANIZING THE KING-dom, some of the *Ikhwan* leaders who had helped him conquer the Hijaz attacked an Iraqi border fort, in defiance of his express orders. Since this was in direct violation of the boundary agreement with the British at al-'Uqayr in 1922, 'Abd al-'Aziz was, reluctantly, forced to take action. He could not tolerate insubordination that threatened the existence of his young state.

The *Ikhwan* were motivated by a number of factors in their rebellion. They were disturbed at 'Abd al-'Aziz's political realism; they saw no reason to honor arrangements with foreign powers that did not adhere to the tenets of Unitarian reform. After conquering the Hijaz, many members of the *Ikhwan* had come into contact with a more cosmopolitan life than they had known, and they looked with suspicion and mistrust on the King's readiness to accept some aspects of it.

During the siege of Jiddah, for example, some of the *Ikhwan* had opposed the use of the telephone, and the King had hesitated before installing a line between Makkah and his headquarters. He reportedly won over the *Ikhwan* by having them listen to verses from the Quran being read over the telephone, arguing that an instrument that carries the Word of God cannot be the work of the devil. Doubts continued to fester, however.

Faced now, in the attack on the Iraqi border, with outright disobedience of his orders by the *Ikhwan*, 'Abd al-'Aziz moved against them. As they were, by the King's own design, elite forces, the fighting lasted for a year and a half. Finally, at a battle near al-Artawiyah in the spring of 1929, 'Abd al-'Aziz defeated them. He brought the rebel leaders to Riyadh and eventually broke the power of all the rebellious *Ikhwan* settlements.

During 1930, King 'Abd al-'Aziz met with King Faysal of Iraq under British auspices. This result was a Treaty of Friendliness and Good Neighborliness that established mutual recognition of Iraq and Najd–Hijaz, as well as mechanisms for dealing with diplomatic representation, tribal raiding and border issues.

During the late 1920s and early '30s, the King was confronted by another, less tractable problem. The economy was based on subsistence farming and stock rearing, and state revenues stemmed from modest customs duties and levies on pilgrims. The march of modernization had begun in the 1920s: Riyadh was expanding as the seat of government, and in 1930 aircraft had begun to appear, along with motor vehicles, radio, telegraphy and telephones. But it was a huge country with tiny financial resources, and matters were made even worse by the world financial crisis. The Wall Street crash of 1929 was followed by the worldwide Great Depression, which began to affect Saudi Arabia in 1931. During the late 1920s, foreign pilgrim numbers had hovered around the 100,000 mark, but slumped to 30,000 in 1932 and 20,000 in 1933. The King was compelled to borrow from the merchants.

In 1931, he remarked with feeling to Harry St. John B. ('Abd Allah) Philby, the British explorer and author who had embraced Islam: "If anyone would offer me a million pounds now he would be welcome to all the concessions he wants in my country." That very year, hope of salvation manifested itself in the person of the American philanthropist Charles R. Crane, who visited Jiddah and offered to commission a survey of the country's oil, water and mineral resources.

The American engineer Karl S. Twitchell was dispatched later that year to perform the survey and traveled in the Hijaz, the north and the eastern region. There he noted the geological similarity of the Dammam area to the formation in Bahrain, where oil prospecting was already under way. By September 1932, when the Kingdom of Saudi Arabia was proclaimed, the stage was set for the deal that was to transform the country from one of the poorest in the world to one of the richest.

The Pilgrimage under the New Saudi Order

Before King 'Abd al-'Aziz's annexation of the Hijaz in 1925–26, the Muslim pilgrimage, or *hajj*, had for centuries taken place under the laissez-faire control of the *sharif*s of Makkah. Once in the Hijaz, pilgrims had been regarded as little more than a source of revenue, and their organization left to guilds of guides who were self-regulating. The pilgrims themselves had to endure much hardship on the way to Makkah; they were often at the mercy of marauding Bedouin, only to be taken advantage of on their arrival in the Holy City. Unsanitary conditions gave rise to diseases, which pilgrims took back to their homelands. During the 19th century and with the arrival of steamships, the colonial powers introduced a number of disease-control measures, including the establishment of quarantine stations in the Red Sea at al-Tur in Sinai, at al-Wajh in the Hijaz and at Kamaran Island off the Yemen coast.

King 'Abd al-'Aziz's first act on taking Makkah was to convene an Islamic Congress on the future of the holy places. He was keenly aware of the need to legitimize Saudi control of Makkah and Madinah in the eyes of the entire Muslim world. The best way to achieve that would be to introduce sound management and strict regulation of the *hajj* to ensure the health and safety of all pilgrims, whatever branch of Islam they subscribed to.

The pilgrimage in 1925 was organized under very difficult conditions, as Jiddah, the main port, was under siege. Despite this, the few pilgrims who made the journey that year reported back favorably on the security, good organization and lack of extortion. The pilgrimage took place under the eyes of an English Muslim, Eldon Rutter. In his account, *The Holy Cities of Arabia*, he comments that 'Abd al-'Aziz's representatives had not only clamped down on shrines and tobacco, but had also put a stop to corruption and unfair charges, enforcing strict price controls on food and water. Rutter vividly describes his audiences with the King, and the uneasy relations between the Najdi warriors and the Makkans.

The positive effects of Saudi governance in establishing both medical facilities and law and order in the desert and cities of the Hijaz were noted by other Western pilgrims in the 1920s and 1930s—most notably by Harry St. John B. Philby, who performed the *hajj* in 1931 and recorded his experiences in *A Pilgrim in Arabia*. Other accounts of the *hajj* during these years by Western Muslim converts were penned by Muhammad Asad (1927), Winifred Stegar (1927) and Lady Evelyn Cobbold (1933).

Ever since, the Saudi Government has given top priority to the administration of the *hajj* for all Muslims. The advent of air transport has boosted annual numbers from an average of around 35,000 in the 1930s to more than 2 million today. The *haram* at Makkah and the Prophet's Mosque at Madinah have been greatly extended, and communications, health and transport facilities completely modernized.

The pilgrimage in the process of modernization: Pilgrims disembark from a large passenger ship in Jiddah in the late 1930s or '40s.

The first all-Saudi crew to bring in an oil well posed proudly in front of Shedgum No. 12. The crew drilled the well to 2,695 meters (8,842 feet) in 121 days, striking oil in February 1954. From left, they are: Ali ibn Ahmed Sulaiman, rigman; Abdullah Jassim Kishi, driller; Jassim ibn Mohammad Sulaiman, assistant driller; and Jassim ibn Mohammad Guidehay.

A 'MODEST' STEP

IN MAY 1933, AT THE KING'S BEHEST, FINANCE MINISTER 'Abd Allah al-Sulayman put his signature to the oil Concession Agreement with Standard Oil of California. In retrospect, the deal seems surprisingly modest: £5,000 (approximately $25,000) as rental for the first year plus a loan of £50,000 over 18 months, all to be paid in gold, with subsequent annual rentals and royalties on any oil production to be paid in foreign currency. But it solved an immediate cash-flow crisis and augured long-term relief from the economic vagaries that plagued the country.

The two American geologists who stepped ashore at the little fishing village of Jubail on the Gulf coast in September 1933 (see page 221) began a search for petroleum that would eventually lead to the discovery of the world's largest oil reserves, and transform Saudi Arabia from a simple desert kingdom into a power in world economics and one of the key political players in the Middle East.

These effects, however, were not felt until after World War II. The search for oil went on during the Depression years of the mid-1930s, when successive test wells failed to live up to expectations. By March 1938, when oil was at last struck in commercial quantities, the clouds of war were gathering in Europe, and the 1939–45 conflict held up the development of production facilities.

Despite the hardships of the time, the 1930s saw the beginnings of devolved government and the apparatus of modern statehood, though the King remained absolutely at the heart of decision-making. In 1932, a Political Com-

Previous spread: (Left) Some 70,000 passionate soccer fans fill King Fahd International Stadium in Riyadh. The stadium's eye-catching exterior resembles a ring of 24 traditional Arab tents with columns supporting a roof covering 47,000 square meters (150,000 square feet), the largest stadium cover in the world. (Right) The goat-hair tents of the Shammar tribe dot the ground at Umm Radmah wells some 250 kilometers (155 miles) northeast of Riyadh in 1936. At one time the tribe migrated annually with its herds of goats and camels between Saudi Arabia and Iraq. Members today are largely settled.

mittee was set up, consisting of 'Abd al 'Aziz's Arab advisors and, from time to time, Harry St. John B. Philby. One of the longest-serving advisors, Yusuf Yasin, once commented: "The King asks us all our advice and sometimes even when we are all agreed he does the opposite and proves to be right." However, the men around him represented departments in embryo, particularly in foreign and financial affairs, headed respectively by Prince Faysal ibn 'Abd al-'Aziz and 'Abd Allah al-Sulayman. These were the seeds from which the Kingdom's bureaucratic structures grew after World War II.

Technical advances helped establish Riyadh as the capital. As well as being the hub of a new network of wireless transmitters in the provinces, it had its own royal and governmental telephone system. By the end of the 1930s, there were more than 300 motor vehicles in the capital, roads were appearing, and the King had built a large new palace complex and seat of government outside the old walled city, at al-Murabba'. Though its buildings were constructed of bricks made of sun-dried mud, the traditional building material in Najd, they were laid out on a grid, presaging town plans of the future. Members of the diplomatic corps remained in Jiddah, but could now travel to Riyadh by car to visit the King at his court.

The radio system, at first so controversial, proved its value in a brief war against Yemen which broke out in 1934 when the Imam Yahya of Yemen disputed Saudi title to the 'Asir region. King 'Abd al-'Aziz dispatched his eldest sons, Sa'ud and Faysal, to deal with the threat and kept in

Several hundred automobiles were in Riyadh by 1937, when this picture was taken at the entrance to King 'Abd al-'Aziz's court.

contact with them via radio. Sa'ud led a column into the highlands, while Faysal followed the coast and captured the port of Hodeida. Yahya abandoned his claim to 'Asir and signed the Treaty of Tayif in May 1934, confirming Saudi possession of Najran, the uplands of 'Asir and Jaizan on the coastal Tihamah.

The Saudi victory and 'Abd al-'Aziz's generous terms to his vanquished foe — he made no attempt to add Yemen to the Kingdom — created a favorable impression throughout the Arab world. A road-building project followed, as a response to the introduction of modern vehicles to transport troops. It also stimulated the development of a standing army, so that by the end of the decade uniformed soldiers could be seen outside government buildings.

The challenge facing the deeply devout King and his successors was how to maintain the country's dedication to its religious, social and cultural heritage, as represented in the historic alliance with the reformism of Shaykh Muhammad ibn 'Abd al-Wahhab, while at the same time developing a modern state. Throughout the 1930s, the King was careful to consult the *'ulama*, who mounted no more serious challenges to the process of modernization. The remnants of the *Ikhwan* were eventually reconstituted as a small force called the *Mujahidin* and the larger National Guard, becoming part of the machinery of state for internal security. As organs of government grew in complexity with new oil wealth after World War II, the religious establishment was given a role within appropriate departments, such as legal affairs, religious education and the supervision of mosques and religious affairs. Like the *Ikhwan*, it was absorbed into the state bureaucracy. This process reached its climax during the reign of King Faysal (1964–75).

WORLD WAR II

BY THE OUTBREAK OF WORLD WAR II IN 1939, U.S. OILMEN HAD developed a flexible, helpful relationship with the Saudi Government. Saudi Arabia in the 1930s and 1940s lacked management and technical skills. It came to regard the California Arabian Standard Oil Company, or Casoc (to which Socal assigned the concession in 1934), as a friend with the know-how to assist with large projects. Casoc responded by giving vital help to the first hospital and public health programs, drilling water wells, setting up agricultural projects and making transport facilities available. After the war, as the Arabian American Oil Company, or Aramco, the enterprise continued to play an important role in the Kingdom's development.

During 1941–42, Casoc operations were reduced to a minimum because of wartime difficulties. Pilgrim numbers fell, and the Kingdom suffered further hardship and even food shortages. At first, the King was able to meet essential expenditures by advances against future oil royalties. Later, Great Britain assumed responsibility for aid to Saudi Arabia and gave it a subsidy of £1 million per year, drawn from the wartime American Lend-Lease funds. (U.S. legislation

Morse and voice radio stations with towers like these shown in old Riyadh in 1950 gave King 'Abd al-'Aziz instant communication across his vast desert Kingdom.

precluded direct American financial assistance to the Kingdom.) In 1943, the Kingdom qualified for Lend-Lease funding itself when President Franklin D. Roosevelt decided that it was "vital for the defense of the U.S.A."

The King maintained a position of benevolent neutrality toward Britain and the United States throughout the war. However, he allowed the Americans to build and use an airfield at Dhahran to maintain, repair and provide other technical services for Allied aircraft. In 1942, the United States opened a legation in Jiddah and in 1944 Saudi Arabia opened a legation in Washington — both later raised to the rank of embassies. In February 1945, the King traveled to Egypt, meeting first with President Roosevelt aboard an American cruiser anchored in the Great Bitter Lake on the Suez Canal, and then with British Prime Minister Winston Churchill and Foreign Minister Anthony Eden at Fayyum Oasis south of Cairo.

These historic meetings confirmed Saudi Arabia's support for the Allies, and in March 1945 the Kingdom officially took the Allied side in the war. During their meeting, King 'Abd al-'Aziz and President Roosevelt also discussed the issue of who should receive the Jewish survivors of Nazi Germany and the countries it had dominated. The King stated that Germany, not Palestine, should bear this responsibility. Roosevelt assured the King that the U.S. Government would make no change in its policy on the Palestine question without full consultation with both the Arabs and the Jews, and that he

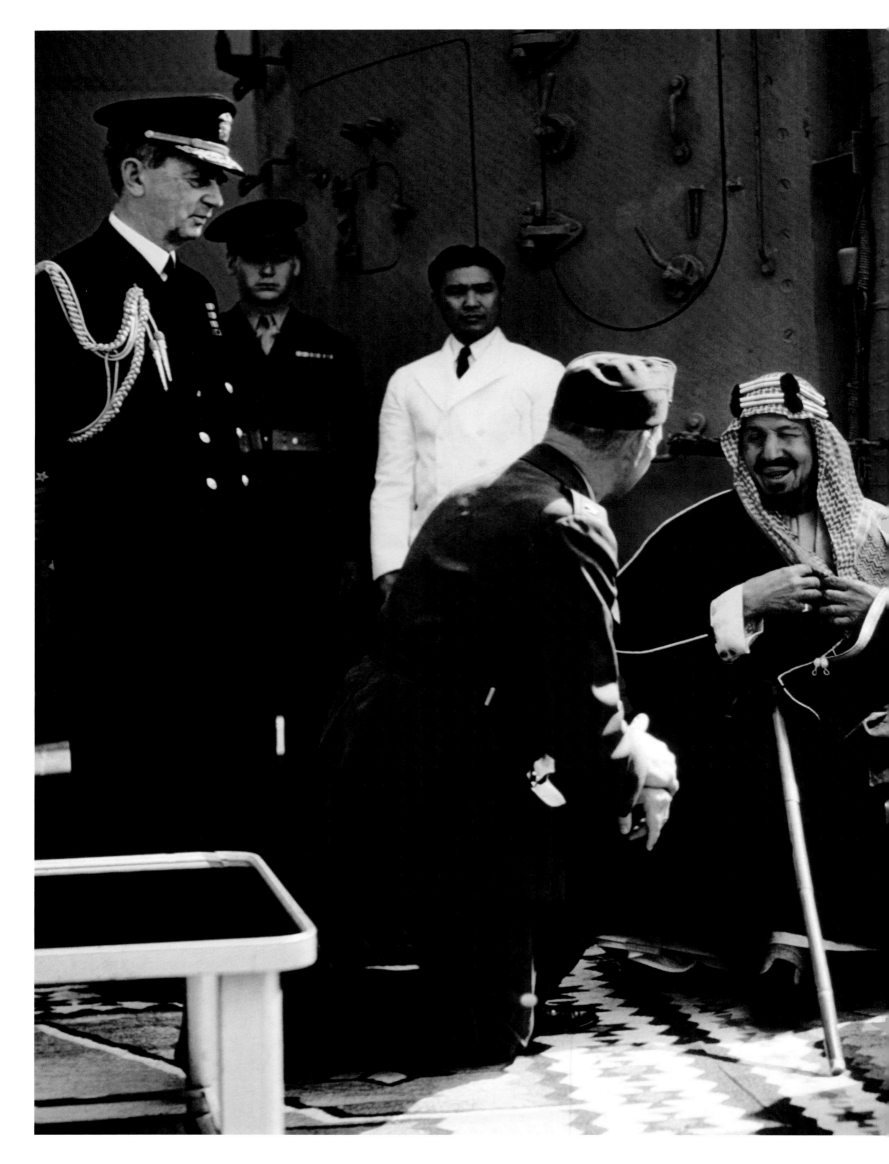

King 'Abd al-'Aziz and U.S. President Franklin Roosevelt met aboard the U.S. cruiser Quincy in the Suez Canal on February 14, 1945, to discuss Middle Eastern and global affairs as World War II neared its end in Europe. An aide to Roosevelt reported the two leaders "hit it off immediately."

Government Revenues

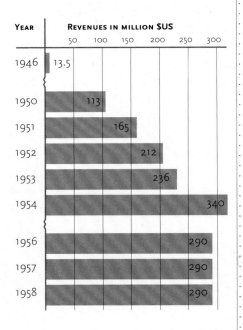

Year	Revenues in million $US
	50 100 150 200 250 300
1946	13.5
1950	113
1951	165
1952	212
1953	236
1954	340
1956	290
1957	290
1958	290

Increasing government revenues through the mid-1950s reflected growing oil production and a change in the oil concession relationship. Beginning in 1950, Aramco agreed to pay a tax to the Saudi Government (the Concession Agreement of 1933 had exempted the company from all taxes) amounting to 50 percent of its net operating income less operating expenses (see page 247). This agreement followed by several months a precedent set in Venezuela and was the first of its kind in the Middle East. In 1952, the agreement was amended so that Aramco paid 50 percent of its gross income.

In this way, the government's income from Aramco operations came to be linked primarily not to the number of barrels of oil produced and sold, but to how much profit the company made. After 1950, therefore, the government showed increasing interest in the prices charged for oil, the cost of operations and the accounting methods used to determine these things, since all of them affected the size of the Kingdom's revenues.

would take no actions which might prove hostile to the Arab people. Two weeks later, Roosevelt reported to the American Congress: "Of the problems of Arabia, I learned more about the whole problem, the Muslim problem, the Jewish problem, by talking with Ibn Sa'ud for five minutes than I could have learned in the exchange of two or three dozen letters." However, Roosevelt died in April 1945, and his successor, President Harry S. Truman, felt under no obligation to keep Roosevelt's promises on Palestine.

THE POSTWAR YEARS

BY THE END OF THE WAR, SAUDI ARABIA'S SITUATION IN THE world had already begun to change. In March 1945, it joined Egypt, Iraq, Lebanon, Syria, Transjordan and a representative of the Palestinian people in signing a Pact of Union of Arab States, the foundation of the Arab League. During the war, a number of the King's sons had visited the United States; one of them, Prince Faysal, later headed the Saudi delegation at the founding of the United Nations in San Francisco — the first of several assignments he was to undertake as his role in formulating the Kingdom's foreign policy expanded.

Oil revenues were starting to mount at a gratifying rate, and at last the King could begin to move more rapidly toward fulfilling his dream of erecting a modern, centrally administered state on the tribal and regional foundations of a traditional society. In 1938, oil production had started with 500,000 barrels. By 1945, it had increased to 21.3 million barrels. In 1938, state revenues stood at around £1.3 million in gold, chiefly from the Hijaz customs and pilgrims. By 1946, revenues had doubled and were set to increase dramatically until the end of 'Abd al-'Aziz's life in 1953 (see table). The new money enabled new ministries to be created: the Ministry of Defense (1946), Interior (1951), Health (1951), Communications (1953), Agriculture and Water (1953) and Education (1953).

One of the country's critical needs was education. Immediately upon unifying the country in 1926, 'Abd al-'Aziz had founded a new school in Makkah. In 1945, he instituted an extensive program of school construction and by 1951 there were 226 schools in the Kingdom, with 1,217 teachers and a total of 29,887 pupils, all supplied with free books and tuition. This was the start of a continuing campaign. In the 1980s during the Third Five-Year Development Plan the Kingdom devoted $35 billion, or 16 percent of the budget, to human resource development. By comparison, $74 billion, or more than 55 percent, of the Seventh Five-Year Development Plan (2000–04) was devoted to that purpose.

Another pressing need was agriculture, a reflection of the King's earlier perception that agricultural settlements were vital to a country where less than one percent of the land is arable and where food supply, as a result, could be problematic. Agriculture has always been important in

The curriculum in the first modern government school in Hofuf in 1951 included science, math, history and geography, along with traditional Arabic language and religious studies. Teacher 'Abd al-Muhsin al-Manqur stands at the back of the class.

Arabia, as the evidence for ancient oasis settlement, dams and irrigation works demonstrates. Already in 1942, 'Abd al-'Aziz had invited a U.S. agricultural mission to visit the country and report on its production potential. He also laid the groundwork for pilot projects to be set up in al-Kharj and elsewhere — projects that became the nucleus of the later government farms and breeding stations. And he strongly backed exploitation of the vast underground water resources in Najd and al-Hasa which were tapped for extensive irrigation projects.

In July 1947, the government announced that it planned to spend some $270 million to build roads, schools and hospitals, and to install power generation plants and irrigation projects. In the early 1950s, escalating revenues enabled Saudi Arabia, with American technical assistance, to launch these and other development programs, although it was still

necessary to arrange credit with Aramco and international banks. Construction was begun on a network of paved roads linking the major cities, a coast-to-coast air service was established, and modern harbor facilities were built in Jiddah. A powerful radio station was installed in Jiddah and authorization given for planning a telephone network that was to achieve the first Kingdom-wide coverage in the 1970s with the construction of a comprehensive telecommunications system based on cable, microwave transmission and satellite ground stations.

Communications is one example of a sector that has been opened to private investment as the Kingdom moves to liberalize its economy. In 1998, the sector was changed from a government entity into the government-owned Saudi Telecom Company, and in 2002 it became a private shareholding company. Competition was introduced in

2004 with the establishment of the mobile phone company Ittihad Ittisalat.

Health was another area close to King 'Abd al-'Aziz's heart. On entering the Hijaz, one of his first measures had been to improve medical facilities for the pilgrims, an act that earned him the gratitude of Muslims everywhere. In 1947, as plans for hospitals were being discussed, he ordered four surplus field hospitals from the U.S. Army to be used in the interim between the planning and construction of permanent ones. These were the first elements in a building program that, in the mid-1970s, brought forth the King Faysal Specialist Hospital and Research Center in Riyadh — one of the foremost in the world — and scores of other hospitals, dispensaries and primary health care centers throughout the Kingdom. Diseases once endemic in old Arabia and borne with resignation by its people, such as malaria, smallpox and trachoma, were virtually eliminated.

This focus on improving health care continues. In 2004, for example, a sophisticated, four-hospital medical city opened in Riyadh. Named after King Fahd, who donated the funds to purchase its equipment, the complex is described as "the most advanced medical facility in the Middle East in treating rare and chronic diseases."

Aramco proved a valuable tool in furthering many infrastructure projects, moving the enterprise far beyond the realm of sister firms worldwide. The company had built its own oil-related infrastructure in the Eastern Province, such as the oil export terminal at Ras Tanura. It also began to offer health, housing and agricultural services and training not directly linked to its core business. The chief example of this was the Aramco-managed project to construct a 600-kilometer (375-mile) railroad from Dammam to Riyadh. Work began in 1947 and was completed in 1951. The immediate result was a rapid advance in the development of the capital, for now it was possible to ship in steel and cement for the first time in large quantities. Adobe was rendered obsolete as a building material, and Riyadh began the rapid expansion whereby today it covers more than 200 times the area of the old town.

King 'Abd al-'Aziz was concerned throughout his long reign to project his prestige as father of his people in a manner appropriate to a deeply traditional society. While creating a modernizing state, however, he remained an absolute ruler. He kept in close touch with the public through the traditional *majlis*, or public reception, meeting regularly with citizens from all walks of life. Through such contacts, and by developing and maintaining the comprehensive welfare state that exists in the country today, successive Saudi monarchs have continued to command the allegiance of the Saudi people.

By 1953, the King had consolidated his own line of descent by fathering more than 50 sons and daughters. His son Prince Sa'ud had been nominated Crown Prince in 1933. In this way, a smooth succession was in prospect.

King 'Abd al-'Aziz died in Tayif on November 9, 1953, after 51 years as leader and head of a land from which he had been exiled as a youth but later had reunited, pacified and developed. In 1900, when he was a young man, his homeland was one of the least known, poorest and most isolated areas of the world. At his death it had taken its place on the world stage. His achievement had been to use the creed of his forefathers to harness centrifugal tribal and local elements into a state, and then to set that state on the road to modernization by moderating the potential conflicts within it. In a sense, the state remained typically Arabian, in that a person's loyalty to tribe, family and region was not diluted by inclusion into the larger nation. Only an individual of unflagging courage, formidable intelligence, rare charisma and — above all — a profound faith in God could have accomplished such an undertaking.

KING SA'UD

KING 'ABD AL-'AZIZ HAD LONG ENVISAGED THE SUCcession passing to his eldest surviving son Sa'ud and then to Faysal. After the conquest of the Hijaz in 1925, Sa'ud had been appointed Viceroy of Najd with special responsibility for tribal affairs, while in 1926 Faysal had been made Viceroy of the Hijaz with responsibility for foreign relations. Both men, therefore, had long experience of government, and they both came to stand for very different approaches to it.

The Saudi Arabian Government Railroad, built under Aramco management, opened in 1951 to link the Arabian Gulf port of Dammam to Riyadh via Abqaiq, Hofuf and Haradh.

An Aramco scientist stocks a canal where mosquitoes breed with larvae-eating minnows during a 1949 anti-malaria campaign. As a result of these efforts, malaria was eliminated from the Eastern Province in the 1950s.

Food

Bedouins have a way of describing a generous man that translates: "He makes coffee day and night." Among a people famous for their hospitality, that rings very true. The preparation of Arabian coffee—flavored with aromatic cardamom seed but unsweetened—was indeed a man's work, and even today the ring of the brass mortar as he pounds the fresh-roasted beans to a powder is music to the ears of expectant guests. For guests of some standing, coffee might be followed by trays heaped with rice and chunks of mutton or, on special occasions, rice-stuffed baby lamb rubbed with spices and roasted whole—all surrounded by circles of flat, unleavened bread. An end to the Arab feast is signaled by the host passing a censer trailing filmy smoke of frankincense or scented wood.

Loyalty to custom and tradition is the essence of all Middle East food. Traditional foods are prepared in centuries-old ways. In detailing the banquets of caliphs in Baghdad, for example, Arab poets of the Middle Ages celebrated Damascus sweets. The same sweets prepared in much the same way are still relished today.

Peninsular Arabs created some of the finest cuisines themselves, while other traditional food creations were borrowed from neighbors. Typically Levantine are two purées eaten with bread as appetizers: *hummus*, made from ground chickpeas, and *baba ghunnuj*, made from mashed eggplant. Both mixtures are rich with *tahinah*, or sesame-seed paste, and pungent with lemon juice and garlic.

The Turkish influence is evident in dishes of tomatoes, peppers, zucchini or eggplant filled with a spicy mixture of rice, pine nuts and currants. *Burghul*, or cracked wheat, mixed with finely chopped parsley, onions, tomatoes and mint, is the main ingredient for the well-known salad called *tabbulah*. Mixed with ground lamb and baked in a variety of shapes, *burghul* is the basis for a meat dish called *kibbah*.

Everywhere one finds members of that vast family of skewered meats and ground meat known as kebabs. And everywhere there is *laban*, the yoghurt of the Middle East, and *labnah*, the rich cream cheese made from *laban* drained through cheesecloth.

Dates have been an Arab staple for centuries. Dates and coffee are frequently offered to a caller, while dates stuffed with almonds are a popular confection. Dates baked into tiny, sugared cookies known as *ma'mul* are essential to the proper celebration of the festival at the close of Ramadan.

Hunayni, a hearty, nearly stiff porridge of ground dates cooked with butter and semolina and flavored with cardamom, is a classic breakfast dish of Najd. Cardamom is also the flavoring for *saliq*, a hot pudding that is the best-known evening rice

dish of the Kingdom. The rice is first half-cooked with meat or chicken broth, and then simmered with milk until it is soft. A hint of *mustaka*, the aromatic resin of the mastic tree, is added, recalling the ancient incense trade.

Makbous, a favorite dish of the Eastern Province, is made with tender, trout-sized *subayti*, a fish that abounds in the Arabian Gulf, along with grouper, king mackerel and succulent shrimp.

To sample the food of Saudi Arabia in its greatest variety, one looks to the Hijaz, where trade and pilgrim caravans have long lent a cosmopolitan air. The best time to sample this rich table is during Ramadan, when a lavish evening meal follows the dawn-to-dusk fast.

The fast is broken with a few sips of water, then a few dates and a thick drink prepared from sheets of dried, pressed apricots chopped and puréed with water. The meal itself begins with a rich soup made from soaked wheat and lamb stock, with

Saudis partake of a traditional meal in the shade of a tent. Families enjoy such weekend or holiday picnics on the beach, in parks or in the desert.

chunks of lamb and spices such as cinnamon, cardamom and the dry, curled leaf of the wormwood bush.

Next comes Egyptian *ful*, broad beans cooked until they are almost puréed and then garnished with tomato, onion and oil. Next is *sanbusak*, paper-thin pastry made up in triangular shapes stuffed with ground meat, onion, a pungent leaf of coriander or a long, spike-like member of the garlic family called *kurrath*. The meal may continue with eggs cooked gently on a bed of fried onion, green pepper and tomato, followed by one or two main dishes. There might be *kabsah*—chicken or lamb sautéed with garlic, onion, tomato, grated carrot and grated orange rind, served atop rice that has simmered in the meat sauce.

It is customary to end such a banquet with a sweet, preferably one that is soft and cold like *muhallabiyah*, a delicate pudding of rice flour and milk, lightly flavored with orange blossom or rose water and decorated with almonds and pistachios.

King Sa'ud ascended to the throne on the death of his father, King 'Abd al-'Aziz, in 1953. He reigned until 1964.

Although oil revenues continued to rise during the early years of Sa'ud's reign, the development program he inherited and pursued put the Kingdom in debt. King Sa'ud in many ways stood for an old-fashioned system of government: He was popular with the people and respected for his traditional virtues of generosity and his love of desert life. As debts mounted, he was forced to rein in spending on government projects.

Government finances and their control became the issue around which relations between King Sa'ud and Crown Prince Faysal revolved. In 1958, Sa'ud granted Faysal full executive powers in financial, internal and foreign affairs. Prince Faysal quickly introduced political and economic reforms, developed a Cabinet system of government through the Council of Ministers (which had originally been established in October 1953, a month before King 'Abd al-'Aziz's death) and granted greater freedom to the Saudi press. In addressing the financial crisis, he insisted on strict austerity, reducing both government expenditures and those of the royal family, and published a state budget for the first time.

During King Sa'ud's reign, the somewhat piecemeal development of government ministries moved ahead. Petroleum and Mineral Resources was set up in 1960, followed by Pilgrimage and Islamic Endowments (1960), Labor and Social Affairs (1962) and Information (1963). Advances were made in education, with the foundation of King Sa'ud University in Riyadh and the opening of the first government girls' schools. The number of students sent abroad to study increased, and many schools and religious institutions were established. In the field of social welfare, the government created a grievance board to ensure impartial hearings on citizens' complaints, granted interest-free loans to farmers, and institutionalized the channeling of *zakah* to help the poor and needy in accordance with Islamic law. A huge housing complex was built in Jiddah for pilgrims to use free of charge during the *hajj*, and the Sacred Mosque in Makkah and the Prophet's Mosque in Madinah were renovated and extended. Roads were paved for the pilgrims' use.

INTERNATIONAL RELATIONS

KING SA'UD BROADENED SAUDI ARABIA'S RELATIONS WITH its neighbors by undertaking a series of trips and official visits to friendly states, among them Egypt. On October 17, 1955, he signed a treaty of defense and friendship with Egypt and the following year, when the French and British attacked Egypt after Cairo nationalized the Suez Canal, Riyadh severed diplomatic relations with London and Paris. In 1958, with the establishment of the United Arab Republic by Egypt and Syria, and Saudi concern over the growing influence of the Soviet Union in the Middle East, relations with Cairo cooled swiftly and did not improve significantly until the early 1970s.

Relations with Jordan and Iraq, still ruled by the descendants of 'Abd al-'Aziz's former opponents the Hashimite *sharif*s of Makkah, improved, and Saudi Arabia also supported Kuwait, its small neighbor to the north, against external threats. In 1958, King Sa'ud and the ruler of Bahrain agreed on a boundary in the waters between their countries.

SOCIAL CHANGE

DURING THE 1950S, WITH THE SPREAD OF EDUCATION AND radio and the growth of newspapers, the Arab public became increasingly aware of events both within and outside their own countries. Saudi Arabia was no exception to these trends. With development came new ideas and forms of political awareness. The growth of jobs in the bureaucracy and armed forces, in the oil fields and on development projects led both to labor migration within the country and to the arrival of job-seekers from other Arab countries. Wealthier Saudis traveled abroad and saw for themselves how other countries organized their affairs.

New social and political groupings emerged within the Kingdom. The most visible politically were the so-called "Free Princes," led by Prince Talal, one of the younger sons of King 'Abd al-'Aziz. Talal saw increased public participation in government as inevitable and favored the formation of a national consultative council.

Another emerging group was formed by educated technocrats, the most prominent of whom was Abdullah H. Tariki. He was educated in Kuwait, Egypt and the United States before returning to work in the Finance Ministry under 'Abd Allah al-Sulayman during the reign of King 'Abd al-'Aziz. Tariki became director general of Petroleum and Mineral Affairs in 1954. Under King Sa'ud, he was appointed first

Educational opportunities expanded during the reign of King Sa'ud and grew further under King Faysal. Here, the first group of students sponsored by Aramco strolls on the campus of the American University of Beirut in 1954. The company has sponsored some 11,000 scholarships for employees and prospective employees to attend colleges and graduate schools in the Middle East, Europe, Asia and the United States since the program began in 1951.

oil minister on the creation of the Ministry of Petroleum and Mineral Resources in 1960. Tariki argued strongly for the renegotiation of national oil agreements and was instrumental in setting up OPEC, the Organization of Petroleum Exporting Countries, that same year. Both Prince Talal and Tariki were voices before their time: The Kingdom now has a Consultative Council, has held municipal elections, and the Concession Agreement was successively renegotiated from 1973 until the company became wholly owned by Saudi Arabia in 1980.

In 1962, King Sa'ud was seriously ill and the responsibilities of government fell more and more upon Faysal, whose powers were much increased over those of 1958. Sa'ud reigned until November 1964 when, because the King's health was declining, the royal family and religious leaders convinced him to abdicate and persuaded Faysal to succeed him.

KING FAYSAL

KING FAYSAL DETESTED EXTRAVAGANCE AND BELIEVED IN CLARITY, sound management and establishing clear priorities. "In one generation," he once remarked, "we went from riding camels to riding Cadillacs. The way we are wasting money, I fear the next generation will be riding camels again."

He set out to modernize the Kingdom, but not in the piecemeal manner of previous administrations. His modernizing cast of mind was combined with a profound faith and with a social conservatism that centered on the cohesion of the royal family and avoidance of upheaval. His motto was: "Change, but change slowly." He set out to apply the Kingdom's growing oil income to a properly planned and comprehensive program of development consistent with Islam and the Kingdom's traditional values.

Born in Riyadh in 1904, Faysal was educated by his maternal grandfather, 'Abd Allah ibn 'Abd al-Latif Al al-Shaykh, a noted religious scholar and descendant of Shaykh Muhammad ibn 'Abd al-Wahhab. In 1918, at the age of 12, he accompanied his father on his military campaign against Hayil and in 1922 he led the campaign in 'Asir.

In 1926, Faysal was appointed Viceroy of the Hijaz as well as chairman of the new Consultative Council there, and in 1930 he became Minister of Foreign Affairs. While holding those posts, he traveled extensively in Europe, including the Soviet Union in 1934. In 1939, he attended a conference on Palestine in London, and in 1943, with his brother Khalid, who would succeed him as King, he made a state visit to President Roosevelt in Washington, D.C. During the 1947 U.N. debate on the Palestine problem, he delivered a historic speech opposing partition. When King Sa'ud succeeded his father, Faysal was appointed president of the Council of Ministers.

On becoming King in 1964, Faysal moved swiftly to improve the machinery of government. He institutionalized government budgets and moved allies to key posts: Prince Khalid was made Crown Prince, while Faysal retained the Foreign Affairs portfolio in the Cabinet. The future King Fahd moved from Education to the Interior Ministry. Two other brothers occupied key posts that they hold to this day: the future King 'Abd Allah was confirmed as Commander of the National Guard and Prince Sultan — today the Crown Prince — became Minister of Defense. Ahmed Zaki Yamani was appointed minister of Petroleum and Mineral Resources. In 1965, the Central Planning Organization was created to mastermind the Kingdom's development. This resulted in the succession of five-year development plans, beginning with the first in 1970–74, that have determined the Kingdom's material progress ever since.

The main sectors to benefit from the new coordinated approach were defense, education and social services, and utilities and infrastructure for transportation, communications and industry. Today's extensive network of modern roads, ports, airports and domestic air routes owes its inception to Faysal's reign. The government also encouraged the development of the non-oil sector in agriculture and industry by providing low-cost industrial sites and special tax and customs incentives. The Kingdom's entrepreneurs began to branch out into plastics, steel, cement, tiles and other services to the construction and automobile trades.

Spending on education increased to around 10 percent of the annual budget. Elementary education had scarcely existed in some regions and female education was unknown in Najd and 'Asir. Faysal's commitment to education, in particular the priority he placed on girls' education with the support of his wife 'Effat, was notable. Elementary and secondary schools sprang up all over the country for both males and females, along with vocational training and institutes of higher education. In the Eastern Province, the University of Petroleum and Minerals (now King Fahd University of Petroleum and Minerals) opened in Dhahran in 1964, and King Faysal University in Dammam opened in 1975.

The King's guiding vision was that Saudi Arabia could modernize economically by importing technical expertise while maintaining its social traditions and remaining faithful to Islam. As modernization rolled forward, the Kingdom's growing oil revenues were also directed toward a wide range of social welfare programs. Faysal established the state bureaucracy as the mechanism of distribution of revenues and systematized its budgets, making welfare benefits, health, housing, education and even employment available to all citizens.

It was vital for the King to keep the religious establishment behind the reforms. This was done by incorporating the 'ulama into the machinery of state, enabling them to participate in government. Faysal also formalized religious education and extended his patronage to the establishment of the Kingdom's two Islamic universities: the Madinah-based Islamic University (founded in 1961) and Imam Muhammad ibn Sa'ud Islamic University in Riyadh (1974). Some technological innovations continued to be contentious, as illustrated by the introduction of television broadcasting in 1965. It was met by resistance that culminated in the storming of the new television station in Riyadh, during which the demonstrators' leader, a nephew of the King, was shot.

INTERNATIONAL RELATIONS

IN 1962, FAYSAL CONVENED A CONFERENCE IN MAKKAH TO find ways to combat secularism in the Arab and Muslim worlds. In 1969, he convened an Islamic summit in Rabat, Morocco, and in 1970 the foreign ministers of 23 Muslim countries gathered in Jiddah to establish the General Secretariat of the Muslim League under Saudi sponsorship. The Organization of the Islamic Conference was set up in 1969, again with Saudi support. Oil wealth enabled Saudi Arabia to initiate a substantial aid program to Muslim countries.

Faysal ibn 'Abd al-'Aziz, the foreign minister and future King of Saudi Arabia, and his brother, future King Khalid (third from left), visited the United States in 1943, meeting with President Franklin Roosevelt at the White House and traveling to San Francisco, where this picture was taken. Late that year, the United States released scarce steel reserves for construction of a new oil refinery at Ras Tanura.

DRESS

Traditional clothing in Arabia has changed little since the advent of Islam. Despite external influences, dress has for the most part retained its authenticity for both men and women. Clothing styles reflect Islamic principles, notably the need for modesty for both genders, particularly in the public sphere. Differences tend to be found only in the quality of materials used and in the fineness of tailoring. Fashion usually exercises an influence only in small details, although it does play a role in women's clothing and in the dress of some young men in urban areas.

MEN'S DRESS

Boys and men wear the *thawb*, a loose-fitting, ankle-length shirt that is usually white. The *thawb* was traditionally made of cotton, but today synthetic materials are more frequently used. Warmer cloth, including wool, is used for the *thawb* in the cool months. The color may vary from white and cream to light gray, or sometimes subdued shades of blue or green.

It is not unusual to see a Western-style suit jacket worn over the *thawb* in winter. The more traditional, flowing floor-length cloak called the *bisht* in eastern and central Saudi Arabia and the *mishlah* elsewhere in the Kingdom is also commonly worn, especially for special occasions. These cloaks are made of finely woven wool or camel hair, and are worn over the shoulders like a cape, enclosing the arms but open in the front. Small slits in the seams allow the hands to extend when desired. They are most frequently black or brown, and more rarely tan or cream, and are edged in cotton cord or in gold and/or silver braid.

Saudi dress is both practical and comfortable. It often combines traditional and Western elements such as the thawb, or ankle-length shirt, and headdress with a suit jacket.

Worn on the head are the *qahfiyah*, *ghutrah* and *'iqal*—the skullcap, the head cloth and the double ring of black rope or cord to hold it. The *qahfiyah* (also known as the *taqiyyah*) is a white, brimless cap frequently worn under the *ghutrah* to help position it and the *'iqal*. The square *ghutrah* comes in plain white or in black-, blue- or red-and-white checks (commonly known as the *shimagh*). The *ghutrah* is folded diagonally to make a triangle and draped with the fold across the forehead and the points hanging down the back of the head and shoulders. One or both ends of the tail of the triangle can be arranged to offer the wearer varying degrees of protection from wind, dust, smoke, sun, heat or cold. Farther north, in the Arab countries of the eastern Mediterranean, the *ghutrah* is called *hattah* or *kufiyah*.

There are few other variations in men's clothing. Western-style business suits are also worn, primarily by Saudis going to work and in urban centers. When Saudis travel abroad, they often wear Western-style business attire. Another variation can be seen in the winter when men in the colder northern region may wear heavy cloaks called *farwah*, a term that means "fur." These are thickly woven *bisht*s, usually in red, brown or black, that are lined with unshaved sheepskin.

Tribesmen in remote areas sometimes belt the *thawb* with a wide leather strap to which a money pouch or a scabbard for an ornamental knife may be attached. In the far southwest, men and women sometimes wear broad-brimmed conical straw hats. In coastal regions, workers such as sailors or farmers often wear a thick knit T-shirt with a brightly patterned cotton sarong called *izar* or *futah* tucked around the waist and reaching to mid-calf.

Sandals complete the traditional male dress, although today Western-style shoes are just as common. All kinds of sandals are worn, but the traditional type has a broad, oval-shaped natural leather strap decorated with geometric patterns of colored or metallic stitching across the top of the foot.

WOMEN'S CLOTHING

As with men, the public dress of Saudi women is fairly similar Kingdom-wide and akin to what is worn in neighboring countries. Like most aspects of life in Saudi Arabia, the teachings of Islam, based on the Quran and the *sunnah*, have affected the public dress code of women. According to Islam, women should dress modestly and avoid showing off their beauty in the presence of men who are not close relatives (i.e., not fathers, husbands, sons, uncles or nephews). To abide by these teachings while wearing whatever they like, women usually wear a wrap that does not attract attention or reveal what is beneath it.

In Saudi Arabia and neighboring countries, the wrap is called the *'abayah*, a cloak slipped over the head and around the shoulders where it can be drawn around the body with the hands. Today, the *'abayah* is almost always black, but in the past it was dyed with indigo. Women often have two types of *'abayah*s—one for everyday wear and the other for special occasions.

Some types of *'abayah*s are worn on the shoulders nowadays. In this case, women should wear a covering for their heads and necks, according to Muslim authorities. This is commonly known as the *misfa'*, *shaylah* or *milfa'*; it is placed

Women's traditional dress varies according to tribe and region. At top (from left) are styles from Najd in central Saudi Arabia, the Tayif area in the west, and Makkah, Madinah and Abha in the southwest.

over the head and wrapped partly around the face and reaches some way down the front. Some scholars say women should also cover their faces. This covering is known as the *ghatwah* or *bushiyah*, or the *niqab* or *burqu'*, depending on whether the face is entirely covered or leaves the eyes uncovered. Together, the *'abayah*, the head cover and the face cover, when used, form the *hijab*. Almost all girls wear a head covering from childhood, even before they begin wearing the veil.

Traditionally, Bedouin women and rural women in 'Asir have not worn the veil when doing daily chores, choosing instead to cover themselves with their *'abayah*s if strangers approached. Bedouin women and villagers traditionally wear the *burqu'* when they come to town. This often takes on the appearance of a mask.

Beneath the *'abayah*, whenever the gathering permits, Saudi women wear traditional dresses referred to as the *thawb*, *darra'ah* or *kurtah*, or the latest fashions from all over the world. Traditional *thawb*s display a rich variety of embroidery, beading and appliqué, depending on a woman's tribe or home region.

Today, there are several ongoing efforts to protect the Kingdom's rich heritage of traditional dress. A Saudi women's organization called *Mansoojat* (which takes its name from the Arabic word for textiles) is preserving traditional costumes and embroidery, and King 'Abd al-'Aziz University in Jiddah offers a master's degree in traditional clothing. Traditional styles are also being incorporated into contemporary dress, keeping the Kingdom's textile heritage alive.

Throughout the 1960s, there was a glut in oil supply and oil prices remained weak — below $2 per barrel (equivalent to around $12.50 today). Faysal's policy was to allow Aramco to produce and sell as much oil as the market would stand. It was good for the state coffers, and Saudi Arabia's cautious approach was underpinned by the recognition that economically producers and consumers were mutually dependent — a policy that continues today.

An Arab attempt to impose an oil embargo after the 1967 Arab-Israeli War failed because consumers could simply go elsewhere for supplies, which meant that the Arab producers would be harder hit by an embargo than consumers. But the war marked the start of a shift in Saudi policy.

In 1971–72, rising oil prices enabled OPEC and Saudi Arabia to adopt a more aggressive stance. In 1971, a higher royalty per barrel was negotiated. In the meantime, Saudi oil production rose to an unprecedented 8 million barrels per day, and in 1972 the Kingdom negotiated the purchase of a 25 percent interest in Aramco's concession rights, effective at the beginning of 1973.

In 1973, on the heels of the October War and the Egyptian crossing into the occupied Sinai Peninsula, Arab oil ministers met in Kuwait to support the military effort with a cut in oil production. Saudi Arabia declared its intention to cease oil supplies to countries that had adopted a pro-Israeli policy. When its full effects were felt, the price of oil rose by 70 percent. The embargo thrust Saudi Arabia into prominence in world affairs and brought the Kingdom into the center of Arab politics.

KING FAYSAL'S LAST YEARS

THE RISE IN THE PRICE OF OIL GAVE A SUDDEN BOOST TO THE Kingdom's economy, increasing gross domestic product (GDP) by two-and-a-half times. This enabled Faysal to accelerate the modernization program embodied in the First Five-Year Development Plan. The period was marked by a very high rate of economic growth, and most of the goals of the development plan were reached or surpassed. One objective was to diversify the economy, reducing the country's dependence on the oil industry for its income. Although there was a substantial increase in the importance of the non-oil sectors of the economy, their contribution to GDP was actually reduced in proportionate terms because of the great increase in income from oil.

Saudi Arabia emerged as a pivotal source of the world's oil supplies during the first development plan, and King Faysal's government faced a problem that was the reverse of his father's and King Sa'ud's. Instead of worrying about how to make ends meet, the government had to cope with a monetary surplus that some Western economists feared could upset finances and currencies around the world. Such fears were exaggerated. Although Saudi Arabia invested a good share of the surplus funds abroad, a substantial percentage was earmarked for aid to other, less fortunate Muslim countries. In addition, the Kingdom began to channel billions of

King Faysal reigned from 1964 to 1975. He was succeeded by his brother Khalid.

dollars into the ambitious Second Five-Year Development Plan to expand the industrial infrastructure of the country.

Saudi Arabia's growing influence and prestige on the international stage masked a vulnerability. A vast country with a relatively sparse population, the Kingdom was experiencing a new affluence but was still relatively underdeveloped. Its development depended on continued growth in the world economy — growth that would strengthen, not diminish, demand for oil. At the OPEC meeting of March 1974, Saudi Arabia was instrumental in stabilizing the oil price at levels beneficial to both producers and consumers.

On March 25, 1975, King Faysal was assassinated in his office in Riyadh by a deranged young relative seeking vengeance for the death of his brother in the anti-television riot of 1965. His murder shocked not only the Kingdom and its people but the world at large, for Faysal had emerged in his last years as a moderating influence politically and economically throughout the Middle East.

KING KHALID

CROWN PRINCE KHALID ACCEDED TO THE THRONE WITHIN three days of Faysal's death.

Born in 1912 in Riyadh, Khalid was exposed to public affairs from an early age. After the conflict with Yemen in 1934, he represented his country at the peace negotiations at Tayif. With Faysal, he had attended a number of international meetings on behalf of Saudi Arabia. In October 1962, Khalid was named Vice President of the Council of Ministers and in 1965 he was designated Crown Prince.

King Khalid came to power at the start of the Second Five-Year Development Plan and his reign coincided with the first peak in Saudi Arabia's oil revenues. However, he and his government had to contend with four crises that threatened the Kingdom's security: the occupation of the Sacred Mosque in Makkah by a group of armed fanatics in 1979; the Iranian revolution the same year that deposed the shah and brought the Ayatollah Khomeini to power; the Soviet invasion of Afghanistan; and the outbreak of the Iran-Iraq War in 1980.

On Khalid's accession, the senior members of the House of Sa'ud chose his brother Fahd as Crown Prince. Fahd had been a minister in the Cabinet since the 1950s and had wide experience in government. The challenge was to manage the rapid change, fueled by oil revenues, that was materially transforming the Kingdom. With the largest-known oil reserves of any country in the world, Saudi Arabia was emerging as an important player in international affairs. King Khalid was a modest and frank man of much personal charm and a strong sense of humor who became the focus of the Saudi people's affection and respect. Because of his ill health, however, Crown Prince Fahd shouldered a large portion of the work of overseeing the Kingdom's development and managing the affairs of state.

DEVELOPMENT

KHALID'S REIGN WAS A TIME OF MASSIVE INFRASTRUCTURE building. By the mid-1970s, the Kingdom's fast-growing economy was outstripping its support systems of roads, ports, electricity and some social services. The second development plan, which began in 1975, and the third, launched in 1980, were full-scale attacks on these bottlenecks. Rapidly expanding oil revenues financed this expensive task, and each plan was funded at more than $200 billion.

The effort was a resounding success: Within a few years, port and road congestion was overcome with the construction of a world-scale national highway system, marine facilities, international airports and expanded telecommunications. In the decade covered by the two plans, paved highways quadrupled in length and port tonnage increased by 10 times, while power generation grew from less than 2 billion to more than 44 billion kilowatt-hours. The number of schools jumped from 5,600 to more than 15,000, with a remarkable average completion rate of more than two schools per day. The number of hospitals nearly doubled, to 176.

A major start was also made on another development phase that aimed to diversify the Kingdom's economy through the development of heavy industry — much of it emphasizing

King Khalid International Airport, gateway to the heartland of Saudi Arabia and Riyadh, opened near the Kingdom's capital in 1983. It was the second of three international airports built to serve the Kingdom, following Jiddah's King 'Abd al-'Aziz International Airport, opened in 1981, and preceding King Fahd International Airport in Dammam, opened in 1999.

petrochemical production based on the fuel and feedstock supplied by the Kingdom's Master Gas System, or MGS, which was also under construction (see page 257). Planners decided to concentrate the new industries in two massive complexes, one at Jubail on the Gulf and one at Yanbuʻ on the Red Sea — each linked by pipeline to the MGS. An independent organization, the Royal Commission for Jubail and Yanbuʻ, was established to coordinate these ventures and provide their special infrastructure requirements.

INTERNAL TENSIONS

KING FAYSAL HAD SOUGHT TO MAINTAIN THE KINGDOM'S values at the center of Saudi Arabian life by state funding for new Islamic universities and by giving the *ʻulama* a role in the government. But the sudden impact of affluence and consumerism upon Saudi Arabia's deeply traditional society was not without upheaval.

A group of fanatics used the end of the 14th Islamic century to proclaim their dissent. As the *Hijri* year 1400 dawned on November 20, 1979, between 200 and 400 armed men revealed themselves to worshipers in the Sacred Mosque in Makkah. Shots rang out and pandemonium ensued. After a protracted siege, the uprising was put down.

INTERNATIONAL RELATIONS

EARLY IN 1979, THE IRANIAN REVOLUTION SHOOK THE REGION. In December, the Soviet Union, already involved in Iraq, sharpened the Cold War by invading Afghanistan. The outbreak of war between Iran and Iraq in September 1980 created insecurity in the Gulf and posed a menace to oil exports.

King Khalid ascended the throne in 1975. His seven-year reign marked a period of enormous infrastructure construction.

The need for security and development prompted the Gulf states to come together to coordinate strategy. In May 1981, Saudi Arabia, Kuwait, Bahrain, Qatar, the United Arab Emirates and Oman formed the Gulf Cooperation Council (GCC). A key GCC objective was to provide a mechanism for

King Khalid inaugurated the Berri Gas Plant, the first plant in the Master Gas System network to be completed, in 1977. It is a few kilometers from Jubail, where the first company geologists landed, and takes its name from the first jabal, or rock outcrop, they visited. King Khalid is accompanied by Crown Prince Fahd (center right in profile), Aramco Board Chairman and CEO Frank Jungers and Minister of Petroleum and Mineral Resources Ahmed Zaki Yamani (left).

Saudi Arabia's paper currency includes
20- and 200-riyal notes issued in
1999 to mark the 100th Hijri anniversary of the Kingdom's founding.

MONEY

The House of Sa'ud issued its first money shortly after the capture of Makkah in 1924. It consisted of copper half-*qirsh* and quarter-*qirsh* coins bearing the *tughra*, or monogram, of 'Abd al-'Aziz, inscribed "Minted in the Mother of All Towns" (a traditional name for Makkah). A new set of quarter-, half- and one-*qirsh* coins was issued the following year in the name of 'Abd al-'Aziz Al Sa'ud, King of the Hijaz and Sultan of Najd.

On January 24, 1928, King 'Abd al-'Aziz established a monetary system based on the Saudi riyal, a silver coin about the size of a U.S. silver dollar, equaling 22 *qirsh* and valued at one-10th of a British sovereign. A new riyal coin, about the size of a U.S. half dollar, was issued in 1936 and eventually valued at 3.75 Saudi riyals to the U.S. dollar.

For many years, Saudi Arabia issued no paper currency. Major transactions were carried out with gold or large quantities of silver riyals. However, with increases in oil production after World War II, handling silver and gold coins in the required quantities became almost impossible. For example, to pay its employees—whose biweekly wages in silver coins might weigh as much as 4.5 kilograms (10 pounds) each—the company had to ship, guard and parcel out 40 tons of silver coins a month.

The Saudi Arabian Monetary Agency (SAMA), the Kingdom's central bank, was established in 1951. SAMA was forbidden by its charter to issue paper money. In 1953, it won government permission to issue "pilgrim receipts"—a sort of traveler's check designed to relieve foreign pilgrims of the need to carry bulky silver riyals. These receipts rapidly displaced gold sovereigns and silver riyals among Saudis, and soon gained the virtual status of official paper currency.

In 1958, after a period of severe inflation, Crown Prince Faysal asked the International Monetary Fund (IMF) to help design and implement a program of fiscal and monetary reform. Government spending was reduced and the riyal devalued.

Saudi Arabia revalued the riyal in 1960, fixing its value in terms of gold at 4.5 riyals to the U.S. dollar and ensuring its stability by providing 100 percent backing in gold and foreign currency. At the same time, it was announced that the riyal would contain 20 *qirsh* divided into five *halalahs*. Thus the currency was, in effect, put on a decimal basis for the first time.

In 1961, the Kingdom accepted the IMF's obligation to make the Saudi riyal a fully convertible currency. That same year, SAMA issued the first Saudi paper currency in denominations of one, five, 10, 50 and 100 riyals. A 500-riyal note was added later. In 1999, in tandem with celebrations for the *Hijri* centennial of the Kingdom's establishment, SAMA began issuing 20- and 200-riyal notes.

Saudi banknotes (printed in Arabic on one side and English on the other) depict crossed swords and a palm tree, the national emblem, and portraits of the reigning monarchs. There are coins of five, 10, 25 and 50 *halalahs*, as well as one-riyal (100-*halalah*) cupronickel coins.

The new industrial city of Jubail, built beginning in the 1970s, boasts fertilizer, chemical, iron and steel manufacturing plants, along with new homes and schools. Jubail is Saudi Arabia's largest industrial city, with a dozen primary industries and some 200 light manufacturing plants. Here, residents turn out for Jubail's annual flower festival.

joint action on security by the Arabian states themselves. The GCC embraced the doctrine of nonalignment. Looking toward a long-term goal of a "Gulf Common Market," the GCC soon took major steps toward freer transit of people and goods and the reduction of customs barriers.

The Iranian revolution created a temporary oil shortage that gave a massive boost to the price of oil, and to the Kingdom's revenues. The Kingdom was wrestling with complex issues on the foreign affairs front when, in the summer of 1982, King Khalid died of a heart attack.

KING FAHD

CROWN PRINCE FAHD IBN 'ABD AL-'AZIZ WAS PROCLAIMED King in June 1982, immediately after King Khalid's death. Prince 'Abd Allah ibn 'Abd al-'Aziz, the Commander of the National Guard, became Crown Prince and First Deputy Prime Minister.

Fahd, who was born in Riyadh in 1921, was already a veteran of many years of distinguished government service, having been appointed the Kingdom's first Minister of Education in 1953. In 1962, he became Minister of Interior and served in that capacity until he was named Crown Prince and First Deputy Prime Minister in 1975. Throughout this period, he worked on developing and implementing many

of the Kingdom's major projects. He served as chairman of a number of high-level committees and councils, including the Supreme Council for Petroleum and Minerals, the Supreme Council for Education and the Royal Commission for Jubail and Yanbu'.

King Fahd served as an inclusive and modernizing monarch who guided the Kingdom through challenging times. His attitude to his people was best expressed by a speech in which he said: "I will be a father to the young, brother to the elderly. I am but one of you: whatever troubles you, troubles me; whatever pleases you, pleases me." His accession coincided with the end of the first boom in Saudi Arabia's oil revenues. The slump in production and income reached its nadir in 1985–86, leading to years of relative austerity. It dealt a blow to the Kingdom's program of economic development, affected GDP and caused some major projects to be frozen.

Demographic pressures accentuated the impact of austerity. In the 1980s and 1990s, the Kingdom had one of the world's fastest-growing populations, so that around 40 percent of today's some 23 million Saudis are under the age of 17. At the same time, the policy of universal education has resulted in an unprecedented number of young Saudi men and women entering the job market. In an effort to increase job opportunities, the government has embarked on a policy of "Saudization" aimed at replacing foreign workers with Saudis as they attain the required standards in education, training and skills. In 2004, foreign workers were estimated to account for as much as half of the country's work force of some 6.5 million.

Progress is being made, but the challenge remains a live one. A growing class of young Saudis has emerged in the cities made up of individuals who have found it difficult to obtain jobs in industry and the service sectors. Many hold degrees in the humanities and from the religious universities. A small minority have turned their backs on modernization and embraced an extreme interpretation of Islam that rejects the status quo in the Kingdom, while the majority believes Islam can be reconciled with cautious and appropriate change. What is or is not appropriate in terms of progress toward greater social freedom, political representation, a more plural society, openness toward the outside world and appropriate material development remains the subject of animated national debate. All shades of opinion emphasize their Islamic credentials, advocating the preservation of what they see as the core Saudi way of life.

DEVELOPMENT

IN SPITE OF THE OIL PRICE SLUMP OF THE MID-1980S, THE government remained determined to proceed with development and was reluctant to cut spending on social welfare pro-

King Fahd ibn 'Abd al-'Aziz reigned from 1982 to 2005, overseeing a number of complex development programs.

grams and education. As a result, successive budget deficits had to be financed by borrowing and drawing on reserves.

King Fahd's reign witnessed completion of the first great wave of macro-scale infrastructure construction envisaged in the first two five-year plans and the fruition of a number of industrial and other developments dependent upon them. Perhaps most notably, major strides were taken in diversifying the Kingdom's sources of income across a growing industrial base, and in achieving self-sufficiency in many primary manufactured and agricultural commodities. To attract private capital, a policy of privatization was introduced at major petrochemical enterprises at Jubail and Yanbu'; these were started by the Saudi Basic Industries Corporation (SABIC), which was set up in the 1970s to mastermind the downstream economic diversification of the oil and refining industries.

By the mid-1990s, the advanced industrial complexes at Jubail and Yanbu' had already passed through a capacity expansion phase. They now hold a seven percent share of the world petrochemical market in competition with the long-dominant plants of North America, Europe and Japan, helping make the Gulf countries the world's largest exporter of petrochemicals and plastics. They also supply a major share of the Kingdom's domestic needs for such manufactured products as construction steel, plastic resins and chemical fertilizers. Secondary industries use these materials to manufacture consumer goods. In 2004, the Royal Commission for Jubail and Yanbu' launched a multi-billion-dollar Jubail-II development plan that will double the size of that industrial city to 11,000 hectares (27,200 acres) and is expected to bring investments of $56 billion and create 55,000 jobs.

Total investment in Saudi Arabia's industrial enterprises, numbering more than 3,600 in 2003, was estimated at more than $66 billion. The huge petrochemical plant investments of SABIC, initially funded by the government because of their massive scale, are now 30 percent privately held.

In line with a trend toward more competition and privatization, a private aviation company began providing flights between Riyadh and Jiddah in 2005, while steps are being taken to privatize the national air carrier, Saudi Arabian Airlines. Other sectors of the economy have also been opened to private investment.

Other development achievements have provided additional public service infrastructure. The second, third and fourth five-year plans, covering 1980–94, concentrated on education, health and social services, and—most recently—defense. Private enterprise and investment were encouraged through incentives. By 2003, the number of public and private hospitals in the Kingdom had grown to more than 340, supplemented by over 2,800 dispensaries and health care centers. Virtually every village had been reached by the electric power grid and all regions had been linked by a country-wide highway network. Among special road projects was the 26-kilometer (16-mile) King Fahd Causeway, an engineering

Saudi dancers stage a traditional folk dance accompanied by song for an audience in Washington, D.C.

MUSIC

Music has long been a vital part of life in the Arabian Peninsula, linked strongly to ancient poetic traditions and to ways of life predating the discovery of oil. Yet it is also part of the modern current, a unique tapestry of rhythms and sounds that enjoys enormous popularity.

The peninsula has interacted with neighboring music cultures for centuries, resulting in a special combination of influences. In recent decades, the pace of musical interchange has increased dramatically. *Khaliji*, or "Gulf," music, as the popular music of the peninsula is known, is one of the most influential styles in the Arab world. Broadcast by radio and satellite television and spread through the Internet, *Khaliji* pop stars and composers are gaining a growing regional following.

The *Khaliji* music style is distinct in its rhythms and accented lyrics. It also reflects more general qualities born of the deep and varied musical heritage of the Bedouin, the cities and towns, the songs of the Gulf pearl divers and traditional women's folk singing. Each style is distinct, but they all borrowed from each other, demonstrating a longstanding cultural exchange among traditional folk cultures within as well as outside the region.

BEDOUIN MUSIC

The traditional songs of the Bedouin, whether laced with poetry or simple folksong lyrics woven over hypnotic, syncopated repetition, exhibit a deep love of the spoken word. The Bedouin sang *nabati*, or folk poems, a cappella as soloists or accompanied by the one-stringed, violin-like *rababah*. The tribes sang poetry in groups, too; these songs included the *Samiri* genre of love poetry and the *'ardah* poems celebrating bravery in battle. The Bedouin also sang simpler songs to celebrate occasions such as weddings. Group singing was set to rhythmic hand clapping, as well as the multi-toned percussion of the *tar*, a hand drum found throughout the Arab world.

URBAN ENSEMBLE MUSIC

Many of the peninsula's cities and towns engaged in long-distance commerce, importing goods from elsewhere in the Middle East, India, Africa and beyond. Traders learned new poems and songs and even instruments in neighboring regions, introducing their discoveries when they returned home. Foreign visitors also brought new musical ideas with them. As a result, urban music styles developed in the peninsula that echo Egypt, the Levant, the coastal towns of Yemen and Oman, Iraq and the Indian subcontinent.

The peninsula's traditional urban song styles include *al-sawt* in most of the Arabian Gulf states, *al-majrur* in the Hijaz in western Saudi Arabia, *al-'awwadi* and *al-sharh* in southern Yemen's Hadhramaut and *al-ghina al-san'ani* elsewhere in Yemen. While the traditions of each region vary, most feature a small ensemble of musicians, percussionists and a lead vocalist playing the Arabian lute, or *'ud*, that performs for friends and family in the salons of private homes.

VILLAGE AND COASTAL FOLK MUSIC

In addition to sophisticated urban music, coastal settlers from Africa and the Indian subcontinent brought folk musical traditions with them and wove them into the local cultural fabric. *Tanburah* music features the eponymous six-stringed lyre and is heavily influenced by the music of East Africa. *Laywah* folk music, spotlighting the *surnay*, a loud, oboe-like wind instrument, and a suite of deep-toned drums such as the *mesendo*, also echoes the music of East Africa.

PEARLING MUSIC

Pearlers from the Arabian Gulf developed a unique song tradition known as *aghani al-ghaws*, or diving songs. In the industry's heyday, more than 1,000 pearling boats went to sea each year from April to September. Ship captains hired a lead musician called a *nahham*, who used songs to motivate the crews. Crewmembers sang specific songs at each stage of work. They entertained themselves at night with a special sub-genre of pearling songs known as *fajri*, songs of the dawn.

Everyone took part as a singer, and added rhythmic clapping or played a percussion instrument. Drummers played a range of instruments including the large earthenware jug, the *jahlah*, as well as finger cymbals. The lead singer wailed out difficult, high-pitched vocal improvisations, while others intoned the *hamhamah*, a distinct bass drone. After the pearling industry died out, retired crews continued to perform their music on shore, preserving the songs for the next generations.

Saudi singer-composer Muhammad 'Abdu is among the best-known performers in the Arabian Peninsula and the Arab world.

Seafarers of the Hijaz region had their own set of songs. They included *al-'ajal*, a highly rhythmic group song played with a small drum called the *mirwas* and the *tar* to motivate sailors. *Al-simsimiyah*, played with a small version of the *tanburah* and different types of drums, is popular on both sides of the Red Sea.

WOMEN'S FOLK MUSIC

For centuries, the women of the Arabian Peninsula, both Bedouin and settled, have sung to celebrate rites of passage such as weddings. Female folk bands continue to entertain women at traditional gatherings. Formerly accompanied by drumming, clapping and the occasional *'ud*, these bands now usually feature electronic keyboards with a special key to make the women's ululating cry of joy, the *zagharid*. Distinctive, multi-layered drumming remains the hallmark of this vibrant music form. Some singers have expanded this genre to perform as soloists in public concerts and to make recordings with full-scale instrumental orchestras.

MUSIC DEVELOPMENTS

An Omani singer made the earliest-known recording of music from the Arabian Peninsula on a wax cylinder in Vienna in 1904, and the Dutch Legation in Jiddah recorded musicians in the Hijaz in 1909. In the 1920s and '30s, companies recorded *sawt* ensembles from Bahrain and Kuwait.

By the 1940s and '50s, listeners in the Arabian Peninsula began to tune their radios to Egypt's popular *Sawt al-Arab* station, becoming part of the audience of pan-Arab superstar singers like Umm Kulthum, Muhammad 'Abd al-Wahhab and Farid al-Atrash. Their use of large orchestras in formal concert halls and recording studios influenced a generation of composers in the peninsula, led by Saudi Arabia's Tariq 'Abd al-Hakim, Talal Maddah, Muhammad 'Abdu, 'Abadi al-Jawhar and Siraj 'Umar.

In the 1960s and '70s, stars from the Arabian Peninsula gained a wider audience in the Arab world. In the 1970s, 'Abdu's song *B'aad*, and Maddah's *Maqadir* achieved widespread popularity. These songs incorporated the Gulf rhythms in the longer song forms developed in Egypt, but were sung in the singer's Saudi accent.

In the 1970s and '80s, many countries set up folklore institutes to teach young people the old music and folk dance traditions. Nearly all the countries of the peninsula today have national folklore troupes.

In the 1990s, a vibrant regional recording industry took root in the Arabian Peninsula. At the same time, music videos spread to the area. *Khaliji* stars like Saudi Arabia's 'Abd al-Majid 'Abd Allah and Jawad al-'Ali have embraced video clips.

Today, young people download the latest pop songs and video clips by Arabian Peninsula song stars. Brides still hire traditional women's folk bands to entertain guests at weddings. Young people study and perform the traditional regional folk arts, preserving traditions. Television and radio stations pulsate with songs, old and new. While the new songs echo the melodies and rhythms of the past, they are clearly moving into the future with an indigenous energy that speaks to a growing local audience.

masterpiece linking al-Khobar in the Eastern Province with the island Kingdom of Bahrain. Funded and maintained by Saudi Arabia, the causeway opened in 1986 and by 2004 was carrying more than 18,000 vehicles daily.

FOREIGN RELATIONS IN THE 1980S AND '90S

EVEN BEFORE ASCENDING THE THRONE, KING FAHD HAD deployed his powers of conciliation on the international stage. In 1981, he brokered the Fahd Plan to resolve the Israeli–Palestinian conflict that was adopted by the Arab League as the Fez Initiative. Serving on the Supreme Tri-partite Committee of the Arab League, he helped to craft the agreement that in 1989 resulted in the signing of the Tayif National Reconciliation Accord that brought peace to Lebanon. In the early 1990s, he supported the U.N.

effort to bring peace to Bosnia and directed a massive Saudi campaign to help ease the suffering of civilians in that war-shattered country.

Closer to home, Saudi Arabia did not become directly involved in the Iran-Iraq War (1980–88). From 1984, the war turned steadily in Iraq's favor, and the United States and Britain, while reluctant to become part of the conflict, were drawn into the "tanker war," sending flotillas to protect Arab oil shipments from possible Iranian attack.

Meanwhile, there was a convergence in U.S.-Saudi policy in Afghanistan, where the Soviet military was deeply involved in the civil war. Young Saudis joined other Muslims in local Afghani militias to resist Soviet occupation, which began in 1979. After Soviet forces withdrew in 1989, many of these men returned home. While the majority resumed a normal

One of the busiest border crossings in the Middle East, the 26-kilometer (16 mile) King Fahd Causeway links Saudi Arabia to the Arabian Gulf island Kingdom of Bahrain. More than 3.5 million vehicles have crossed the $1.2 billion causeway since it opened in 1986.

Powerful lights illuminate a work site at the Sacred Mosque in Makkah. Saudi Arabia spent nearly $19 billion between 1986 and 1996 to expand facilities around the Sacred Mosque and the Mosque of the Prophet in Madinah, Islam's two holiest sites.

EXPANDING THE HOLY PLACES

Pilgrims have made their way to Makkah overland and by sea, often enduring great hardships along the way, for some 1,400 years, and it has always been a priority of Muslim governments to look after the safety and welfare of pilgrims. Today this is the responsibility of the Government of Saudi Arabia, and the task is formidable. In 1925, some 25,000 foreign pilgrims made the *hajj*. Today the annual number of pilgrims to Makkah is more than 2 million, and each year the number rises.

Improvements to the physical facilities of the holy places themselves have been a continuing high priority. Each successive Saudi monarch has taken a special personal interest in a long series of amplifications of the areas of the Sacred Mosque in Makkah and the Mosque of the Prophet in Madinah. Two years before his death, King 'Abd al-'Aziz initiated a building program to increase the Sacred Mosque area by some 60 percent. Later, King Faysal built some 35,000 square meters (nearly nine acres) of open plazas around the mosque, and this area was later doubled by his successor, King Khalid.

This concern for the pilgrimage and the holy places was enshrined in the official title adopted by King Fahd, who in 1986 dropped the traditional "His Majesty" in favor of *Khadim al-Haramayn al-Sharifayn*, "The Custodian of the Two Holy Mosques." His successor, King 'Abd Allah, retained that title.

Between 1985 and 1996, Saudi Arabia spent more than 70 billion riyals ($18.7 billion) on the expansion of the Mosque of the Prophet in Madinah and the Sacred Mosque of Makkah.

The project at the Mosque of the Prophet—the most extensive ever—increased its size 10-fold. Six new 105-meter (336-foot) minarets brought the mosque's total to 10; seven new entrances were added; and a series of 27 domes, each 15 meters (48 feet) in diameter and capable of being electronically opened and closed, was incorporated into the new roof. Awnings like giant umbrellas open automatically to shade the courtyards of the mosque and protect worshipers from the sun.

The western gallery of the Sacred Mosque was extended into an area that had previously been an open esplanade. The new extension is entered through a monumental gateway flanked by two new minarets, bringing the total number of minarets to nine. The extension has 18 smaller entranceways and is supported by 500 marble columns within the mosque itself. The mosque now encloses 356,000 square meters (88 acres), including the rooftop prayer areas and open plazas.

This expansion project permits access to more worshipers—up to a million at a time. The floor is paved with specially designed heat-resistant tiles and the entire complex is cooled by one of the world's largest air-conditioning plants, for temperatures in the summer consistently exceed 40°C (104°F). Worshipers can ascend to the rooftop prayer area by escalator.

Al-Khobar, just a fishing hamlet in 1933 when the oil explorers arrived in the Eastern Province, is now a booming metropolis. It is bordered by a new corniche, built on land reclaimed from the Arabian Gulf, that extends many kilometers along the Arabian Gulf coast.

life, some had adopted a radical and violent way of thinking that was broadly rejected by their families, by their communities and, eventually, by their governments. Some of those men returned to Afghanistan and supported the Taliban regime when it took power in 1996. Among them was Osama bin Laden, who established the terrorist body al-Qaeda as the focus of a loose network of groups dedicated to forcing their extreme doctrines on Muslim nations and the world. The Saudi Government had earlier stripped Bin Laden of his Saudi citizenship as a result of his extremist activities.

Saudi Arabia faced a crisis on its northern border in August 1990 when Iraq invaded Kuwait. When Iraq refused to comply with a U.N. Security Council resolution to withdraw by January 15, 1991, a coalition of forces from around the world— including the GCC states, Egypt, Morocco, Syria and others, joined Saudi Arabia and the United States in enforcing the U.N. sanction. In a brief war, they ejected Iraqi forces from Kuwait, though not before severe damage had been caused in that country and the region when Iraqi forces blew up oil wells and released large amounts of oil into the Gulf.

Reforms of 1992–93

Legislation introduced by Royal Decrees of King Fahd in 1992 and 1993 further modernized and defined the system of government while broadening the bases for decision-making. The Basic System of Government, issued in March 1992, has many characteristics of a Western-style constitution. However, its first article states that the constitution of the Kingdom is the Quran and the *sunnah* of the Prophet Muhammad.

The Basic System, among other provisions, defines eligibility for the throne, establishes the judiciary as an independent authority subject only to the *shari'ah*, or religious law, and sets forth general rules for the state financial system. Another series of provisions acts, in effect, as a bill of citizens' rights, guaranteeing rights of private property, the inviolability of the home and protection from arbitrary penalties.

In Saudi Arabia, as it did once throughout the Islamic world, the *shari'ah* regulates many matters covered in Western countries by civil and criminal law. The *shari'ah* is considered to be divine law, and is interpreted and administered by the *qadi*s and *'ulama*; as a result, the judiciary system in the Kingdom has a considerable degree of independence from other branches of government. In matters not expressly prohibited or enjoined by the *shari'ah*, the King, through the Council of Ministers and a number of commissions and advisory bodies, administers a relatively large body of regulations covering such areas as public health, customs, commerce, company law and labor—all increasingly important as the process of modernization moves ahead.

One important provision of the Basic System created an advisory body called the *Majlis al-Shura*, or the Consultative Council. The council, as defined by Royal Decree in 1993, consisted of 60 members (raised to 90 in 1997, 120 in 2001 and 150 in 2005) appointed for four-year terms; it is charged to advise the Council of Ministers on matters of economic and social development, international agreements and interpretations of legislation. On December 29, 1993, King Fahd opened the first session of the council, whose members represented a broad spectrum of leaders with extensive experience in the academic world, public administration and various technical fields. The majority hold advanced academic credentials, many from well-known Middle Eastern and Western universities. Notably, the council encompasses conservatives and liberals, bringing them together in the same debating arena.

Provincial Administration

Another major component of these legislative developments, issued in March 1992, was a more detailed definition of the Kingdom's system of provincial administration. The Law of the Provinces provided for greater participation at the local and regional level in the Kingdom. It included the establishment of provincial councils with members of recognized stature and expertise appointed from both the private and public sectors. These bodies function primarily to advise the executive branch on regional development matters.

Originally, Saudi Arabia was divided into broad geographical regions for administrative purposes. The main divisions were Najd, covering a large part of the interior and including Riyadh; the Hijaz, containing the Holy Cities of Makkah and Madinah, and Jiddah, the Kingdom's main port on the Red Sea; 'Asir, the mountainous district administered from Abha and including Najran; and al-Hasa (later called the Eastern Province), named after al-Hasa Oasis but including Dammam, al-Khobar, Dhahran, Abqaiq and Ras Tanura.

This traditional administrative division of the Kingdom evolved over the years. Today the country is divided into 13 provinces, which do not necessarily correspond with the earlier geographical regions. They are: 'Asir, al-Baha, the Eastern Province, Hayil, al-Jawf, Jaizan, Makkah, al-Madinah, Najran, the Northern Frontier, al-Qasim, Tabuk and Riyadh. Each is governed by an appointed *amir*. The provinces are subdivided into districts, often centered on cities or towns. The provincial governors are responsible to the Ministry of the Interior and have access to other ministers to facilitate economic development in their areas.

The majority of Saudis, conservative and liberal alike, welcomed the new laws. They viewed them as steps to reinforce stability in the Kingdom, confirm citizens' rights, encourage greater participation in public affairs and provide for a more accountable government.

Stern Challenges

On the economic front, the cost of the 1991 Gulf War and slumping oil prices forced the government to borrow heavily abroad for the first time to maintain its budget commitments. The situation worsened until, in early 1998, with the price as low as $10 per barrel, the government was forced to cut back on public expenditure. Saudi Arabia's oil revenue had slumped in 1998 to just $32 billion from a

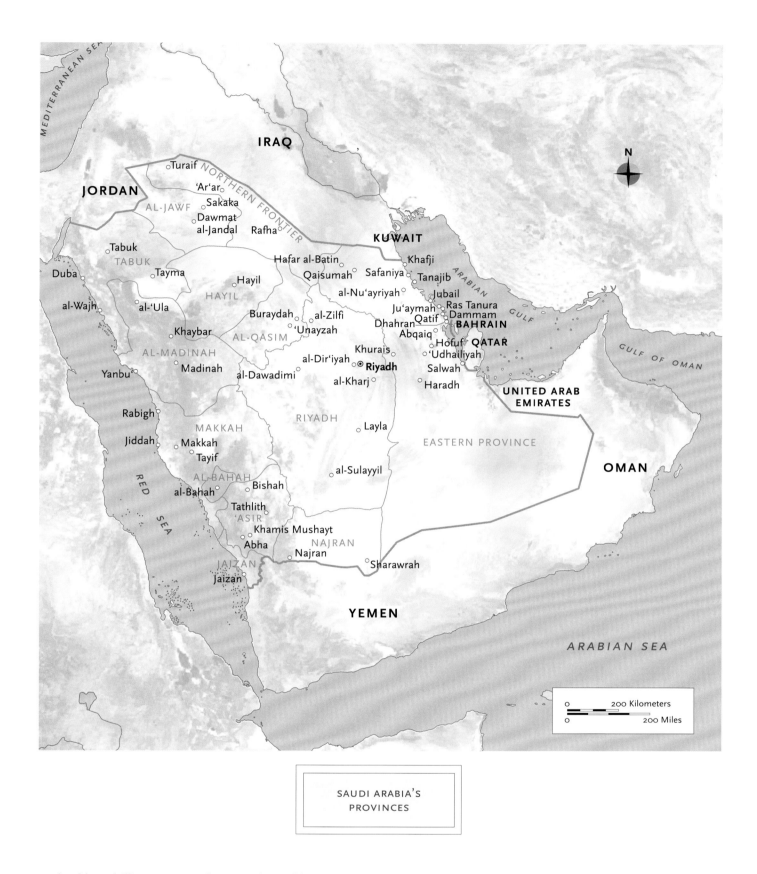

MEDITERRANEAN SEA

IRAQ

N

JORDAN

Turaif

NORTHERN FRONTIER

'Ar'ar

Sakaka

AL-JAWF

Dawmat
al-Jandal

Rafha

KUWAIT

Tabuk

Hafar al-Batin

Khafji

TABUK

Tayma

Qaisumah

Safaniya

Tanajib

Duba

ARABIAN GULF

al-Nu'ayriyah

Jubail

Hayil

HAYIL

Ju'aymah

Ras Tanura
Dammam

al-Wajh

Buraydah

al-Zilfi

Dhahran

Qatif

al-'Ula

'Unayzah

BAHRAIN

Khaybar

AL-QASIM

Abqaiq

QATAR

AL-MADINAH

al-Dir'iyah

Khurais

Hofuf

Madinah

al-Dawadimi

Riyadh

'Udhailiyah

Yanbu

al-Kharj

Salwah

Haradh

UNITED ARAB
EMIRATES

Rabigh

RIYADH

Layla

GULF OF OMAN

MAKKAH

EASTERN PROVINCE

Jiddah

Makkah

OMAN

Tayif

al-Sulayyil

RED SEA

AL-BAHAH

al-Bahah

Bishah

Tathlith

ASIR

Khamis Mushayt

NAJRAN

Abha

Najran

JAIZAN

Sharawrah

Jaizan

YEMEN

ARABIAN SEA

0   200 Kilometers

0   200 Miles

SAUDI ARABIA'S
PROVINCES

peak of $119 billion in 1981, the equivalent of $213 billion in 1998 dollars.

By the middle of the next decade, the situation was reversed as oil prices crossed the $70-a-barrel mark in the face of high demand—particularly by consumers in the Far East—and weather-related production losses in the United States. Oil export revenues rose to $116 billion in 2004. Per capita oil revenues stood only at about $4,500, compared with approximately $22,500 in 1980, due to a near-tripling of the Kingdom's population.

Safeya Binzagr of Jiddah is one of the best-known painters in Saudi Arabia. She has presented exhibitions in Paris, Geneva and London, as well as Saudi Arabia.

SAUDI WOMEN TODAY

Significant changes have taken place in the lives of Saudi women in a relatively short span of time. Today, Saudi women are homemakers, teachers, doctors, nurses, engineers, geologists, information technology experts, filmmakers and poets. They are television and radio broadcasters, journalists, artists, lawyers and heads of corporations. They are fashion designers, interior decorators and security guards.

The history of Saudi women is indissolubly linked to Islam and, more broadly, reflects how religion, culture and tradition determined how women lived. In the centuries preceding the revelation of Islam, women in Arabia were mostly relegated to the margins of community life and had a low social status. Here, as in many other parts of the world, a patriarchal culture with its characteristic features of male domination prevailed. There were some notable exceptions, such as Khadijah bint Khuwaylid of Makkah, a successful trader who sent caravans as far as Syria and who became the Prophet Muhammad's first wife.

The dawn of Islam elevated the position of women throughout Arabia. Islam teaches that the souls of men and women are equally precious, and thus equal in the eyes of God. One of several verses from the Quran illustrates this concept: "Whoever works righteousness, man or woman, and has faith, verily to him will We give a new life that is good and pure, and We will bestow on such their reward according to their actions." (The Quran 16:97)

Islam mandated a broad spectrum of inalienable and well-defined rights for women. They included her right to own property and dispose of it as she saw fit; the right to choose a husband, and to propose marriage orally or in writing; the right to keep her maiden name after marriage; and the right to be the sole owner of her dowry (*mahr*), which not only provides some economic protection to a woman but also symbolizes her respected status and financial rights.

Furthermore, women earned respect and honor by playing an integral role in spreading the message of Islam. Stories of notable women were told and retold. These begin with the Prophet's first wife Khadijah, the first person to embrace Islam. There is also the unique and much-quoted 'Aishah bint Abu Bakr al-Saddiq, who is renowned for the vast knowledge of religion and jurisprudence she gained from her marriage to the Prophet. Other notable women in early Islam include Umm 'Umarah Nusaybah bint Ka'b, whose bravery in battle became legendary, and the poetess al-Khansa Tumadir bint 'Amr, whose elegies for her brothers and sons are lauded for their stylistic elegance and tenderness.

As Arabian society became more cosmopolitan with the rapid expansion of Islam, women assumed a larger role alongside men, sharing decisions on family affairs. This extended across society, encompassing Bedouin women and women in rural communities and cities. In the cities, as men left to pursue commerce in the expanding Muslim world, women took charge of household matters. The respect for, and decision-making authority accorded to, female elders is attested in literature and is part of the culture of the Arabian Peninsula.

The status of Arab women in the first century of Islam is described by some scholars as the closest to the spirit of Islam. Women participated more fully in society than ever before and their position in the community rose to a level that has not been seen since. Over time, the values and customs of the older, ingrained culture reemerged. Eventually, this led to the segregation of women becoming the norm in Arabia.

For at least the last half century, growing numbers of Saudi women have been working to regain the position they held in society during the early period of Islam. A short list of professionals with national and international reputations attests to the growing success of this effort. They include Dr. Thurayya 'Ubayd, executive director of the U.N. Population Fund, artist Safeya Binzagr and filmmaker Haifaa al-Mansour.

Fayzah Dabbagh, the first Saudi woman to study abroad in 1956, went on to become the first dean of the Girls College of Education in Jiddah. Other well-known women include Professor Samirah Islam, in Jiddah, and Dr. Selwa al-Hazzaa, chief of ophthalmology at King Faisal Specialist Hospital in Riyadh.

Naelah Mousli was the first Saudi woman to earn a petroleum engineering degree and to hold a managerial position at the national oil company, Saudi Aramco. Other successful professionals include international businesswoman Lubna Olayan, the first woman elected to the board of a Saudi public company, and business consultant Nadia Ba 'Ishin.

Key characteristics of what has been dubbed "the modern Saudi woman" include a devotion to education and a spirit of self-motivation. Society has come to support

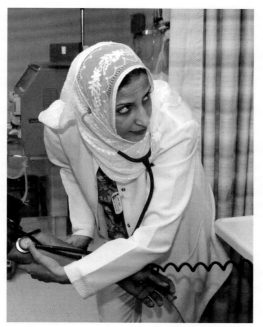

Maryam al-Moalem, a senior staff nurse midwife, is a key member of the medical team at Saudi Aramco's Dhahran Health Center.

Hanadi Hindi was the first woman licensed to pilot jet aircraft in Saudi Arabia. She was hired in 2004 to fly private jets for the Kingdom Holding Company, fulfilling what she said was a childhood dream.

the ambitions that drive women to succeed in the modern world—be they housewives helping with their children's education at home or women pursuing fulltime professional careers while tackling homemaking duties.

Women's issues have been studied, written about and freely discussed in Saudi Arabia and elsewhere in recent years. The major obstacles to women participating fully in business and contributing directly to economic growth have been identified, and steps to deal with them are part of a national dialogue in which women actively participate. The government issued separate identification cards for women in 2001 and enacted reforms allowing women to own or operate a business without having a male agent in 2004.

Several factors are driving these social changes. They include the need for women to supplement the family income in the face of the rising cost of living, and the fact that some 60 percent of university graduates are female. There are now some 4.7 million working-age women in the Kingdom.

Her Highness Princess 'Effat Al-Thunayyan, the wife of the late King Faysal, was a pioneer in the movement to educate girls. She opened the first private school for girls in Jiddah in 1962. There were much earlier efforts to teach girls reading, writing, math and basic science in some cities and towns. Older women and male scholars taught girls to recite the Quran. Some students with basic skills tutored other girls, starting a chain reaction that created a generation of literate women in such cities as Jiddah, Makkah, Madinah and Tayif in western Saudi Arabia.

The daughters of a number of families with a background in scholarship or business pursued higher education. This was particularly true in the cosmopolitan cities in western Saudi Arabia. Families with sufficient resources sent their girls to schools and universities in neighboring Arab countries in the 1950s and, beginning in the late 1960s, to Europe and the United States. On their return, they became pioneers in several fields, working as doctors, pharmacologists and college professors.

Today, many women take advantage of higher-level educational opportunities at home. By 2004, about 275,000

Saudi Aramco reservoir simulation engineer Amal al-Awami uses 3-D visualization technology in Dhahran to evaluate "maximum reservoir contact" oil wells—wells with drill pipes that branch out for five kilometers (3 miles) or more inside a reservoir.

women were enrolled in their sections of the Kingdom's eight universities and in more than 80 women's colleges.

Meanwhile, Saudi chambers of commerce and industry, and the private sector, have established new training establishments for women. These provide education in fields ranging from computer science and web-page design to nursing, hospital management, and English and secretarial skills, answering a demand for new skills and absorbing newly trained university graduates as teachers.

Of course, adjustments are required as women broaden their working horizons. There are long hours for ladies in new fields such as banking and demanding shift schedules for doctors and nurses. Many teachers have to travel to remote regions and reside in villages where new schools opened — an unprecedented step in a conservative society.

Saudi women own some 20,000 firms— about five percent of all registered businesses in the Kingdom. The number of women registered in local chambers of commerce and industry is rising. The Jiddah chamber has more than 2,000 female members out of a total membership of 50,000, and in 2005

Dr. Thurayya 'Ubayd, executive director of the U.N. Population Fund, speaks at a news conference in New York.

elected two women to its 12-member board. In Riyadh, the figure is 2,400 out of 35,000 members, a fourfold increase in women's membership in 10 years. Businesswomen in the Eastern Province chamber number more than 1,000 out of a total 14,000.

The Jiddah Chamber of Commerce and Industry recently established the Khadijah bint Khuwaylid Center to provide services for businesswomen, to facilitate business opportunities and to offer guidance in running businesses. The center is named after the first Muslim businesswoman.

Increased use of information technology in the Kingdom has accelerated women's entry into the work force. This has been accomplished at banks, in particular, by opening women's branches. New opportunities for online and home businesses have blossomed through the use of the Internet.

Most women who work or are preparing to enter the work force must adapt quickly to a very different lifestyle than they, or their society, originally envisioned. They are drawing both from their heritage and from newly available resources to help them meet the challenges faced by their counterparts the world over.

In late 1995, King Fahd suffered a stroke. Although he continued to fulfill the monarch's role as the leader of the Kingdom, Crown Prince 'Abd Allah assumed major responsibilities in running the day-to-day affairs of the country.

Under the leadership of King Fahd and the Crown Prince, the Kingdom took effective steps to resolve outstanding border disputes with its Gulf neighbors and Yemen and launched a rapprochement with Iran. Saudi Arabia reiterated its long-standing position emphasizing that a just resolution to the Israeli-Palestinian conflict is central to the resolution of other Middle Eastern problems. In 2002, 'Abd Allah announced a peace plan calling for Israel to withdraw to its pre-1967 borders and the Palestinians to establish their independent state with Jerusalem as its capital; in return, the Arab states that have refused to recognize Israel since 1948 would establish normal diplomatic and trade relations with it.

The events of September 11, 2001, when al-Qaeda terrorists hijacked and crashed four passenger aircraft in the United States, killing several thousand people, shocked the world community, Muslims and non-Muslims alike. The fact that 15 of the 19 hijackers were of Saudi origin intensified the challenges already facing the Kingdom.

Saudi Arabia condemned the crimes, emphasizing that Islam is a religion of mercy, peace and respect for all, and adopted stiff laws to combat the threat of terrorism. At this critical time, in addition to strained financial conditions stemming from low oil prices, the government's steps toward administrative, political, social and economic reform had created more ambitious reform-seeking voices at home. The shock of September 11 accelerated the movement toward reform.

In October 2001, a U.S.-led coalition invaded Afghanistan, acting under a U.N. Security Council resolution calling for the Taliban rulers to hand over al-Qaeda leaders and close their training camps, quickly toppling the government. In March 2003, the United States and several other countries launched a war against Iraq after Baghdad failed to comply with U.N. Security Council Resolution 1441, which called for a full disclosure of the country's program to develop weapons of mass destruction. Saudi Arabia, which had argued strongly in favor of diplomatic efforts to resolve the impasse over Resolution 1441, did not participate in the war.

Saudi Arabia also suffered a series of terrorist attacks that took the lives of Saudis and expatriates. The government cracked down firmly on extremists, while granting amnesty to members of radical groups who disavowed violence and rejoined civil Saudi society. The campaign to marginalize and isolate the violent fringe continues with impressive success.

To face these challenges and others, the Kingdom has speeded up and intensified the processes to modernize education, the media and the legal system, and has introduced political reforms. A decree in June 2003 enlarged the role of the *Majlis al-Shura* so that it can propose, debate and suggest revisions to (though not pass) legislation without prior

'Abd Allah ibn 'Abd al-'Aziz became King in 2005. He had served as Crown Prince since 1982.

approval. In a move toward more open government, sessions of the *Majlis al-Shura* have been televised.

In tandem with these developments, the King 'Abd al-'Aziz Center for National Dialogue was established in Riyadh in July 2003, and dialogue sessions have been held in cities across the Kingdom to promote open discussion about modernization and development issues, in line with the country's Arab identity and *shari'ah*. Key issues being addressed are the development of education, tackling violence and extremism, and the role of women and youth in development.

King 'Abd Allah

KING FAHD DIED IN AUGUST 2005 AND HIS BROTHER CROWN Prince 'Abd Allah ibn 'Abd al-'Aziz was immediately proclaimed the sixth King of Saudi Arabia. Upon his succession, he decided to maintain the title "The Custodian of the Two Holy Mosques," as adopted by King Fahd. Prince Sultan ibn 'Abd al-'Aziz was designated Crown Prince and Deputy Prime Minister.

Born in Riyadh in 1924, 'Abd Allah received his early education at the royal court. Influenced by his father, King 'Abd al-'Aziz Al Sa'ud, he developed a profound respect for religion, history and the Arab heritage. He also spent years with Bedouin tribes observing, practicing and absorbing their traditions.

'Abd Allah took a prominent role in politics beginning in the 1950s. In 1962, he was named Commander of the National Guard by King Faysal, whose piety and frugality he shares. He became Second Deputy Prime Minister in 1975 on the succession of King Khalid and was designated Crown Prince when Fahd became King in 1982.

King 'Abd Allah has proven to be a cautiously reform-minded regent, calling for greater participation by women in society. He is keen to combat growing unemployment by accelerating growth. To do this, he favors gradually liberalizing the economy through privatization and by opening Saudi Arabia to foreign investment. He supported the Kingdom's preparations to join the World Trade Organization, efforts that bore fruit late in 2005. As Crown Prince, he traveled widely throughout the Kingdom. In 2005, he closely monitored the election process for half the membership of the country's municipal councils.

King 'Abd Allah is experienced in international diplomacy, and he has worked to strengthen Saudi Arabia's relations with countries around the globe. He has been a strong voice in promoting the Kingdom's defense of Arab and Islamic issues, and in furthering its efforts to achieve world peace, stability and security.

CHALLENGES OF THE FUTURE

SAUDI ARABIA'S POPULATION GROWTH — 2.5 PERCENT PER annum — and the fact that about 40 percent of its citizens are age 17 or younger provide a challenge for the future. The government is intent on creating jobs for the young and understands the need to build a competitive and efficient work force. The Seventh Five-Year Development Plan (2000–04) focused on economic diversification and on increasing the role of the private sector in expanding the economy and providing jobs. It aimed at an average GDP growth rate of 3.16 percent each year, and set a target of creating more than 800,000 new jobs for Saudis, while continuing programs to decrease reliance on foreign workers across the board. The Eighth Five-Year Development Plan focuses on technology and employment opportunities for university graduates, as well as boosting growth and income.

While exercising Saudi Arabia's role as the world's major oil producer, the country's leaders understand that prosperity depends on the quality and the fullest use of the Kingdom's human resources: the better educated its people and the more choices open to them under the rule of law, the more the country will flourish.

Islam plays a profound role in the lives of the Saudi people. The vast majority of the people reject extremism and wish to build their futures in a society that respects tradition, yet dares to open new doors for growth and development. In this fashion, they are following in the footsteps of King 'Abd al-'Aziz, the strong, devout leader who laid the foundations more than a century ago for the country that bears his family's name.

Youngsters play in park in Dhahran in a scene recognizable the world over. The children are celebrating 'Id al-Fitr, the holiday that caps the month of Ramadan. Nearly half the Kingdom's population is 17 or younger.

CHAPTER 7

WILDLIFE AND CONSERVATION

A nocturnal hunter, the small Ruppell's sand fox survives the searing heat by hiding in burrows carved deep into gravel plains between the dunes. Ranging freely at night, it searches for small rodents, reptiles and insects, and consumes more plant material than most other carnivores.

A UNIQUE ECOLOGY

THE RUB' AL-KHALI, OR "EMPTY QUARTER," IN SOUTHERN Saudi Arabia is the largest continuous sand desert on earth. Bigger than France, Belgium and Holland together, this sea of sand has come to symbolize a timeless Arabia. To think of Saudi Arabia as "empty" is incorrect, however, for its desert and mountain regions, its plains and plateaus, and its seas and seashores contain a surprising variety of highly adapted inhabitants.

While the ecology of the region has undergone dramatic transformation in the last half-century as a by-product of modernization, it remains an evolutionary process millions of years in the making. The Arabian Peninsula was once a part of Africa, but broke from the continent beginning some 36 million years ago. At the end of the last Ice Age, some 12,000 years ago, rising sea levels filled the Red Sea and the Arabian Gulf, isolating Arabia from Africa and what today is Iran. Rising seas also transformed the natural world of Arabia by altering birds' migratory pathways, creating new marine habitats and dramatically shaping the evolution of Arabia's flora and fauna. The result was a uniquely Arabian ecology with a number of endemic species.

Those species provide the focus for much of the current conservation thrust in the Kingdom. Conservation efforts have been undertaken in response to an urgent need to protect endangered species and to reintroduce species that have disappeared in the wild. Unsustainable hunting and habitat reduction have had catastrophic consequences for many of Arabia's larger animals, including the cheetah, leopard, gazelle, oryx, ibex, dugong, ostrich and sea turtles, as well as the houbara bustard.

Previous spread: (Left) At the height of the summer, Arabian Gulf islands like Karan host one of the largest tern breeding colonies in the world. Up to 28,000 pairs of lesser-crested terns and as many as 34,000 pairs of bridled terns nest here, as do hundreds of hawksbill and green turtles. (Right) The diminutive lily Gagea reticulata is often found in sand around the edges of rocky outcrops in eastern Saudi Arabia. According to some reports, its tiny bulbs were once gathered by Bedouins as food in times of famine.

Some gazelle subspecies, such as the 'afri, have been lost forever. Others, like the Arabian sand gazelle (rim) and mountain gazelle (idmi), once the most widespread species on the peninsula, have been hunted to the brink of extinction. The Arabian ostrich for centuries played an integral role in Bedouin life. Valued for its meat, oil, feathers and eggs (whose shells were invaluable vessels for water storage), it is now extinct—the last sighting reported in 1938. Similar stories are repeated throughout the countries of the Arabian Peninsula.

In 1986, a Royal Decree created Saudi Arabia's National Commission for Wildlife Conservation and Development (NCWCD) to develop and implement strategies to preserve wildlife. Since then, 17 Protected Areas have been set up in different parts of the country and the NCWCD has nominated 56 terrestrial and 47 marine habitats for protected status. It is envisaged that some eight percent of the Kingdom needs to be fully protected and managed if the full diversity of habitats is to be maintained. Crucially, at a time when 16 species are now considered rare or endangered following population collapse over the last 50 years, the NCWCD and its two captive-breeding centers at Tayif in the Hijaz Mountains and al-Thumamah near Riyadh are working to reintroduce large mammals such as the ibex, oryx, gazelle and leopard, along with birds like the houbara bustard and red-necked ostrich.

Captive breeding and reintroduction are critical to preserving the region's ecology, but such measures are only part of the wildlife and habitat conservation strategy. Education and international cooperation are other vital components of the conservation picture. Saudi Arabia is among 150 countries that are signatories to the Convention on Biodiversity at the Earth Summit in Rio de Janeiro in 1992, the first global agreement on species conservation and sustainability. The Kingdom is also a party to the Convention on International Trade in Endangered Species (CITES), which protects certain plants and animals by regulating and monitoring their international sales.

An Al Murrah tribesman who is a ranger with the National Commission for Wildlife Conservation and Development uses his keenly honed tracking skills to protect wildlife on one of the Kingdom's reserves.

DESERTS

THE ARABIAN PENINSULA LIES AT THE CENTER OF A HUGE swathe of desert extending from Morocco to China. Sand deserts comprise one-third of the peninsula's land mass, but there are also stone, limestone and salt deserts (the remains of ancient lakes and shallow seas), as well as volcanic wasteland. All are subject to extremes of temperature and harbor little moisture. But these deserts support life on a reduced scale and contain many of nature's most intriguingly adapted animals and plants.

Saudi Arabia's generally harsh climate means that it sustains a relatively small number of plant species. The Eastern Province, for example, hosts about 500 species, compared with some 3,500 in the smaller Lebanon-Palestine area, which borders on several different floristic regions and includes a variety of landforms. Another feature of Arabian desert vegetation is the relative rarity of endemic species. Most wild plants did not arise in this region but migrated to it as conditions became favorable.

The terrain and climate of the Arabian desert system are relatively uniform, as is the plant life there. By contrast, higher altitudes in the southern parts of the peninsula—in the highlands of 'Asir and Yemen, and the mountains of Oman—host a surprisingly different and varied range of species.

Some areas, such as the central and western deserts, support scattered acacia trees and a number of annual herbs or low shrubs that have adapted to the hot, usually dry climate. Some have "learned" to store water in fleshy stems or in roots buried deep in cooler sands. The great dunes of the Rub' al-Khali may appear devoid of moisture, but once occasional rain has seeped to a depth of two meters (6.5 feet), the moisture is effectively stored there and available to plants. Consequently, most have extensive root systems. Four-fifths of the mass of some plants is below the surface and their roots extend 30 meters (100 feet) into the sand.

Most desert plants limit their surface area by seasonally restricting the number and size of leaves, through which water would otherwise evaporate. Others have leaf surfaces covered with fine hairs that reflect heat and curb water losses. Some species, called halophytes, have developed a tolerance to salty soils and mineral-rich water that would kill their less adapted relatives.

Many plants also produce well-protected seeds. In some cases, they can remain dormant for years before germinating and sprouting rapidly when rain arrives. Many live out their entire life cycle in a single rainy season that may last only a few weeks.

Conspicuous among the plants that have adapted to the Arabian desert in eastern Arabia are a sedge and a perennial grass that are common in the coastal sands. Farther inland, the 'arfaj shrublet is the dominant species over large expanses of land, while a saltbush called rimth is prevalent in poorly drained areas where groundwater is salty. Both provide important pasturage for camels, and the rimth sup-

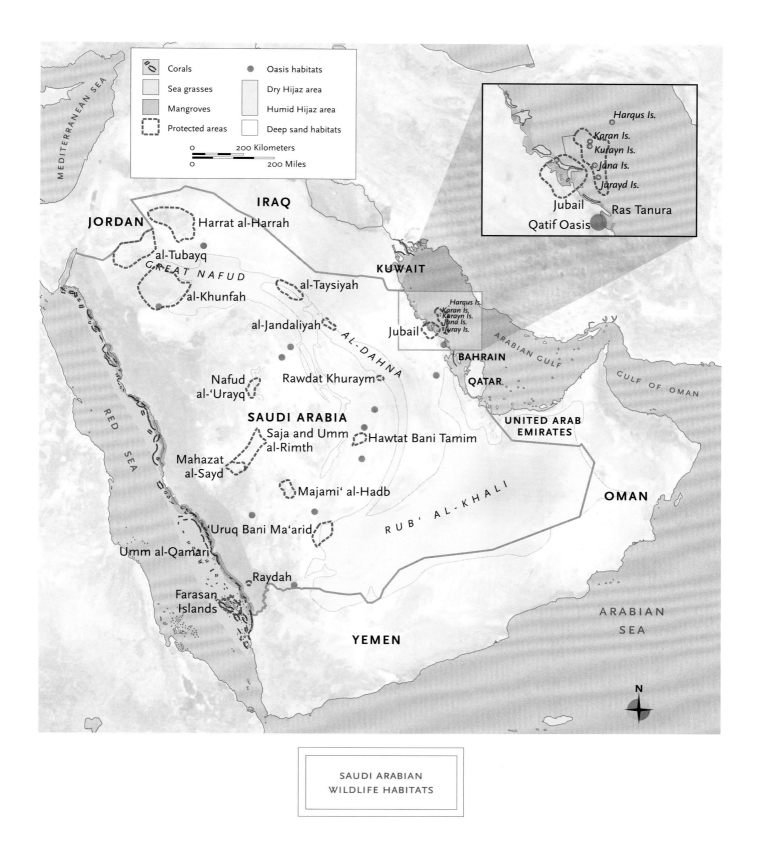

SAUDI ARABIAN
WILDLIFE HABITATS

plies the salt that grazing animals need. Southwestern Arabia has native cactus-like plants, but these are euphorbias, stapelias and aloe, not true cacti.

Although some Bedouin once ate a score or more different wild herbs in times of famine, few are now important as food. The seeds of the fleshy-leaved *Mesembryanthemum* are sometimes collected and ground into flour for making bread in northern Arabia. During their brief season, *faq'* (known as "desert truffles," but different from the species in Europe) are a sought-after delicacy.

Many desert plants produce flowers whose beauty is out of proportion to their modest numbers and small size.

Clockwise from top left: This eagle owl chick, a desert resident, was photographed in northeastern Saudi Arabia; the Agama lizard is usually found on rocky terrain; the sand boa, a harmless and gentle nocturnal snake of sand habitats, may grow to about 45 centimeters (18 inches) long.

Fragrant yellow spikes of broomrape, a root-parasitic plant sometimes called "desert candle," brighten roadsides in eastern Arabia in the spring, and delicate desert camomile grows in scattered carpets on the sand. To the north and west, on the rocky steppes, dense growths of wild iris color depressions where rain has pooled. Elsewhere, tiny lilies grow, as does the mauve *khuzama*, a member of the mustard family. The fruiting of the *'abal* bush marks the height of the spring flowering season on the deep sands. The small annual *kaff Maryam* (Mary's hand) is likened in Arab tradition to the hand of Christ's mother, clenched in the pains of childbirth. Its small branches drop their leaves at the end of spring and roll inward like closed fingers, protecting the seeds in a firm brown ball.

The deserts host small mammals such as the strikingly patterned black-and-white ratel, or honey badger; the porcupine; the desert hedgehog; and the jerboa, the ecological equivalent of the American kangaroo rat. Hares are found throughout the country and are still hunted in the traditional way — with falcons and saluki dogs. Sand cats, two species of spiny mouse, gerbils, *jirdh*s (sand rats) and bats also inhabit the deserts.

Occupying a pivotal position between Africa, Asia and the Palearctic regions of northern Europe, the Arabian Peninsula witnesses one of the world's great wildlife spectacles: During the spring and fall, millions of birds migrate over the remotest desert regions, and along the Red Sea and Arabian Gulf. Flocks of bee-eaters flash their bright colors as they cross the Rub' al-Khali, for example. Lone steppe eagles journeying from Russia to southern Africa join up in September to cross the Bab al-Mandab strait between Yemen to Djibouti and Eritrea at a rate of 40,000 a day.

Ravens, eagles, hawks and falcons — especially kestrels — are common seasonal residents. The largest of the vulture family, the magnificent lappet-faced vulture, ranges well into the Rub' al-Khali. The bird depends on a diminishing number of tall acacia trees to nest and roost. It is flourishing in protected areas like 'Uruq Bani Ma'arid in the western Rub' al-Khali and Mahazat al-Sayd 160 kilometers (100 miles) east of Tayif, where the natural plant balance is preserved.

The windswept northern volcanic plains, or *harrat*, are favored by seven members of the lark family and contain the largest concentration of breeding larks in the Palearctic region. Some, like the hoopoe lark (also known as Umm Salim), the crested lark and the desert lark, are familiar to desert travelers throughout Arabia. Like other desert birds, most have modified their color to blend in better with their nesting zone.

Arabia hosts some 40 species of land snakes, most of which are harmless. Common in the Eastern Province are the sand boa, Gray's whip snake, the Arabian leaf-nosed snake, the variable sand snake, the diademed sand snake and the Moila snake. The latter is sometimes mistaken for a hooded cobra, but it belongs to a different family and is not dangerous to man. The true cobra, the hooded variety, is found in southwestern Arabia. The black cobra, which has no hood, is highly venomous, but also very rare. According to Bedouin folklore, it can change itself at will into

Clockwise from top left: The Arabian oryx, hunted to extinction in the wild in the 1970s, is making a comeback in protected areas in the Kingdom; a wildlife reserve ranger prepares to take off to monitor radio-collared oryx; the root-parasitic broomrape, the "desert candle"; the sand cat has paws covered below by a dense mat of hairs, probably an adaptation to walking on loose sand.

any shape it chooses—a camel, a woman, a horse—to lure humans to their doom.

The Kingdom's deserts also support many kinds of lizards. The *dabb*, or spiny-tailed lizard, is a common type. This heavy-bodied, plant-eating species grows to a length of 50 centimeters (20 inches). Bedouins say its meat tastes like chicken.

The sand-swimming skink, called *dammusah* in Arabic, moves through the sand like a fish through water. Geckos, small, soft-bodied lizards with fleshy tails, are welcome guests in some houses because of their efficiency in hunting insects. The *nadus* is a small, reddish, snake-like reptile that lives under the surface of the sand, its eyes reduced to nearly functionless dots.

An insect commonly encountered in the desert is the dung beetle—the scarab made famous in ancient Egyptian art. Barely able to fly, it collects small balls of dung in which to lay its eggs. The desert also supports a variety of arachnids, ranging from the velvety red rain mite to the camel spider—a harmless creature that can grow to 15 centimeters (six inches) in diameter and is often mistaken for a tarantula—and the scorpion. The latter is nocturnal and carries a painful, but rarely life-threatening sting.

The greatest conservation success in the desert has been the reintroduction of the Arabian oryx back into its primary habitat, the Rub' al-Khali. The oryx, the largest of Arabia's cloven-hoofed mammals, is a white antelope which may have given rise to the legend of the unicorn. (Viewed

from the side, its two straight horns look like one.) It lived in parts of the Rub' al-Khali and the Great Nufud sand desert of northern Arabia for thousands of years, successfully exploiting one of the world's harshest environments. The arrival of hunters in motor vehicles in the 1930s tipped the balance against the oryx, however, and by 1972 it had been hunted to extinction in the wild.

A core NCWCD program is to restore the Arabian oryx population as part of "Operation Oryx." In 1962, the Fauna and Flora Preservation Society in London organized the capture of two males and a female near Sanaw in the Aden Protectorates (now part of Yemen). The animals were shipped to the Phoenix Zoo in Arizona, where they were joined by pairs donated by King Sa'ud of Saudi Arabia, the ruler of Kuwait and the Zoological Society of London. Those nine animals became the nucleus of a "world herd" from which, by 1978, oryx were being returned to Arabia for captive-breeding programs, including one at the National Wildlife Research Center (NWRC) in Tayif.

After initial successes in Jordan and Oman, Operation Oryx bore fruit in the Kingdom in 1990 when the first oryx were released into the 2,244-square-kilometer (866-square-mile) Protected Area of Mahazat al-Sayd. The area was fenced to exclude grazing livestock and, when the first batch of oryx survived, more followed. By 1993, seventy-two oryx from foreign, private or national collections, and nearly as many from the captive-breeding program, were released into the enclosed zone. In 1995, these oryx were released into the unfenced Pro-

189

New wetlands created by treated waste-water from cities have created oases for bird life like that at al-Hair watercourse near Riyadh. Moorhens, mallard, herons and more than 100 pairs of black-winged stilts are familiar residents.

A farmer harvests ripening dates at al-Dir'iyah. Some 150 date species are found in the Arabian Peninsula. Their wild precursor grew here long before man built permanent settlements. There are more than a million date palm trees in Saudi Arabia today.

tected Area of 'Uruq Bani Ma'arid. The 220-strong herd there in 2004 attested to the program's success.

The NCWCD is targeting other species for conservation, too. The King Khalid Wildlife Research Center at al-Thumamah is charged with the conservation of ungulates like the *idmi* and *rim* gazelle, while alongside the oryx at the NWRC in Tayif there are enclosures for breeding red-necked ostriches, the nearest genetic kin to the extinct Arabian ostrich. The NCWCD is also considering the reintroduction of leopards into their native mountain habitats.

OASES

IN A LAND WITH VIRTUALLY NO RIVERS OR LAKES, AND GENERally very limited rainfall, the oases have always been magnets for wildlife. More than 250 non-native bird species from all over the Palearctic region to the north winter in Arabia or pass over on their way to wintering grounds in Africa. Cuckoos, thrushes, warblers, swallows, wagtails, wheateaters, bee-eaters, raptors and cranes, along with large numbers of shorebirds and waterfowl, are among the migrants.

The yellow vented bulbul, a songbird with a sulphur-yellow bottom, is the most common year-round oasis denizen. There are also constantly chattering sparrows and the occasional ring-necked parrot.

Today, cities provide moist new microclimates inhabited by an impressive variety of plants, birds and insects seldom seen before in Arabia, and a number of migrants have become winter residents. Wetland birds like black-crowned night herons breed in great numbers in Riyadh's al-Hair watercourse, an inland lake filled with treated wastewater. Other species like the gray heron, white stork and the black-winged stilt winter there, and reptiles, amphibians and introduced fish species like tilapia abound.

Al-Hasa, Saudi Arabia's largest oasis, supports pond turtles and frogs. Asiatic jackals inhabit al-Hasa wetlands, which are also a breeding ground for birds such as the little bittern and ruddy shelduck.

The most familiar and valuable plant in the oases is the date palm. It provides a staple food and valuable wood and fiber by-products that are still sometimes used for weaving and thatching. The date palm is so much a part of life in Saudi Arabia that it appears in the Kingdom's emblem. Rice, melons, grapes, pomegranates, oranges and other tree fruits are also cultivated. A wide range of vegetable crops have been introduced in the oases, where tamarisk trees have often been planted to serve as windbreaks.

Other domesticated plants include wheat, barley, sorghum and millet—the main grains of the Kingdom—and alfalfa, a common oasis fodder crop. Previously restricted to the natural oases, such crops are now cultivated in man-made oases: huge, irrigated circles in the desert. Wheat production was supported by generous government subsidies and free water drawn from deep underground aquifers. However, these subsidies have been cut as part of an effort to conserve the Kingdom's non-renewable water resources. Projects have also been undertaken to use seawater to irrigate commercial crops of samphire, a salt marsh plant known as *Salicornia* to botanists, which has edible stems and produces seeds that can be pressed into vegetable oil.

THE ARABIAN GULF

NUTRIENT-RICH WATERS FROM IRAQ'S RIVERS IN THE NORTH and from the Arabian Sea in the south mix in the Arabian Gulf to create a highly productive marine environment. High temperatures result in a net evaporation rate of 1.5 meters (4.9 feet) a year. This, combined with restricted circulation through the narrow Strait of Hormuz, results in remarkably high seawater salinity, averaging 4.3 percent in open waters and climbing as high as seven percent in some back bays.

The waterway's shallow depth—averaging around 35 meters (just over 100 feet)—along with clear waters and good light penetration, encourages the growth of coral reefs and seagrass beds. Seagrass and coastal mangroves provide a coastal nursery for many species of marine organisms. These, in turn, support the food chain sustaining a variety of fish and birds.

Salt marshes and algae-covered mud flats span some 1,000 square kilometers (400 square miles) of the Kingdom's Gulf

CLIMATE

The arid climate prevailing over much of the Arabian Peninsula is due largely to its place on the map. Simply put, it lies within a broad band of territory where the pattern of atmospheric circulation restricts rainfall, leaving deserts in its wake. It may not rain for years in the vast southern sand desert called the Rub' al-Khali, the Empty Quarter, and summertime temperatures in the shade can climb to 50°C (122°F) there and elsewhere.

Still, there is a surprising diversity of climate in Saudi Arabia and its neighbors. On the southern fringes of the peninsula, rainfall turns mountaintops and the seaward sides of mountain ranges green, and farmers have long grown crops in terraced fields. Even in the desert, sudden storms can turn normally dry *wadi*s into destructive torrents. In northern Saudi Arabia, winter temperatures may drop below freezing and snow may fall on the inland desert plateau.

The peninsula's location between the 15th and 30th parallels of latitude in the Northern Hemisphere places it within a major, worldwide system of atmospheric circulation known as the Hadley Cell. After dropping most of its moisture as rain in the tropics, warm air from the equatorial regions rises to the upper atmosphere and moves toward higher latitudes—both to the north and the south. It begins to descend when it reaches about the 30th parallel, warming and losing any remaining ability to form clouds or rain. Then it flows back along the earth's surface as a dry stream toward the equator, where it acquires another load of warm moisture and buoyancy, and begins the cycle all over again.

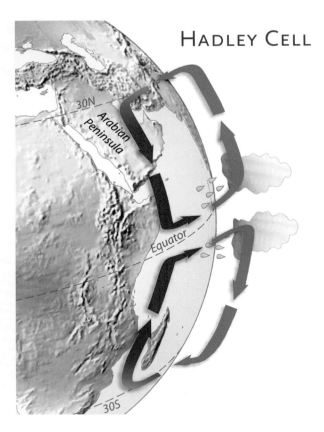

HADLEY CELL

The descending northern branch of this circular pattern, striking northern Saudi Arabia and the Sahara, forms a band of high pressure called the "subtropical high." This suppresses uplift and cloud formation, leading to desert conditions across North Africa, the Arabian Peninsula, Iran and the northwestern Indian subcontinent.

On the Arabian Peninsula these conditions reach their extreme in the Rub' al-Khali, where long-term average annual precipitation is typically less than 25 millimeters (one inch). Another particularly dry region lies in the northwestern quarter, along and inland from the Red Sea. Over large parts of the rest of the peninsula, rainfall ranges between 50 to 150 millimeters (two to six inches) a year. In a few favored areas of the southwest, it is markedly greater.

In the winter, Arabia plays host to polar continental air masses moving in from Central Asia on the northeast, leading to cooler and generally cloud-free conditions. From time to time, low-pressure storm centers originating as far away as the North Atlantic and traversing the Mediterranean region move in from the northwest, bringing clouds and rain, often followed by clear skies and chilly northerly winds. These "Mediterranean depressions" track across northern Arabia and often reach the Arabian Gulf coast, on rare conditions penetrating as far south as the northern and central Rub' al-Khali. Overall, winter is a time of fine weather across much of Arabia.

Spring is an important rainfall season for large parts of Arabia, particularly the central regions. Rising temperatures and the clash of maritime and continental air masses may cause rapid mixing and the convectional rise of moisture. This can lead to violent thunderstorms. Such storms generally cover a limited area and are short-lived, but they can turn *wadi*s into raging rivers and cause local flooding.

Summer conditions set in by May, with important changes in regional pressure patterns. A stable low-pressure area develops over the heating Asian land mass east and northeast of the peninsula. This leads to a counterclockwise circulation marking the start of the *shamal* season. Surface winds, sometimes gusting to 65 kilometers per hour (40 mph), sweep out of the north (in Arabic, *shamal*), often carrying dust from as far away as the Mesopotamian flood plain in Iraq.

The term *shamal* can refer to the especially strong north-northwest winds of early summer, usually peaking in June, that may continue for days, bringing harsh conditions with blowing dust. True sandstorms, with sand grains rising more than waist-high, are rare, even in Arabia's extensive dune areas. The great bulk of sand transport—even with strong winds—takes place within half a meter (less than two feet) of the ground.

In eastern Arabia along the Gulf coast, the *shamal* period is followed in August-September by doldrums characterized by extremely high humidity which greatly accentuates the summer heat. It can be particularly severe when the southeast wind called the *kaws* sweeps up the Gulf from the south, gathering moisture from its heated waters. Before air conditioning became common, this was tradi-

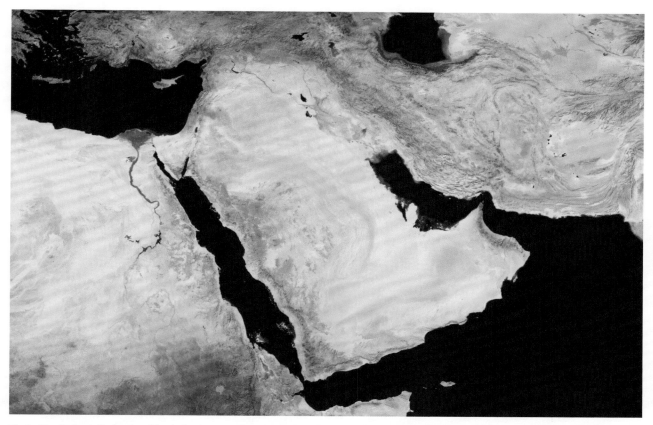

The Arabian Peninsula lies in a broad band of territory stretching across Africa all the way into Asia where atmospheric circulation patterns make rainfall rare – resulting in largely desert conditions.

tionally the most trying period for the coastal inhabitants. Bedouins and townsmen alike scanned the southern horizon before dawn – as they still do today – for the annual rise at the end of August of the bright star Canopus, known to the Arabs as *Suhayl*. Its appearance traditionally marks the end of the hottest period of summer, although full relief may yet be two months away.

The Arabian Gulf is subject to big seasonal changes in temperature because of its relative shallowness, averaging only 35 meters (115 feet). Offshore water temperatures vary from 16°C (60°F) in winter to 32°C (90°F) in summer. Coastal bays and lagoons have even greater fluctuations, ranging from a high of 40°C (104°F) in summer and a low of 5°C (41°F). The Red Sea, by contrast, has an average depth of 490 meters (1,600 feet) and its surface water temperatures experience an average seasonal range of only about 5°C (10°F).

Over most of Arabia, *wasmi* (autumn) rains are rare. When they do occur as early as October, however, they are considered particularly beneficial by the Bedouins. If the rains are followed later by well-spaced episodes of winter rain, conditions are ripe for an all-too-rare phenomenon called the *rabi'*. This literally means "spring," but is commonly used to refer to the widespread growth of lush annual desert herbs after the rain, providing nourishment for livestock.

A few parts of Saudi Arabia and its neighbors to the south are exceptions to the desert-climate pattern. The Kingdom's mountainous southwestern province of 'Asir benefits from tropical circulation associated with the southwest monsoon of the Arabian

Sea. Rain falls in summer as well as in spring, and annual precipitation may total 250 millimeters (10 inches) or more. Rainfall is even more copious in the highlands of neighboring Yemen.

The mountain wall of 'Asir and Yemen, rising above the coast of the southern Red Sea, deflects moist westerly winds upward where they cool and release their water as rain. Most of this precipitation falls on the tops and coastal side of the mountains; the inland sides are rain-starved and slope down in an abrupt transition to desert.

The southwest monsoon strikes the southern coast of Arabia most directly in Dhufar, the southern province of the Sultanate of Oman. From June through August, heavy, moisture-laden winds flow over upwellings of cooler, deeper water in the Arabian Sea, impinging on the coast. This leads to the formation of a summer-long cap of clouds and mist over the coastal zone and seaward slopes of the backing mountains. The landward sides of these mountains are dry and merge with plains leading directly to the Rub' al-Khali. Desert patterns are broken again in northern Oman, where Jabal al-Akhdar ("The Green Mountain") rises to nearly 3,000 meters (about 10,000 feet). Moisture intercepted here provides annual rainfall of some 350 millimeters (14 inches) for a small area of upland villages cultivating temperate-zone crops.

Tornadoes or hurricanes are very rare. Southern coastal regions may be struck by tropical cyclones that veer north of their usual paths in the Arabian Sea in May-June or October-November. Occasionally, such storms have brought winds topping 90 knots (around 170 kilometers, or 100 miles, per hour), along with torrential, flooding rains.

193

(Clockwise from left) The tiny red Anthias is the signature fish of the Red Sea and its most populous reef inhabitant; a young volunteer plants a mangrove on the Arabian Gulf coast as part of a Saudi Aramco conservation program; a green sea turtle prepares to lay her eggs on a secluded Arabian Gulf beach.

coast, providing a home for invertebrates such as shrimp that offer a feast for birds and animals. Up to 2 million birds, representing as many as 70 species, stop in the Gulf region to feed on their annual migrations. Sand beaches used by nesting green turtles form another vital marine habitat of the Gulf.

The Gulf's habitats suffered enormously during the 1991 Gulf War, and they continue to be impacted as urban development spreads along the coast. However, restoration is possible and evidence of this can be seen in some affected areas like Jubail and Tarut Bay where mangroves have been extensively replanted, due partly to pioneering work in the field by Saudi Aramco. The mangroves offer vital shelter for mollusks, crabs, juvenile shrimp and fish, as well as important nesting sites for birds.

During the war, nearly 700 kilometers (435 miles) of the Kingdom's Gulf coastline were flooded by oil released from Iraqi and Kuwaiti terminals. Drifting south, it sank into the wet sands and formed layers of tar that poisoned the breeding hatcheries of myriad species. The disaster could have been much worse without the dedicated joint efforts by Saudi Aramco, the Presidency of Meteorology and Environment, and the NCWCD. Teams from Saudi Aramco worked around the clock to protect vital water-intake channels for power-generation, water-desalination and other facilities, and recovered more than 1.2 million barrels of oil from the Gulf—the largest amount ever reclaimed from a spill. As a result, hundreds of kilometers of beaches and intertidal areas were saved.

While the Gulf had been earmarked for protection several years before the war, officials stepped up conservation plans after this disaster. The NCWCD, the Regional Organization for the Protection of the Marine Environment, the Gulf Cooperation Council and the European Union cooperated to create a Marine Habitat and Wildlife Sanctuary that includes the coral islands of Harqus, Karan, Kurayn, Jana and Jurayd, and the Jubail and Abu 'Ali coastal areas.

The islands are the main nesting sites for green and hawksbill turtles, but birds are their most prominent inhabitants. Socotra cormorants are the first to arrive during the winter, building nests in the sand and laying chalky blue eggs. Four species of terns also breed on the islands, including 28,000 pairs of lesser-crested terns, the world's largest colony. An even greater number of bridled terns—up to 34,000 pairs—also breed here. For this species, the islands are the most vital breeding areas on earth.

(Clockwise from top left) The pincushion starfish is frequently found in the northern Red Sea; a young Socotra cormorant displays for its mother to receive food; a Saudi Aramco diver carries out a survey in the Arabian Gulf.

More than 4,000 species of marine life, including fish, echinoderms like starfish and sea urchins, mollusks and algae live in the Gulf. The most common game fish is the *hamur*, a grouper weighing up to 20 kilograms (45 pounds). Another is the *kan'ad*, a king mackerel which also reaches 20 kilograms. The *qidd*, or barracuda, can weigh up to 10 kilograms, and the *sayyafi*, or sawfish, can tip the scales at more than 100 kilograms (220 pounds). A variety of tuna called the *jihabah* and spiny lobsters and sea crayfish are also sought by fishermen.

Whales and dolphins are occasionally seen in the Arabian Gulf, and several species of sharks live in its waters. Several kinds of sea snakes are also common.

THE RED SEA

MOST VISITORS TO THE RED SEA FIND THAT, LIKE OTHER SEAS, its water is blue. Only occasionally does the waterway live up to its colorful title. When conditions are right, the sea's algae population explodes into bloom, and when those millions of tiny plants die they may, indeed, turn parts of the sea a deep, rusty red.

The Red Sea lies in a vast trench. Some 10,000 years ago, it was much like the salty waters of the Dead Sea in which little marine life could survive. As the icecaps melted at the end of the last Ice Age, water poured from the Indian Ocean through the Strait of Bab al-Mandab. Perfect conditions for coral to grow in the Red Sea were reached only 6,000 or 7,000 years ago. Though marine life began to thrive, not one of the species was endemic.

The Red Sea is surrounded by semi-desert. No rivers debouche there and it receives little rainfall. There is minimal flooding, erosion or stream-borne pollution to cloud its surface and the water is remarkably clear. Substantial land filling over coral reef shelves for expanding cities and Jiddah's sewage disposal troubles have posed problems, however.

The Red Sea contains one of the most extensive coral-reef systems on earth. While this makes for exciting diving, dive tourism is minimal as most tourists visit Saudi Arabia for religious reasons. The efforts of the NCWCD, the Presidency of Meteorology and Environmental Protection, and Red Sea environmentalists aim to prevent damage to the marine environment and coastal areas before the first signs of it appear.

Hamadryas baboons like this big male are the only wild primates in Arabia. Some 350,000 live along the escarpment that extends from the moist 'Asir region north into the dry desert mountains of the Hijaz.

The Farasan Islands are a good example. This large coral archipelago lying 40 kilometers (25 miles) off the coast from Jaizan covers nearly 700 square kilometers (270 square miles) and has hundreds of low-lying islands and islets. The largest island, Kabir, is only 66 kilometers (41 miles) long, and rises to just 72 meters (236 feet). The NCWCD designated these islands a Protected Area in 1989 to guard their enormous biological diversity: 231 species of fish, 49 species of reef-building coral, three species of dolphin and various mollusks and crustaceans. The islands are also home to the Farasan gazelle, Saudi Arabia's largest wild gazelle population.

The islands' dense mangroves and their seven species of seagrass are also protected. The NCWCD is working to restore degraded mangrove thickets by replanting mangrove seedlings grown in nurseries. By protecting mangroves, the NCWCD is protecting huge numbers of breeding seabirds, including ospreys and sooty falcons. The mangroves also provide fodder for camels and goats, and fuel for humans.

THE WESTERN MOUNTAINS

WESTERN SAUDI ARABIA IS DOMINATED BY THE HIJAZ AND 'Asir mountain chain running the length of the Red Sea. Peaks rise to 3,000 meters (nearly 10,000 feet), plunging steeply to the Tihamah plains that bank the Red Sea. Evaporating moisture from the Red Sea rises against the mountain walls to precipitate and feed the rich variety of flora and fauna. The mountains block the clouds, preventing rain from reaching the interior.

Rainfall in the 'Asir region may reach 500 millimeters (nearly 20 inches) annually, five times the average of the Kingdom as a whole. A thousand years ago, the mountains supported a dense growth of juniper trees. Today, around 2.7 million hectares (6.67 million acres) remain. The forest is most prolific along the peaks of the 'Asir range, where the junipers are draped with dew-trapping lichens. Lower down are wild olive trees, acacias and, lower still, wild fig trees. The southwestern Arabian mountain woodlands are home to 2,000 plant species, of which 170 are endemic, and shelter around 34 mammal species and 245 bird species.

The mountains form a continuous band of lush greenery, ideal for the movement of species and seed dispersal between Africa and the northerly zones of Asia and Europe. Consequently, a vast array of the mountain flora and fauna is African in origin, including between 250,000 and 350,000 hamadryas baboons — an endangered species in Africa. However, most Arabian mammals are smaller than their African counterparts as a result of sparser vegetation.

Some species that are rare or have disappeared from the region are now targeted for captive breeding and reintroduction programs. The leopard is a high priority for breeding at the NWRC in Tayif, for reintroduction in the more northerly Hijaz Mountains.

The juniper forest is protected at the Raydah reserve in the 'Asir Mountains. Covering nine square kilometers (3.5 square miles), the reserve also provides habitat for nine of the 10 indigenous bird species of Saudi Arabia, including the Yemen thrush and Arabian red-legged partridge. Hamadryas baboons, caracal lynx, wolves, wildcats, mongoose and eagles also inhabit the reserve, which is a planned site for the reintroduction of *idmi* gazelle.

196

FALCONRY

The Bedouin holding a falcon on his gloved hand is an enduring image of the Arabian Peninsula, symbolizing a harmonious link between man and animal. Nomads learned how to domesticate birds to hunt long ago and falconry is believed to be one of the earliest hunting partnerships. A good falconer exhibited not only skill, but also admirable self-reliance. The traditional quarry — hares, houbara bustards and even gazelles — provided a welcome addition to the Bedouin's diet.

The Arabian falconer's favorite bird is the *saqr* falcon. Its prize quarry is the houbara bustard, a large bird, camouflaged and wary, that prefers to walk in areas where it is hidden. With a 1.2-meter wingspan (four feet) and distinctive dark spots on its wings, the bustard in flight is easily visible to a falcon.

Falconry was always dictated by the rhythm of the seasons and the arrival of both the falcon and bustard on their migratory journeys. Wild *saqr* falcons were caught during the autumn migration and Bedouins spent weeks training them, until the falcons could be let loose to return from flight on command.

Traditionally, falcons were captured in October, and then trained for two months for a hunting season that started in December. When the season ended in late spring, the falcons were released to continue their migration. Kept captive, they simply died of heat in the summer months.

The advent of automobiles and four-wheel-drive vehicles had devastating consequences for falcons and bustards. The ability to drive to remote places turned falconry into a one-sided sport. By the 1970s, so many migrant falcons were being trapped that *saqr* numbers started to dwindle. The sport also put increasing pressure on the bustard. Guns sometimes replaced falcons in the hunt, and accessories such as night-vision binoculars and satellite phones helped to tip the balance against the quarry.

Conservation efforts were launched in the 1980s and the bustard became the "flagship quarry" of the National Commission for Wildlife Conservation and Development (NCWCD). In 1989, the National Wildlife Research Center in Tayif painstakingly bred the first birds using artificial insemination and hand-reared the chicks. The experiments worked and by 2000, when 314 birds were reintroduced, the survival rate had climbed to between 45 and 50 percent.

While the intention may have been to breed bustards for quarry, the project may also help save the bird from extinction in Arabia. Unfortunately, the same cannot be said for the falcon. Although a falcon-breeding project funded by Prince Khalid al-Faysal in the 'Asir Mountain region did prove that falcons could be bred and released in large numbers, it has ceased operations. Among the challenges facing the project was the fact that Saudis take pride in training the wild falcon to take wild prey, thus rendering captive-bred birds of little interest. Instead, hunters turned to imports.

In 2003, the Ornithological Society of the Middle East announced that at least 6,400 *saqr* falcons were imported from as far away as Mongolia and sold in the region. The NCWCD is attempting to limit imports by requiring Convention on International Trade in Endangered Species permits for falcons. Permits are only issued within the official three-month season beginning at the start of December.

The spread of falcon hospitals is another positive sign. Today, veterinary support is available peninsula-wide. Such facilities help ensure that falcons no longer die needlessly and also gather knowledge and statistical data, and monitor the legality of birds in the country.

A falconer in northern Saudi Arabia readies his bird for the hunt in the early 1950s.

CHAPTER 8

TAPPING THE
TREASURE

An American family displays the range of their household's contents – from clothes to toys to furnishings – that are made from oil-based polymers.

THE WORLD'S BIGGEST BUSINESS

PETROLEUM IS THE WORLD'S BIGGEST BUSINESS. FROM ITS roots in northwestern Pennsylvania where drillers first struck oil 150 years ago, the petroleum industry has grown into a global concern generating more than $2 trillion in annual revenue. Petroleum is the lifeblood of industry, a major force in the global economy and a crucial element in the well-being of nations.

The world uses more crude oil than any other liquid except water. More than 83 million barrels of oil were consumed worldwide each day in 2005. The United States used a quarter of that total, some 21 million barrels of 42 gallons each, or the equivalent of almost three gallons of oil daily for every person in the country. China was a fast-rising second, consuming nearly 6.6 million barrels a day, and Japan was third at 5.4 million barrels daily. A total of 18 countries consumed more than 1 million barrels a day, accounting for over 75 percent of the world's consumption.

Petroleum products fuel and lubricate almost every machine that moves, from lawn mowers to jet airplanes. Oil and natural gas provide more than 60 percent of the world's energy needs. The electricity they generate powers appliances and equipment ranging from coffeemakers to heart-lung machines.

Thousands of products are derived from petroleum. There is, for instance, more petroleum in a computer than in the crankcase of a car. Natural gas, transformed into fertilizers, greatly increases the world's food supply. Petroleum

Previous spread: (Left) Using advanced tools such as this 3-D image of the world's largest oil field – Ghawar – geoscientists in Dhahran have improved recovery rates from oil and gas fields by up to 50 percent and greatly enhanced the search for new petroleum deposits. (Right) Chief geologist Max Steineke led the search for oil in Saudi Arabia. Relying on basic tools and an understanding of the earth, he laid the foundations for uncovering the Kingdom's petroleum treasure.

CRUDE OIL

Crude oil is a mixture of different hydrocarbons that are separated into products (distillates) in a refinery. Crude oil is classified according to density, or specific gravity. The lighter the crude oil, the more valuable products it yields when refined. Premium light products include gasoline and jet fuel; diesel fuel is a medium product; and asphalt is a heavy distillate.

Density is defined in terms of the American Petroleum Institute (API) density scale. This is an inverted scale with the lighter crudes having higher numbers. Crude oil varies from API 5° to 55°. Those with gravities exceeding 32° are considered light. Those with gravities below 24° are heavy. Saudi Aramco produces crude oil in five ranges: Arabian Super Light (greater than 40°), Arabian Extra Light (36°-40°), Arabian Light (32°-36°), Arabian Medium (29°-32°) and Arabian Heavy (less than 29°).

Bottles display (right) oil as it comes out of the ground and (left) a refined motor oil product.

Crude oil is also categorized according to its sulfur content. Sulfur is contained in hydrogen sulfide gas, which is corrosive and poisonous. Oil is considered "sweet" or "sour," depending on its sulfur content; "sour" crude oil contains more than one percent sulfur.

About 75 percent of the Kingdom's production is light gravity, premium oil. The world's largest field, Ghawar, produces mostly Arabian Light crude oil, while Safaniya, the world's largest offshore field, produces Arabian Heavy. The fields in central Saudi Arabia produce Arabian Super Light, with minimal sulfur content. The Shaybah field and sections of the Abqaiq field produce Arabian Extra Light.

is an integral part of thousands of other products, ranging from heart valves and compact discs to athletic shoes, deodorants and eyeglasses.

Saudi Arabia is the world's largest supplier of crude oil. At the start of the 21st century, the Kingdom reigned as the world's leader in oil production, export and oil reserves, and one of the top 10 refiners. The Kingdom provided more than 11 percent of the oil consumed worldwide in 2005, boosting production to meet increasing demand and continuing its long record as a dependable supplier. In addition to oil, Saudi Arabia ranks fourth in the world in natural gas reserves, and is a major gas producer and the top exporter of natural gas liquids, or NGL.

Saudi Arabia was a relative latecomer to the petroleum business. Serious exploration didn't begin in the Kingdom until 1933, nearly 75 years after drillers completed the world's first oil well in the United States. The first commercial well in Saudi Arabia wasn't drilled until 1938 and large-scale production didn't kick off until after World War II.

Today, the Saudi Arabian Oil Company (Saudi Aramco), the Kingdom's national oil enterprise, is responsible for approximately 260 billion barrels of crude oil reserves, all but the small fraction in the Kingdom's onshore portion of the Saudi-Kuwait Partitioned Zone. Saudi Aramco's spare capacity makes Saudi Arabia the only country capable of significantly boosting production to meet spikes in demand and help maintain stability in the world oil market. The Kingdom's oil policy, implemented by Saudi Aramco, calls for maintaining a surplus production capacity of between 1.5 and 2 million barrels per day. In late 2005 the company launched its largest expansion in 25 years, a $20 billion program to raise maximum sustained production capacity from 10 million to 12.5 million barrels of oil per day, while adding 180 million standard cubic feet of ethane production for the Kingdom's industries.

THE GOLDEN CORRIDOR

THE MAJORITY OF THE WORLD'S PETROLEUM RESERVES ARE concentrated in a golden corridor of oil-rich land some 2,735 kilometers (1,700 miles) long and half that wide extending from eastern Turkey south through the Arabian Gulf to the Arabian Sea. Nine nations along that corridor — Turkey, Iraq, Kuwait, Saudi Arabia, Iran, Bahrain, the United Arab Emirates, Qatar and Oman — hold more than 60 percent of the world's proven oil reserves and 40 percent of proven natural gas reserves.

The golden corridor is the child of plate tectonics. Millions of years ago, the Arabian Plate impacted and slid under the larger Eurasian Plate, creating a huge basin where most of the Middle East's oil and gas is found today. The basin extends from the Strait of Hormuz north to the Turkish-Armenian frontier. It runs parallel to Iran's Zagros Mountains and encompasses the Arabian Gulf and the territory several hundred kilometers on either side.

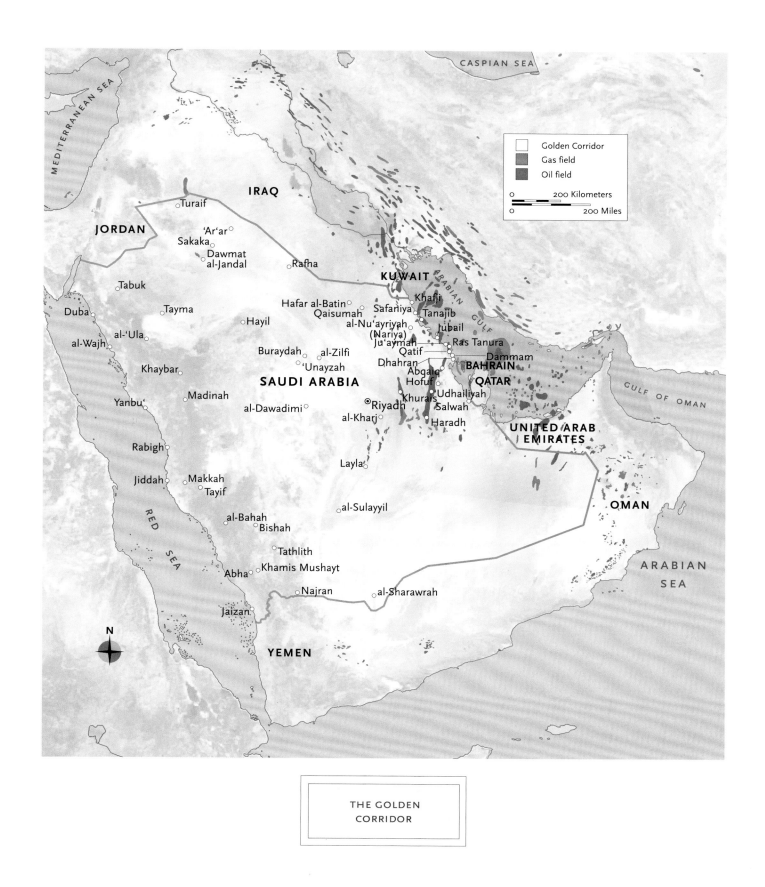

Legend:

- Golden Corridor
- Gas field
- Oil field

0   200 Kilometers

0   200 Miles

CASPIAN SEA

MEDITERRANEAN SEA

IRAQ

JORDAN

Turaif

'Ar'ar

Sakaka

Dawmat al-Jandal

Rafha

KUWAIT

Tabuk

Tayma

Hayil

Hafar al-Batin

Qaisumah

Safaniya

Khafji

Tanajib

Duba

al-'Ula

al-Nu'ayriyah (Nariya)

Jubail

al-Wajh

Khaybar

Buraydah

al-Zilfi

Ju'ayman

Ras Tanura

Qatif

Dhahran

Dammam

'Unayzah

SAUDI ARABIA

Abqaiq

BAHRAIN

Yanbu'

Madinah

Hofuf

QATAR

al-Dawadimi

Riyadh

Khurais

Udhailiyah

ARABIAN GULF

al-Kharj

Salwah

Haradh

UNITED ARAB EMIRATES

Rabigh

GULF OF OMAN

Jiddah

Makkah

Tayif

Layla

al-Sulayyil

al-Bahah

Bishah

OMAN

Tathlith

Abha

Khamis Mushayt

ARABIAN SEA

Najran

al-Sharawrah

Jaizan

RED SEA

N

YEMEN

THE GOLDEN
CORRIDOR

203

Oil seeps, like this one that blackened a Red Sea beach south of Muwaylih near the Gulf of Aqaba in 1931, drew prospectors into several unsuccessful exploration attempts on the west coast of Arabia in the early 20th century.

Most geologists believe that crude oil and natural gas are the residue of tiny plants and animals that accumulated on the bottom of seas, lakes and coastal areas over millennia. Buried under successive layers of sediment, this organic material was converted into hydrocarbons by enormous pressure and heat. Much of this material migrated to the surface and evaporated away. But when it was trapped under the surface by a lid of impermeable cap rock, it formed the oil and gas fields that punctuate the map of the Middle East today.

The origin of oil is still a subject of some debate. For years, a few scientists have argued that crude oil was created by chemical actions within the earth itself. They believe most of the oil known today leaked out of vast reservoirs of oil buried 480 kilometers (300 miles) or more beneath the earth's surface.

ANCIENT OIL SEEPS

THERE ARE HUNDREDS OF OIL SEEPS AND SPRINGS, GAS SEEPS, asphalt veins and oil-impregnated rock outcrops around the world. Some ancient people worshiped at them, while others feared them as the blood of the earth. For many,

however, they were a valuable source of medicine, adhesives and building material.

Archeological discoveries and ancient written records testify to the use of natural asphalt from oil seeps in the Middle East more than 5,000 years ago. Natural asphalt is a sticky, dark, semisolid substance — also known as tar or bitumen — that oozes to the surface through fissures in the earth. It is the residue left after the gas and liquids in oil evaporate. Sumerians, Assyrians and Babylonians used natural asphalt as building mortar, medicine, a waterproofing material and an adhesive to attach handles to knife blades and ax heads.

Three-thousand-year-old Chinese texts mention the use of natural gas from seeps. Some 2,500 years ago, the Chinese fitted bamboo poles with metal tips to drill as deep as 150 meters (500 feet) for natural gas in limestone formations near modern-day Chongqing. The gas was burned to dry rock salt found in the same limestone formations.

Babylonians in what is now Iraq were using asphalt from oil seeps to pave roads in 600 BC. The prototypes for the basket in which Moses floated down the Nile and the ark in which Noah saved animals from the flood were probably waterproofed with asphalt. The sailing ships that rode seasonal winds from the Arabian Gulf and Red Sea south to Africa and east to India were caulked with strips of cotton rolled in asphalt. Great quantities of asphalt were distributed commercially from a famous oil seep at Hit about 145 kilometers (90 miles) west of present-day Baghdad. The Greek historian Herodotus reported that it was used as medicine to check bleeding, treat cataracts, toothache and chronic cough, and relieve diarrhea, rheumatism and fever.

Natural gas sometimes escaped from seeps. When ignited, it could burn for years. The natural flows of asphalt and gas at Baku on the west coast of the Caspian Sea in today's Azerbaijan were some of the most spectacular in the world. Stories of eternal fires have emanated from Baku for more than 2,500 years. Zoroaster considered it a holy site and instructed his followers, the Zoroastrians, to "pray in the presence of the fire."

Seeps also provided the raw material for a weapon that for centuries played a key role in warfare. In the *Iliad*, Homer describes a fiery liquid, probably a mixture of oil and sulfur, that the Trojans poured onto Greek ships. King Cyrus of Persia used a similar substance to set alight watchtowers and housetops in his conquest of Babylon in 539 BC. The Byzantines devised an oil-based compound, similar to modern napalm, that ignited spontaneously and used it to destroy the Arab fleets that attacked Constantinople in the 7th and 8th centuries. This substance—known to the Arabs as "Greek fire"—adhered to surfaces, burned furiously and could not be extinguished by water alone.

Oil was well-known in the early Muslim world. Around the year 900, the Persian physician and scientist al-Razi wrote a handbook on how to distill *neft* (anglicized to "naphtha") from natural asphalt. About the same time, Arab scholars in Basra, in present-day Iraq, theorized that *neft* was the result of chemical reactions between water and underground rocks.

Little more was learned about oil or its origins until the advent of the Industrial Revolution in Europe and America nearly 2,000 years later. Then things changed rapidly. First, oil proved to be a better lubricant than lard for the new, hot-running steam engines of the 19th century. In 1848, the Scottish chemist James Young discovered that a brightly burning fuel called kerosene—superior to anything then available for lighting homes and offices—could be distilled from oil.

Young's discovery created a huge demand for oil. In 1859, Edwin L. Drake struck oil at 21 meters (69.5 feet) at Titusville, Pennsylvania, proving that drilling for oil could be profitable and touching off the first of the cyclical price swings that have bedeviled the industry ever since. In 1859, oil prices rose to $10 a barrel—the equivalent of more than $217 in 2005 prices. Two years later, after other producers copied Drake's method and flooded world markets with oil, prices plunged to 52 cents a barrel, or around $12 in 2005 dollars.

The petroleum industry was turbulent, wasteful and disorganized in its early years. Between 1860 and 1880, John

More highly refined fuel increased the power and reliability of internal combustion engines, making gasoline-powered cars the popular choice of families such as this one in a 1923 Ford Model T.

GASOLINE

In 1913, chemists at Standard Oil of Indiana pioneered "thermal cracking," a discovery that launched the modern petroleum industry. This technique used intense heat of up to 343°C (650°F) and high pressure to break large hydrocarbon molecules into smaller molecules, resulting in a product called "motor spirits" and nearly doubling the share of gasoline that could be refined from a barrel of oil.

This, combined with the discovery of the additive tetraethyl lead in the 1920s, resulted in a plentiful supply of high-octane gasoline to power internal combustion engines without excessive knock. Although electric- and steam-powered cars were built through the 1930s, the gasoline-fueled internal combustion engine reigned supreme in the automobile industry. (Tetraethyl lead was used as an anti-knock agent for nearly 50 years, until the passage of antipollution legislation led to its replacement by unleaded fuel in many countries.)

Of equal importance, thermal cracking enabled refiners to manipulate hydrocarbon molecules to increase the output of many other desirable products, such as diesel fuel, naphtha and kerosene. Thermal cracking, and later catalytic cracking, led to a host of new products such as synthetic rubber, synthetic fabrics and, eventually, plastics.

THE SEARCH FOR OIL AND GAS

The search for oil and gas is carried out on land, at sea and by air. Exploration involves a full integration of geology, geophysics, advanced drilling techniques and engineering, and uses massive amounts of data that are processed by the world's most powerful computing systems.

Until the 19th century, man rarely searched for oil methodically. In some places, he detected it seeping into pools or glistening on the surface of streams. Elsewhere he could scarcely miss it: The "pitch lake" in Trinidad, for example, is estimated to have held some 200 million barrels of heavy oil and asphalt that could simply be dug by hand.

Beginning in the late 1800s, geologists noted that oil seeps seemed to originate in or near the upward-folded layers of rock known as "anticlines" and speculated that oil was trapped in these structures. An anticline is one type of trap in which the strata are bent to form a solid rock structure that resembles—roughly speaking—an upside-down bowl.

Over millions of years, petroleum flows up through porous rock layers and into the anticlinal trap. It is held in place because the structure is "capped" by a layer of impermeable rock. In Saudi Arabia, the cap rock is a crusty white mineral called anhydrite; elsewhere it is often shale. There are several kinds of structural traps, but anticlines are generally the most important in the search for oil because they are easier to detect and are likely to contain more oil than other types.

The folds of rock that form traps do not necessarily reveal themselves on the surface and the search for hydrocarbons must rely on a variety of methods to deduce what lies underground. The basic tool in this search is an understanding of the earth itself. This involves disciplines such as stratigraphy (the study of the origin, composition and distribution of rock strata), petrology (the classification and occurrence of rocks) and paleontology (the study of fossilized animal and plant remains from ancient geological periods).

Since the 1930s, exploration methods based on the science of geophysics (the study of the physics of the earth) have played an important role in the search for oil and gas. Geophysical data are collected through magnetic, gravity, electrical and seismic measurements. These may be used alone or together to map subsurface structures. The use of computer systems that manipulate millions of pieces of data simultaneously has added enormously to the hydrocarbon discovery and recovery process.

The magnetometer detects minute variations in the earth's magnetic field. Since sedimentary rocks are practically nonmagnetic, while igneous rocks have strong magnetic effects, differences in the local magnetic field are used to determine the size, shape and thickness of sedimentary strata, which may hold hydrocarbons. Magnetic surveys are often made by specially equipped aircraft that gather data continuously over wide areas. In 2003, Saudi Aramco completed the world's largest aeromagnetic survey covering nearly 1.7 million linear kilometers (some 1 million miles) of the Kingdom, using nine aircraft flying simultaneously.

The gravity meter measures tiny differences in the earth's gravitational field. Variations between the gravity values of the sedimentary rocks and the underlying "basement" rocks enable earth scientists to determine the shape, size and distribution of subsurface sedimentary structures that may hold oil or gas.

While the magnetometer and gravity meter can play important roles in exploration, advances in geophysical technology have made the seismic survey the most widely used method for studying subsurface strata. The traditional seismograph is a device that records and measures vibrations in the earth produced by earthquakes. In oil and gas exploration, instruments working on the same principle are used to record and measure manmade vibrations or shock waves.

The most common method used by Saudi Aramco today is to vibrate a heavy metal pad on the ground. The pad is mounted on the underside of specially equipped trucks that move along surveyed lines; they stop at regular intervals to lower the pad and generate a series of shock waves.

The energy travels down through the earth and a very small portion is reflected back by each of the interfaces between layers of rocks of different densities. The time it takes a shock wave to travel down and back to the surface is measured with an accuracy of up to a thousandth of a second by precisely placed geophones. When these data are processed on computers, geoscientists can construct images of reservoirs buried five or more kilometers (three miles) below the surface.

Offshore seismic surveying is carried out by seismic recording vessels. Hydrophones are towed in "streamers" behind single boats, and air guns are used to release sharp pulses in the water. The resulting data are recorded while the boat is moving and sent for processing. In another technique, both geophones and hydrophones are placed on the seabed; once again, air guns provide pulses of energy. Transition zone surveys combine land and marine operations and are the most complex to carry out.

Computing systems generate 3-D models of subsurface formations that can be viewed from almost any geometric perspective. This technology offers insights into geologically complex areas, resulting in improved discovery rates for initial, "wildcat" wells; more accurate reserve estimates; reduced drilling risks; and enhanced reservoir development strategies. Saudi Aramco has conducted 3-D seismic surveys over all of its major producing fields—onshore and offshore—as well as in new exploration areas where there is currently no production.

While these surveying techniques are far advanced over the methods used in the early days of the oil industry, they cannot guarantee the presence of oil or gas. The only certain way is to drill a well and see what is there.

The most primitive method was digging a well by hand, and this technique was used in some parts of the world up to the early 20th century. The next step was drilling by percussion. This consisted of suspending a large sharpened drilling tool at the end of a rope and dropping it repeatedly into the hole being drilled. With

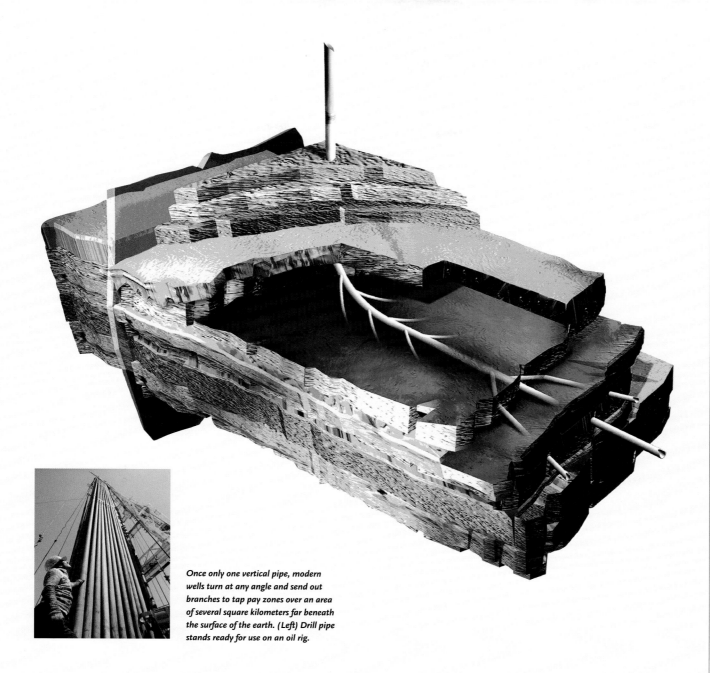

Once only one vertical pipe, modern wells turn at any angle and send out branches to tap pay zones over an area of several square kilometers far beneath the surface of the earth. (Left) Drill pipe stands ready for use on an oil rig.

the advance of mechanization in the early 19th century, the efficacy of this method was greatly increased by using steam power, enhanced by the use of steel cable instead of a rope.

Rotary drilling was developed late in the 19th century. This used a steel drill bit attached to a long string of drill pipe that rotated at the bottom of a hole, offering a much faster drilling rate. The cone bit provided the next advance. It consisted of three steel cones fitted with exceptionally hard, durable teeth that rotate as the bit is turned and grind their way though successive layers of rock.

The cutting tool is only one of the essential elements in drilling a well, however. Another is a means of shoring up the sides of the hole to prevent a cave-in. Today, lengths of steel pipe that are screwed together form a well casing that lines the well bore and acts as a channel through which the broken rock from around the rotating drill bit can be brought to the surface.

One more essential element in the drilling process is known as "mud"—which actually consists of water to which the driller adds one or two special types of solids mixed with chemicals to produce the exact consistency and weight required. This fluid, which is pumped into the hole, serves two purposes. It lubricates the teeth of the drill bit and carries out debris from the bottom of the hole.

Drilling varies enormously from country to country and location to location in terms of difficulty, cost and techniques required. Wells do not have to be vertical; modern drilling techniques can aim curved holes precisely to reach pockets of oil at considerable lateral distance from the rig on the surface. They can also be multilateral, that is, have a number of holes stemming from the main hole to capture as much oil as possible from oil-bearing strata, increasing recovery rates.

Saudi Aramco's Geosteering Center, which opened in Dhahran in 2005, employs the latest drilling, well-logging, satellite data transmission and computer-aided visualization technology to maximize production. Here, experts guide drillers at the rig to follow oil- or gas-bearing strata by means of detailed data obtained from the wells as they are being drilled, using software developed by the company.

Six operators control the directional drilling of up to 12 wells simultaneously, penetrating and tracking oil or gas reservoirs as thin as 1.5 meters (five feet) over long horizontal distances deep underground. The ability to increase the contact of the well bore with the reservoir greatly increases the potential production of a well.

Oil erupts from the first successful well drilled in the Middle East, at Masjid-i-Suleiman in Persia in 1908.

MASJID-I-SULEIMAN

The discovery of oil at Masjid-i-Suleiman in west-central Persia (today's Iran) opened the oil era in the Middle East. The 1908 strike was the first in a "golden corridor" of oil-rich territory that came to include eastern Saudi Arabia 30 years later. The discovery was financed by William Knox D'Arcy, an Englishman whose syndicate was soon after reorganized as the Anglo-Persian Oil Company (later British Petroleum). Exploration was inaugurated in 1901 and almost abandoned just prior to the discovery. The first oil shipment was made in 1912 from Abadan, where a refinery was completed the same year. D'Arcy, who struck it rich in the Australian gold rush in the 1880s and who loved horse racing and opera, sat on the board of the Anglo-Persian Oil Company until his death in 1917, but he never saw the land his venture so altered.

D. Rockefeller put his hand to organizing the petroleum industry in the United States, creating a company that controlled refining, transportation and distribution activities right down to the consumer.

Rockefeller's methods angered competitors. But he and his associates created a structure that through its very size and efficiency was able to stabilize petroleum prices, fueling the growth of American industrialism. It also enabled the United States to hold its own in the keen competition for international petroleum markets that developed among British, Dutch, Russian and American companies in the 1880s. In 1911, the Supreme Court upheld anti-trust legislation that broke Rockefeller's organization into more than 30 independent companies. One of them, Standard Oil of California (Socal), would discover oil in Saudi Arabia.

By the start of the 20th century, a host of new uses had been found for products refined from petroleum. Oil-fired furnaces began to replace coal- and wood-burning steam engines in railroad trains, at the bottom of mines and in farm fields, mills and industrial shops. By converting from coal to oil, ships could travel farther and faster than ever before. The British and German navies began to make the switch as early as 1905. Oil's supremacy was sealed by the development of the internal combustion engine, fueled by gasoline, to power automobiles, trucks and even airplanes. So it was that investors eagerly scoured the world for what was already being referred to as black gold.

THE OIL INDUSTRY IN THE MIDDLE EAST

A WEALTHY ENGLISHMAN NAMED WILLIAM KNOX D'ARCY brought the oil industry to the Middle East. In 1900, the government of Persia—as Iran was then known—was in dire financial straits. The shah sent a representative to Europe to sell a petroleum concession. He wowed D'Arcy with tales of "incalculable riches" awaiting discovery in Persia.

In the spring of 1901, D'Arcy dispatched a representative to Tehran where a 60-year concession agreement covering three-fourths of the country was negotiated. In return, D'Arcy paid the Persian Government £20,000 (equal to about $100,000) up front, plus another £20,000 in paid-up shares in his exploration company. He also agreed to a royalty equal to 16 percent of the company's annual profits.

This wasn't the first modern bid to explore for oil in the Middle East. Petroleum possibilities in Persia had been investigated as early as 1850, along oil seeps and potential oil-bearing formations running for 1,125 kilometers (700 miles) along the foothills of the Zagros Mountains. D'Arcy's team relied on the 1890 field report of a French geologist who had found "two unquestionably petroliferous territories" at the northern end of the Arabian Gulf. D'Arcy hired George B. Reynolds, a British engineer who had recently managed a drilling team for Royal Dutch/Shell

Internal combustion engines powered lethal new weapons in World War I, among them airplanes, submarines and tanks. Ample oil supplies from the United States tipped the balance of power in favor of the Allied forces.

on the island of Sumatra (now part of Indonesia), where oil had been discovered in 1885.

By 1908, with no oil in sight, D'Arcy's syndicate voted to withdraw. But Reynolds believed he was on to something and continued working at a site called Masjid-i-Suleiman, a name that means "Suleiman's mosque." On May 26, 1908, before the order to withdraw could be enforced, Reynolds's crew brought in the first commercial well in the golden corridor, initiating the flow of Middle Eastern oil to the world. The Masjid-i-Suleiman oil field eventually produced over 1 billion barrels of oil.

In April 1909, D'Arcy incorporated the Anglo-Persian Oil Company. The company laid out and supervised construction of a 210-kilometer (130-mile) pipeline to Abadan at the northern end of the Gulf, where a 2,400-barrel-a-day refinery was built. Shortly after that, the British Government contracted Anglo-Persian to supply oil to the Royal Navy. Five years later, just six days before the start of World War I, the British Government purchased a 51 percent interest in the company, which later became British Petroleum.

WORLD WAR I

WORLD WAR I PROVED THAT PETROLEUM WAS CRUCIAL TO national power—even survival. Trucks replaced horses, tanks substituted for cavalry, and pilots in flimsy bi-wing aircraft dueled above the battlefield. In Paris, taxicabs were mobilized to transport soldiers to the front. Historian Barbara Tuchman called it "the first war that petroleum won." When the war started in 1914, the British military had just 800 motor vehicles. By the war's end four years later, the Allied forces of Britain, France and the United States fielded 56,000 trucks, 36,000 cars, 15,000 planes and 2,300 tanks, giving them unprecedented mobility and power.

The Allies received ample petroleum from the United States during the war. The Central Powers, including Germany, the Austro-Hungarian Empire, Romania, Bulgaria and the Ottoman Empire, lacked a single reliable source of oil. (Although the Ottomans controlled what is now Iraq, oil wasn't discovered there until after the war.) They rationed oil and diesel fuel, and canceled some operations for lack of

209

fuel. Petroleum supplies would prove crucial again a generation later during World War II.

At the end of World War I, the United States called for a
joint commission to recommend what should be done with
pieces of the shattered Ottoman Empire. President Wood-
row Wilson appointed two commission members—Charles
R. Crane, heir to a plumbing company fortune and former
minister to China, and Henry C. King, president of Oberlin
College in Ohio. Britain appointed two members but soon
withdrew them. The other powers declined to participate.
Nevertheless, the U.S. commissioners toured the Middle
East, visiting Turkey, Syria, Egypt, Lebanon and Palestine to
sample public opinion.

The King-Crane Commission recommended that local
populations determine their own governments, that Jewish
immigration to the Middle East be limited and that the
project to make Palestine a virtual Jewish commonwealth
be abandoned. However, delegates to the Versailles Peace
Conference ignored the commission's insightful report.

The commission's tour did ultimately have a notable
effect. While in Cairo, Crane asked for the names of the
most important leaders in Arabia. First on the list was
'Abd al-'Aziz Al Sa'ud, then the *amir* of Riyadh. Crane jot-
ted his name down in a black notebook. A dozen years
later this simple act would have dramatic impact
in Saudi Arabia.

THE RED LINE

THE TIES THAT BOUND THE ALLIES DURING WORLD
War I began to fray soon after the armistice as the
Europeans maneuvered for spheres of influence
and access to resources in the Middle East. They
were motivated in part by fears of imminent oil
shortages based on memories of periodic scarci-
ties during the war, and heightened by a soaring
demand for petroleum products.

Demand for oil in the United States (where consumption increased by 90 percent between 1911
and 1918) spurred American oil companies to look
overseas for petroleum supplies. One focus was the
new British mandate of Mesopotamia—soon to be
renamed Iraq—which had been cobbled together
from the old Ottoman provinces of Mosul, Baghdad and Basra.

In 1920, England, France and the Netherlands
formed the Iraq Petroleum Company (IPC), group-
ing the Anglo-Persian Oil Company with Royal
Dutch/Shell and Compagnie Française des Pétroles,
to protect their petroleum interests in the region.
To ensure access to Middle Eastern oil, Britain stationed a squadron of warships in the Arabian Gulf,
where they had established a network of treaties
with states and tribal leaders.

American companies complained they were being
excluded from exploration in the region by their former
European allies. In a bid to participate in Middle East oil
development, five American firms formed the Near East
Development Corporation (NEDC) in 1922. Finally, in
1928, an agreement was struck under which shareholding
in IPC was adjusted to include the new American group.
NEDC and each of the IPC members held a 23.75 percent
share, and the remainder went to Calouste Gulbenkian—a
Turkish Petroleum Company shareholder, oil pipeline deal-
maker and fine art collector—who earned the name "Mr.
Five Percent."

At the same time, IPC members sketched a red line around
the borders of the old Ottoman Empire and bound members not to undertake oil operations there except through
the IPC. All the major oil fields of the Middle East except
Persia and Kuwait eventually found themselves within the
"red line." This agreement established a framework for Middle East oil development.

Iraq's oil potential had been proved in 1927, when drillers brought in a well that flowed at 95,000 barrels a day at
Baba Gurgur in the Kurdish provinces around 240 kilometers (150 miles) north of Baghdad. It took nine days and
four lives to bring the gusher under control. It was located

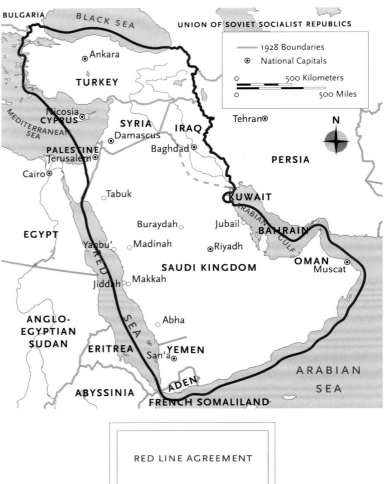

RED LINE AGREEMENT

Fred Davies of Bapco oversaw the successful search for oil in Bahrain in 1932 and thought much larger quantities of oil might be found in nearby Saudi Arabia. He was proved right in 1938 and later became the chairman of the board of Aramco, the Arabian American Oil Company.

within 1.5 kilometers (a mile) of a fiery gas seep into which the King of Babylon was thought to have cast his enemies 25 centuries before. IPC members were preoccupied with finding new markets for the flood of oil from Iraq and not especially concerned when a non-member company, Standard Oil of California, or Socal, received a concession to explore for oil on Bahrain, within the Red Line zone.

BAHRAIN

MAJOR FRANK HOLMES, A NEW ZEALAND MINING ENGINEER and entrepreneur, caught oil fever as a soldier stationed in Basra, in what is now southern Iraq, during World War I. He remained in the region after the war and helped set up the Bahrain office of Eastern and General Syndicate, a London-based finance group. In 1923, Eastern and General received a concession from 'Abd al-'Aziz Al Sa'ud to explore for oil in eastern Arabia, on the condition that it not sell any part of the concession to the Anglo-Persian Oil Company, an IPC member. The syndicate hired a veteran Swiss geologist to reconnoiter the area. He found no sign of oil in the region, classifying exploration there as "a pure

gamble" and convincing almost everyone that there was no oil in Arabia. The concession eventually expired for lack of financial backing.

Unfortunately for Holmes, the geologist apparently missed features such as the Dammam Dome, the structure that would draw Socal geologists to the mainland a decade later. Things broke Holmes's way in 1925, however, when Shaykh Hamad ibn 'Isa Al Khalifah, the ruler of Bahrain, contracted Eastern and General to drill for water. Drilling proved so successful that the ruler offered the syndicate an option to explore for oil. The British Colonial Office approved the agreement. No one believed there was oil in Bahrain, but Holmes had seen streaks of oil in the water wells.

Established Middle East oil companies were not interested in financing exploration work in Bahrain, so Holmes headed to the United States to seek a backer. Gulf Oil Corporation gave him a hearing in New York and contracted Eastern and General to carry out a geological survey of Bahrain. The survey confirmed the possibility of oil, but Gulf—a partner in the Red Line Agreement—could act only in unison with the other members. Try as it might, Gulf could not convince IPC to undertake exploration in Bahrain.

In 1928, a Gulf representative mentioned the Bahrain geological report to a Socal officer at an oil-industry convention in Chicago. Socal had been actively seeking overseas supplies for the past decade and had spent millions of dollars on unsuccessful forays in the Philippines, Colombia and Alaska. It seized the new opportunity and won the Bahrain concession almost by default after England gave the company a grudging go-ahead to explore in Bahrain, then a British protectorate. Socal could do this because it was not a party to the Red Line Agreement. It created the Bahrain Petroleum Company (Bapco), a British firm registered in Canada, to comply with a rule that oil development in the area be carried out only by British interests.

Drilling began in October 1931 near Jabal Dukhan (literally, "the hill of smoke") that at 131 meters (431 feet) was the highest spot on the island. Seven months later, drillers struck oil at 609 meters (2,000 feet). It was a good investment: The well flowed at up to 1,400 barrels a day, and Socal had spent just $650,000 to bring it in. Notably, the oil came from source rocks older than the productive Miocene age limestone formations in Persia and Iraq. Until then, geologists at established Middle East oil companies believed that oil would be present only in areas with similar limestone formations.

A young Socal geologist named Fred A. Davies supervised the Bahrain exploration program. Standing atop Jabal Dukhan when the sun was low in the evening, Davies could see the outline of a *jabal* on what would soon be named Saudi Arabia, 40 kilometers (25 miles) to the west. "Naturally we were curious and wanted to look around over there," Davies later wrote to a friend. "We had a strong desire to examine the geology. We thought there might well be oil possibilities in the vastly larger area of the mainland."

THE CONCESSION AGREEMENT

THE ECONOMIC DEPRESSION THAT BEGAN WITH A "CRASH" IN prices on the New York Stock Exchange in October 1929 did not spare the Kingdom of the Hijaz and Najd and its Dependencies, precursor of Saudi Arabia. The Kingdom's economy was undeveloped. No real budget existed and no paper currency circulated. The government drew most of its income from fees paid by pilgrims to Makkah, and the number of pilgrims plummeted, slashing the government's main source of revenue.

By the early 1930s, the Kingdom was nearly broke. "The country's treasury would have fit in the King's saddlebags," a British official reported. The desperate finance minister, 'Abd Allah al-Sulayman, declared a moratorium on the Kingdom's debts and commandeered the gasoline stocks of two private companies in Jiddah as a ready source of cash.

In the midst of the financial crisis, Charles R. Crane, the same philanthropist who had served on the King-Crane Commission after World War I, called on King 'Abd-al-'Aziz. It was the first link in a chain of events that would transform the Kingdom beyond most men's wildest dreams. Crane arrived in Jiddah on February 25, 1931, and was welcomed in style. The King greeted him at the two-story Khuzam Palace on the outskirts of the port city.

Crane had wanted to meet Ibn Sa'ud, as King 'Abd al-'Aziz was known in the West, for 12 years, ever since an Egyptian scholar put his name at the top of a list of promising Arab leaders. Crane and Ibn Sa'ud had corresponded occasionally, but they had never met. Harry St. John B. Philby, an acquaintance of the King, heard Crane was in Cairo and suggested that it might be a good time to invite the American philanthropist for a visit.

During Crane's weeklong stay, Ibn Sa'ud told the American that he gave first importance to the safety, health and

Charles Crane (seated, right) and Henry C. King headed a 1919 commission that recommended self-determination for the residents of the former Ottoman Empire after World War I. Crane later met with King 'Abd al-'Aziz, setting in motion the events that led to the discovery of oil in Saudi Arabia.

CHARLES R. CRANE

Charles R. Crane was born to wealth in Chicago, Illinois, in 1858, heir to the family's plumbing company fortune. This in itself was not so unusual. What was unusual was what Crane did with his money and his life.

For much of his life, he roamed the world noting worthy causes in a black notebook and writing checks, sometimes in six figures, to support them. The range of his beneficence was remarkable. For example, he helped finance famine relief in China and rescued the now-famous Marine Biological Laboratory at Woods Hole, Massachusetts, from bankruptcy. He supported classical music groups in Russia, artists in Eastern Europe and polar exploration. He was also an influential advisor to U.S. presidents from William Howard Taft to Harry Truman during the first half of the 20th century. He served as the first U.S. ambassador to Czechoslovakia, and cochairman of the King-Crane Commission, which — unsuccessfully — recommended self-determination for the people of the Middle East after World War I.

The Middle East had held a special place in his heart ever since his first visit to Cairo in 1878 at age 20. Crane paid for translations of the Quran into English and the restoration of the mosaics at Hagia Sophia, the great Byzantine basilica in Constantinople (now Istanbul) that was turned into a mosque in the 15th century. He was a trustee and supporter of Robert College in Istanbul and the Constantinople College for girls. He helped finance school construction in Egypt and hospitals in Basra and Muscat.

Described by the president of Robert College as "an unusual and eccentric genius who devoted himself to learning about the nature of other peoples and collecting unusual and interesting personalities as friends, just as other collectors gather books or paintings," Crane had a special talent for altering the lives of people and even the direction of nations.

It could well be said that his weeklong meetings with King 'Abd al-'Aziz Al Sa'ud in Jiddah in 1931 helped launch Saudi Arabia's transformation into a modern state. With the King's approval, Crane assigned Karl S. Twitchell, a Vermont-born mining engineer working for him in Yemen, the task of sizing up the potential of the Kingdom's natural resources. Twitchell, in turn, contacted the oil company that discovered oil in Saudi Arabia.

The faith and austere way of life of the people of Saudi Arabia appealed mightily to Crane. As he wrote to his son John: "The peninsula of Arabia is the home and natural habitat of prophets, and I wanted to get as near as possible to the conditions of life out of which appear every now and then a great prophet. Naturally one does not expect a prophet to grow out of the complicated machinery of the modern state."

The irony is that Crane set in motion a process that brought riches to Saudi Arabia and also resulted in the establishment of a modern state, with all the "complicated machinery" required to run it.

economic prosperity of his people. Spiritual values were ultimately more important, he said, but they could scarcely flourish in people who had to live with disease, insecurity and poverty.

When the King mentioned water shortages, Crane asked if any artesian wells had been drilled. Ibn Sa'ud said that while he had ordered test borings at Ras Tanura on the Gulf, the ground in the central province of Najd was so hard and stony he was reluctant to seek tests until experts had examined the territory and reported on the chances for success. Crane offered to assign Karl S. Twitchell, a mining engineer he employed on projects in Yemen, to visit and give his advice. The King gratefully accepted.

Crane described King 'Abd al-'Aziz in glowing terms in a letter to U.S. President Franklin D. Roosevelt. Ibn Sa'ud was "the most important man who has appeared in Arabia since the time of Mohammad," he noted. He wrote to his son: "The King was all that I could possibly have wished. He is a magnificent man, six feet three or four, powerful in every way but of great charm. While he plays a strong, uncompromising role, he is most generous to his former enemies...."

Twitchell arrived in Jiddah in mid-April. At the King's request, he scouted throughout the Hijaz, the country's westernmost territory, but found no geological evidence to justify drilling for water. He had, however, seen the ruins of some ancient gold mines at Mahd al-Dhahab that he felt might be associated with those of the legendary King Solomon. Later, Twitchell helped restore the mines to working condition.

In December 1931, Twitchell traveled across the Arabian Peninsula to al-Hasa, the Kingdom's easternmost province, prospecting for water and other resources. It was a 1,600-kilometer (1,000-mile) trip over harsh terrain that no American had ever traversed. Twitchell journeyed with a military escort and some 30 support personnel in a convoy of Ford trucks and cars, via Riyadh, to the oasis city of Hofuf and up and down the Gulf coast. Then he crossed to Bahrain, met with the ruler and returned to Hofuf in early January.

Two days later, Ibn Sa'ud arrived in Hofuf accompanied by 'Abd Allah al-Sulayman, the finance minister, and Yusuf Yasin, his chief secretary, to hear Twitchell's report. His findings on the water possibilities in central Arabia were disappointing: no geological evidence jus-

Mining engineer Karl Twitchell's auto caravan crossed the Arabian Peninsula for the first time in 1931. Twitchell looked for water and noted the possibility of oil in al-Hasa, today's Eastern Province.

'ABD ALLAH
AL-SULAYMAN

Originally from the heartland of Arabia, 'Abd Allah al-Sulayman studied trade and bookkeeping in Bombay before he was named finance minister by King 'Abd Al-'Aziz in 1932. He had a reputation for making a little money go a long way, and he proved a shrewd manager for the Kingdom's Depression-era economy. Although he was not able to convince Socal to provide the immediate £100,000 loan he regarded as vital to pay off Saudi Arabia's debts, he did succeed in securing more than that amount contingent upon the discovery of commercially useful oil resources. But his far more lasting legacy is that he ensured in the 1933 Concession Agreement that Saudi Arabia would continue to receive substantial proportions of all future oil revenues. It was this framework that in time brought his country unprecedented prosperity and full ownership of the oil enterprise.

tified drilling artesian wells. The Eastern Province was different. He saw numerous springs and a huge oasis supporting thousands of date palm trees and dozens of farm fields at Hofuf.

Twitchell was also intrigued by the possibility of oil in al-Hasa. Two-thirds of the province consisted of a sedimentary rock formation, which, under certain conditions, was favorable for oil prospects. Twitchell had seen no oil seeps or other indications of oil, but neither had he seen anything to preclude oil. He recommended the King wait and see what happened on Bahrain, where drilling was under way. In essence, his thoughts mirrored those of Socal's Fred Davies. If oil was found in Bahrain it was likely there was also oil in al-Hasa, and in much larger quantities.

The discovery of oil on Bahrain in May 1932 abruptly changed the King's focus from water to oil. He was not, he told his friend the *amir* of Kuwait, anxious to grant a concession for foreigners to look for oil. Yet, given the Kingdom's financial difficulties, he had no choice.

At the King's request, Twitchell agreed to try and interest oil companies in exploring in al-Hasa. Despite Socal's recent success in Bahrain, it was not an opportune time to sell an oil exploration deal. In addition to the worldwide Depression, the oil market was saturated. The oil companies in Persia and Iraq had more than they knew what to do with, and there was a huge output from new fields in east Texas and Oklahoma. Prices had collapsed from around $2 a barrel in the 1920s to less than 15 cents.

Twitchell journeyed to New York in the summer of 1932 and began making the rounds. He had little tangible evidence in favor of an ambitious new exploration project. There were no specific structural features that he knew of to indicate the presence of oil in al-Hasa or anywhere else in Arabia. The only geological information specific to al-Hasa was the 1923 Eastern and General Syndicate report calling exploration in al-Hasa "a gamble." Oil in Bahrain did not guarantee that the same favorable conditions existed on the mainland.

What geological evidence there was for the remainder of the peninsula consisted mostly of published notes by desert travelers. During the early 1900s, there had been reports of oil-bearing shale in northern Arabia and oil seeps at outcroppings in the northwest. The Shell Company had acquired a concession for the Farasan Islands in the southern part of the Red Sea in 1912. Shell drilled around oil seeps, but found no oil and abandoned the sites.

Twitchell went first to NEDC headquarters in New York. Its parent, IPC, was the most powerful oil consortium in the world. NEDC couldn't move without the approval of the other IPC companies, all signatories of the Red Line Agreement. But NECD's participation soon became a moot point.

A Socal representative contacted Twitchell and arranged for him to meet a member of the company's board of directors in New York. Socal supplemented Twitchell's meager

Socal lawyer Lloyd Hamilton (left) and Harry St. John B. Philby played important roles in paving the way for oil exploration to begin in Saudi Arabia. They are pictured in Jiddah in 1933.

deal to advise Socal in negotiations on a concession agreement.

In November 1932, Socal contacted Philby and asked him to request permission for a geological examination of al-Hasa, but King 'Abd al-'Aziz was unwilling to allow a survey prior to negotiating a concession. In January 1933, Twitchell and Maurice E. Lombardi, the Socal board member he'd seen in New York, sailed to London, where they met Lloyd N. Hamilton, a lawyer in charge of the company's London office. Together, they worked up a proposed concession agreement. Then Hamilton and his wife, along with Twitchell, his wife and son, traveled to Jiddah.

Philby, perhaps reasoning that competition for a concession would be in the best interests of the Kingdom, told friends at the Anglo-Persian Oil Company and its parent, IPC, about Socal's growing interest in Saudi Arabia. IPC decided to join the bidding.

'Abd Allah al-Sulayman and Hamilton began negotiations February 19, 1933, seated across the table from one another in a dimly lit room on the second floor of Khuzam Palace. IPC's representative, Stephen H. Longrigg, joined the talks a few days later.

From the beginning, it was evident that a key element in the negotiations would be the amount of cash the companies were willing to pay up front for concession rights.

geological information with reports from Davies in Bahrain and concluded the odds of finding oil on the mainland were "good to excellent," wrote Reginald Stoner, the head of Socal's Production Department. Furthermore, Stoner believed that this was an especially good time to seek more reserves because there was plenty of oil around and prices were low.

On September 19, 1932, a Royal Decree changed the name of the Kingdom of the Hijaz and Najd and its Dependencies to the Kingdom of Saudi Arabia, after the ruling House of Sa'ud. A few days later, Socal offered Twitchell a hefty payment to work as an advisor on conditions in Arabia. He agreed, after making sure that Crane had no objection. At the same time, Socal's chief lawyer made similar overtures to Philby, who eventually negotiated a lucrative

Shaykh al-Sulayman opened the negotiations by suggesting the equivalent of £100,000 in gold (about $500,000) for the concession. Hamilton countered with an offer of £20,000 in gold. Longrigg offered only £10,000 in rupees, not gold, and even this would be contingent on a positive report by his company's geologists. There were major differences between the two firms' approach to the negotiations: Socal was after new oil resources, while IPC did not believe there was oil in eastern Saudi Arabia and merely wanted to keep the American company from intruding into the Middle East.

Negotiations recessed in April. When they restarted in May, al-Sulayman announced that the government had reduced its demands to an initial payment of £50,000 in gold plus an annual rent of £5,000 in gold. Hamilton said he had

Shaykh 'Abd Allah al-Gosaibi and his brothers were
the agents for Socal, providing living and working quarters for early oil prospectors in Jubail and
Hofuf when exploration commenced in 1933.

received authority from San Francisco to make a new, "very liberal" final offer. Longrigg never returned to Jiddah, for IPC's directors would not match Socal's original offer. He and others in the IPC consortium thought that if any oil were in Arabia it would be found in the west, near the Red Sea, not in al-Hasa.

The negotiations swiftly concluded. The Concession Agreement was signed in Jiddah on May 29, 1933, by Shaykh al-Sulayman and Hamilton. The Hamiltons left almost immediately, but Twitchell stayed to attend to the next steps.

Socal agreed to an immediate loan of £30,000 in gold, plus another loan of £20,000 in gold 18 months later. (The loans were the equivalent of about $250,000.) In addition, Socal agreed to yearly rentals of £5,000 in gold (about $25,000) and royalties of four shillings in gold (about $1) per ton of oil produced. The company promised to provide the government with an advance of another £50,000 in gold if oil in commercial quantities was found. The agreement called for an immediate start of exploration, for drilling to begin as soon as a suitable structure was found, and for construction of a refinery after oil was discovered. It was the immediate loan of £30,000 pounds in gold that sealed the deal, Twitchell later wrote.

Socal obtained the exclusive right to prospect for and produce oil in eastern Saudi Arabia for the next 60 years, and preferential rights to explore for oil elsewhere in the Kingdom. The term eastern Saudi Arabia referred to some 829,000 square kilometers (320,000 square miles) of territory running from the border with Iraq on the north through the forbidding Rub' al-Khali, or Empty Quarter, in the south. It extended inland from the Gulf coast to the western edge of the Dahna, a wide band of red sand connecting Saudi Arabia's two huge deserts, the Great Nafud in the north and the Rub' al-Khali.

Royal Decree Number 1135 "granting a concession for the exploration of petroleum" was issued on July 7, 1933, and proclaimed in the official gazette on July 14. The agreement contained 37 separate articles. One of them, Article 23, opened the industrial age to thousands of Saudis. It read: "The enterprise under this contract shall be directed and supervised by Americans who shall employ Saudi nationals as far as practicable, and in so far as the

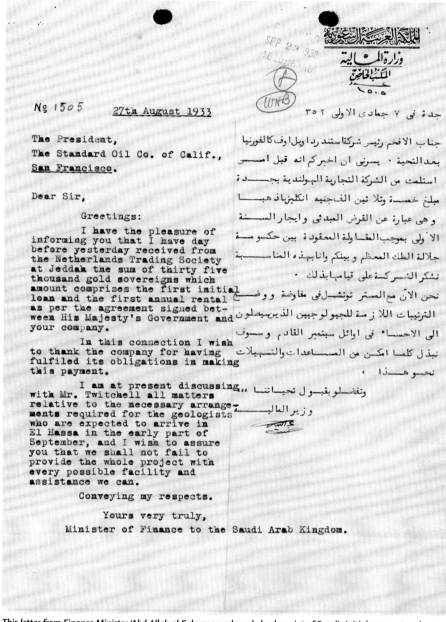

This letter from Finance Minister 'Abd Allah al-Sulayman acknowledged receipt of Socal's initial payment and promised "every possible facility and assistance" in the search for oil.

Company can find suitable Saudi employees it will not employ other nationals." A second paragraph made it clear that the labor laws of Saudi Arabia, not those of any other country, applied to company workers.

Socal had made a daring move. It was 1933 and a "bank holiday" had just been declared in the Depression-wracked United States. Oil was selling for pennies a barrel. And the company was sending men and hundreds of thousands of dollars in equipment halfway around the world to search for oil where most experts thought none existed.

Ibn Sa'ud was also taking a big risk. Needing money to keep the Kingdom solvent and meet the pressing needs for his people, he opened Saudi Arabia to large-scale Western involvement for the first time.

DISCOVERY!

SOCAL DIDN'T WAIT LONG TO START WORK. ON SEPTEMBER 23, 1933, a launch carrying its first geologists from Bahrain chugged into the little harbor at Jubail. At the dock, the local *amir*, an escort of soldiers and a throng of other people waited to welcome Robert "Bert" Miller and Schuyler B. "Krug" Henry to Saudi Arabia. Karl Twitchell had crossed the Arabian Peninsula from Jiddah to meet Miller and Henry in Bahrain, and was also on the launch. Like him, Miller and Henry had grown beards and wore Arab dress to avoid appearing too different from the local people, most of whom had never seen a Westerner.

After a few customary cups of coffee, the geologists piled into one of the two Ford sedans Twitchell had rented from the Saudi Government and drove off to inspect a hill called Jabal al-Berri (which later gave its name to the Berri oil field). A crowd followed on camels and donkeys and soon caught up. The geologists' car was stuck in the sand. Amid much laughter, Miller and Henry accepted a camel ride to the *jabal*. It was a novel start to the Saudi Arabian oil venture.

Miller, Socal's chief geologist in Saudi Arabia, Henry and the others who would soon join them faced a daunting task: exploring a vast, roadless territory that was as large as Texas and Louisiana combined. All they knew about the eastern part of Saudi Arabia came from Twitchell, a few books by Western explorers and an old British War Office map of the Arabian Peninsula.

The geologists stayed in rooms provided by Socal's local agents, the prominent al-Gosaibi merchant family. During the first week, they explored west to the village of al-Hinnah and south to Qatif, accompanied by a retinue of guards, cooks, interpreters, drivers and mechanics. They spent a day on Tarut Island just off the Qatif Oasis. Then they headed south to inspect the geological feature most responsible for their presence, a 137-meter (450-foot) hill of broken brown limestone known locally as Jabal Dhahran.

221

What Miller and Henry found at Jabal Dhahran whetted their prospecting appetites. The formation was nearly identical to the one in Bahrain where Bapco had struck oil. "When we drove around the structure, we could see right away that it was a textbook illustration of a dome," Miller later said. "... it was like a carbon copy of Bahrain Island. To get two structures like that was a rather marvelous thing."

The first thing Miller had to do was establish a headquarters. The offices set aside for Socal at Hofuf in the al-Hasa Oasis area were fine, but the bridges that crossed the many canals there were inadequate for motor traffic. In addition, malaria was endemic in the Hofuf area, as it was in the oasis town of Qatif to the northeast. So Miller set up business in Jubail, a relatively cool and breezy town with facilities to receive supplies from Bahrain.

Although Miller and Henry had prospected in places as remote as the Aleutian Islands in Alaska and the rugged back country of Peru, they felt quite isolated in Saudi Arabia. Few Saudis spoke English. The "roads" were camel trails crisscrossing the gravel plains and winding between sand dunes. They were some 1,200 kilometers (750 miles) from Jiddah, soon to be the location for Socal's administrative office in the Kingdom, and they were half a world away from their base of supplies in Richmond, California. There were no shops or warehouses to supply equipment; hardly as much as a nail or a pair of pliers was available anywhere in this part of the Kingdom. Their transport consisted of the two cars Twitchell had rented from the government.

They could use the government's rudimentary wireless communication system, with stations in Jubail, Qatif, Hofuf and Riyadh. However, no messages could be sent across the international border to Bahrain, some 120 kilometers (75 miles) away. Communication with Jiddah or the United States involved several relays in a language unfamiliar to the inexperienced operators. What came out at the other end often made no sense.

Reinforcements arrived quickly. Geologist J.W. "Soak" Hoover landed in October, bringing three Ford V-8 touring cars, a mechanic, a helper and two drivers. Before the end of the year, three more Americans joined the party: Hugh L. Burchfield, Felix Dreyfuss and Socal's chief geologist, J.O. "Doc" Nomland, who stayed for a month and returned to the United States. As soon as the newcomers were settled, Twitchell left for Jiddah with the two rented cars on his fourth and final trip across Arabia. As his last assignment with the company, he helped Bill Lenahan set up a Socal office in Jiddah.

Miller wasted no time in getting on with exploration. In October 1933, he dispatched Hoover and Henry south to begin detailed mapping at Jabal Dhahran. They used a plane table and alidade to determine locations and a barometer to measure elevation, using high tide at the Arabian Gulf, 10 kilometers (six miles) to the east, as sea level. On November 8, Socal assigned the concession to a subsidiary called California Arabian Standard Oil Company (Casoc). After more geologists arrived in November, Miller established a branch office in Hofuf to serve as a staging post for exploration in southern areas. There, data collected by field parties were transferred onto maps of the concession area.

The company also introduced an advanced new technology—aerial photography—to further the search for oil in the Kingdom. The development of large, high-speed aerial cameras in the 1920s had made accurate airborne mapping possible. The Concession Agreement permitted the use of airplanes for exploration, and this proved critical because of the vast size of the concession.

Casoc ordered a custom-built, single-engine monoplane from Fairchild Aviation in the United States and assigned geologist Richard Kerr, an ex-Navy pilot, to do aerial photography. Charley Rocheville, Kerr's co-pilot and mechanic, designed an extra gas tank that increased cruising range to 565 kilometers (350 miles). Kerr worked with the research division of Eastman Kodak in Rochester, New York, to devise a process for developing aerial films in the water temperatures of up to 49°C (120°F) in Saudi Arabia.

The plane was sent by sea to Alexandria, Egypt. Kerr and Rocheville then flew it to Jubail via Cairo, Gaza, Baghdad, Basra and Kuwait. When they landed in Jubail, they were arrested and the plane was padlocked. There had been no official approval for a landing there. The misunderstanding was soon cleared up,

Pioneer geologists (left to right) J.W. "Soak" Hoover, Hugh Burchfield, J.O. "Doc" Nomland, Bert Miller, Schuyler B. "Krug" Henry and Felix Dreyfuss pose at headquarters in Jubail in 1934.

The company's Fairchild 71, specially equipped for aerial photography, arrived at Jubail in March 1934. Aerial photography, then in its infancy, greatly simplified mapping of a concession area the size of Texas and Louisiana combined.

but Casoc was on notice that the government considered airplanes and aerial photography a sensitive subject.

Work to correct existing maps began at once. Some points in old maps of al-Hasa proved to be off by as much as 40 kilometers (25 miles). By the end of 1935, parts of the concession area from the northern Rub' al-Khali all the way to its northwest boundary with Iraq had been photographed from the air. While Kerr photographed the target of most interest—Jabal Dhahran—extensively from the air, Hoover and Henry detailed the structure on the ground. Two other geologists worked out of a camp at 'Uray'irah southwest of Hofuf. Another geologist and his party mapped the area running from west of Jubail as far south as Qatif.

It took a small army to support exploration parties. A well-equipped field team included 15-20 cargo camels, two trucks and a touring car, a guide, a cook and a cook's helper, a houseboy, a mechanic and mechanic's helper, an automobile driver, four camel drivers and an escort of 15-30 armed Bedouin guards. The government supplied the people, and Casoc paid their salaries.

For many Saudis, the first contact with these exploration parties proved unforgettable. Nassir M. Al-Ajmi, who would join the oil company and rise to the rank of executive vice president, and later president general of the Saudi General Railways Corporation, came from a Bedouin family. In his autobiography, *Legacy of a Lifetime*, he recalled his introduction to geologists and their equipment in the 1940s in the desert southwest of Hofuf:

> *The first time I saw a vehicle was a frightening experience. ... it was springtime and I was playing with other children next to our encampment when we heard a strange noise. We saw an odd-looking thing rushing toward us with a cloud of dust behind it. We ... hid inside the tent. As we peeked through the holes to observe the noisy, strange-looking creature, we noticed two or three unfamiliar-looking people wearing funny clothes and deep plates or funneled pots over their heads. It was an exploration party asking for water and seeking directions.*

Geologists had their own share of surprises in the field. Hoover and Henry were the first to report what was to

MAPPING THE FUTURE

Geologists Krug Henry and Soak Hoover didn't limit their 1934 exploration report to drilling prospects. They also addressed how any oil found could be exported. "It is believed that a shipping terminal for heavy draft craft could be developed at Ras Tanura without great difficulty," they wrote. "The distance by land from Jabal Umm Er Rus [on the Dammam Dome] to Katif (Qatif) is approximately 70 kilometers. There is at present a good road from the village of Dammam to Katif, a distance of about 21 kilometers. The greatest difficulties of road-building would probably be encountered between Ras Tanourah and El Katif, this being in part a sand dune region. It would also be necessary to construct a road around Katif to the West as the streets of the village are too narrow for trucks."

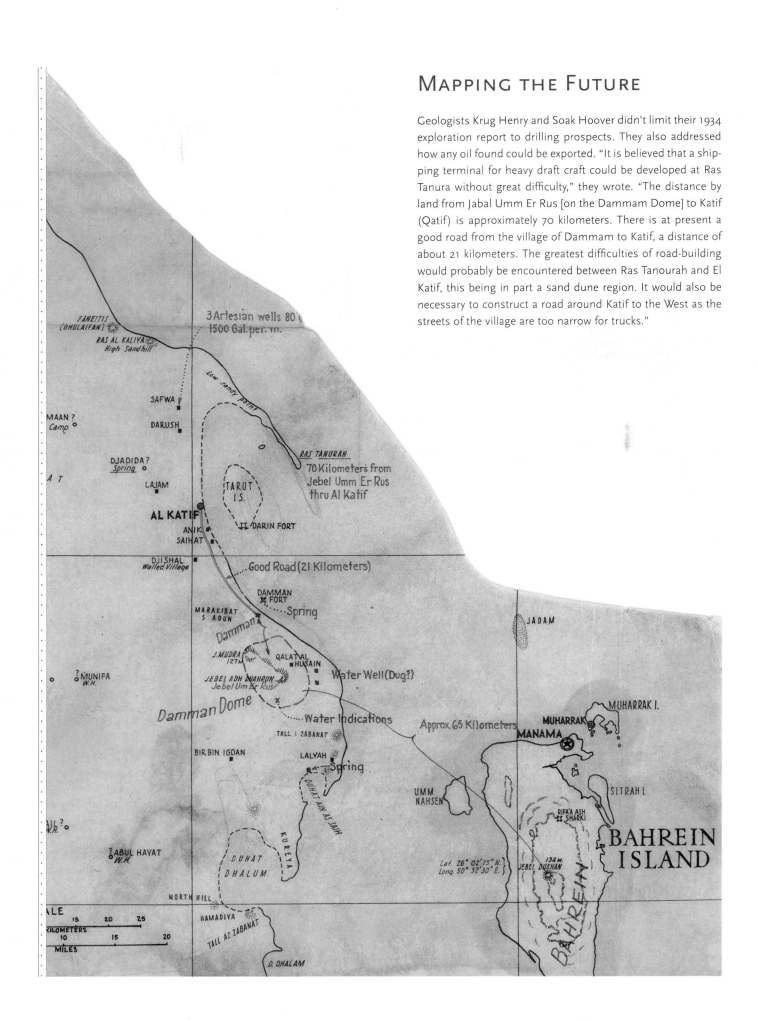

Soak Hoover (left) and Jerry Harriss camp on the Abqaiq structure in 1936. They ate canned food, supplementing their diet by hunting and by purchasing provisions from passing Bedouins.

become a recurring problem. In 1934, returning to Jabal Dhahran from a brief trip outside the area, they found their wooden survey stakes gone, apparently taken for firewood. Many geologists would have to redo their survey points because the stakes they had placed the day before were used for firewood that night. The problem didn't go away until the company switched to metal survey stakes.

In the spring of 1934, Hoover and Henry finished detailed mapping of Jabal Dhahran, which Hoover in his report on the geological structure renamed Dammam Dome. Dammam was the larger of two coastal settlements in the immediate vicinity (the other was al-Khobar) and "dome" indicated the geological structure that might be favorable for the accumulation of oil. Although it was company policy to use local names whenever possible, Hoover thought Jabal Dhahran might be confused with Jabal Dukhan, the site of the first commercial well in Bahrain. The geologists built a cairn of stones to mark the place where they hoped to drill the company's first well.

The Concession Agreement included a provision for suspending work during the hottest part of the year, and most members of the Casoc team spent the summer of 1934 in the cool hills of Lebanon, writing their field reports and completing maps. The first geological reports were more comprehensive than later ones, describing road-building conditions, weather, access to ports, observations on local culture and anything else that might be relevant

to starting a new oil venture. Henry and Hoover produced a report that recommended test drilling at the Dammam Dome, and geologist Hugh Burchfield followed up with a report suggesting that oil would probably be found at the 610-meter (2,000-foot) level, just as it had in Bahrain. After mulling over the costs, Casoc management in San Francisco gave the green light to drill.

Several newcomers joined Casoc in the autumn of 1934. Among them were geologist Max Steineke and petroleum engineer Floyd Ohliger, both of whom would play important roles in the new oil venture. Ohliger's first assignment was to build a pier at al-Khobar to receive supplies from Bahrain, a job that required the first large-scale hiring of Saudis. Ohliger and a Saudi supervisor, Ahmad al-Somali, put every able-bodied man they could find to work gathering a crusty, shell-like stone called *furush* which was exposed along the shore at low tide. Soon, a tongue of rough stone stretched out far enough from shore to receive small cargo boats. Supplies could now be unloaded onto the pier rather than carried to shore on the heads of workmen, and visitors no longer had to wade to land through waist-deep water.

The early explorers found much to admire in the Saudis they met, delighting in Saudi hospitality and respecting the average man's devotion to his religion. Many formed long-lasting friendships. The Bedouin guide Khamis ibn Rimthan was so widely admired for his dignity and loyalty,

GEOLOGY OF ARABIA

Saudi Arabia is made up of two distinct geologic regions. The oldest is the Arabian Shield, on the western side of the Arabian Peninsula. The youngest is the Arabian Shelf, located in the middle and eastern side of the peninsula.

The Arabian Shield is composed of Precambrian igneous and metamorphic rocks that are 550 million years to 2 billion years old. Igneous rocks formed when molten magma cooled and lithified into solid stone. Metamorphic rocks formed from preexisting rocks that were altered and welded by heat and pressure. Both types of rocks were created when tectonic plates of the earth's crust collided.

The Arabian Shield is part of a greater Afro-Arabian Shield, which was split by the Red Sea Rift 36 million years ago. During rifting, the western side of the Arabian Peninsula was uplifted, tilted and eroded down to Precambrian crystalline basement rocks. The shield bulges eastward at its midsection and occupies about one-third of the Arabian Peninsula. In some regions, lava flows dating from 24 million years ago to the recent past have extruded onto the shield. This igneous-metamorphic complex slopes gently eastward and is covered in its eastern part by strata of the Arabian Shelf.

The Arabian Shelf is composed of generally younger sedimentary rocks. In the distant past, most of the Arabian Peninsula lay beneath a vast, shallow sea. The sea spread north and west, intermittently covering regions now occupied by Iraq, Jordan, Lebanon and Syria, in addition to most of Saudi Arabia. The remains of organisms that lived in shallow marine water and fine carbonate mud were deposited as sediment. As the sea alternately flooded and retreated over time, it exposed sediments deposited earlier to erosion and then covered them again. Through these long, slow processes of nature, the sediments were lithified into sedimentary rock, largely limestone, while the organic matter they contained was transformed by heat and pressure into petroleum.

The oldest Arabian Shelf sedimentary rocks were deposited some 550 million years ago, at the beginning of the Paleozoic Era. They outcrop on the eastern flank of the Arabian Shield and, along with the progressively younger, overlying sedimentary rocks, dip gently and thicken toward the Rub' al-Khali desert and Arabian Gulf. These sedimentary rocks now lie some 6,500 meters thick (21,000 feet) beneath the shoreline of the Arabian Gulf. Through time, erosion has worn away and exposed softer rock formations at their thinner western edge, leaving more resistant layers standing high above the surrounding terrain. These escarpments are composed of Paleozoic, Mesozoic and Cenozoic outcrops. Most notable is the Tuwayq Escarpment, the long, curved belt of westward-facing cliff west of Riyadh. Resistant limestones cap each scarp, and many of these rock units continue without significant interruption for hundreds of kilometers in a north-south trend across the Arabian Shelf.

The largest accumulations of hydrocarbons in Saudi Arabia occur in carbonate sedimentary rocks of the Arab Formation that were deposited in the Late Jurassic Period, 150 million years ago, when dinosaurs walked the earth. The environment began to change at that time. Shallow marine seas deposited porous and permeable beds of limestone. With time, the seas became restricted and—through a process of evaporation—deposited beds of nonporous anhydrite. Alternate transgressions and regressions of the sea resulted in four sedimentary cycles during which shallow marine carbonates were overlain by beds of anhydrite. These limestones form the four members of the Arab Formation. They are of paramount importance, especially the highly porous and extremely prolific Arab-D member, for they contain the world's largest reserves of petroleum.

Millions of years after deposition and lithification of these sedimentary rocks, tectonic forces deformed the strata into folds of rock called anticlines. Oil accumulated in these structural traps, with overlying beds of impermeable anhydrite acting as a vertical seal.

Drilling began at Dammam Well No. 1 on the Dammam Dome by March 1935, and a small camp (later named Dhahran) sprouted nearby. Three years later, deep well Dammam No. 7—not far from No. 1—struck oil in commercial quantities.

The Dammam field, the first oil field discovered in Saudi Arabia, is a dome-shaped uplift, the result of upward movement of a deeply buried salt plug. Arab-C limestone is the primary reservoir in the field.

The majority of the known oil and gas fields in Saudi Arabia, however, are in anticlines formed when tectonic forces folded the sedimentary rocks. Major deformation occurred during tectonic events in the Cretaceous and Eocene periods, some 92 million and 35 million years ago, respectively. Large, broad anticlinal folds were formed as the Arabian plate collided with the Asian plate. The general trend of these anticlines in Saudi Arabia is north-south. The En Nala anticline forms Ghawar, the world's largest oil field, extending for more than 280 kilometers (175 miles) and up to 26 kilometers (16 miles) wide.

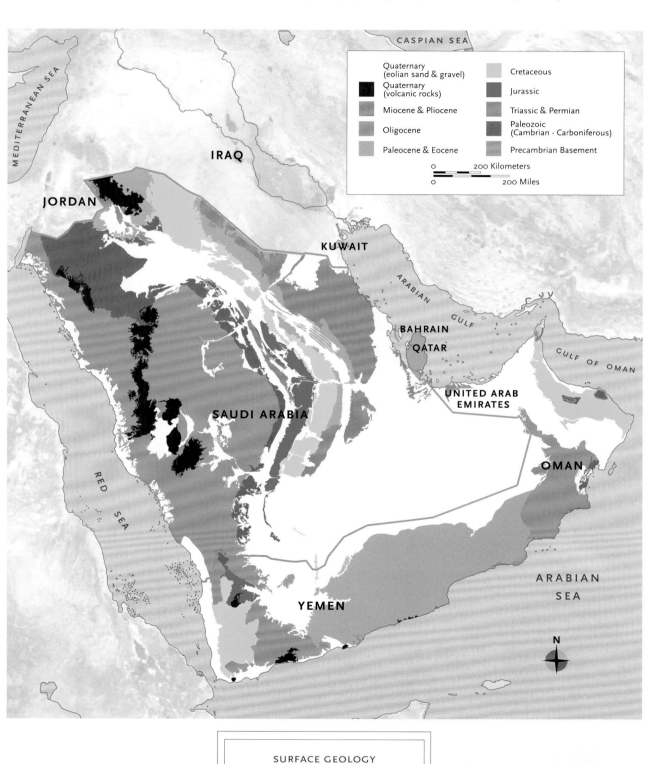

SURFACE GEOLOGY
OF THE ARABIAN PENINSULA

Les Hilyard and his Saudi crew pose at Dammam No. 7. Drilling of No. 7 as a deep test well began December 7, 1936. Fifteen months later it came in big, launching the oil industry in Saudi Arabia.

as well as his uncanny ability to navigate across unmarked terrain, that an oil field was later named after him.

Casoc sent an operations group from Bahrain to prepare for test drilling the Dammam Dome, and a community began to take shape around the site of well Dammam No. 1, where drilling began in April 1935. Infrastructure included offices, living quarters for Americans, housing for Saudi workers and a sand road to the pier at al-Khobar.

Casoc's expectations for success appeared to be realized when, as the drill bit at Dammam No. 1 reached the level where oil had been struck in Bahrain, a cable arrived at corporate headquarters in San Francisco saying oil was flowing at a rate of more than 6,500 barrels a day. The message was garbled, however, and it turned out that production was only 100 barrels daily. Even that soon turned from oil to mud and water.

Drilling of Dammam No. 2 started in February 1936. By mid-June, it was flowing at an average of 335 barrels a day and a week later—after acid treatment—it produced at a rate of 3,840 barrels a day. San Francisco was jubilant and approved four more wells in the Dammam Dome and a wildcat—an initial, speculative well—32 kilometers (20 miles) to the northwest. In July, plans were made to drill Dammam No. 7 as a deep test well into a zone that had shown gas, but little oil, in Bahrain. Disappointingly, Dammam No. 2 fizzled after a promising start, and seven more wells, including No. 7, spudded December 7, 1936, produced little or nothing.

Nevertheless, Casoc continued adding men and supplies. A community known as Dhahran (after Jabal Dhahran) was growing around the Dammam Dome. Ralph Wells, a driller hired in the spring of 1936, described landing at al-Khobar. There he boarded a balloon-tired Ford sedan, which scraped its bottom many times on the rocks of the pier before reaching shore and continuing to Dhahran. He wrote in his diary:

> Seven miles [11 kilometers] of sandy road brought us to the camp. It now consists of two bunkhouses with large rooms, a small emergency hospital, an office building with six rooms, a bosses' house of several rooms, a mess house and recreation club combined, a machine and blacksmith shop, an ice plant and a few other minor buildings. Two wells are now being drilled not far from camp. There is not a tree, bush or anything but spotted dry bunches of stiff grass anywhere.

The first two wives arrived in the spring of 1937, moving into the first air-conditioned, two-bedroom portables in Dhahran. The cottages sat on stone and sand, without a bush or grass around them. Residents could see a derrick among the distant *jabals* and a few power poles. Four more wives and the first four children in the community came in September.

Several important developments occurred around this time. Although Casoc had nothing yet to show from Saudi Arabia, its parent, Socal, had oil to sell from holdings elsewhere in the Middle East and Netherlands East Indies (now Indonesia) and needed more marketing facilities. At the same time, the Texas Company (later Texaco) had extensive marketing facilities in Africa and Asia but needed more accessible production. The companies combined their interests located between Egypt and the Hawaiian Islands in a new firm named Caltex. In 1936, this company became a half-owner of Casoc, providing additional funds for the operation in Saudi Arabia.

Meanwhile, Casoc appointed Max Steineke chief geologist in 1936. In 1937, he crossed the Arabian Peninsula in both directions, gathering information that became the basis for all future geological profiles of the country.

By this time, however, management's patience was wearing thin. Casoc had spent five years and as much as $9 million in Saudi Arabia without any return. That compared with just seven months and $650,000 that Bapco invested to discover oil in Bahrain. Dammam No. 7 was already more than 1,370 meters (4,500 feet) down, more than twice the depth of the production zone in Bahrain. There were rumors about abandoning the search for oil in the Kingdom.

In November 1937, Casoc ordered drilling halted everywhere but on Dammam No. 7. No. 7 had seen its share of troubles, including cave-ins, stuck drilling bits, lost circulation and accidents. Now Casoc was betting everything on it.

Steineke returned to San Francisco for consultations early in 1938. He spent two days with Fred Davies—called in from New York—poring over geological maps with Socal's chief geologist and the production manager. Other news complicated matters: In late February, there was word of the first oil strike in Kuwait, where a gusher at Burgan, 400 kilometers (250 miles) north of Dammam Dome, was producing oil at 1,128 meters (3,700 feet), or 305 meters (1,000 feet) *above* the level Dammam No. 7 had reached.

Davies and Steineke faced Casoc's board of directors March 2. The company had pulled out of expensive foreign wildcats before, directors said, and perhaps it should do so again. Then they put the big question to Steineke, who knew more about the Arabian Peninsula's stratigraphy than anyone else in the world: What were the prospects in Saudi Arabia? Keep drilling No. 7, he advised.

Another, possibly final, board meeting was scheduled for March 4. That very day, cabled news from Floyd Ohliger in Dhahran turned an air of unease and uncertainty into euphoria. On March 3, Dammam No. 7 had struck oil at 1,441 meters (4,727 feet) in the Arab Formation and was flowing at a rate of 1,585 barrels a day. San Francisco telegraphed its congratulations and a request for more tests. The flow of oil continued to increase, stabilizing at 3,690 barrels a day three weeks later. A barge carried the first offshore shipment of Saudi oil from al-Khobar to Bahrain on September 3, 1938, and commercial production was declared on October 16. Dammam wells No. 2 and 4 were soon deepened and they also turned out to be good producers. The Dammam oil field thus entered the books as Saudi Arabia's first commercial drilling success.

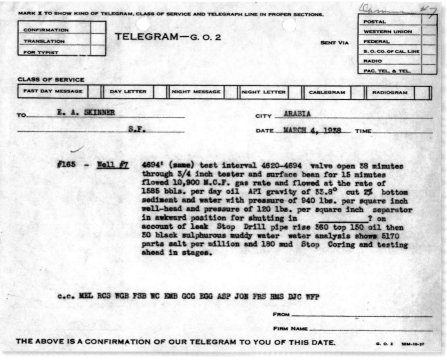

Floyd Ohliger, assistant general manager in Dhahran, on March 4 triumphantly cabled Casoc news of the oil strike at Dammam No. 7. The message announced the beginning of the oil industry in the Kingdom.

Entering the
Oil Era

WITHIN WEEKS OF THE DISCOVERY, JAPAN AND GERMANY HAD established diplomatic relations with Saudi Arabia, and their envoys were trying to buy out the concession or otherwise win the right to explore for oil in Saudi Arabia. The Japanese offered a sum of "astronomical proportions" for a concession, according to U.S. Government reports. The Germans and Italians proposed arms deals in exchange for exploration rights.

The United States had no diplomatic ties with Saudi Arabia when Casoc discovered oil. However, the fact that Americans and Saudis were already living and working together in Dhahran, the town that was growing up on the Dammam field, helped counterbalance the diplomatic contacts between Riyadh and its new oil-hungry suitors. Besides, under the terms of the concession, Casoc had preferential rights to explore for oil in other areas of the Kingdom. The company exercised those rights and, after detailed negotiations, a supplemental Concession Agreement was signed on May 31, 1939.

This supplemental agreement gave Casoc exclusive rights for 60 years to an additional 314,166 square kilometers (121,300 square miles) of territory, expanding the concession to 1,139,600 square kilometers (440,000 square miles), about the size of today's France, Germany and United Kingdom combined. In return, the company agreed to pay a bonus of £140,000 plus an additional £20,000 in yearly rental. The government reaffirmed Casoc's preferential rights and agreed not to negotiate with anyone for five years on rights in central Saudi Arabia, an area IPC had expressed an interest in exploring.

Casoc hastened to spread exploration parties over its expanded concession. Steineke's earlier investigations of the stratigraphy of the Arabian Peninsula pointed to oil else-

King 'Abd al-'Aziz takes the salute of officers of the tanker D. G. Scofield on May 1, 1939. The King had just opened a valve sending oil through a pipeline to begin loading the first oil tanker to call at Ras Tanura.

where in eastern Arabia, and work by paleontologist Richard A. Bramkamp and geologist Tom Barger in 1938 reinforced that deduction. It came at Dahl Hit, a sinkhole where they found a tar seep and the same thick anhydrite outcrop that overlay the commercial producing zone in Dammam No. 7, about 385 kilometers (240 miles) to the east. The anhydrite acted like a giant lid; its presence in both places meant oil might be found in a wide swath of the concession.

By the end of the year, Casoc had explored 453,250 square kilometers (175,000 square miles) or about 40 percent of the total concession area. About 129,500 square kilometers (50,000 square miles) of it had been mapped in detail. Test drilling was under way at Abu Hadriya, 160 kilometers (100 miles) northwest of the Dammam Dome, at Ma'aqala, about 240 kilometers (150 miles) to the southwest, and at Abqaiq, 72 kilometers (45 miles) to the southwest.

IPC went to work in the other side of the Kingdom. It obtained a 60-year concession to explore for oil in a 100-kilometer-wide band (62 miles) centered on the Red Sea shoreline. The only drilling activity was on the Farasan Islands, where the Shell Company had drilled a quarter century earlier, but no oil was found and IPC abandoned its concession in 1939.

In later years, the King enjoyed entertaining American visitors with his own tongue-in-cheek explanation about why he preferred to have Americans operate the concession. "First," he said, "you are good oilmen. You found oil in Bahrain when others said it was not there. Second, you treat Arab employees as equals. Third, yours is a big, powerful country more interested in business than political advantage. Fourth, and lastly, you are very far away!"

On September 1, 1939, just three months after the supplemental agreement was signed, Germany invaded Poland and World War II began. Work continued full steam ahead in Saudi Arabia. Casoc extracted 3.6 million barrels of oil from seven wells in the Dammam Dome in 1939, the first full year of production. The work force expanded from 635 employees to 3,641—more than 95 percent of them Saudis. At Dhahran, Saudi-American teams constructed a stabilizer plant to remove poisonous hydrogen-sulfide from the crude

A seismic crew and a shot-hole drill deploy at Abu Hadriya, about 160 kilometers (100 miles) northwest of Dhahran in 1939.

Festooned with celebratory flags, the D.G. Scofield is ready to receive Saudi oil from storage tanks visible on shore. With a capacity of 81,224 barrels, the Scofield was less than one-20th the size of a modern oil tanker.

oil, built 80 kilometers (50 miles) of pipeline, lengthened the al-Khobar pier and established a small marine terminal south of al-Khobar. They built a spare-parts storehouse and other support facilities, including a hospital, and erected a building to house the local government's police force and a jail.

Just southwest of the industrial area, a fenced-in community of prefabricated houses was home to 700 American men, women and children. A new power plant and a central plant for cooling Dhahran's houses was up and running, along with a commissary. A community of thatched dwellings called Saudi Camp mushroomed in a hollow alongside the Dhahran–al-Khobar road. Laborers who lived there walked a kilometer (half a mile) or more to work in the shops in Dhahran or at the Dammam Dome oil field. Some workers walked all the way from al-Khobar, about 10 kilometers (six miles) to the east.

After some debate, Casoc built a terminal and a small, "tea kettle" refinery with a capacity of 3,000 barrels a day at Ras Tanura, a long, low sand spit stretching out to water that was deep enough for an oil tanker to berth. A 25-centimeter (10-inch) oil pipeline linked Ras Tanura to Dhahran, some 65 kilometers (40 miles) to the south. The terminal consisted of five oil-storage tanks, a pumping station and a short submarine line to pipe oil to ships. The company shipped 2 million barrels of oil from this facility in 1939.

King 'Abd al-'Aziz himself oversaw the transfer of the first Saudi oil to a tanker that spring. In late April, the King and an entourage of nearly 2,000 people traveled from Riyadh to Dhahran in a caravan of some 500 cars. They set up a city of white tents near the Dammam Dome and spent two days feasting and inspecting company facilities. On May 1, the King and his party traveled to Ras Tanura to supervise the loading of the *D.G. Scofield*, named after the co-founder of Socal. After opening the valve through which the first tanker load of oil flowed out of Saudi Arabia to the world market, the King boarded the flag-bedecked tanker, saluted the crew and dined in the officers' mess. The royal party visited a wildcat well at Abu Hadriya on the way back to Riyadh.

The year was not without its tragedies. On July 8, 1939, Dammam Well No. 12 exploded, erupting in a spectacular fireball hot enough to melt the metal derrick. Five workers were killed. It took 10 days to extinguish the blaze, which consumed some $10 million worth of oil. The cause of the company's first major industrial accident was never established.

Almost all Saudis who came to work at the company were entering the industrial world for the first time. For many, the idea of selling their labor for a certain number of hours a day to "earn a living" was something new. Up until

Saudi employees learn to read the numbers used on indicator dials in the giant Kenworth trucks they will be driving across the desert.

then there had been no clear separation between work and non-work time; the two had blended together in the traditional way of a rural society. Most were unaware of the rules of the workplace and unfamiliar with some of the simplest industrial tools.

The turnover rate among Saudi employees reached 75 percent during the early years. Every year, in season, many Bedouins returned to their flocks and many pearl divers to their pearling boats. Men accumulated enough money to buy a goat, a sheep or a camel and left for home unannounced.

Training took place on an ad hoc basis. An unexpected side effect was that each crew of workers had, in effect, a unique language as each American supervisor developed his own way of communicating with his crew. When a Saudi employee switched job locations and bosses, he had to learn the "talk" all over again.

By 1940, Casoc was on the verge of becoming one of the major oil producers in the world, with lavish plans for expansion. There were promising signs of a big field at Abqaiq where drill stem tests showed a well flowing at

9,720 barrels a day. In addition, there was a major new discovery at Abu Hadriya. This was another "almost-missed-it" story. Well No. 1 was down to 3,050 meters (10,000 feet) without a sign of oil, and San Francisco cabled orders to suspend the Abu Hadriya operation. But the drilling crew conveniently "lost" the cable, kept going and in October 1940 struck oil at 3,083 meters (10,115 feet). The strike was particularly significant because it showed that similar deep structures in Saudi Arabia might yield oil.

That same month, World War II intruded and everything changed in Dhahran. During the night of October 19, 1940, Italian long-range bombers dropped about 80 bombs on Bapco facilities in Bahrain and two or three dozen 27-kilogram (60-pound) fragmentation bombs on Dhahran. Although there were no injuries, and repairs to a small oil flow line and water main cost only around $100, the psychological damage was considerable. Women and children began to leave almost immediately. In six months, more than half of the American men were gone, and the Saudi payroll was down by 40 percent. Italian Prime Minister Benito Mussolini apologized for the Dhahran raid, saying the only target was Bahrain where British naval ships refueled, but few people believed him.

The Axis powers clearly had their eyes on the Middle Eastern oil fields. By the summer of 1942, German troops under General Erwin Rommel were nearing Alexandria in Egypt. If Egypt fell, Rommel would have a clear path to the Arabian Peninsula. Italian troops in Ethiopia, across the Red Sea from Saudi Arabia, also posed a threat. At the same time, German forces in the Soviet Union were closing in on the huge oil fields at Baku.

As the war news worsened, Casoc pulled exploration teams from the field, closed the Dhahran stabilizer plant and shut down the new refinery at Ras Tanura. Workers built 25 air raid shelters. Plans were developed to disable oil wells and evacuate employees across the Rub' al-Khali to British bases at Aden in southern Yemen. The company kept a fleet of vehicles fueled and ready if the need arose. Ten of the 16 wells in the Dammam Dome were sealed shut, but Socal was still able to ship 12,000 to 15,000 barrels of oil a day by barge to Bahrain to fuel British naval vessels.

Just as in World War I, fuel shortages caught up with the Axis forces. Just prior to his defeat at the decisive battle of El Alamein in October 1942, Rommel wrote to his wife: "Shortage of petrol! It's enough to make one weep."

In 1942, the Casoc work force dropped to 1,766 (including 1,600 Saudis and 82 Americans), the lowest level of the war. No supply ships reached the ports serving Dhahran in the last seven months of the year. Still, the mood in the company was markedly more upbeat following the Allied victories in Africa and Russia. In Dhahran, an American named Steve Furman established a farm to provide employees with fresh vegetables, chickens, eggs and even beef, from herds driven on the hoof 1,600 kilo-

meters (1,000 miles) from Yemen by a Saudi named Mutlaq. Furman, one of the famed "100 men" who oversaw company operations during the war, built an incubator to hatch chicks; it was the first such equipment seen by Saudi farmers in the area, where a thriving poultry industry later developed.

Casoc formed the Arab Contracting Department during the war and encouraged entrepreneurial Saudi employees like Mutlaq to become contractors in the lines of work in which they had been trained. At first, pinched for spare vehicle parts, the company contracted with Bedouins to haul supplies by camel caravans. Later, it tendered contracts for construction, purchasing and food supply. The idea was to contract out support services to free employees for their main job, maintaining the oil fields.

More than one Saudi contractor who started as a laborer became a multimillionaire. Suliman Saleh Olayan was an example. He joined Aramco in 1937 as a stockman, left a decade later to form his own trucking company, and parlayed his earnings and business acumen into a New York-based conglomerate of 50 companies worth an estimated $8 billion at his death in 2002.

The war took a dramatic toll on the Kingdom's finances. With oil production at a trickle and the number of foreign pilgrims to Makkah down to just a few hundred, Saudi Arabia was once again almost broke. Casoc appealed to U.S. President Franklin D. Roosevelt for financial aid to Saudi Arabia. Without help, Casoc warned, the concession might be lost. After lengthy discussions, the administration decided not to provide any direct assistance for Saudi Arabia. Britain did, using funds allocated by the United States through the wartime Lend-Lease program. After America entered the war in 1941, however, U.S. sentiments about direct funding for Saudi Arabia changed.

In the winter of 1942-43, an acute shortage of high-octane airplane fuel curtailed a number of missions by U.S. fighter planes and bombers. Fears of an energy crisis were rife. Taking into account the concern of his Cabinet and military brass, Roosevelt first endorsed a plan for a U.S. Government purchase of a majority stake in Casoc. But that idea was dropped in the face of fierce opposition from Casoc and other U.S. oil companies.

Then, anticipating a prolonged war in the Pacific and the need to fuel it, Roosevelt in 1943 allocated scarce steel for a large, new Casoc-financed refinery and terminal project in Ras Tanura. Casoc began actively recruiting employees in the United States and Saudi Arabia, and quickly moved men and supplies to the building site. The centerpiece of the project was a 50,000-barrel-a-day refinery, a tank farm, a marine terminal and a submarine pipeline to Bahrain. Gearing up for the project, Casoc's board of directors decided to incorporate the company under a new name. On January 31, 1944, it became a Delaware-registered corporation called the Arabian American Oil Company, better known by its acronym: Aramco.

Construction of the 50,000-
barrel-a-day Ras Tanura Refinery
dominated company activities in
the immediate postwar years. To
build the refinery required more of
everything: employees, pipelines,
storage tanks, terminals, crude-oil
stabilization plants, trucks and
welding machines.

A truck convoy is loaded with pipe destined for use in building the 1,700-kilometer (1,054-mile) Trans-Arabian Pipeline, also known as Tapline. The pipeline, completed in 1950, connected the oil-handling center at Abqaiq to a tanker terminal at the Mediterranean port of Sidon, Lebanon.

Postwar
Expansion

Burgeoning global demand for oil in the years immediately following World War II fueled the first great Aramco expansion period. The other engine of the company's development would fire up later, in the form of an increasing role on the part of the Saudi Government in the operations of the enterprise.

Highlighting the growing importance of oil in world politics, U.S. President Franklin Roosevelt interrupted his return home from a World War II summit conference at Yalta to meet with King 'Abd al-'Aziz on February 14, 1945, aboard an American cruiser anchored in the Suez Canal. The meeting underscored the value Washington placed on a good relationship with the Kingdom. As the foreign affairs correspondent for *The New York Times* wrote of the meeting: "The immense oil deposits in Saudi Arabia alone make that country more important to American diplomacy than almost any other smaller nation."

No one then knew just how "immense" the Kingdom's oil deposits were, but Roosevelt was aware that a leading American geologist, Everette Lee DeGolyer, had toured the Middle East a year earlier and returned convinced that "there is enough oil in the Middle East to supply world requirements for many years to come." DeGolyer conservatively estimated Saudi Arabia's oil reserves at 5 billion barrels. However, he speculated privately that Saudi reserves could be well over 100 billion barrels, more than four times the United States' proven reserves of 23 billion barrels, the largest known cache of oil at the time. "The center of gravity of world oil production is shifting to the Middle East," DeGolyer wrote, and "is likely to continue to shift until it is firmly established in that area."

World War II ended with Japan's unconditional surrender on September 2, 1945. At that time, the United States was the world's leading oil producer, satisfying domestic

Many workers were housed in tents in busy Abqaiq, a focus of drilling activity, in 1946.

demand for products like gasoline while exporting oil, too. But by 1947 America was importing two percent of its oil requirements, and imports grew at a more or less steady rate after that. The need for reliable sources of crude oil, made clear during World War II, became a permanent driver of America's global strategic policy.

Far from declining after the war, as most experts had predicted, oil consumption skyrocketed, jumping by nearly 50 percent, from about 2.5 billion barrels in 1945 to 3.7 billion barrels in 1950. The U.S. Government lifted gasoline rationing 24 hours after the Japanese surrender and American motorists took off on a joyride. Between 1945 and 1950, the number of cars on American roads increased from 26 million to 40 million, total miles driven tripled, and gasoline prices rose from 20 cents to 29 cents per gallon, or the equivalent of about $2.25 a gallon in 2005 dollars.

In Western Europe, oil consumption rose from 830,000 barrels a year in 1948 to 3 million barrels in 1956, nearly a fourfold increase. Those figures reflected the rapid pace of European recovery under America's Marshall Plan. About 20 percent of the aid in the Marshall Plan went to imports of oil — including oil from Saudi Arabia — and oil equipment. "Without petroleum, the Marshall Plan could not have functioned," said a U.S. Government report. In Asia, oil use increased by 25 percent in the five years after World War II, with a rapidly growing Japanese economy leading the way.

Around the globe, oil was replacing coal in industrial boilers, in electrical power plants and as the preferred home-heating fuel. It was the only source of fuel for growing numbers of airplanes, cars and trucks. In 1946, world consumption of oil and natural gas combined surpassed coal for the first time, but it would be another 20 years before oil alone took over from coal as the world's leading energy source.

The years following World War II were a defining period for Aramco, the time when the company took its place among the world's major oil firms. Aramco's average daily oil production soared 25-fold, from 20,000 barrels in 1944 to more than 500,000 barrels in 1949. The company celebrated its first 1 million-barrel production month in December 1944, and its first 2 million-barrel month in September 1945.

Between 1945 and 1950, the number of producing wells increased from 24 to 80, including 44 wells in the Abqaiq area and 30 around the Dammam Dome. The company struck oil at Qatif in 1945, at 'Ain Dar in 1948 and at Haradh, 330 kilometers (235 miles) south of Qatif, in 1949, highlighting the breadth of oil deposits in eastern Saudi Arabia.

By 1949, Saudi Arabia had become the fifth largest oil-producing nation in the world and was pushing Iran to become the top oil-exporting country in the Middle East. Aramco executives calculated that the company held more oil reserves than the combined U.S. reserves of its two founding firms, Socal (later renamed Chevron) and the Texas Company (later Texaco).

Aramco had invested over $80 million in the concession, and it was apparent that millions more would be required. In November 1948, two more major oil companies — Standard Oil of New Jersey and Socony-Vacuum (later renamed Exxon and Mobil, respectively) — acquired shares in Aramco. They contributed both money and new outlets for Aramco oil, most notably in Europe. Phenomenal growth and expansion followed, the result of cooperation among four of the largest oil companies in the world. This fruitful partnership would last until the establishment of the Saudi Arabian Oil Company (Saudi Aramco) 40 years later.

Expanded ownership also led to erasure of the 1928 Red Line Agreement and an end to British dominion over much Middle East oil development. With help from the U.S. State Department, Standard Oil of New Jersey and Socony-Vacuum, both Iraq Petroleum Company members, convinced the British Government to terminate the agreement that had obligated all IPC partners to participate jointly in the development of oil in the region.

To be a world-class oil producer required world-class facilities, and Aramco set about building these at a feverish pace. Some projects had nothing to do with oil production and everything to do with promoting good will and protecting the concession. Major projects undertaken or completed by the company between 1945 and 1950 included:

• A 50,000-barrel-a-day oil refinery at Ras Tanura. Work on its two 25,000-barrel-a-day distillation plants and dozens of related facilities dominated company activities from 1944 to 1946. By 1951, the refinery was turning out a total of 160,000 barrels a day of gasoline, diesel, kerosene and fuel oil, more than three times its original capacity.

• A 55-kilometer (34-mile) submarine pipeline from al-Khobar to Bahrain capable of delivering 40,000 barrels of oil daily to the Bapco refinery. Completed in 1945, it was considered the world's longest submarine pipeline until it was revealed that the Allies

An oil rigger works in Abqaiq in 1949. His job combined the skills of a heavy-load handler and a tightrope artist.

secretly laid submarine pipelines across the English Channel to France and Belgium in 1944 to supply oil to troops in Europe.

• Al-Kharj Agricultural Project, 87 kilometers (54 miles) south of Riyadh. In the mid-1940s, Aramco engineers supervised construction of an irrigation system for a 1,215-hectare (3,000-acre) farm on behalf of the Saudi Government. Aramco also provided logistical and communications support to the project to raise crops, poultry, sheep, goats and dairy cattle.

• The Trans-Arabian Pipeline (Tapline), a 1,700-kilometer (1,054-mile) oil pipeline from the Eastern Province to Sidon, Lebanon, on the Mediterranean Sea. Begun in 1948 and completed in 1950 at a cost of about $200 million, Tapline was the world's longest pipeline and largest privately financed construction project. It ran across northern Saudi Arabia and through portions of Jordan and Syria before reaching Sidon. Tapline was shut down to Sidon in 1983; deliveries continued to Jordan until 1990.

• A 580-kilometer (360-mile) railroad linking the port of Dammam to Riyadh, via Abqaiq, Hofuf and Haradh. The line, financed, designed and built for the Saudi Government under Aramco management, opened October 20, 1951, after a ceremony in Riyadh at which King 'Abd al-'Aziz presided. In conjunction with the railroad project, Aramco designed and supervised construction of the Kingdom's first deep-water port on the Gulf coast at Dammam.

Those super-sized projects were in addition to "routine" construction projects such as an oil-gathering facility at Abqaiq, new pipelines from Abqaiq to Ras Tanura, a health center and an administration building in Dhahran, permanent masonry housing at company facilities for some 2,000 Saudi employees and 1,125 kilometers (700 miles) of improved roads.

That work could not have been completed, nor the remarkable production figures achieved, without an accompanying increase in manpower. The number of Aramco employees soared from 2,800 in 1944 to over 20,200 in 1948. During those years, the company routinely signed on more than 500 Saudi workers a month and in one peak month—October 1947—it added nearly 2,000 to the payroll. In 1945 alone, Aramco hired 10,683 new workers, an average of 890 a month.

Nearly 80 percent of the employees were Saudis, most without work experience. Assimilating so many untrained employees proved challenging. Increasingly, Aramco also looked overseas for skilled workers—not only Americans, but Indians, Pakistanis, Yemenis, Sudanese, Lebanese, Egyptians and, in 1945, nearly 2,000 Italians evacuated from Eritrea.

King 'Abd al-'Aziz paid his final visit to Aramco in January 1947, arriving at Dhahran in a fleet of six airplanes. He and his large entourage encamped in a tent city south of

Dhahran, exchanged magnificent banquets with the ruler of Bahrain and toured the new refinery at Ras Tanura. On January 25, the aging king, seated on an outdoor platform, met and chatted with about 150 American families, occasionally lifting a child into his lap. It was a memorable day for the residents of Dhahran.

Meanwhile, geologists doggedly continued exploring the concession. Up to nine specialized geological parties were in the field in a single season in the late 1940s. Saudi Arabia did not readily display its wealth. The broad, dome-like surface structures that overlay many oil fields were not apparent to the naked eye. They came to light only gradually, through painstaking surveying, structure drilling and geophysical work.

It is often said that the world's largest oil field—Ghawar—was discovered in 1949 when oil was found at Haradh. But the story of Ghawar's "discovery" spans at least nine years, starting in 1940 when a young geologist named Ernie Berg, in his second season with the company, was mapping a barren area on the edge of the Rub' al-Khali desert 320 kilometers (200 miles) southwest of Dhahran. Berg and his partner camped at a water well called 'Ain Haradh, where they were to meet their boss, Max Steineke, the next day.

Berg was enthusiastic about the map on which he was working. He had noticed that a dry riverbed, called the Wadi al-Sahba by the Bedouin, suddenly turned south for no apparent reason. He was sufficiently curious to take measurements of every rock outcrop he could find and to map the area accordingly—something not normally done on reconnaissance missions. Berg's map indicated the *wadi* was diverted by a dome, one so broad and low that it only became apparent when a large area was plotted. Steineke examined the map and concurred in its significance. It was the first sign of the huge structural uplift that later became known as the Ghawar oil field.

Exploration was suspended during World War II, and Haradh was put on the back burner while oil fields closer to Dhahran were developed. The company finally began drilling at Haradh in 1948 and struck oil the next year. This discovery, along with detailed survey mapping of the area to the north and the oil strike in the same formation a year earlier at 'Ain Dar No. 1 more than 250 kilometers (155 miles) to the north, gave geologists solid evidence of a huge geological structure. But it wasn't until 1957—after scores of probes with portable structure-drilling rigs—that the company could confirm the Ghawar field's size. Encompassing six previously discovered fields, it was about 280 kilometers long (174 miles) and up to 26 kilometers wide (16 miles). By that time, Berg had left Aramco. His former

Clockwise from far upper left: Farmers show off their harvest at the Aramco-assisted al-Kharj Agricultural Project around 1950. Two 25,000-barrel-a-day distillation plants were the heart of the Ras Tanura Refinery project, completed in 1946. Aramco designed and supervised construction of the Kingdom's first deep-water harbor at Dammam and its first railroad, linking the port to Riyadh.

partner, Tom Barger, who would become company president and CEO, wrote later that "most people had forgotten that Ernie Berg was the discoverer of the Ghawar Field."

Ghawar contained an estimated 80 billion barrels of oil. At the rate of oil consumption in 1957 (about 7 billion barrels annually) that was enough to supply the entire world with oil for about 11 years. A U.S. Government report hailed Ghawar as "the greatest commercial prize in history." But that wasn't all.

In 1951, Aramco sank the first offshore well in the Arabian Gulf: Safaniya No. 1, drilled in shallow water about 3.2 kilometers (two miles) off the coast around 225 kilometers (140 miles) north of Dhahran, near the border with Kuwait. Dick Kerr, the aviator and one of the pioneer geophysicists,

cited its oil potential as early as 1939 when he drew a red arrow at Safaniya's location on a map and wrote, "Possible high area offshore."

When put into production in 1957, the field produced 50,000 barrels of oil daily from 18 wells. Eventually, Safaniya and the offshore Khafji field, in what was then the Neutral Zone between Kuwait and Saudi Arabia, proved to be part of a single giant field with estimated reserves of 25 billion barrels of oil, the largest offshore field in the world. In 1957, another offshore giant, Manifa, was discovered with estimated reserves of 11 billion barrels. As *Oil and Gas International* magazine commented in 1962: "Superlatives and the Saudi Arabian oil industry are inseparable."

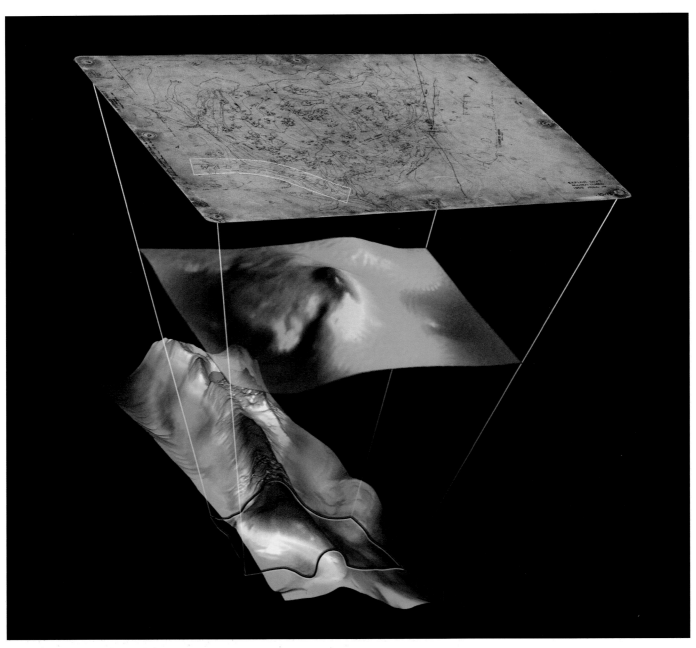

The bend in the Wadi al-Sahba, shown on geologist Ernie Berg's 1940 map (top), provided the first clue of the giant Ghawar oil field. The 3-D model of the Ghawar reservoir vividly presents the field, which lies 1,648 meters (5,000 feet) to 2,472 meters (7,500 feet) beneath the earth's surface. The colors represent depths below sea level, from red down through yellow and green. The portion of the field that Berg identified lies toward the bottom left.

A tutor helps Saudi youngsters with an English lesson in Dhahran. No Saudi employee could climb the job ladder without first learning English, the language of the company and the industry.

THE JABAL SCHOOL

Education took place on several levels at Aramco. The Jabal School opened April 8, 1944, in a converted bunkhouse on Dhahran's dusty main street. Its main purpose was to teach English, arithmetic and basic science to Saudi youngsters employed by Aramco in such jobs as office boys and telephone operators. It was also open to non-employees approved by the *amir* of the Eastern Province. The rules were difficult to enforce, however, and some students simply walked in and attended classes.

The Jabal School functioned alongside the company's "Volunteer Schools" for adults, but it differed in at least two important ways. First, it was for boys under 18, not men. Second, and perhaps most important, young employees attending the Jabal School spent two to four hours a day in class, worked the rest of the day and were paid a full day's wages. Without that extra money, many boys who were helping to support their families could not have afforded to stay in school. By contrast, Saudi employees who wished to attend "Volunteer Schools" did so after working hours, without pay.

Ali I. Al-Naimi, who rose through the company's ranks and, in 1995, became Saudi Arabia's minister of Petroleum and Mineral Resources, was an illiterate nine-year-old Bedouin boy when he walked into the Jabal School in the mid-1940s. He studied there for two years before becoming an Aramco office boy, and then went on to earn a high school diploma and university degrees on company scholarships.

"I saw this teacher—he had a huge red beard—and he was pointing to a picture behind him," Al-Naimi recalled of his first day at the Jabal School. "Everyone was shouting: 'This is a fox.' So I said, 'This is a fox.' That's how it all started."

The Jabal School began with two classrooms and 70 students, some as young as eight years old. Within a year, enrollment had doubled and the school was partitioned into four classrooms. Eventually, enrollment grew to more than 200 students with makeshift classrooms in the Accounting Office, next door to the original school, and at a palm-branch *barasti* in Saudi Camp. A similar school was opened at Ras Tanura in 1946. Along the way, new courses were added: shorthand, typing, hygiene, safety and—since there were so few schools for Saudis outside—Arabic reading and writing.

In 1949, the Dhahran and Ras Tanura schools were quietly shut down and eligible employees were absorbed into the company's new Industrial Training Centers.

Although the Jabal School only operated for five years, it occupies a special niche in company history. It is the place where some of the company's first Saudi managers and supervisors were introduced to letters and numbers. School was a new and exhilarating experience for these youngsters. As one former student put it: "We were a group of excited Saudis. This was a new adventure, a new language, a new environment, a new life!"

245

PEOPLE AND PRODUCTION

THE 1950S AND 1960S WERE REMARKABLE FOR THE SPEED OF change in the economic and social character of Aramco. These were tumultuous times in the Middle East. The partition of Palestine in 1947 had ignited a struggle that would last for decades to come; in 1951, the government of Iran nationalized the Anglo-Iranian Oil Company and its non-Iranian personnel were evacuated from the country; and the shadow of the Cold War spread into the region. Though none of these events directly involved Saudi Arabia or Aramco, everyone took notice and, inevitably, was affected.

Aramco's relationship with its Saudi employees and the Saudi Government steadily evolved and matured during this era. In 1950, the company and the government reached a new financial arrangement that gave the latter a 50 percent share in Aramco's net operating income. For the first time, the government's income was tied through Aramco to the world oil market. Until then, the government had been paid a fixed royalty per barrel of oil and changes in oil prices had no direct impact on the state's income. Two years later, in 1952, the agreement was modified to give the government a 50 percent share in the company's gross income. Under this arrangement, Aramco's payments to the government leapt from $57 million in 1949 to $170 million in 1952.

At the same time, the Kingdom began to pay special attention to the pace of Saudi development. The government placed great stress on training programs for Saudi workers and on improvements in their living and working conditions. Starting in 1950, the company dropped the term "Saudi Camp," and "senior staff"—a title given employees in the upper pay grade levels—was no longer limited to expatriates. The first three Saudis reached senior-staff status in 1950.

Then, in what it called "a significant policy change," Aramco moved its headquarters from New York to Dhahran in 1952.

The first all-Saudi GOSP operations crew began running Abqaiq GOSP 3 in 1950. A year later, Saudi crews were running three other Abqaiq-area GOSPs.

EMPLOYEES

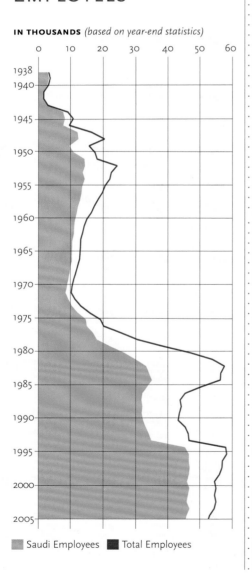

IN THOUSANDS *(based on year-end statistics)*

Saudi Employees   Total Employees

President Robert L. Keyes and Fred A. Davies, the chairman of the board of directors, took up residence in Dhahran during the year. This was the same Davies who, as a young geologist in 1931, had directed the drilling of the discovery oil well in Bahrain and had hoped for the chance to do the same a few kilometers across the Gulf on the Arabian Peninsula.

The company put the development of Saudi employees on a new footing. It kicked off the five-year Aramco Production Training Program in 1949, aiming to qualify half of the 8,000 unskilled Saudi workers for skilled and semiskilled positions. At the heart of the initiative was the "one-eighth-time training" program, so called because it required all organizations—from Exploration to Finance—to devote an hour out of each work day to training Saudis.

The program proved a remarkable success. The number of Saudis classified as journeymen (those with some basic work skills) increased from just 84 in 1949 to more than 1,100 in 1954. The number of Saudi employees at the semiskilled level (those with some technical competency) increased fourfold, from 1,600 to 6,500.

Aramco moved higher education for Saudi employees to the forefront at the same time, initiating a college scholarship program in 1951. Ten Saudi employees a year were awarded full college scholarships, covering tuition, room and board, a clothing allowance and 75 percent of their salaries while enrolled at the American University of Beirut, Aleppo College in Syria or other accredited institutions in the Middle East.

Behind those training numbers are stories of individual and collective advancement. For example, Abqaiq gas-oil separator plant (GOSP) No. 3 became the first such facility operated around-the-clock by a Saudi crew in 1950. An all-Saudi crew brought in Shedgum Well No. 12 in early 1954. In June 1955, Ibrahim al-Muhtasib from Jiddah became the first Aramco scholarship student to earn a four-year diploma when he graduated from American University of Beirut with a degree in commerce.

The term "Saudization" was fixed in the vocabulary and minds of almost all employees around this time. Everyone knew that Saudis were being trained to replace Americans and other expatriates. But the word had no specific meaning as to how many Saudis should be working and in what positions. Clarification came on January 25, 1953, when the company president, Robert L. Keyes, made it clear that Saudis were to be trained to occupy the maximum number of jobs at "all" levels.

By the early 1950s, the company's massive postwar construction program was coming to a conclusion. Oil production, treatment and transportation facilities had nearly caught up with demand. Most of the critical infrastructure—pipelines, a refinery, roads and housing—had been built. Production continued to climb, but fewer employees were needed to keep the company running.

Between 1944 and 1952, the company's oil production surged from 7.79 million barrels to 301.9 million

A Pioneer Outside the Oil Fields

Initially, Saudi communities where Aramco operated could offer almost nothing in terms of services, manufactured products or entertainment for employees and their families. The company thus had to serve as a major supplier of goods and services to its employees for some time. Aramco employees washed their clothes at company laundries. Much of the food for expatriate employees was imported and warehoused by Aramco and sold in company commissaries. Employees banked in company cash offices, com-

![school children playing outdoors]

Between 1953 and 2005, the company built, equipped and maintained 139 schools for boys and girls. Upon completion, each school was turned over to the government for operation. This school is in al-Khobar.

pany newspapers and periodicals were printed at the company print shop, and company cars were owned and maintained by Aramco.

Soon, Aramco was pioneering activities in several fields outside its core business that benefited Saudis inside and outside the company. The motivation was more than altruistic: It helped lay the foundations for future growth in the communities in which Aramco operated, and eventually across the Eastern Province, greatly strengthening the company's base of operations. The wide scope of these activities set Aramco apart from other international oil companies.

One field was home ownership. In 1950, an Aramco committee visited oil companies in Iran and Venezuela to study their approaches to employee housing. The committee developed a plan—instituted in 1951—under which Saudi employees could become owners of land made available by the government and developed by the company, and then receive long-term, company-subsidized loans to pay for construction of homes. The Home Ownership Program, which proved to be one of the company's outstanding initiatives for employees, also spurred the local construction business.

The company also mounted a technical assistance program to help local entrepreneurs get off to a good start, resulting in a number of successful business enterprises. A separate agricultural assistance program offered advice to local farmers in places like Qatif and al-Hasa. The company actively cooperated with the Ministry of Agriculture to establish an experimental farm near Hofuf and also worked to stabilize a sand-dune field that had threatened to engulf several al-Hasa villages.

Next, Aramco began building schools for the children of its Arab and Muslim employees in the Eastern Province. Under an agreement with the Saudi Government reached in 1953, the company constructed the schools and paid for their operation, while the government supplied the curriculum and teachers. This arrangement lasted for more than 50 years.

The company also became a television broadcaster. When Saudi Aramco's television station, HZ-22 TV—Channel 3—went on the air in 1957, it was the first Arabic-language channel in the Kingdom. Arabic dialogue was dubbed in, while English-speakers listened to a radio soundtrack broadcast simultaneously. The station went off the air in 1998, after a number of other channels had begun broadcasting.

In addition, Aramco undertook an aggressive program of preventive medicine, with a major emphasis on reducing industrial accidents and disease among its workers and their families. In the 1940s and '50s, the company joined with the Saudi Government to tackle the pernicious problem of malaria, with impressive results. A tuberculosis-prevention program in the 1950s and '60s achieved excellent results. In the mid-1950s, the company and the Harvard School of Public Health launched a program to study trachoma, with the aim of finding a vaccine against the blinding eye disease. Aramco donated over $1 million for trachoma research between 1955 and 1974, with significant progress in fighting the spread of the disease in the Kingdom.

The Home Ownership Program, launched in 1951, gave rise to neighborhoods of company-financed homes near major company facilities in the Eastern Province. More than 53,000 homes have been financed under the program.

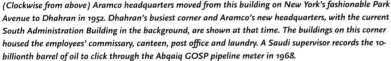

(Clockwise from above) Aramco headquarters moved from this building on New York's fashionable Park Avenue to Dhahran in 1952. Dhahran's busiest corner and Aramco's new headquarters, with the current South Administration Building in the background, are shown at that time. The buildings on this corner housed the employees' commissary, canteen, post office and laundry. A Saudi supervisor records the 10-billionth barrel of oil to click through the Abqaiq GOSP pipeline meter in 1968.

barrels a year. During the same period, the number of employees climbed from 2,800 to 24,120, a high mark that would not be reached again for another quarter-century. In 1954, production climbed to 348 million barrels, or some 953,000 barrels a day, enough to earn Aramco the title "world's largest oil producer," The Associated Press reported. The Kuwait Oil Company grabbed the title in 1955 and held it until 1971, when Aramco took the top place back — and kept it.

On the price front, crude oil stabilized in the 1950s at $2.50 a barrel. It remained in the $1.80 to $3 range — the equivalent of $18 to $25 a barrel at 2005 prices — through the 1960s.

Saudi Arabia's first commercial gas well, Dammam No. 43, went into production in December 1956. No. 43 reached

Khuff gas — gas not associated with oil — at 2,637 meters (8,650 feet). It yielded more than 12 billion standard cubic feet of gas before being shut down in September 1969.

In the mid-1950s, the training emphasis began to shift. Now, rather than turning Saudi recruits into semiskilled workers, the goal was to prepare them to acquire higher-level skills involved in producing, refining and delivering Aramco products. This took place at new facilities called Industrial Training Centers built between 1955 and 1957 in Dhahran, Ras Tanura and Abqaiq.

Saudis had already taken over a large percentage of the company's day-to-day work. For example, when a Consolidated Shops building opened in Dhahran in early 1956, it combined 15 smaller shops employing sheet metal specialists, pipe fitters, electricians, welders, and similarly skilled

The first two Saudis elected to the Aramco Board of Directors, Abdullah H. Tariki, director general of Petroleum and Mineral Affairs, and Hafiz Wahbah, ambassador-at-large (third and fourth from right, respectively), are shown at their first board meeting in October 1959 in Dhahran.

and semiskilled workers. Seventy percent of the 162 workers in the building were Saudis.

As Aramco expanded in the 1950s, so did the Saudi Government. Along with the gradual development of a modern state bureaucracy grew the notion that the government should not only receive money from the oil industry, but also have a hand in running it. The first step in this direction came in 1959 when two Saudis were elected to the company's board of directors: Abdullah H. Tariki, the director general of Petroleum and Mineral Affairs; and Hafiz Wahbah, a former ambassador of Saudi Arabia in London.

Events on the international stage now coalesced to impinge on Aramco's concession. In 1959 and again in 1960, the company and other major oil producers cut the posted price of oil without consulting their host governments. The price of oil fell from $2.12 a barrel in early 1959 to $1.84 a barrel by the mid-1960s. Oil-industry publications estimated the resulting losses to Saudi Arabia and Iraq, Kuwait and Iran, the three other major oil-producing countries in the Middle East, totaled about $235 million a year.

The oil companies argued that the cuts were the result of a surplus of oil in the world market, but the producer governments were determined to have more say in oil-production policy. In 1959, members of the Arab League organized the Arab Petroleum Congress, the first Arab forum to discuss oil-related policies. This was followed in 1960 by the creation of the Organization of Petroleum Exporting Countries, or OPEC. The founding countries were Iraq, Kuwait, Iran, Venezuela and Saudi Arabia.

251

The Ras Tanura tank farm stores millions of barrels of crude oil for delivery by tanker to terminals around the world.

New Arrangements

Between 1949 and 1972, oil consumption worldwide increased from 8.7 million barrels a day to 42 million barrels a day. Oil use in the United States shot up more than fivefold to 17 million barrels daily, but this paled in comparison with the other industrialized regions. In Western Europe, oil use increased 15-fold; in Japan it was 137 times higher than it had been in 1949. As economies and wages grew, people purchased cars, appliances and houses that relied either directly or indirectly on oil to power, heat and cool. The number of motor vehicles in the United States increased by two and a half times to 119 million; outside America, the number of vehicles soared by eight and a half times to 161 million.

Technological advances enabled refiners to transform oil and natural gas into the raw materials for new kinds of plastics that replaced traditional materials in household products and automobiles. Refiners nearly doubled the yield of gasoline, diesel, jet fuel and heating oil that could be extracted from a barrel of oil.

Coal shortages after World War II led governments across Western Europe to promote a switch to oil. Environmental factors also entered the picture. A "killer smog"—essentially a blanket of soot from coal burned in home fireplaces—enveloped London during the December 1952 holidays, contributing to an estimated 4,000 deaths. Afterward, the British Government offered grants and other encouragements for homeowners to switch from coal to oil, gas or electrical heating. A similar blanket of smog overlying the city of New York in the summer of 1965 was blamed for 12 deaths. Before long, the utility serving North America's largest city converted its power plants from coal to oil.

"King Coal" had been toppled from its throne after a century and a half as the world's leading source of energy. In 1950, coal provided 75 percent of the energy used in the Western world, compared with 23 percent for petroleum. By 1972, the figures had flip-flopped and oil provided 60 percent of the energy compared with 22 percent for coal.

Between 1960 and 1970, as oil use in non-Communist countries around the world soared by 21 million barrels per day, Aramco's oil production increased by 2.3 million barrels a day—to about 3.5 million barrels daily. In other words, Aramco's added production satisfied almost 11 percent of the increase in oil demand during that decade in what was referred to as the Free World.

The company's 1970 annual report told a familiar story: Crude oil production increased by 19 percent during the year; proven oil reserves—the largest in the world—grew by 3.3 million barrels to 88 billion barrels; and the payroll was down by nearly 400 to 10,606 employees, 80 percent of them Saudi (remarkably, nearly 80 percent of the Saudis had been with the company for 15 years or more). It was the 29th consecutive year of increases in both production and petroleum reserves, and the 18th straight year of reductions in employment. Company planners saw no reason for this pattern to change.

Aramco produced 1.29 billion barrels of oil in 1970. Almost 50 percent of the company's exported oil—or some 630 million barrels—went to Europe, 38 percent to Asia and just one percent to the United States. For the first time, the company's annual payments of taxes and royalties to the Saudi Government exceeded $1 billion and shipments of crude oil and petroleum products from Ras Tanura terminal topped 1 billion barrels.

Meanwhile, an oil revolution was at hand. The era of oil abundance, market stability and production-price controls by the so-called Seven Sisters—Chevron, Exxon, Mobil and Tex-aco (the four Aramco partners), and Shell, British Petroleum and Gulf—was coming to an end.

World oil demand had nearly caught up with production capacity. Oil industry observers estimated that in 1972 there were as few as 500,000 barrels between the demand for oil and the amount the industry could supply on any given day. The United States relied on imported oil to satisfy 14 percent of total energy consumption in 1972, up from just one percent two years earlier. By 1972, Europe depended on foreign oil for 65 percent of its requirements. Japan was 90 percent dependent.

In fact, U.S. production peaked in 1970 at 9.63 million barrels a day. During the two world wars, and in every crisis in between, America's spare capacity had been the most important element in ensuring the energy security of the Western world. Now, that spare capacity was gone, marking a sea change in the dynamics of oil and politics.

The tight supply-demand balance worked to make Saudi Arabia an ever more important player on the world stage. The Kingdom's share of Free World oil exports—all but a small portion provided by Aramco—climbed rapidly, from 11 percent in 1970 to 21 percent in 1973. Saudi Arabia replaced the United States as the swing producer on which others relied, a position the Kingdom still holds.

In reaction to events related to the fourth Arab-Israeli war, Arab members of OPEC initiated an oil embargo in October 1973 (see page 162) to the surprise and shock of the major oil importing countries. The average price of a barrel of oil quadrupled, climbing to $12 a barrel by early 1974 (equal to an increase from $13.04 to $47.05 a barrel in 2005 dollars). The increase was unprecedented. For 30 years prior to 1974, oil prices had hovered between about $2 and $4 a barrel; fluctuations of $1 or more were considered major adjustments.

Saudi Arabia became an Aramco shareholder around this time through a series of "participation" agreements.

Ahmed Zaki Yamani, the Kingdom's minister of Petroleum and Mineral Resources, put forward the theory of participation in June 1968. Its premise was that the government should share not only in the income of the company, but also in the ownership of its assets and its top-level direction. "It is inconceivable in the political and economic context of the second half of the 20th century that so important a national resource as oil, representing ... most of the country's national income, should remain under the ownership of foreign companies," Yamani explained.

On December 20, 1972, after long negotiations, participation became a reality when the major oil concessionaire companies operating in the Arabian Gulf signed a "general agreement" with their host governments. As a signatory, at the beginning of 1973 the Saudi Government acquired a 25 percent interest in

An oil tanker loads at the Ras Tanura terminal, one of more than 3,000 tankers to do so in 1970. In contrast to the tanker, the basic design of the passing dhow is centuries old.

Successful oil operations made the Kingdom the key player in the industry by the early 1970s.

The University of Petroleum and Minerals opened as a two-year college in 1965 and was renamed King Fahd University of Petroleum and Minerals in 1986. Next to company head-quarters in Dhahran, it was the first university of petroleum technology in the Middle East. Aramco released the land for the school from its concession and contributed $15 million toward the construction of a stunning new campus that opened in 1970.

Aramco's crude oil concession rights, production and pro-duction facilities. After further discussions, the government's interest increased to 60 percent at the beginning of 1974, and talks continued toward a full buyout.

Government participation in Aramco dovetailed with the opening of another period of expansion and growth. In the period from 1972-75, Ras Tanura grew into one of the larg-est oil ports in the world. Abqaiq, once targeted as a small, bachelor-only community, came to resemble a boomtown with the rapid addition of two-man trailers, prefabricated efficiency apartments and new family and bachelor housing as the company ramped up its oil-processing capacity.

The camp in 'Udhailiyah—atop the central part of the giant Ghawar oil field 125 kilometers (78 miles) southwest of Abqaiq—was taken out of mothballs and expanded to provide living space for around 1,500 employees involved in the development of facilities to inject water into the Ghawar field to ensure optimal production.

Water injection was required because—like most fields in Saudi Arabia—oil wells in Ghawar flow due to pressure exerted by gas dissolved in crude oil. Oil is not pumped out. Since not all the available oil may have been produced when this pressure decreases and the oil flow slows, water is injected as a pressure-maintenance tool.

Between 1972 and 1974, oil production climbed 70 percent to 8.2 million barrels a day. Government participation also accelerated the replacement of expatriates by Saudi work-ers. By 1974, some 5,500 Saudis were enrolled in company training programs, nearly double the number in 1972. This included nearly 300 Saudi employees attending colleges and universities in Saudi Arabia and the United States on com-pany scholarships. Aramco reported that it was operating "the largest industrial training program in the world."

Saudis began to enter top executive echelons during the 1970s. Ali I. Al-Naimi was among the first. In April 1975, he was elected to the new post of vice president, Producing and Water Injection. Among his critical jobs was maintain-ing pressure in the company's two largest oil fields, Ghawar and Abqaiq.

There was a new emphasis on programs to prepare Sau-dis for management positions and professional jobs in fields such as engineering and geology—posts heretofore filled by expatriates. Aramco already had on its doorstep one of the first universities in the Middle East to specialize in petroleum technology: the University of Petroleum and Minerals. The school was located on 600 hectares (1,500 acres) adjacent to company headquarters. During a visit by King Fahd ibn 'Abd al-'Aziz on December 25, 1986, the school was renamed King Fahd University of Petroleum and Minerals.

Far from fewer employees, as had been predicted at the start of the decade, Aramco's work force nearly doubled between 1970 and 1975 to about 19,500 people. This came as soaring worldwide demand for oil, coupled with increased oil prices, boosted Saudi Government earnings from oil sales in 1974 to $27.8 billion, 90 percent more than in 1972. The added income provided the revenue for an extraordinary government program that launched Aramco into a period of even faster and steeper growth.

In February 1975, the Saudi Government unveiled a new Five-Year Development Plan. The plan assigned top priority to construction of a multibillion-dollar, Kingdom-wide network of diversified industries. The government asked Aramco to design, develop and operate a gas-gathering and -processing system to fuel this vast new industrial network.

Like everything else in the plan, the size of the Master Gas System, or MGS, was staggering. The project's price tag was estimated at $10 billion to $15 billion and it would require more than 30,000 men to build. It would be one of the largest engineering and construction projects, if not the largest, ever taken on by an oil company. The engineering or preparation phase alone would require some 2,500 engineers and craftsmen and take nearly 200 million man-hours to complete. Aramco called the MGS, the keystone of the country's massive new development program, "the most ambitious energy project in history."

The company had been extracting NGL from oil at Abqaiq since the early 1960s, sending it by pipeline to Ras Tanura for further processing, storage in refrigerated tanks and sale locally or overseas. But the new system would capture and process virtually all gas that came to the surface with crude oil. Instead of being flared, as most had been in the past, the gas would be treated at new facilities and pipelined to industrial centers to serve as a fuel or feedstock for domestic petrochemical, fertilizer and steel industries. It would also supply the energy to power water-desalination plants and electrical generators, and provide more NGL for export. When completed in 1982, the MGS harnessed about 3.5 billion standard cubic feet of gas per day—the energy equivalent of 750,000 barrels of crude oil.

The MGS included gas-gathering facilities in four big oil fields in the Eastern Province; major gas-processing facilities in the Eastern Province and across the Kingdom on the Red Sea; and export terminals at Ju'aymah and Ras Tanura on the Arabian Gulf and Yanbu' on the opposite coast.

In 1976, the company had three of the largest construction projects anywhere going full steam ahead at the same time: the MGS; the offshore Zuluf GOSP-2, the biggest facility of its kind in the world; and the Qurayyah Seawater Treatment Plant, also the largest of its type in the world.

Aramco accepted yet another large and challenging project in August of 1976. After several months of negotiations between the company and the government, a Royal Decree created the Saudi Consolidated Electric Company

King Khalid cuts the ribbon at the official opening of the Berri Gas Plant in October 1977. Accompanying him are Minister of Petroleum and Mineral Resources Ahmed Zaki Yamani (center) and Aramco Board Chairman Frank Jungers.

At government request, Aramco created a huge new electrical power network under the name Saudi Consolidated Electric Company (SCECO). By 1982, SCECO had built about 4,800 kilometers (3,000 miles) of circuits and had a capacity of 5,800 megawatts – nearly three times larger than that of Los Angeles. SCECO became a model for similar companies in other regions of the Kingdom.

(SCECO), an entity formed by consolidating Aramco's electrical network and the bulk of the company's generating facilities with 26 small private power companies. Aramco established, operated and managed SCECO for its first five years and trained Saudis to run the company, which today is part of the national Saudi Electric Company.

One of SCECO's mandates was to provide electrical power for the industrial areas being developed at Jubail Industrial City which—along with Yanbu' on the other side of the country—would house industries fed by the MGS. SCECO was also charged to supply electricity to some 100,000 people in 200 widely scattered communities. Its original service area was about 285,000 square kilometers (110,000 square miles), roughly the size of New Zealand.

Between 1972 and 1980, daily oil production increased from 5.75 million barrels to 9.66 million barrels and the government's annual oil revenue ballooned from $2.63 billion to $89.16 billion. About 43 percent of the exported oil went to Europe, 33 percent to Asia, and 18 percent to the United States. Exports to the United States climbed to 1.73 million barrels a day, 98 percent more than in 1972.

To handle all this work, Aramco boosted the number of employees to a record 46,870, including 26,321 Saudis, in 1980. The company augmented the work force by some 20,000 men supplied by scores of local contractors.

In February 1979, Riyadh announced an agreement for full Saudi Government ownership of the company. The final agreement was signed in 1980, retroactive to 1976. The government purchased the remaining shares in Aramco from the American partners, ending the concession arrangements that began with Socal in 1933. However, Aramco continued to operate and manage the country's oil fields on the Kingdom's behalf.

Workers place sections of the 1,170-kilometer (725-mile) NGL pipeline, an integral part of the Master Gas System, on its path from the Eastern Province across the mountains of western Saudi Arabia to Yanbuʻ on the Red Sea. The pipeline – the longest and most advanced of its kind – runs parallel to the East-West Crude Oil Pipeline system, linking production and processing facilities in the Eastern Province to the west coast.

Saudi Arabia opened a new chapter in the history of the oil industry in the 1980s, culminating in the establishment of the Saudi Arabian Oil Company, or Saudi Aramco, in 1988.

BECOMING SAUDI ARAMCO

No one at Aramco in 1980 could foresee an end to the company's growth spree, or anticipate the daunting new challenges that lay just ahead.

With the outbreak of the Iran-Iraq War in 1980, the price for Saudi light crude more than doubled, climbing from $12.70 to $30 a barrel (equivalent to an increase from $29.81 to $70.42 in 2005 dollars). The Saudi Government's oil income increased by 77 percent from 1979.

Several big projects completed in the early 1980s signaled the Kingdom's determination to take its energy destiny in its own hands. In Dhahran, two sleek, seven-story office facilities—the Exploration and Petroleum Engineering Center (EXPEC) and the Engineering Building—opened in 1982. Within a few years, EXPEC, the adjacent EXPEC Computer Center (ECC) and the associated Laboratory Research and Development Center enabled the company to nearly eliminate its dependence on others for technological support in the exploration and producing arena.

The ECC consolidated advanced computer services previously performed by employees in Europe and the United States. More than 250 computer operators, programmers and technicians moved to Dhahran, forming by far the largest contingent of computer experts ever assembled by any company in Saudi Arabia. At their fingertips were advanced reservoir simulators, precision geological map plotters and the largest computers then made.

This juxtaposition of earth scientists, petroleum engineers and computer experts in EXPEC and the ECC brought major benefits. These facilities enabled experts to work together on site to find the most effective and efficient ways to discover, recover and use the Kingdom's hydrocarbon wealth. They also provided a primary point

(Above) A wide-angle lens portrays the gleaming Exploration and Petroleum Engineering Center, or EXPEC (right), and the Engineering Building, opened in 1982. The adjacent EXPEC Computer Center houses some of the most advanced equipment in the world for efficiently finding, producing and maintaining oil and gas fields. (Right) Geoscientists study computer-enhanced seismic data to determine promising drilling sites.

to transfer advanced technology to Saudi Arabia's oil and gas development program.

At the government's urging, Aramco launched a new Saudi recruiting campaign. The company sent recruiters for the first time to Saudi universities and high schools, and extended employment offers to Saudis attending colleges in the United States. The campaign was a success: Aramco hired 327 Saudi college graduates in 1980, more than the *total* number hired in the previous 20 years. Over a third of those graduates came from schools in Saudi Arabia, a sign of the progress made in developing the Kingdom's higher education system. The company also hired nearly 1,300 Saudi high school graduates in 1980, more than it had brought on board in the previous decade.

The company stepped up programs to recruit and train Saudi women. In 1980, the company, with government approval, began awarding college scholarships to talented women employees and to outstanding graduates from women's high schools.

In 1983, the company celebrated the 50th anniversary of the signing of the Concession Agreement and the start of the oil industry in Saudi Arabia. On May 16, King Fahd ibn 'Abd al-'Aziz visited Dhahran to inaugurate the flag-adorned EXPEC building. On November 8, the board of directors capped the anniversary year by electing Ali I. Al-Naimi the first Saudi president of Aramco, effective January 1, 1984.

Just a year before, Dammam Well No. 7, where Saudi and American workers exuberantly witnessed the Kingdom's first commercial oil discovery, had been shut down. The well had averaged 1,600 barrels of oil a day over its 45-year career and produced a total of 32 million barrels since that remarkable day—March 3, 1938—when it "came in big." But demand had slackened, and other wells were more profitable.

The era of record high oil prices and record expansion ended almost as suddenly as it had begun. The price of oil reached $42 a barrel in 1981 (the equivalent of $89 a barrel in 2005 dollars) before a worldwide oil surplus developed and prices plummeted. In 1982, the Kingdom's income from oil revenue dropped by $38 billion. Saudi Arabia and other OPEC countries agreed to sharp production cutbacks in a bid to stabilize prices. They succeeded—for a time. Saudi Arabian light crude sold for $34 a barrel through January 1983, but thereafter prices fell precipitously, bottoming out at under $10 a barrel in 1986.

The world was awash in oil. The soaring demand—and higher prices—of the 1970s encouraged the development of new oil resources around the world. Mexico and Libya pumped up exports, and new oil poured in from fields in the North Sea and Alaska. Egypt, Malaysia, Angola, the Soviet Union and China became significant exporters. The years of high oil prices enabled coal and nuclear power to reclaim portions of the electrical generation and industrial energy market. Oil's share of the total worldwide energy market declined from 53 percent in 1978 to 43 percent in 1985. Conservation also had an impact. By 1985, the United States was using 25 percent less oil per day than in 1973. Japan became 31 percent more energy efficient during the same period. In 1982, non-OPEC production surpassed that of OPEC. The call for OPEC oil was about 13 million barrels a day in 1982, forty-five percent below 1979 levels.

Aramco cut production from 9.66 million barrels a day in 1980 to just over 3 million barrels a day in 1985, the lowest level since 1969. Falling oil prices led to sharp reductions in the work force, particularly among expatriates. By 1985, the company had 51,500 employees, 16 percent below the peak of 61,227 workers in 1982. The company began a "phased withdrawal" of families from 'Udhailiyah in 1985 to prepare for a complete shutdown of that community. Facilities were carefully "mothballed" for future use, and the focus on Saudization of the work force continued.

It had been a great run, however: Between 1970 and peak production in 1980, the company added 27 new oil fields to the 31 fields previously discovered. Year-to-year oil production increases of 25 percent or more were common during the decade. NGL production rose from 52,118 barrels a day in 1970 to nearly 450,000 barrels daily in 1981, before declining in tandem with crude oil output.

On November 8, 1988, one era ended and another era began. On that date Aramco ceased to be the producing agent for Saudi oil. In a meeting at Riyadh that evening, the Council of Ministers approved a charter for a new national oil enterprise—the Saudi Arabian Oil Company. A Royal Decree issued by King Fahd ratified that decision, establishing a new company that took over all the responsibilities of Aramco.

The new charter seemed little more than a technicality since, as a practical matter, the Saudi Government gained control of Aramco in 1980 when it purchased, retroactive to 1976, substantially all of the assets of the company from its American shareholders. For most people, it meant only that the company had a new name—in common parlance Saudi Aramco instead of Aramco. Yet it heralded momentous strategic change for the enterprise.

The change had been presaged seven months earlier, in April 1988, when John J. Kelberer, the last American board chairman and CEO of Aramco, stepped down, turning over the helm to new Saudi leadership. Minister of Petroleum and Mineral Resources Hisham M. Nazer was named chairman of Aramco's board of directors, and Aramco President Ali I. Al-Naimi assumed the additional title of CEO. Executive Vice President Nassir M. Al-Ajmi was next in the chain of com-

King Fahd inaugurates Aramco's Training Center in Ras Tanura in 1984. The huge facility included 57 classrooms and 41 shops. To the King's left is Minister of Petroleum and Mineral Resources Hisham M. Nazer and to his right are John J. Kelberer, Aramco CEO, and Ali I. Al-Naimi, president.

Traders bid, or ponder their next move, in the oil futures' pit of the New York Mercantile Exchange.

NYMEX TRADING

On March, 30, 1983, the New York Mercantile Exchange (NYMEX) began trading crude oil on its commodities market. For years oil prices had been pegged to a number set by a handful of major producers. Now oil prices increasingly depended on minute-by-minute transactions between hundreds of traders and speculators in the volatile commodities arena. Oil was bought and sold at either spot prices—that is, for immediate delivery—or as futures, meaning delivery in a month or more. At the end of 1983, more than half of internationally traded crude oil was sold in the spot market or sold at prices keyed to the market. In 1986, Saudi Arabia linked its oil price to the spot market. Today, Saudi oil prices are tied to spot markets in the United States, Dubai and Oman, and to Brent futures contracts in Europe.

mand, followed by five senior vice presidents, all of them Saudis. Kelberer remained on the board of directors and served as its vice chairman until his retirement a year later.

The passage from Aramco to Saudi Aramco could hardly have been smoother. Kelberer and Al-Naimi discussed the arrangements during a quiet dinner in Dhahran at Hamilton House, the Cape Cod-style visitor's lodge named after Lloyd Hamilton, the Socal lawyer who negotiated the original Concession Agreement in 1933. The changeover was announced in an open letter from Al-Naimi to employees in mid-November 1988. It read, in part:

"The most important asset that Saudi Aramco will have upon assuming its responsibilities will be the human resources of the current work force, its depth of experience, its technical competence and its loyalty.... Working together, we can preserve the many Aramco accomplishments of the past, ensure the success of Saudi Aramco and continue to contribute to the future prosperity of the Kingdom."

The Saudi Aramco Board of Directors held its inaugural meeting March 14, 1989. For the first time since the beginning of the oil enterprise in the Kingdom, the board met without the presence of the American firms that were the former partners in the concession.

In the past, the company had been primarily concerned with exploration and producing. Under its new leadership, Saudi Aramco began to expand into an integrated energy company, engaged in every aspect of the industry, from exploration to delivery and sale of petroleum products to customers in the Kingdom and around the world. In rapid order the company:

- Enlarged exploration activities, previously limited to the eastern part of the country, to cover about two-thirds of the Kingdom, an area almost as large as Germany, France and Spain combined.
- Moved into the downstream oil business overseas when a subsidiary, Saudi Refining Inc. (SRI), signed a joint venture with Texaco to create Star Enterprise to refine, distribute and market petroleum products under the Texaco trademark in the eastern and southeastern United States.
- Took over direct marketing of gas and crude oil in Saudi Arabia.
- Undertook a multibillion-dollar program to restore production capacity to 10 million barrels of oil a day. This called for reactivation of facilities mothballed earlier in the decade, construction of new facilities, significant upgrades of existing facilities and the addition of a substantial number of employees.

The changes soon began paying off. Saudi Aramco discovered high-value Arabian Super Light crude oil and gas at al-Hawtah in central Saudi Arabia, south of Riyadh, in 1989—only a year after operations began in the area. It was the first of 42 oil and gas discoveries that would be made in central Saudi Arabia and elsewhere over the next 16 years.

Star Enterprise, launched with Texaco, Inc. in 1989, included three refineries, around 50 product-distribution terminals and 11,000 Texaco-branded service stations in 23 eastern and Gulf Coast states. It was the first of several major refining-and-marketing joint ventures for Saudi Aramco around the globe.

These included discoveries of hydrocarbons in the northwest region of the Kingdom. Exploration between 1991 and 1993 revealed gas fields in the Jawf basin, in the Midyan region near the Gulf of Aqaba and the Umluj area, about 150 kilometers (95 miles) north of Yanbu'.

Oil prices had begun creeping up in the latter half of the 1980s. In 1987, prices climbed by more than $4 a barrel, ending a five-year downward spiral, and in 1988 Saudi Aramco increased oil production to 4.93 million barrels per day, the most in six years. Oil prices, which had fluctuated between $15 and $18 a barrel, shot up to more than $40 a barrel after Iraq invaded Kuwait in August of 1990.

To help stabilize prices, Saudi Aramco ramped up its program to restore production that had been shut down a few years earlier. The company increased oil output by more than 60 percent to 8.5 million barrels a day during the last five months of 1990. That made up for about 75 percent of the 4.6 million barrels a day in oil exports lost due to an international embargo on sales from Iraq and occupied Kuwait. Prices quickly fell back to the $20 level.

Saudi Aramco dramatically extended its international reach in the 1990s. In 1991, the company purchased a 35 percent interest in SsangYong Oil Refining Company (now S-Oil Corp.) in the Republic of Korea. S-Oil Corp. markets petroleum products throughout that country and exports refined petroleum products to Japan and other Pacific Rim

nations. In 1994, Saudi Aramco purchased a 40 percent interest in Petron Corporation, the largest refining-and-marketing company in the Philippines. From 1996 to 2005, the company participated in a refining-and-marketing joint venture with Motor Oil (Hellas) Corinth Refineries and its affiliate Avinoil in Greece.

In the United States, SRI, Saudi Aramco's partner with Texaco in Star Enterprise, linked up in a new joint venture with Texaco and Shell in 1998 to establish Motiva Enterprises LLC. This company combined the strength of Star Enterprise with Shell's marketing advantages in the eastern and Gulf Coast regions of America. SRI and Shell became 50-50 partners in Motiva in 2002 after Texaco's merger with Chevron.

Saudi Aramco invested millions of dollars in very large crude carriers (VLCCs) during the 1990s through its subsidiary Vela International Marine Limited, gaining the capability to deliver a significant portion of its exports to depots around the world. Vela took delivery of 15 new VLCCs—two in 1993, 10 in 1994 and the remainder in early 1995. By 2004, the Vela fleet numbered some 70 company-owned and chartered tankers, most of them in the VLCC category. These included four new double-hulled supertankers, each capable of carrying 2 million barrels of oil. This fleet delivers about one-third of Saudi Aramco's daily production.

In June 1993, the government merged the Saudi Arabian Marketing & Refining Company, or Samarec, into Saudi

HISTORY OF THE CONCESSION AREA

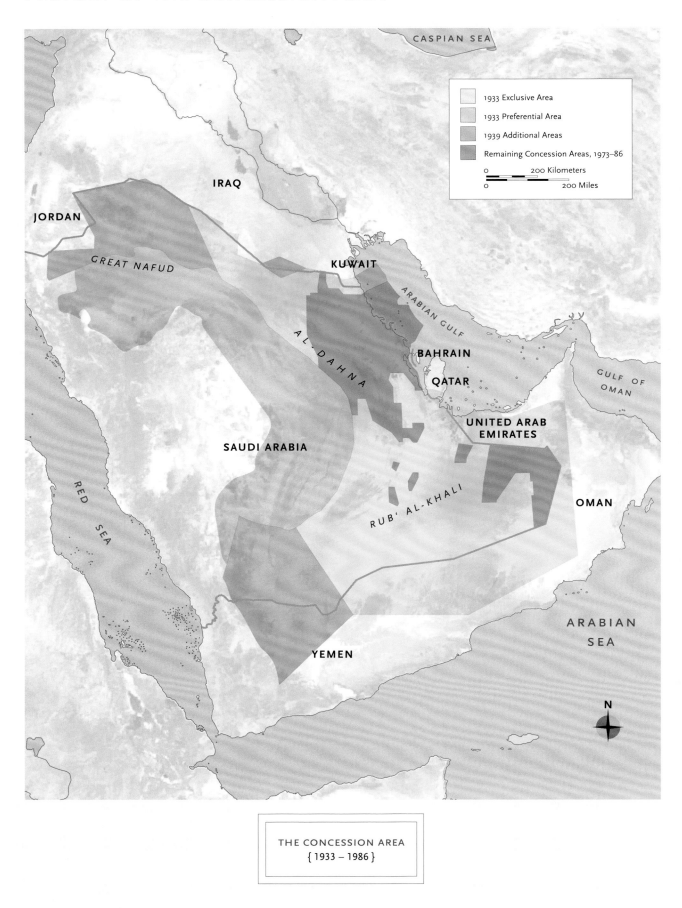

Legend:
- 1933 Exclusive Area
- 1933 Preferential Area
- 1939 Additional Areas
- Remaining Concession Areas, 1973–86

0 — 200 Kilometers
0 — 200 Miles

CASPIAN SEA

IRAQ

JORDAN

GREAT NAFUD

KUWAIT

ARABIAN GULF

AL-DAHNA

BAHRAIN

QATAR

GULF OF OMAN

UNITED ARAB EMIRATES

SAUDI ARABIA

RUB' AL-KHALI

OMAN

RED SEA

ARABIAN SEA

YEMEN

N

THE CONCESSION AREA
{ 1933 – 1986 }

The concession area granted to Socal by the Saudi Government in 1933 (left) consisted of an exclusive area covering all of eastern Saudi Arabia as far as the westerly edge of the Dahna, and a further area of preferential rights extending west as far as "the contact between the sedimentary and igneous formations." In 1939, the concession was extended to include areas in the far northwest and southwest of the Kingdom, as well as Saudi Arabia's interests in two Neutral Zones to the northeast. The concession area was reduced by subsequent relinquishments until, in 1973, it consisted of six separate "retained areas" covering a total of 220,000 square kilometers (84,950 square miles).

In 1986, Aramco was reassigned oil exploration rights to all of the territory of the original concession and its supplemental areas within the Kingdom's modern boundaries (below). In 1990, the Red Sea coastal strip with adjacent waters was added to the prospective area. This gave the company exploration responsibility for all parts of the Kingdom which have sedimentary rock strata and which thus could potentially hold hydrocarbons. The company's operations now extend Kingdom-wide. (See the Saudi Aramco operations map on page 275.)

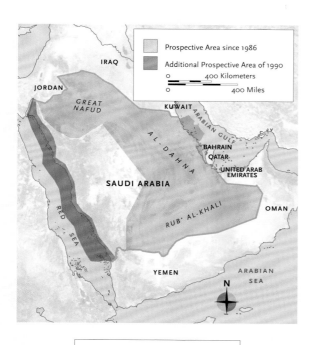

PROSPECTIVE AREAS
{ 1986 – PRESENT }

Aramco. Headquartered in Jiddah, Samarec was responsible for domestic refining, international product marketing and the distribution of petroleum products throughout the Kingdom. Its facilities included refineries at Jiddah, Riyadh and Yanbuʻ, and joint-venture shares of three other refineries: at Jubail with Shell and across the Kingdom at Yanbuʻ with Mobil and at Rabigh with Greece's Petrola (the latter now a wholly owned Saudi Aramco facility). Saudi Aramco also absorbed Samarec's Kingdom-wide network of storage facilities and airport refueling units and its international marketing system, with offices in London, Tokyo, Singapore and New York. The company offered all Samarec employees transfers to Saudi Aramco and nearly 10,000 of the 11,500 workers made the move. This boosted Saudi Aramco's payroll almost overnight to more than 57,000 employees, about 85 percent of them Saudi.

In 1994 the company completed work to restore its sustained production capacity to the 1980 level: 10 million barrels a day. This involved a series of onshore and offshore oil and gas projects in the Eastern Province, as well as expansion of the strategic East-West Crude Oil Pipeline system and the Yanbuʻ Crude Oil Export Terminal.

In the mid-1990s, the company initiated three multi-billion-dollar projects that highlighted its intention to maintain its record as a reliable energy supplier: development of the Shaybah oil field deep in the Rubʻ al-Khali desert, and construction of the company's first two gas plants to process exclusively non-associated natural gas—gas found independent of oil.

These projects went ahead even in the face of low oil prices. The Shaybah development project proved particularly important when oil prices began to climb sharply early in the next decade, giving the Kingdom the added capacity to help meet fast-rising demand.

Crude oil at Shaybah is "extra light," making it especially valuable for export and for blending (and thus lightening) heavier crude oils. The lighter the crude, the easier it is to refine into premium transportation fuels. As of 2005, Shaybah's remaining reserves were estimated at 17.6 billion barrels of oil and 30 trillion standard cubic feet of gas. The field's initial designed production rate was 500,000 barrels a day.

Shaybah was unique not only due to the huge amount of materials and effort that went into development of the remote site, but because the team in charge of the task was 90 percent Saudi. In the past, expatriate professionals had handled such major projects. Shaybah was a breakthrough. It was the "pinnacle of Saudization," the company said.

The Shaybah development project was completed in 1998, a year ahead of the original schedule and at a cost of $1.7 billion—$800 million under budget. The field is linked by pipeline to facilities at Abqaiq some 640 kilometers (395 miles) to the north, where its crude oil production is stabilized and blended with crude from other fields for export.

The Central Producing Facility in the Shaybah field is nestled among dune mountains deep in the Rub' al-Khali. The field produces 500,000 barrels per day of Arabian Extra Light crude oil, the equivalent of the daily energy requirement of more than 10 million households.

(Above) The work force at Shaybah in the Empty Quarter numbers 750 men. Operators inside and outside the control room handle duties around the clock. (Below) A 640-kilometer (400-mile) pipeline, shown under construction in 1997, carries premium Arabian Extra Light crude oil from Shaybah to Abqaiq. There, it is stabilized and blended with other Arabian Extra Light production, and sent on for export from terminals at Ras Tanura or Ju'aymah on the Gulf.

A NEW CENTURY

NOWHERE HAS THE POWER OF OIL AND GAS TO CHANGE A SOCI-ety been more spectacularly shown than in Saudi Arabia. In the span of a single lifetime, petroleum transformed the Kingdom from a materially impoverished, isolated land into one of the 25 richest and most influential nations in the world.

At the beginning of the 21st century, Saudi Arabia made two significant changes in response to evolving energy conditions in the Kingdom and around the world. First, in 2000, the government moved to streamline energy deci-sion-making at the highest level by creating the Supreme Council for Petroleum and Mineral Affairs to oversee Saudi Arabia's general energy strategy. The new government body replaced the Supreme Council of the Saudi Arabian Oil Company. That same year, for the first time, the Kingdom invited major foreign oil companies to bid on gas explora-tion and development projects inside Saudi Arabia.

In 2003, Saudi Aramco signed a deal with Royal Dutch/ Shell and France's Total for gas exploration, development and production on more than 200,000 square kilometers (77,200 square miles) of the southeastern Rub' al-Khali. Shell holds a 40 percent stake in the South Rub' al-Khali Company Limited (SRAK), and Total and Saudi Aramco have 30 percent each. Minister of Petroleum and Mineral Resources Ali I. Al-Naimi called the historic deal "an impor-tant step and strong beginning in the area of global invest-ment in gas exploration and production."

The company's gas-exploration partnerships expanded the next year, when Russia's Lukoil, China's Sinopec and a consortium of Italy's Eni and Spain's Repsol YPF received licenses to explore for and produce non-associated gas in the northern Rub' al-Khali. Saudi Aramco has a 20 percent inter-est in each of the three ventures—Lukoil Saudi Arabia Energy Limited, Sino Saudi Gas Limited and EniRepSa, respectively. Lukoil Saudi Arabia is exploring in a 30,000-square-kilo-meter area (11,600 square miles) just south of the Ghawar

271

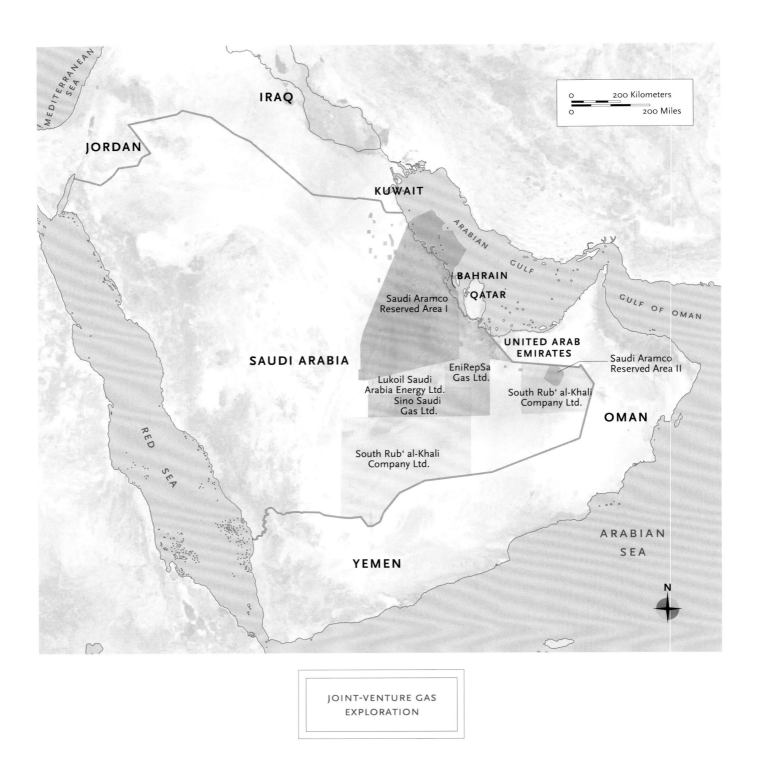

oil field, while Sino Saudi's territory covers 39,000 square kilometers (15,600 square miles) and EniRepSa encompasses 52,000 square kilometers (20,100 square miles).

The projects will take years to complete, but when work is finished some 60 percent of the Rub' al-Khali will have been scoured for hydrocarbons. Under the agreements, Saudi Aramco will take over and develop any oil and associated gas discoveries made by the foreign companies. All non-associated gas will be sold to Saudi Aramco.

This work began at a critical time. Gas consumption in the Kingdom rose from 3.1 billion standard cubic feet a day in 1998 to more than 9 billion standard cubic feet daily in 2005—meaning that Saudi Arabia had become the largest per capita consumer of gas in the world. Demand is expected to nearly double by 2012.

The gas-exploration initiative is one facet of the company's multi-pronged Gas Program, which centers on the Master Gas System. Initially, the MGS processed only the gas produced in association with crude oil. In 1984, the system was enlarged to gather non-associated gas. This was a boon to the Kingdom's industries because the supply of non-associated gas did not depend [CONTINUED ON PAGE 279]

ENVIRONMENTAL ACCOUNTABILITY

Saudi Aramco invests millions of dollars annually in environmental activities. "Environmental accountability today stands as one of the most important measures of a company," Saudi Aramco's president and CEO has said. "If an organization is not active in safeguarding the earth's natural resources, its best efforts in all other business areas are diminished."

Saudi Aramco has mapped out global oil spill contingency plans to deal with potential spills from its fleet of supertankers. It has developed regional and global plans to respond to any spill of crude or other oil products on land. Saudi Aramco's Environmental Protection Program covers its operations across the Kingdom, and includes everything from refinery maintenance to fire drills, and safety inspections to driver training. Every plant and tanker has an emergency response plan and highly trained emergency response teams.

Saudi Aramco finances marine studies by the Research Institute of King Fahd University of Petroleum and Minerals in Dhahran, including a Bio-accumulation Monitoring Program to assess the impact of hydrocarbons and heavy metals on clams, oysters and other marine creatures. The company has built water-treatment plants to remove oily contaminants in water discharged into the Arabian Gulf, and it has helped replant mangrove thickets that once lined Gulf inlets, providing a haven for small marine creatures. Two old Marine Department vessels were carefully scuttled in 1999 and 2004 to provide new habitat for marine life on the generally featureless Arabian Gulf floor.

Saudi Aramco's environmental record goes back more than four decades to the 1960s and development of the Kingdom's first environmental protection plan, intended to monitor and control the quality of the air, groundwater, land and marine environment in areas of company operations.

In the 1970s, the company became the first organization in the Kingdom to monitor air quality. The construction of the Master Gas System, or MGS, starting in the late 1970s is one of the most vivid examples of how conservation, environmental protection and economic growth can go hand in hand. Before the MGS, gas produced with oil was flared into the atmosphere from hundreds of wells. When the MGS began operation in the early 1980s, this gas was collected and sold as fuel for local industries and electrical generating stations, or as feedstock for new industries, instead of being flared. In addition, the company extracts millions of metric tons of raw sulfur annually from associated gas — which has significantly reduced air pollution from the release of sulfur dioxide into the environment. Now the sulfur is exported for use in industry and agriculture around the world.

Today, according to the Saudi Government, air pollution in the Kingdom's cities is the lowest in the Middle East. Saudi Aramco operates 10 air-quality-monitoring and meteorology stations to ensure that its facilities continue to meet national and company air-quality standards.

Aramco developed its first oil-spill response plan in 1980. In 1991, the company organized a massive effort to recover more

Crewmen on a vessel off Rabigh on the Red Sea practice deploying yellow booms that would be used to corral floating oil for cleanup in the event of a spill.

than 1 million barrels of oil released into the Arabian Gulf by Iraqi troops during the Gulf War — the most oil ever collected from a spill. That same year the company, concerned about air pollution, cut the percentage of lead in the gasoline it produced by 50 percent. In 2001, Saudi Aramco became the first company in the Middle East to produce and sell only unleaded gasoline.

Each of these steps served as an example to the public and other industries in the region, as well as a possible blueprint for the government's environmental regulations. Saudi Aramco's environmental protection policy is a clear statement of the company's concern for clean water, air and land: "The company will assure that its operations do not create undue risks to the environment or public health, and will conduct its operations with full concern for the protection of the land, air and water from harmful pollution. The company will promote environmentally sound waste-disposal practices and cost-effective waste minimization through source reduction, reuse and recycling." Saudi Aramco favors cooperative efforts to improve the environmental performance of oil, involving technology developers, national laboratories, academic institutions and related industrial sectors, such as automobile and electric-power-equipment manufacturers.

At Saudi Aramco's new Research and Development Center in Dhahran, scientists are working to improve petroleum's environmental performance. At the same time, the company has identified several more strategic technology areas for the industry. One entails the production of ultra-clean fuels from crude oil that contains sulfur, using innovative and cost-effective technologies. A second involves economically managing the issue of greenhouse gas emissions, going beyond carbon sequestration. Another is devising technically and economically viable ways of reforming oil to produce hydrogen. The aim is to develop cleaner-burning fuels, new generations of higher-efficiency, lower-emission engines and more environmentally friendly oil-use technologies to help secure the world's energy future.

OIL AND GAS OPERATIONS

Saudi Aramco's oil and gas operations are divided geographically into two areas. Southern area oil operations, which includes the world's largest oil field—Ghawar—are administered from Abqaiq, a major processing center for crude oil and natural gas liquids (NGL) located about 65 kilometers (40 miles) southwest of Dhahran. Southern area gas operations, which include the company's largest gas plants, are directed from 'Udhailiyah, 125 kilometers (78 miles) southwest of Abqaiq. Oil and gas fields in the central region, south of Riyadh, are attached administratively to the southern area.

Northern area gas and oil operations are administered from Ras Tanura, site of the company's largest refinery. The refinery complex, about 65 kilometers (40 miles) north of Dhahran, includes marine terminals for both oil and liquefied petroleum gas (LPG).

The Operations Coordination Center in Dhahran is the hub of the company's enormous, around-the-clock energy supply effort serving customers in the Kingdom and around the globe.

Crude oil from the largest fields in the southern area is piped from gas-oil separator plants (GOSPs) to Abqaiq for further processing. Most of the crude oil from GOSPs in the northern fields goes to Ras Tanura. Oil and gas from central Arabia are sent west for export at Yanbu' on the Red Sea via the transpeninsular East-West Pipeline system. Where compression facilities have been added to a GOSP, "raw" gas condensate—composed of all the readily condensable hydrocarbons present in the separated gases and some impurities such as hydrogen sulfide—is piped downstream for processing.

Saudi Aramco operates nearly 20,000 kilometers (12,500 miles) of pipelines to carry oil, gas, gas condensates or refined products. Crude oil leaving GOSPs, with the exception of that from the offshore Safaniya and Zuluf fields in the north, the central Arabia fields and the Shaybah field in the Rub' al-Khali, is sour. It contains hydrogen sulfide, which in gaseous form is poisonous and when dissolved in water forms a highly corrosive acid. Sour crude can be shipped by pipeline. It can also be used as refinery feedstock, when the hydrogen sulfide is removed as part of the refinery operation. However, it must be "sweetened" before it can be transported by tanker. This is done in a process called stabilization, in which the hydrogen sulfide gas is boiled off.

Sour crude from the southern area is stabilized at Abqaiq, which handles nearly 70 percent of all crude produced by Saudi Aramco. The portion of the northern area crude that requires stabilization is processed at Ras Tanura. First, however, a final stage of separation brings the crude from the pressure of 3.5 bars (50 pounds per square inch) at which it leaves most GOSPs down almost to atmospheric pressure. This is accomplished in

large spherical vessels called spheroids, in which most of the remaining dissolved gases are released.

Spheroid gas separated from crude during the stabilization process and gas piped from the GOSPs can be compressed and then cooled and liquefied to recover additional natural gas condensate. The condensate is then fed into "stripper" columns to remove the light gases such as ethane and methane, as well as hydrogen sulfide. The natural gas condensate, now in the form of stabilized NGL, is mixed with the NGL recovered from the gas in the gas plants and sent by pipeline to fractionation facilities.

Saudi Aramco has two wholly owned and five joint-venture refineries in the Kingdom. The largest is the 550,000-barrel-a-day Ras Tanura Refinery. Refineries consist of a number of plants that break oil down into such products as jet fuel, gasoline, kerosene, naphtha and diesel oil. Other plants remove the last traces of sulfur compounds from stabilized NGL and fractionate it into ethane gas and three main liquid components. The two lightest liquids, propane and butane, are commonly referred to as LPG. The third NGL product is natural gasoline.

Crude oil and products can be shipped from the marine terminal at Ras Tanura, with its two loading piers and four offshore Sea Islands, which provide berths for vessels of up to 500,000 deadweight tons. A terminal at Ju'aymah, northwest of Ras Tanura, can load the largest crude carriers now in service from moorings in deep water 11 kilometers (seven miles) out in the Gulf. Large storage tanks at both terminals provide loading flexibility. The crude tank farm at Ju'aymah holds 25 million barrels, while the tank farm at Ras Tanura stores over 30 million barrels of crude and products—more than five times the daily oil production of the United States. The crude oil export terminal at Yanbu' provides alternative outlets to Western markets. The terminal has the capacity to ship 4.2 million barrels of oil a day. Smaller terminals meet the coastal shipping needs of the Rabigh and Jiddah refineries.

All of the oil operations, from wellhead to terminal, are links in a long and intricate chain, with each operation dependent on many others. A change in reservoir pressure, the shut-down of a processing unit for maintenance or modification, an emergency of some kind, fluctuating requirements for various grades of crude or different products, or even a few days of unusual weather can affect production planning and ship scheduling. These factors and more are constantly balanced at the Operations Coordination Center in Dhahran, which monitors virtually every aspect of Saudi Aramco's oil, gas, NGL and electric power operations.

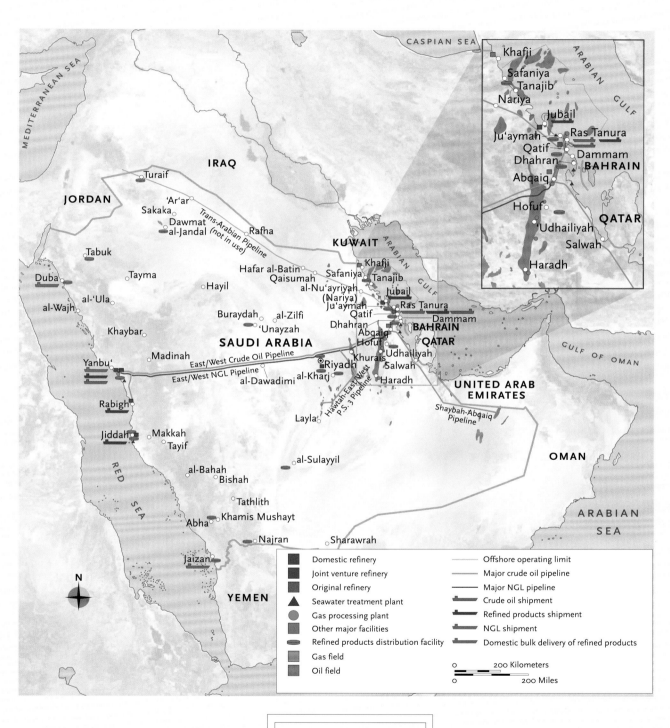

SAUDI ARAMCO
OPERATIONS

OIL OPERATIONS

The crude oil produced by Saudi Aramco from both onshore and offshore fields first goes to gas-oil separator plants for removal of gases, after which it is sent for further processing at stabilizers or refineries. Most of the crude oil is delivered to tankers at Ras Tanura, Ju'aymah or Yanbu'. Saudi Aramco also delivers crude oil within Saudi Arabia for use as a fuel to feed refineries turning out products for domestic use and export. See map of Saudi Aramco operations on page 275.

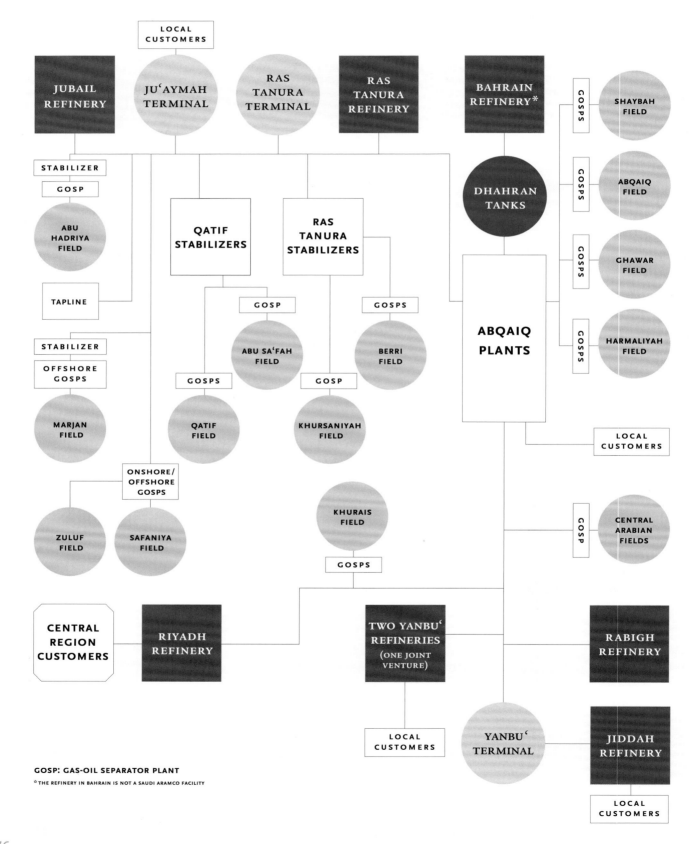

GOSP: GAS-OIL SEPARATOR PLANT

* THE REFINERY IN BAHRAIN IS NOT A SAUDI ARAMCO FACILITY

GAS OPERATIONS

Gas produced with crude oil is collected at gas-oil separator plants. There, impurities are removed, hydrogen sulfide is recovered for conversion into elemental sulfur, and sweet, dry gas is extracted for use as an industrial fuel or feedstock. From gas-processing centers at Shedgum and 'Uthmaniyah, natural gas liquids (NGL) and ethane are piped to plants at Yanbu' and Ju'aymah for fractionation into their separate components. After removal of the ethane, the NGL is further fractionated into LPG (propane and butane) and natural gasoline. Gas produced independently of crude oil is processed at the Haradh and Hawiyah gas plants for delivery into the sales gas system. NGL from the Berri Gas Plant goes to Ju'aymah or Ras Tanura for fractionation. LPG is exported from Yanbu', Ju'aymah and Ras Tanura. In the fractionation plants, ethane is produced in gaseous form for use as a petrochemical feedstock in the industrial complexes at Yanbu' and Jubail. Some butane is used as a feedstock at the Jubail Industrial Complex.

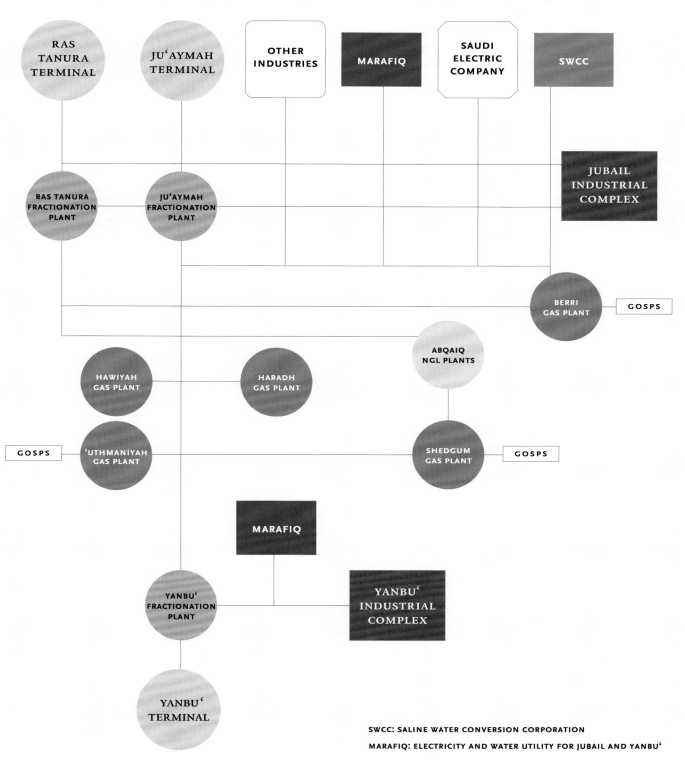

SWCC: SALINE WATER CONVERSION CORPORATION

MARAFIQ: ELECTRICITY AND WATER UTILITY FOR JUBAIL AND YANBU'

The huge Haradh Gas Plant, shown here, and a sister facility at Hawiyah are the latest additions to the Kingdom-wide Master Gas System. Both plants process non-associated gas, which is produced independently of crude oil and is a significant component of the Kingdom's energy supply.

[CONTINUED FROM PAGE 272] on fluctuating crude oil production. Tapping these gas reserves meant domestic utilities that provided power for industries and homes could switch from crude oil to cleaner-burning gas, freeing more-valuable crude oil for export.

The addition of two giant facilities to the MGS, the Hawiyah Gas Plant in 2001 and the Haradh Gas Plant in 2003, more than doubled its capacity, to 9.4 billion standard cubic feet a day. As with the Shaybah mega-project, the Hawiyah and Haradh project teams were almost entirely Saudi. Both new plants handle non-associated gas. Today, the MGS adds the equivalent of more than 1.3 million barrels of oil a day to the world energy supply.

Industries using gas produced by Saudi Aramco accounted for some 15 percent of the Kingdom's total GDP in 2003, providing nearly 40,000 jobs. NGL processed and distributed by the expanded MGS provides feedstock to industries that produce more than 50 petrochemical products and rack up international sales of some $10 billion a year.

Between 1999 and 2004, electrical power generated by gas-powered plants in the Kingdom shot up by about 15 percent—to about 40 percent of the total generated. Saudi Arabia's Industry and Electricity Ministry believes the country will need an additional 20 gigawatts of electrical power by 2019, nearly double the 2004 generating capacity. The vast majority of this increase will come from natural gas-fired turbines or cogeneration plants, in line with the government's plans to expand gas utilization and free more oil for export. Cogeneration plants use technology borrowed from jet engines to produce steam and electricity from power-station exhaust that is otherwise wasted.

GLOBAL REACH

ANOTHER KEY FOCUS FOR SAUDI ARAMCO IS TO MEET THE needs of rapidly growing markets in Asia and the Far East, the destination for nearly half of the company's oil exports in 2005, while continuing to be a dependable supplier to traditional customers in North America and Europe. Saudi Aramco was the largest exporter of oil that year to China, India, Japan, the Republic of Korea and Taiwan. The company was the third largest oil supplier to the United States, behind Canada and Mexico.

Company subsidiaries Saudi Petroleum Overseas Co. Ltd. in London; Saudi Petroleum International, Inc. in New York; and Saudi Petroleum Ltd., with offices in Tokyo, Beijing and Singapore, market crude oil, LPG, refined products and sulfur. The company's overseas support subsidiaries are Aramco Services Company in Houston, Texas, and Aramco Overseas Company in Leiden, the Netherlands, with branches in Tokyo, Hong Kong and Seoul.

Saudi Aramco strengthened its ties to the Far East in 2004 and 2005 by signing three milestone agreements. In 2004 the company acquired nearly 10 percent of Showa Shell Sekiyu

Saudi Aramco President and CEO Abdallah S. Jum'ah and Sumitomo Chemical Co. President and CEO Hiromasa Yonekura celebrate after signing an agreement to upgrade the Kingdom's Rabigh Refinery into a major refining and petrochemical complex.

K.K., a Royal Dutch/Shell refining-and-marketing arm in Japan. Saudi Aramco agreed to provide Showa Shell with a minimum of 300,000 barrels a day of oil. In 2005 the company increased its stake to 15 percent of Showa Shell Sekiyu.

Saudi Aramco linked up with Fujian Petrochemical Co. Ltd. and ExxonMobil China Petroleum and Petrochemical Co. Ltd. to jointly fund and design a $3.5 billion refining and chemical complex in southeastern China's Fujian Province. The project will substantially expand an existing refinery by adding 160,000 barrels a day of refining capacity capable of processing high-sulfur Arabian crude.

Saudi Aramco also signed a multibillion-dollar joint-venture agreement with Sumitomo Chemical Co., one of Japan's most innovative and technically advanced chemical businesses, to develop Rabigh Refinery, on the Kingdom's west coast, into a major refining and petrochemical complex. The complex, due to come on stream in 2008, will produce ethylene and propylene used in manufacturing products ranging from synthetic rubber to baby oil.

In May 2006, Saudi Aramco signed memorandums of understanding with Total of France and ConocoPhillips of the United States to build two export refineries at Jubail and Yanbu', respectively. The 400,000-barrel-a-day plants—both planned to start up in 2011—will convert heavy grade crude oils into high-quality, ultra-low sulfur products, especially transport and heating fuels, that meet all U.S. and European product specifications. In April, Motiva Enterprises LLC, Saudi Aramco's joint venture with Shell in the United States announced significant progress toward expanding refining capacity. Plans call for boosting capacity by 325,000 barrels a day at Motiva's Port Authur, Texas, refinery to increase supplies of transportation fuels for the U.S. market.

TECHNOLOGICAL REVOLUTION

DURING THE FIRST SIX YEARS OF THE 21ST CENTURY, SAUDI Aramco produced some 13 billion barrels of crude oil and more than 25 trillion standard cubic feet of gas. At the same

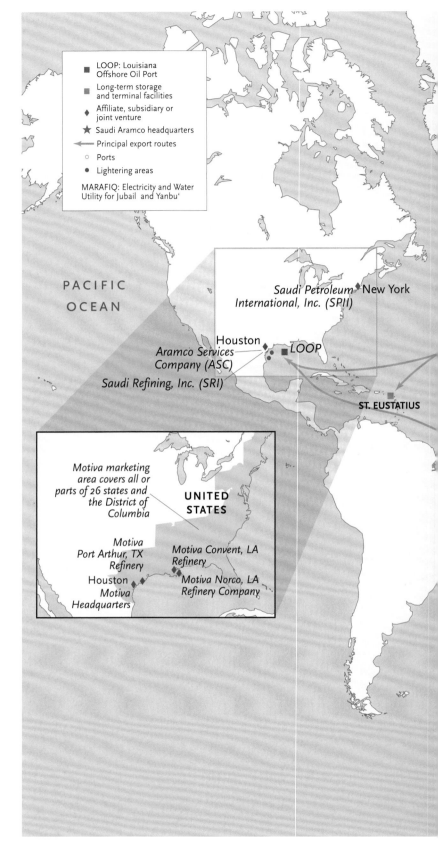

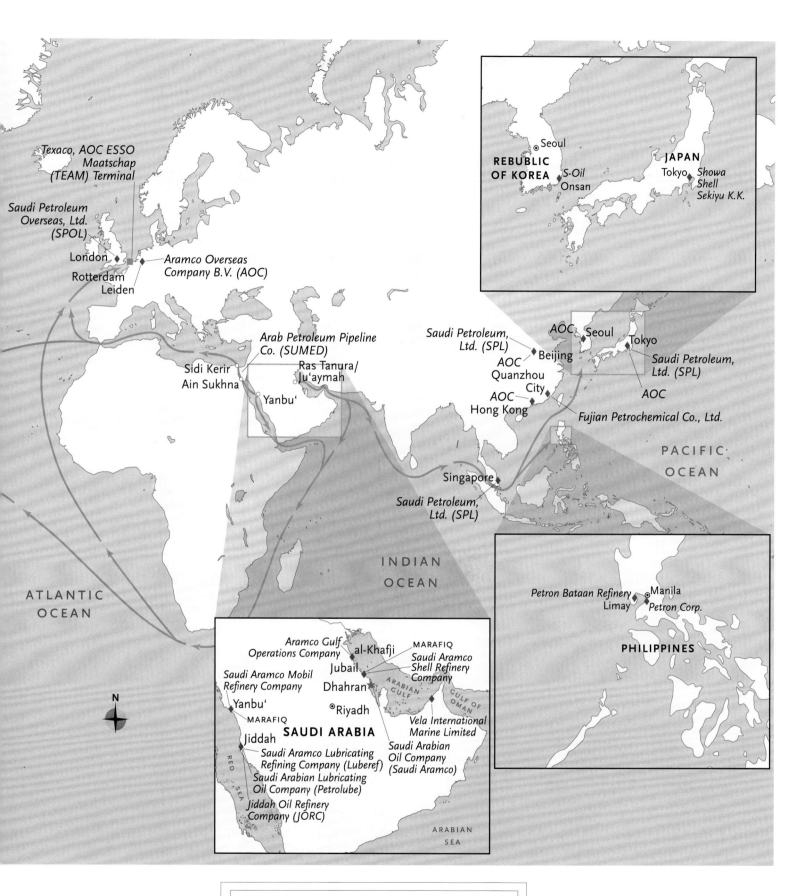

Texaco, AOC ESSO
Maatschap
(TEAM) Terminal

Saudi Petroleum
Overseas, Ltd.
(SPOL)

London
Rotterdam
Leiden

Aramco Overseas
Company B.V. (AOC)

Arab Petroleum Pipeline
Co. (SUMED)

Ras Tanura/
Ju'aymah

Sidi Kerir
Ain Sukhna

Yanbu'

Saudi Petroleum,
Ltd. (SPL)

AOC
Seoul

Beijing

AOC
Quanzhou
City

AOC
Hong Kong

Fujian Petrochemical Co., Ltd.

Tokyo

Saudi Petroleum,
Ltd. (SPL)

AOC

REBUBLIC
OF KOREA

Seoul

S-Oil
Onsan

JAPAN

Tokyo
Showa
Shell
Sekiyu K.K.

PACIFIC
OCEAN

Singapore

Saudi Petroleum,
Ltd. (SPL)

INDIAN
OCEAN

ATLANTIC
OCEAN

Petron Bataan Refinery
Limay

Manila
Petron Corp.

PHILIPPINES

N

Aramco Gulf
Operations Company

al-Khafji

MARAFIQ

Saudi Aramco Mobil
Refinery Company

Jubail

Saudi Aramco
Shell Refinery
Company

Dhahran

ARABIAN
GULF

GULF
OF
OMAN

Yanbu'

Riyadh

MARAFIQ

SAUDI ARABIA

Vela International
Marine Limited

Jiddah

Saudi Aramco Lubricating
Refining Company (Luberef)

Saudi Arabian Lubricating
Oil Company (Petrolube)

Jiddah Oil Refinery
Company (JORC)

RED
SEA

Saudi Arabian
Oil Company
(Saudi Aramco)

ARABIAN
SEA

SAUDI ARAMCO SUBSIDIARIES, AFFILIATES, JOINT
VENTURES AND PRINCIPAL EXPORT ROUTES
{ GAS-EXPLORATION JOINT VENTURES, SEE PAGE 272 }

281

AN EXPANDING ENTERPRISE

Saudi Aramco has grown from essentially an exploration and production company prior to the 1990s into an integrated global petroleum enterprise. The company not only markets and exports crude oil, petroleum products, natural gas liquids and sulfur — it also participates in joint ventures and other affiliates at home and abroad to refine crude oil and sell its products.

Combining Saudi Aramco's capabilities as a supplier with its partners' knowledge of local markets and customers' needs, the company's international affiliates now operate in North Africa, Asia, the Pacific Rim and the United States.

The company's shipping subsidiary Vela International Marine Limited sails one of the world's largest fleets of crude carriers, consisting of some 70 company-owned and chartered vessels.

Along with its five domestic refineries in the Kingdom, Saudi Aramco's interests include joint-venture refineries with Shell in Jubail and ExxonMobil in Yanbu'. These and its joint-venture and shareholder interests in refineries in the United States (Motiva Enterprises LLC) and the Far East (S-Oil in the Republic of Korea, Petron in the Philippines, and Showa Shell Sekiyu K.K. in Japan) have a combined processing capacity of 4.2 million barrels per day, placing the company in the top rank of world refiners.

(Clockwise from top) In the late 1990s the company's joint-venture partner in the Republic of Korea, SsangYong (today's S-Oil Corp.), completed a major project to convert heavy oil residue into higher-value light products at its 525,000-barrel-a-day Onsan Refinery. Employees of Motiva Enterprises LLC, a refining-and-marketing joint venture with Shell in the United States, confer at a Motiva product terminal in New Haven, Connecticut. Motiva Enterprises succeeded Star Enterprise, Saudi Aramco's first international joint venture in 1998. Saudi Aramco bought 40 percent of the shares of Petron Corporation, the major refining and marketing company in the Philippines, in 1994. Petron operates 1,200 gas stations.

Saudi Aramco sails one of the world's largest fleets of crude carriers. The double-hulled supertanker Leo Star — with a capacity of 2.3 million barrels of oil — is among the newest of 21 very large crude carriers and seven product vessels owned by the company's shipping subsidiary, Vela International Marine Limited.

"Let the Genie Out of the Bottle"

"I want to be the one who lets the genie out of the bottle," said the president and CEO of Saudi Aramco, Abdallah S. Jum'ah.

He was speaking at a meeting of the company's senior executives in 1998, a time when the oil industry was in a state of flux. Oil prices were extremely low. A barrel of Saudi Arabian premium light sold for as little as $10 that year.

"Companies worldwide were changing, and we needed to change with them," Jum'ah recalled. "We were asking ourselves: 'What do we want to be? Where do we want to go? How do we want to move forward?'"

That's when Jum'ah called for the release of the fabled genie. "What I meant by that statement was that I wanted the brain power of the company released," he explained.

The years that followed were highlighted by a series of multi-billion-dollar oil and gas projects—Shaybah, Hawiyah, Haradh and Qatif Producing Plants—constructed for the first time under the direction of Saudi managers rather than expatriate contractors. Both Hawiyah and Haradh won the prestigious Project of the Year Award from the U.S.-based Project Management Institute.

"Mega-projects have become a characteristic of Saudi Aramco, and they were needed," Jum'ah said. "Our people have become masters at the management of major projects. That didn't happen by accident. We put a lot of emphasis on teamwork and breaking down the barriers between organizations.

"That is one aspect of the change we went through. The second aspect is a series of programs—changing the image of the company with a new logo, promoting self-development, articulating our corporate values. I think today people realize that to be successful you have to uphold those values."

An Innovation initiative launched in 2002 encouraged employees to submit ideas for improving work processes and conditions. The campaign generated thousands of suggestions in its first two years; a number of these resulted in patents, and hundreds more were under review.

"I am very happy to say the genie is out of the bottle now," Jum'ah said. "And the genie is doing a fantastic job for the company."

Jum'ah grew up living in a *barasti*—a home of thatched palm-leaf walls and roof—in the village of al-Khobar, in the shadow of Aramco's headquarters. His father, a former pearl diver, was blind. "Our life depended on the income generated by my two older brothers who were working in the company," he said.

He traces his respect for learning to his mother, who, although illiterate, could recite the Quran from memory. She ran a small religious school in their modest home. Jum'ah and his brothers expanded the curriculum by teaching reading, writing and arithmetic.

Jum'ah attended high school in Dammam, working summers as an office boy in Aramco's Engineering Department. He received a college scholarship, awarded by the government and financed by Aramco, and graduated from the American University

New graduates of Saudi Aramco's three-year Professional Development Program receive congratulations from Abdallah S. Jum'ah, company president and CEO. The program's regimen of classes and job assignments has helped prepare high-potential Saudi employees for key jobs since 1980.

of Beirut in 1968 with a degree in political science. He went right to work for Aramco and began climbing the corporate ladder.

In 1976, Jum'ah attended the Harvard University management program, something he calls "an eye-opening experience." He moved steadily up through management and executive ranks with Aramco. Jum'ah was senior vice president of International Operations when he was elected president and CEO in August 1995—the first leader of the company not trained as an engineer or geologist. That, perhaps, gave him a slightly different management touch.

The Saudi people, like Jum'ah, whose lives are inextricably linked to the petroleum industry, are not likely to be careless with the God-given natural resources on which the Kingdom relies.

"The reality of the matter causes us to operate these reserves differently than an international company," Jum'ah said. "An international company would deplete the reserves for a quick economic return. Once they get their economic reward, they would look for something else. We look at our oil and gas reserves as our children. We nurture and protect them.

"Saudi Arabia is the cornerstone of the oil industry. The world is looking for us to deliver. Thank God we have always been able to deliver. I can tell you that in our history there was not a single barrel that was promised on a certain date to any customer in the four corners of the world that was not delivered on the date promised. God willing, that will not change."

time, the gas reserves it manages increased by 12 percent, to 239.5 trillion standard cubic feet, and crude oil reserves held steady at about 260 billion barrels.

That is not as strange as it may sound. The world has consumed about 820 billion barrels of oil since the first strike in Pennsylvania in 1859, almost three-quarters of that total—or 600 billion barrels—since 1973. Yet the world's proven oil reserves are 50 percent greater now than they were in 1973, and 10 times greater than in 1950.

Between the start of production in 1938 and 2005, the company produced around 106 billion barrels of oil, more than 86 billion barrels of that since 1973 alone. However, the company's proven and probable oil reserves increased almost every year, more than doubling from 1973 to 2005.

Part of the reason for this seeming paradox is that new oil fields continue to be discovered in hydrocarbon-rich eastern and central Saudi Arabia—Yabrin in 2003; Abu Sidr in 2004; and Du'ayban, Halfa and Muraiqib in 2005. In addition, the company discovered the Awtad, Fazran and Midrikah gas fields during that same period. Simply put, people are working smarter—using human ingenuity and a growing platform of knowledge to meet the world's energy needs.

Saudi Aramco and the oil industry are in the midst of a technological revolution. New techniques and advanced tools have greatly enhanced the success rate for finding new oil and gas, while increasing the average yield from existing wells by as much as 50 percent. Information technology—the computer and its offshoots—combined with work in the laboratory has had a lot to do with it.

Sophisticated computer systems analyze and compare billions of bits of seismic data to create vivid three-dimensional simulations of the earth's interior—and then project the images onto a screen like a motion picture. Saudi Aramco engineers can manipulate reservoir models, peel away layers of earth, turn the image around and upside down, and even draw in and "produce" a virtual oil well before it is ever drilled. The information gained from simulations is used to select new well locations, schedule field maintenance, maximize oil and gas recovery, and optimize production rates throughout the lifetime of a reservoir.

Until 2002, however, no computer technology in the world was powerful enough to image the world's largest oil field, Ghawar. That year, Saudi Aramco scientists achieved the first complete 3-D picture of the Ghawar and neighboring Abqaiq and Harmaliyah reservoirs. To accomplish this breakthrough, company scientists worked for years on new mathematical algorithms and a new computer language that enabled a string of 128 computer processors—similar to those used in ordinary desktop computers—to work together like a single supercomputer. The giant in-house simulator was named POWERS, an acronym for Parallel Oil, Water and Gas Reservoir Simulator.

The POWERS' 3-D model was formed from a composite of almost 10 million separate images covering an area of about 7,000 square kilometers (2,700 square miles) and included 3-D views of 3,400 wells drilled in Ghawar field and nearby formations since 1940. Previously, areas of Ghawar were imaged separately, which did not properly account for

Specialists in Saudi Aramco's new Geosteering Center in Dhahran communicate with crews at the well site to direct the drill bit as it cuts through the earth, combining advanced computer technology with software developed in-house to reach and track oil and gas deposits far underground.

The new Research and Development Center in Dhahran provides facilities including laboratories, pilot plants and workshops for 330 scientists. They answer questions such as, "How can petroleum fuels burn cleaner and more efficiently?"

interactions among the various regions, limiting the accuracy of predictions. Results of the new Ghawar simulation showed a good agreement with measured well pressures, and oil, water and gas production rates.

Improvements in computerized measurement-while-drilling also help optimize exploration and production capabilities. Sophisticated downhole tools—the equivalent of a drill bit with a computer attached—spinning through the rock and muck in a well bore, often at temperatures above 150°C (300°F), send data to the company's Geosteering Center many kilometers away. Employees at the center track the bit's progress and the conditions it is encountering. Engineers and geologists there use this information to direct drilling crews at the well site, while watching the work progress on screen.

Directional drilling enables Saudi Aramco geologists to approach a reservoir from the angle that seems most promising, twisting and turning the bit to cut through any number of different reservoirs, or even make a U-turn to tap previously inaccessible areas. In the Ghawar field, for example, directional drill strings fan out like branches of a tree to cover an area about four kilometers (2.5 miles) in circumference.

To keep on pace in scientific and technical matters, Saudi Aramco has built an ultra-modern Research and Development Center in Dhahran. The major portion of the center, opened in 2004, houses some 300 scientists working on issues such as how to combat corrosion, how to maximize yields from gas and oil reservoirs, and on techniques for blending different grades of crude to produce lighter products. This work goes hand in hand with the company's efforts to steadily improve the environmental performance of all operations.

How Long Can Oil Last?

OFF AND ON AGAIN OVER THE LAST 150 YEARS THE INCREASING demand and problematic nature of oil resources—where are they and how can they be produced—has prompted people to ask: "How long can the oil last?" Occasionally, fears of an international oil shortage escalate into something like a panic.

In 2003, oil prices topped $30 a barrel for the first time in nearly 20 years, prompted by increased demand in Asia, war in Iraq and problems in producing countries such as Nigeria and Venezuela. In January 2004, confidence in the industry was shaken when Royal Dutch/ Shell announced it had overstated its proven oil and gas reserves by 3.9 billion barrels, or 20 percent. A month after that, a U.S. energy analyst published a report saying that Saudi Arabia could suffer production declines in the next five to 10 years.

Saudi Aramco promptly went on record to stress its reliability, explaining that its overall oil reserves were not in decline, and that the amounts of proven reserves were, if any-

Saudi Arabia and World Energy

Saudi Arabia and the other countries around the Arabian Gulf are endowed with about 60 percent of the world's petroleum reserves and produce far more than they consume. On the other hand, the industrialized nations of the West and the rapidly growing economies in Asia, such as China and India, use far more petroleum than they produce. They cover the deficit by purchasing millions of barrels of oil daily from the Middle East. The balance sheet for natural gas liquids (NGL) is similarly lopsided. The countries of the Middle East and Russia combined control an estimated 65 percent of the world's natural gas resources.

The United States runs a huge energy deficit. It used nearly 25 percent of all the oil consumed in the world during 2005, but produced only eight percent and held only about 2.5 percent of the total oil reserves. Western Europe, with about 1.6 percent of world reserves, produced 6.5 percent of the world's oil but used around 17.5 percent. The ledger was even farther out of balance for Japan, which has practically no oil production or reserves but consumed 6.4 percent of the world's oil output. The rest of the Asia and Pacific region used 22.7 percent of the world's oil against production of 9.8 percent, with reserves of about 3.5 percent. Fast-growing China used 8.5 percent of the oil consumed in 2005, while its reserves accounted for less than 1.5 percent of the world total.

By contrast, the world's leading oil supplier, Saudi Arabia, exported more than 7.2 million barrels a day in 2005, providing nearly 20 percent of the world's total oil exports. The Kingdom's neighbors on the Arabian Gulf are also net exporters. When

Saudi Arabia's exports are combined with those of its fellow Gulf Cooperation Council (GCC) states—Kuwait, Bahrain, Qatar, the U.A.E. and Oman—they account for nearly 30 percent of world oil exports. When the export contributions of other Middle Eastern countries are added, the total reaches some 45 percent.

The world will continue to rely on Saudi Arabia and other countries in the Middle East to fulfill its energy needs in the foreseeable future. The combined oil reserves of Saudi Arabia and its neighbors—Iran, Iraq, Kuwait, Qatar and the U.A.E.—amounted to approximately 730 billion barrels, or 61 percent of the world total, at the end of 2005. The Kingdom's reserves accounted for more than a third of the region's rich holdings.

Saudi Arabia's oil reserves are expected to last for at least 70 years, so the Kingdom takes a long-term view when it shapes its national oil policies. It consistently strives to maintain oil market stability. To help achieve that objective, Saudi Arabia maintains surplus production capacity of between 1.5 and 2 million barrels per day, which can be brought on stream whenever dictated by market circumstances.

Russia holds the world's largest natural gas reserves, an estimated 1,680 trillion standard cubic feet. Next in line are Iran, Qatar and Saudi Arabia, which among them have 50 percent more gas reserves than Russia. Saudi Arabia has reserves of nearly 240 trillion standard cubic feet. The Kingdom is the world's largest exporter of NGL—289 million barrels in 2005—and is engaged in major gas exploration projects with international partners in its southern area.

2005 Oil Reserves (billions of barrels)

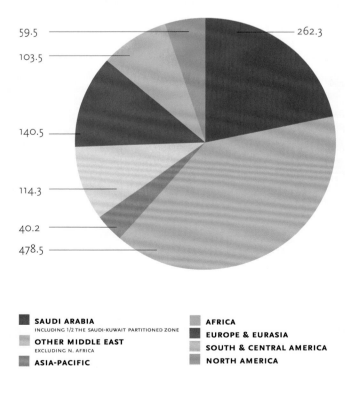

59.5	
103.5	262.3
140.5	
114.3	
40.2	
478.5	

SAUDI ARABIA
INCLUDING 1/2 THE SAUDI-KUWAIT PARTITIONED ZONE

OTHER MIDDLE EAST
EXCLUDING N. AFRICA

ASIA-PACIFIC

AFRICA

EUROPE & EURASIA

SOUTH & CENTRAL AMERICA

NORTH AMERICA

2005 Oil Production (million barrels per day)

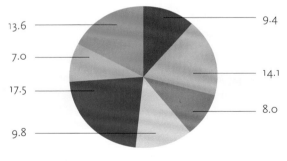

13.6	9.4
7.0	14.1
17.5	8.0
9.8	

2005 Oil Consumption (million barrels per day)

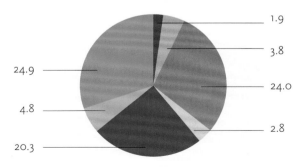

24.9	1.9
4.8	3.8
20.3	24.0
	2.8

Variance between world consumption and production statistics is due to factors including stock changes, consumption of non-petroleum additives and substitute fuels, and rounding of figures.

Source: Saudi Aramco; BP Statistical Review of World Energy

With a push of a throttle-like switch, King 'Abd Allah, then Crown Prince, officially inaugurated the Haradh Natural Gas and Oil Development Project in January 2004, significantly adding to the Kingdom's energy production capabilities. Minister of Petroleum and Mineral Resources Ali I. Al-Naimi stands to his right.

thing, conservatively stated. The company said that it could continue to produce oil at the 2005 rate—about 9 million barrels a day—for the next 70 years. Furthermore, by conservative estimate, there are more than 100 billion barrels of oil still to be found in unexplored areas of the Kingdom. That adds up to a century's worth of oil at 2005 production rates. Similarly, OPEC's 11 member countries, Saudi Arabia among them, with proven reserves totaling 900 billion barrels, can supply oil at 2005 levels for many years to come.

High demand and shortage fears continued, however, and oil prices climbed to more than $70 a barrel for the first time in early 2005. It was the highest price in the 21-year history of oil futures trading on the New York Mercantile Exchange, but still well below peak levels in 1979-80 when oil reached $40 a barrel—the equivalent of $85 in 2005 prices. Saudi Arabia pledged to increase its oil production capacity to 11 million barrels a day—up from 10 million barrels—to help calm the market. The Kingdom "seeks to stabilize the market and curb the escalation of prices that could be detrimental to the growth of the global economy, particularly that of developing countries," said the minister of Petroleum and Mineral Resources, adding that Saudi Arabia is "ready and capable of making up for production shortfalls occurring anywhere in the world."

Saudi Aramco had already underscored that commitment late in 2004 with the inauguration of the multibillion-dollar Qatif Producing Plants project, which added 500,000 barrels of oil a day to the world oil market, plus 370 million standard cubic feet per day of associated gas. Still more major increases are planned from other Eastern Province oil fields over the next few years as part of a long-range program to boost production capacity to 12.5 mil-

lion barrels a day. Oil production from the Shaybah field, for example, will be raised by 50 percent to 750,000 barrels a day, while some fields held in reserve for decades will be brought on line. (Only 11 of the company's 82 oil fields and 14 gas fields were in production at the end of 2005.)

To protect its extensive infrastructure and enhance the safety of its employees, Saudi Aramco has bolstered its security forces to more than 6,000 men and installed multiple protective systems. In addition, special government forces monitor and participate in guarding the company's vital installations, helping to ensure Saudi Aramco's ability to sustain production as world energy needs require.

What does the future hold? It is generally agreed that demand for energy will increase by at least two percent annually during the coming decades, mainly to satisfy increased demand in Asia. Saudi Aramco President Abdallah S. Jum'ah told an interviewer in 2005 that he expects oil to maintain a 39 percent share of the energy mix, with natural gas increasing to a 24 percent share and replacing coal as the No. 2 energy source by 2010.

The most recent U.S. Geological Survey report estimates the amount of oil still in the ground at nearly 2.3 trillion barrels, or about 75 percent more than has already been produced. Much of it will be hard to reach. But anyone betting against its recovery may be joining a long list of people who have underestimated the resources of human ingenuity, energy, adaptability and creativity.

Saudi Aramco offers bountiful examples of all those traits. The company is setting a global standard for efficient conversion of the resources bestowed upon the country by God into prosperity for the Saudi people and fuel for an energy-hungry world.

THE PEOPLE OF SAUDI ARAMCO

Saudi Aramco, ranked No. 1 among the world's petroleum companies for 17 consecutive years since 1988 by *Petroleum Intelligence Weekly*, relies on its employees for success. During the last seven decades, the enterprise has grown enormously, discovered huge reserves of oil and gas, and produced billions of barrels of crude oil and trillions of standard cubic feet of gas. It has built and operated world-class petroleum facilities, and become a reliable partner in refining, marketing and distribution joint ventures around the world. And it has established itself as the reliable source for about 10 percent of the world's daily oil needs. At the heart of the company's achievements are its people.

Saudi Aramco employed a cosmopolitan work force of some 53,000 persons at the end of 2005. The majority—about 87 percent—were Saudis. The company's 7,000 expatriate employees hailed from more than 50 countries. At the core of the work force are geologists, scientists, engineers, plant operators and other professionals with the know-how to build, maintain and operate the company's vital parts. But it also takes a variety of other employees—including accountants, lawyers, materials-supply experts, personnel advisors, pilots and medical professionals—to keep the enterprise humming.

Saudi Aramco strives to provide its employees and their families with the support and services they need to lead comfortable, healthy, productive lives, and to continue to excel in their jobs. This includes medical, social and recreational, and educational services, as well as rewarding benefits.

Thousands of employees and their families live in appealing, company-built and company-maintained communities that are often compared to California suburbs. They have recreation facilities one would expect to find in such towns: a golf course, riding stables, soccer fields, baseball diamonds, tennis courts and swimming pools.

The Home Ownership Program also makes the company an appealing place to work. Thousands of attractively designed houses have been built by Saudis with loans from the company, mostly in neighborhoods developed by the company close to its major Eastern Province facilities. More than 53,000 homes have been built since the program began in 1951.

However, Saudi Aramco is known best for the extensive employee-development opportunities it offers. In fact, Saudi Aramco can be seen as a school of sorts, for it operates one of the largest corporate training programs in the world. More than 3,000 individuals took part in the Apprenticeship Program during 2005, bringing the total to almost 16,500 since 1988. From 1951 through 2005, the company sponsored more than 10,000 four-year college scholarships and some 900 advanced-degree scholarships for both employees and potential employees in the Kingdom and abroad. In addition to other overseas venues, Saudis have begun studying in China, Japan and the Republic of Korea, where the company has important business activities.

Through company medical facilities or approved hospitals inside and outside the Kingdom, Saudi Aramco provides its

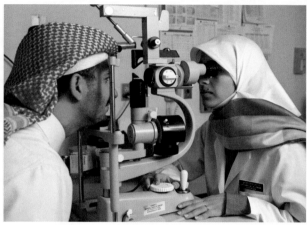

employees and their dependents—who number close to half a million—with comprehensive and superior quality medical care and health services.

The company and its employees are also well known for providing outreach programs to the community at large. At the Saudi Aramco Exhibit in Dhahran, some 200,000 Saudis and foreign visitors annually explore the secrets of the petroleum industry and see how the heritage of Arab-Islamic scientists and scholars of the past relate to today's civilization. This learning center also organizes special programs for students and their parents. The company's Mobile Libraries have served millions of schoolchildren across the Kingdom for many years. Saudi Aramco has also linked up with local charities to provide orphans and needy children in the Kingdom with school supplies.

Employees have strong ties to Saudi Aramco, reflected in the fact that a worker's average length of service with the company is more than 17 years. These ties remain strong even after employees retire. There are social organizations of retirees in Saudi Arabia and around the world. Saudi Aramco regularly organizes get-togethers for former employees in the Kingdom and supports gatherings organized by annuitants in the United States, Pakistan and India, for example. The AramcoBrats organization—a U.S.-based umbrella group for the offspring of company employees—has approximately 5,000 members in more than 50 countries, highlighting the depth and breadth of the Saudi Aramco connection.

(Clockwise from far left) Young geologists get tips from a veteran in the field. Six Saudi Aramco students pose with their Korean-language teachers in Seoul. Saudi Aramco is training specialists to work in its joint-venture operations in the Far East and around the globe, including its partnership with S-Oil in the Republic of Korea. Runners go through their paces in Ras Tanura. Youngsters who benefited from Saudi Aramco's outreach program for orphans and needy schoolchildren enjoy a company-sponsored holiday outing. An employee discusses cycling safety in a company community. First-class medical care for employees and their families is a Saudi Aramco priority.

(Clockwise from left) A Saudi schoolgirl learns about the astrolabe, a sophisticated instrument that was used mainly for navigation at sea, at the Saudi Aramco Exhibit in Dhahran. The spacious Exhibit relates the heritage of Arab-Islamic scholars of the past to the technology of the modern petroleum industry, set against the background of the natural history of Saudi Arabia. Volunteers from Aramco Services Company (ASC), a Saudi Aramco affiliate, work on a Habitat for Humanity home-construction project for a family in its base in Houston, Texas. Like its parent company, ASC has been actively involved in public service projects for many years. Trainees leave a math-science class at an Industrial Training Center in Ras Tanura. The company has provided training for thousands of individuals to meet company needs at centers like this, starting in the mid-1950s.

293

A Saudi Aramco employee pauses on his way to the top of a crude oil tank at Tanajib, a hub for offshore activities in the northern Gulf coast region.

The giant Qatif Producing Plants project, inaugurated
late in 2004 on Saudi Arabia's east coast, processes
800,000 barrels of oil and 370 million standard cubic feet
of gas per day from the onshore Qatif and offshore Abu
Sa'fah fields — the largest project of its kind ever built.
It is a key component of Saudi Aramco's commitment to
supply energy to the Kingdom and the world.

Experts find clues to new petroleum deposits and ways to increase production at existing wells in ancient rock samples stored at Saudi Aramco's Core Labratory in Dhahran. In the foreground, geoscientists Robert Lindsay and Mokhtar al-Khalid study a core sample of rock 150 million years old from the world's largest oil field, Ghawar.

The 550,000-barrel-a-day Ras Tanura Refinery, the largest in the Kingdom, stands on the site of a basic "tea kettle" refinery built in the late 1930s to process Saudi Arabia's first crude oil production. The refinery is being considered for development into an integrated refinery-petrochemical complex.

A supertanker several football fields long moves into mooring position at Ras Tanura's Sea Island terminal. Saudi Aramco's terminals on both coasts of the Kingdom load more than 9,000 tankers annually — millions of barrels of oil per day — for consumers around the globe.

Motiva Enterprises LLC, a 50-50 refining-and-marketing joint venture between Saudi Aramco subsidiary Saudi Refining Inc. and Shell in the eastern and southern United States, owns and operates three refineries in Texas and Louisiana, including this plant in Convent, Louisiana. The facilities have a total capacity of 780,000 barrels daily, with plans to expand capacity to approximately 1,100,000 barrels a day.

This view of Saudi Aramco's Dhahran core area highlights the growth of the company over some 70 years. The original horseshoe-shaped Administration Building, center, that opened in the 1940s (see page 250) is now surrounded by new exploration and producing, engineering, computer and administrative facilities. The core area is fronted by red-roofed community housing, with high-rise apartments to the rear. Just behind the apartments at top is the site of Dammam Well No. 7, the Kingdom's first commercial oil well.

Index

310

FURTHER READING

The selection of books for further reading about the subjects covered in this volume does not pretend to be more than an introduction to the vast number of works that have been published about Saudi Arabia, the Arabian Peninsula and Islam. The books listed are all in English and they have been chosen for their intrinsic worth, readability and availability. Although most of the authors are specialists, the books are, with a few exceptions, general works written for the nonspecialist.

Brief descriptions of certain books are provided, especially where titles do not clearly indicate the matter covered. All the books listed are recommended, although they are not, of course, of equal merit. The selection is by design weighted in favor of books on the Arabs and the Arabian Peninsula.

A good source of well-illustrated articles on a wide variety of subjects connected with the Arab and Muslim worlds is *Saudi Aramco World**, a magazine published six times a year. Its subject matter is very broad, ranging from the history, geography and culture of Saudi Arabia, to topics such as the Arab role in science and technology, and Islam in China. Written in an authoritative, journalistic style, it provides good source materials for use in the classroom, as well as use by the general reader.

Readers seeking more detailed information about Saudi Aramco should consult the company's Web site: www.saudiaramco.com. Those who are interested in the latest scientific and engineering developments at the company may consult *Journal of Technology*.** The magazine, published quarterly for professionals, presents papers aimed at advancing knowledge in the hydrocarbon industry.

---

* Subscriptions are available to a limited number of readers, free of charge. Readers from Saudi Arabia may send subscription requests to Public Relations, Saudi Aramco, Box 5000, Dhahran 31311, Saudi Arabia. Readers from all other countries should send subscription requests to *Saudi Aramco World*, P.O. Box 469008, Escondido, California, 92046-9008. Back issues of *Saudi Aramco World* from 1960 onward may be accessed online at www.saudiaramco.com.

** Individual subscriptions may be requested from Pubic Relations, Saudi Aramco, JOT Distribution, Box 500, Dhahran 31311, Saudi Arabia. Complete issues of *Journal of Technology* are available in "publications" at www.saudiaramco.com.

THE MIDDLE EAST AND THE ISLAMIC WORLD: SURVEYS AND COMPILATIONS

Coon, Carleton S. Caravan: *The Story of the Middle East*. Revised ed. Huntington, N.Y., 1976.

E. J. Brill. *Encyclopaedia of Islam*. New ed. 12 vols. Leiden, The Netherlands, 1960-2004.

Al-Faruqi, Isma'il R. and Lois Lamya'. *The Cultural Atlas of Islam*. New York and London, 1986.

Glassé, Cyril. *Concise Encyclopaedia of Islam*. New York, 1989.

Hayes, John R., editor. *The Genius of Arab Civilization: Source of Renaissance*. 2nd ed. Cambridge, Mass., and London, 1983.

Held, Colbert C. *Middle East Patterns: Places, Peoples, and Politics*. 3rd ed. Boulder, Colo., 2000, 2005.

Lewis, Bernard, editor. *The World of Islam: Faith, People, Culture*. London, 1976.

Lunde, Paul. Islam: *Faith, Culture, History*. London, 2002.

Malone, Joseph J. *The Arab Lands of Western Asia*. Englewood Cliffs, N.J., 1973.

Mansfield, Peter. *The Arabs*. 3rd ed. London and New York, 1991.

Robinson, Francis. *The Spread of Islam*. Oxford and New York, 1976.

_____. *Atlas of the Islamic World Since 1500*. New York and Oxford, 1982.

Schacht, Joseph, and C. E. Bosworth, editors. *The Legacy of Islam*. Oxford, 1979.

The Legacy of Islam and the handsome books edited by Hayes and Lewis contain excellent essays by specialists on many aspects of Middle Eastern and Islamic civilization. Coon writes as an anthropologist, Malone as a political scientist and Mansfield as a journalist. Lunde's book is a concise, well-illustrated compendium on Islam and Islamic society. *The Encyclopaedia of Islam*, having been nearly completed in its new edition by 2004, contains much broader subject matter than indicated by its title. Scholarly articles address geography, people and tribes, the arts and history, and include considerable material on the Arabian Peninsula. It is the standard reference book for Islamic subjects.

THE MIDDLE EAST AND THE ISLAMIC WORLD: HISTORY

Antonius, George. *The Arab Awakening: The Story of the Arab National Movement*. London, 1938; New York, 1965.

Atiyah, Edward. *The Arabs*. London, 1955; New York, 1968.

Brockelmann, Carl. *History of the Islamic Peoples*. Translated by Joel Carmichael and Moshe Perlman. New York, 1960.

Chaudhuri, K. N. *Trade and Civilization in the Indian Ocean: An Economic History from the Rise of Islam to 1750*. Cambridge, 1985.

Esposito, John L. *The Islamic World: Past and Present*. 3 vols. Oxford and New York, 2004.

Fromkin, David. *A Peace to End All Peace: Creating the Modern Middle East 1914-1922*. New York, 1989.

Hitti, Philip K. *The Arabs: A Short History*. Princeton, 1949.

_____. *History of the Arabs*. 10th ed. New York, 2002.

Hodgson, Marshall G. S. *The Venture of Islam: Conscience and History in a World Civilization*. 3 vols. Chicago and London, 1974.

Holt, P. M., Ann K. S. Lambton and Bernard Lewis, editors. *The Cambridge History of Islam.* 4 vols. Cambridge, 1977.

Hourani, Albert. *A History of the Arab Peoples.* London and Cambridge, Mass., 1991.

Hourani, Albert, Philip S. Khoury, and Mary C. Wilson. *The Modern Middle East: A Reader.* Berkeley, 1994.

Ibn Khaldun. *The Muqaddimah: An Introduction to History.* Translated by Franz Rosenthal. New York, 1958.

Kirk, George E. *A Short History of the Middle East: From the Rise of Islam to Modern Times.* 6th ed. New York, 1960.

Lapidus, Ira M. *A History of Islamic Societies.* Cambridge, 1990.

Lewis, Bernard, editor and translator. *Islam: From the Prophet Muhammad to the Capture of Constantinople.* 2 vols. New York and London, 1974.

Mansfield, Peter, and Nicholas Pelham. *A History of the Middle East,* 2nd ed. London, 2003.

Mas'udi. *The Meadows of Gold: The Abbasids.* Translated by Paul Lunde and Caroline Stone. London, 1989.

Monroe, Elizabeth. *Britain's Moment in the Middle East,* 1914-1956. London, 1963.

Nicolle, David. *Historical Atlas of the Islamic World.* New York, 2003.

Sinor, Denis, editor. *The Cambridge History of Early Inner Asia.* Cambridge and New York, 1990.

Toynbee, Arnold J. *The Islamic World Since the Peace Settlement.* London, 1927.

The works of Brockelmann, Hourani and Hodgson are scholarly and thorough. Antonius writes of the political renaissance of the Arabs in this and the last century. Hitti brings his history of the Arabs down to the establishment of the Ottoman Empire in Egypt in 1517. Bernard Lewis's two volumes entitled *Islam* are a fascinating compilation of translations from Arabic, Persian and Turkish literature up to the 15th century. The books by Toynbee and Kirk are particularly valuable for their treatment of the Palestine problem. The first part of Nicolle's atlas deals in some detail with the Arabian Peninsula.

THE RELIGION OF ISLAM

Ahmad, Kurshid, editor. *Islam: Its Meaning and Message.* Ann Arbor, Mich., 1976; and Leicester, U.K., 1980.

Ali, Abdullah Yusuf. *The Holy Qur-an: Text, Translation and Commentary.* 2 vols. Lahore, Pakistan, 1934; New York, 1946; and other editions.

Amin, Mohamed. *Journey of a Lifetime: Pilgrimage to Makkah.* London, 1978.

Amin, S. M. *The Holy Journey to Mecca.* Naples, 1976.

Arberry, Arthur J. *The Koran Interpreted.* 2 vols. London and New York, 1955.

Armstrong, Karen. *Islam: A Short History.* New York, 2000.

'Azzam, 'Abd-al-Rahman. *The Eternal Message of Muhammad.* Translated by Caesar A. Farah. New York, 1964.

Cook, Michael. *The Koran: A Very Short Introduction.* Oxford, 2000.

Crone, Patricia. *Meccan Trade and the Rise of Islam.* Princeton, 1987.

Donner, Fred M. *The Early Islamic Conquests.* Princeton, 1981.

Esin, Emel, and Haluk Doganbey. *Mecca the Blessed, Madinah the Radiant.* London, 1963.

Esposito, John L. *Islam: The Straight Path.* New York and Oxford, 1991.

Gibb, Hamilton A. R. *Mohammedanism: An Historical Survey.* 2nd ed. London, 1961

Guellouz, Ezzedine, and Abdelaziz Frikha. *Mecca: The Muslim Pilgrimage.* New York and London, 1979.

Hamidullah, Muhammad. *Introduction to Islam.* Paris, 1969.

Hodgson, Marshall G.S. *The Venture of Islam: Conscience and History in a World Civilization. Vol. 1: The Classical Age of Islam.* Chicago and London, 1974.

Hourani, Albert. *Europe and the Middle East.* Berkeley and London, 1980.

Ibn Ishaq. *The Life of Muhammad.* Translated by Alfred Guillaume. Oxford, 1955.

Lippman, Thomas W. *Understanding Islam: An Introduction to the Muslim World.* New York, 1990.

Lings, Martin. *Muhammad: His Life Based on the Earliest Sources.* London, 1991.

Maududi, Abul A'la. *Towards Understanding Islam.* Chicago and Leicester, U.K., 1980.

Nasr, Seyyed Hossein. *Ideals and Realities of Islam.* Boston, 1972; London, 1985.

Peters, F.E. *Hajj: The Muslim Pilgrimage to Mecca and the Holy Places.* Princeton, 1994.

_____. *Muhammad and the Origins of Islam.* Albany, N.Y., 1994.

Pickthall, Mohammed Marmaduke. *The Meaning of the Glorious Qur'an: An Explanatory Translation.* New York, 1988.

Rippin, Andrew. *Muslims: Their Religious Beliefs and Practices.* 2nd ed. London and New York, 2001.

Ruthven, Malise. *Islam: A Very Short Introduction.* Oxford, 1997.

Ruthven, Malise, and Azim Nanji. *Historical Atlas of the Islamic World.* Oxford, 2004.

Savory, R. M. *Introduction to Islamic Civilization.* Cambridge, 1976.

Schacht, Joseph. *An Introduction to Islamic Law.* Oxford, 1964.

Schimmel, Annemarie. *Islam: An Introduction.* Albany, N.Y., 1992.

Von Grunebaum, G. E. *Muhammadan Festivals.* New York, 1951.

Watt, W. M. *Muhammad at Mecca.* Oxford, 1953.

_____. *Muhammad at Medina.* Oxford, 1956.

Zakaria, Rafiq. *Muhammad and the Quran.* London, 1991.

There are many translations of the Quran. Each has its strong points. Those by Arberry and Pickthall are particularly good. Abdullah Ali's translation is especially useful for its explanatory notes. The newcomer to the subject is well advised to start a study of Islam with a general introduction, such as is provided by 'Azzam, Gibb or Hamidullah. Von Grunebaum's book is a pleasant introduction to the Muslim at prayer and on pilgrimage.

Esin and Doganbey are Turkish Muslims who describe the Holy Cities by word and picture.

ARCHEOLOGY AND THE ANCIENT NEAR EAST

Baines, John, and Jaromir Malek. *Atlas of Ancient Egypt.* Oxford and New York, 1988.

Bibby, Geoffrey. *Looking for Dilmun.* London, 1984.

Bienkowski, Piotr, and Alan Millard, editors. *Dictionary of the Ancient Near East,* London, 2000.

Burney, Charles. *The Ancient Near East.* Ithaca, N.Y., and Oxford, 1977. (The title of the British edition is *From Village to Empire.*)

Eph'al, Israel. *The Ancient Arabs: Nomads on the Borders of the Fertile Crescent, 9th–5th Centuries BC.* Jerusalem and London, 1982.

Groom, Nigel. *Frankincense and Myrrh: A Study of the Arabian Incense Trade.* London, 1981.

Hoyland, Robert G. *Arabia and the Arabs from the Bronze Age to the Coming of Islam.* London, 2001.

Al Khalifa, Shaikha Haya Ali, and Michael Rice, editors. *Bahrain Through the Ages: The Archaeology.* London, 1986.

Maigret, Alessandro de. *Arabia Felix: An Exploration of the Archaeological History of the Yemen.* London, 2002.

Potts, D. T. *The Arabian Gulf in Antiquity.* 2 vols. Oxford, 1990.

Retso, Jan. *The Arabs in Antiquity: Their History from the Assyrians to the Umayyads.* London, 2002.

Rice, Michael. *The Archaeology of the Arabian Gulf.* London, 1994.

Roaf, Michael. *Cultural Atlas of Mesopotamia and the Ancient Near East.* Oxford and New York, 1990.

Saudi Arabian Ministry of Education, Department of Antiquities and Museums. *An Introduction to Saudi Arabian Antiquities.* Riyadh, 1975.

Simpson, St. John, editor. *Queen of Sheba: Treasures from Ancient Yemen.* London, 2002.

Taylor, Jane. *Petra and the Lost Kingdom of the Nabataeans.* London, 2001.

Thompson, Andrew. *The Origins of Arabia.* London, 2000.

Bahrain Through the Ages: The Archaeology details discoveries relating to Bahrain and the Arabian Gulf area. Readers should also consult the *Atlal* series of journals published by the Saudi Arabian Department of Antiquities and Museums from 1977, which provide detailed information on excavations and surveys in the Kingdom.

SCIENCE, LITERATURE AND THE ARTS

Allen, Roger. *An Introduction to Arabic Literature.* Cambridge, 2000.

Binzager, Safeya. *Saudi Arabia: An Artist's View of the Past.* Lausanne, Switzerland, 1979.

Blunt, Wilfrid. *Splendours of Islam.* London and New York, 1976.

Brend, Barbara. *Islamic Art.* London and Cambridge, Mass., 1991.

Burckhardt, Titus. *Art of Islam: Language and Meaning.* London, 1976.

Du Ry, Carel J. *Art of Islam.* Translated by Alexis Brown. New York, 1970.

Eiland, Murray L. *Oriental Rugs: A Complete Guide.* Revised ed. Boston, 1976.

Facey, William. *Back to Earth: Adobe Building in Saudi Arabia.* Riyadh, 1997.

Gibb, H. A. R. *Arabic Literature: An Introduction.* 2nd ed. Oxford, 1974.

Grabar, Oleg. *The Mediation of Ornament.* Princeton, 1992.

al-Hassan, Ahmad Y., and Donald R. Hill. *Islamic Technology: An Illustrated History.* New York and Cambridge, 1987.

Hawley, Walter A. *Oriental Rugs, Antique and Modern.* New York, 1913; 1970.

Haywood, John A. *Modern Arabic Literature, 1800-1970: An Introduction, with Extracts in Translation.* London, 1971.

Irwin, Robert, editor. *Night & Horses and the Desert: An Anthology of Classical Arabic Literature.* Woodstock, N.Y., and New York, 1999.

Jayyusi, Salma Khadra, editor. *The Literature of Modern Arabia: An Anthology.* London and New York, 1988.

Johnson-Davies, Denys. *Arabic Short Stories.* London, 1983.

Al-Khan, Waheed A. *Laiwa Music of the Gulf. Vol. 3.* Doha, Qatar, 1989.

King, David A. *Astronomy in the Service of Islam.* Aldershot, U.K., and Brookfield, Vt., 1993.

King, Geoffrey. *The Traditional Architecture of Saudi Arabia.* London, 1998.

Kritzeck, James. *Anthology of Islamic Literature: From the Rise of Islam to Modern Times.* New York, 1964.

Lichtenstadter, Ilse. *Introduction to Classical Arabic Literature: With Selections from Representative Works in English Translation.* Boston, 1974.

Lings, Martin. *The Quranic Art of Calligraphy and Illumination.* London, 1976; Boulder, Colo., 1978.

Nance, Paul. *The Nance Museum: A Journey into Traditional Saudi Arabia.* Lone Jack, Mo., 1999.

Nicholson, Reynold A. *A Literary History of the Arabs.* 2nd ed. Cambridge, 1969.

Peters, F. E. *Mecca: A Literary History of the Muslim Holy Land.* Princeton, 1994.

Rice, David Talbot. *Islamic Art.* London, 1991.

Ross, Heather Colyer. *The Art of Arabian Costume: A Saudi Arabian Profile.* London, 1993.

_____. *The Art of Bedouin Jewelry: A Saudi Arabian Profile.* London, 1994.

Safadi, Yasin Hamid. *Islamic Calligraphy.* London, 1978.

Scerrato, Umberto. *Islam.* New York, 1976.

Schimmel, Annemarie. *Calligraphy and Islamic Culture.* New York and London, 1984.

Tahan, Malba. *The Man Who Counted: A Collection of Mathematical Adventures*. London and New York, 1993.

Touma, Habib H. *The Music of the Arabs*. Portland, Ore., 1996.

Topham, John, et al. *Traditional Crafts of Saudi Arabia*. Revised ed. London and Riyadh, 2005.

Gibb, Lichtenstadter and Nicholson offer introductions to the literature of the Arabs, and Kritzeck and Haywood have compiled anthologies of that literature in translation. Brend, Burckhardt, Du Ry and Rice survey the visual arts, while Blunt and Scerrato accent architecture. Allen's book is an abridgement and revision of his more detailed earlier work, *The Arabic Literary Heritage*, 1998.

CLASSICS

Arabian Nights. Many editions, but the most famous translations are by Richard F. Burton and Edward William Lane.

Burkhardt, John Lewis. *Notes on the Bedouins and Wahábys*. 2 vols. London, 1831; New York and London, 1967.

_____. *Travels in Arabia*. 2 vols. London, 1829; London, 1993.

Burton, Richard F. *Personal Narrative of a Pilgrimage to Al-Madinah and Meccah*. 2 vols. London, 1893; New York, 1964.

Doughty, Charles M. *Travels in Arabia Deserta*. 2 vols. London, 1921; New York, 1979.

Lawrence, T. E. *Seven Pillars of Wisdom*. London and New York, 1991.

Niebuhr, Carsten. *Travels through Arabia and Other Countries in the East*. Translated by R. Heron. 2 vols. Edinburgh, 1772, 1774; Reading, U.K., 1994.

Palgrave, William Gifford. *Narrative of a Year's Journey through Central and Eastern Arabia (1862-63)*. 2 vols. London, 1865; 1969.

Pelly, Lewis. *Report on a Journey to the Wahabee Capital of Riyadh in Central Arabia*. Bombay, 1866; Cambridge and New York, 1978.

Sadleir, George F. *Diary of a Journey Across Arabia (1819)*. Cambridge, 1977.

As the entries above indicate, a number of publishers have recently been bringing out new editions of some of the best-known older books on Arabia and the Middle East — in some cases 100 years and more after they were first published. The books by Burton, Doughty and Lawrence listed here are classics of the English language, quite apart from their merits as authorities on Arabian matters. None of these works is easy reading, but any effort by the reader will be well rewarded.

THE ARABIAN PENINSULA AND THE GULF

Al-Abbasi, Ali Bey [Domingo Badia y Leblich]. *Travels in Africa and Asia during the Years 1803-7*. 2 vols. London, 1916. Reprinted as *Travels of Ali Bey in Morocco, Tripoli, Cyprus, Egypt, Arabia and Turkey*. Reading, U.K., 1993.

Ajmi, Nassir. *Legacy of a Lifetime: An Essay on the Transformation of Saudi Arabia*. London, 1995.

Almana, Mohammed A. *Arabia Unified: A Portrait of Ibn Saud*. London, 1980; New Brunswick, N.J., 1985.

Armerding, Paul L. *Doctors for the Kingdom: The Work of the American Mission Hospitals in the Kingdom of Saudi Arabia — 1913-1915*. Grand Rapids, Mich., and Cambridge, 2003.

Al-Ayaf, Abdulaziz Khalid. *Eastern Province of Saudi Arabia: A Picture Memory 1930-2003*. Dammam, Saudi Arabia.

Azzi, Robert. *Saudi Arabian Portfolio*. Manchester, N.H., 1978.

Barger, Thomas C. *Out in the Blue: Letters from Arabia — 1937 to 1940*. Vista, Calif., 2000.

Belgrave, Charles. *Personal Column*. London, 1960.

Beling, Willard A., editor. *King Faisal and the Modernisation of Saudi Arabia*. Boulder, Colo. and London, 1980.

Bidwell, Robin. *Travellers in Arabia*. Reading, U.K., 1995.

Bin Sultan, Khaled. *Desert Warrior: A Personal View of the Gulf War by the Joint Forces Commander*. London, 1995.

Bogary, Hamza. *The Sheltered Quarter: A Tale of a Boyhood in Mecca*. Austin, Texas, 1991.

Brent, Peter. *Far Arabia: Explorers of the Myth*. London, 1977.

Buchan, James. *Jeddah: Old and New*. London, 1991.

De Gaury, Gerald. *Faisal, King of Saudi Arabia*. London, 1966.

Dickson, H. R. P. *Kuwait and Her Neighbours*. London, 1956.

Facey, William. *Dir'iyyah and the First Saudi State*. London, 1997.

_____. *Riyadh, The Old City*. London, 1992.

_____. *The Story of the Eastern Province of Saudi Arabia*. London, 1994

Facey, William, and Gillian Grant. *The Emirates by the First Photographers*. London, 1996.

_____. *Kuwait by the First Photographers*. London, 1996.

_____. *Saudi Arabia by the First Photographers*. London, 1996.

Freeth, Zahra, and H. V. F. Winstone. *Explorers of Arabia: From the Renaissance to the End of the Victorian Era*. London, 1978.

Guise, Anthony. *Riyadh*. London, 1988.

Hapgood, David. *Charles R. Crane: The Man Who Bet on People*. New York, 2000.

Al-Hariri-Rifai, Mokhless. *The Heritage of the Kingdom of Saudi Arabia*. Washington, D.C., 1990.

Hattox, Ralph S. *Coffee and Coffeehouses: The Origins of the Social Beverage in the Medieval Near East*. Seattle, 1985.

Hawley, Donald. *The Trucial States*. London, 1970.

Hill, Ann and Daryl. *The Sultanate of Oman: A Heritage*. London and New York, 1977.

Hopwood, Derek, editor. *The Arabian Peninsula: Society and Politics*. London, 1972.

Ingrams, Harold. *Arabia and the Isles*. 3rd ed. London, 1972.

Kelly, J. B. *Britain and the Persian Gulf, 1795-1880*. Oxford, 1968.

Keane, John F. T. *Six Months in the Hijaz, 1877-1878*. Beirut, 2005.

Kiernan, Reginald H. *The Unveiling of Arabia: The Story of Arabian Travel and Discovery*. London, 1937; New York, 1975.

Lippman, Thomas. *Inside the Mirage: America's Fragile Partnership with Saudi Arabia*. Boulder, Colo., 2004.

Long, David E. *The Persian Gulf: An Introduction to Its Peoples, Politics and Economics*. Revised ed. Boulder, Colo., 1978.

Mauger, Thierry. *Undiscovered Asir*. London, 1993.

Meade, Frances. *Honey and Onions: A Life in Saudi Arabia*. Philadelphia. 2004

Monroe, Elizabeth. *Philby of Arabia*. London, 1973.

Al-Muqaddasi. *The Best Divisions for Knowledge of the Regions (Ahsan al-Taqasim fi Ma'rifat al-Aqalim)*. Translated by Basil Collins. Reading, U.K., 2001.

Nasir-i Khusraw. *Naser-e Khosraw's Book of Travels (Safarnama)*. Translated by W. M. Thackston Jr. New York, 1986.

Nicholson, Eleanor. *In the Footsteps of the Camel: A Portrait of the Bedouins of Eastern Arabia in Mid-century*. London, 1983.

_____. *Through the Lion Gate*. Philadelphia. 2002.

Pesce, Angelo. *Jiddah: Portrait of an Arabian City*. London, 1974.

Peterson, J. E. *Oman in the Twentieth Century: Political Foundations of an Emerging State*. London and New York, 1978.

Philby, Harry St. John B. *Arabia of the Wahhabis*. London, 1928, 1977.

_____. *Arabian Days*. London, 1948.

_____. *Arabian Jubilee*. London, 1952.

_____. *The Empty Quarter: Being a Description of the Great South Desert of Arabia Known as Rub' al-Khali*. London, 1933.

_____. *The Heart of Arabia*. London, 1922.

_____. *A Pilgrim in Arabia*. London, 1946.

_____. *Sa'udi Arabia*. London, 1955.

Rentz, George S. *Birth of the Islamic Reform Movement in Saudi Arabia: Muhammad Ibn 'Abd al-Wahhab (1703/4-1792) and the Beginnings of Unitarian Empire in Arabia*. London, 2005.

Rihani, Ameen. *Around the Coasts of Arabia*. London, 1930.

_____. *Ibn Sa'Oud of Arabia: His People and His Land*. London, 1928.

_____. *Maker of Modern Arabia*. Westport, Conn., 1983.

Sabini, John. *Armies in the Sand: The Struggle for Mecca and Medina*. London, 1981.

al-Saud, Noura bint Muhammad, Al-Jawharah Muhammad al-'Anqari, and Madeha Muhammad Ajroush. *Abha, Bilad Asir: Southwestern Region of the Kingdom of Saudi Arabia*. Riyadh, 1989.

Sheean, Vincent. *Faisal: The King and His Kingdom*. Tavistock, U.K., 1975.

Stacey International. *The Kingdom of Saudi Arabia*. New ed. London, 2005.

Teitelbaum, Joshua. *The Rise and Fall of the Hashemite Kingdom of Arabia*. London, 2001.

Trench, Richard. *Arabian Travellers*. London, 1986.

Troeller, Gary. *The Birth of Saudi Arabia: Britain and the Rise of the House of Sa'ud*. London, 1976.

Twitchell, Karl S. *Saudi Arabia*. 3rd ed. Princeton, 1958.

Vassiliev, Alexai. *The History of Saudi Arabia*. London, 1998.

Wilson, Arnold T. *The Persian Gulf: An Historical Sketch from the Earliest Times to the Beginning of the Twentieth Century*. Oxford, 1928; London, 1954.

Winder, R. Bayly. *Saudi Arabia in the Nineteenth Century*. New York etc., 1965.

Winstone, H. V. F. *Captain Shakespear*. London, 1976.

Beling's book is a compilation of papers on Saudi Arabia. Belgrave's autobiographical work is about the author's years as an advisor to the ruler of Bahrain, while Kelly and Winder collect detail for the historian. Ingrams's *Arabia and the Isles* is about the area known as Hadhramaut. Brent, Freeth and Kiernan write of the development of knowledge of Arabia by European explorers. The books by Azzi, Buchan and Guise consist mainly of beautiful color photographs. Philby's historical works are sound, and his records of exploration are valuable compendiums of information. Rihani's book *Ibn Sa'Oud* is a firsthand account of the Saudi State in the 1920s by an American of Arab descent who was with King 'Abd al-'Aziz at the conference of al-'Uqayr in 1922. Facey's books on the Eastern Province and Dir'iyah are photographic reports with much descriptive and historical text; his book on Riyadh features a more detailed text. Facey and Grant's well-printed compilations of early photographs provide a picture of old Arabia that is now difficult for a newcomer to imagine. The work by Rentz (an Arabist who worked for Aramco) is a Ph.D. dissertation long used by scholars and now published for the first time. Its subject is the 18th-century beginnings of the First Saudi State. Barger's book consists of letters he wrote to his young bride in America when he was a young geologist exploring in Saudi Arabia (he later became president of Aramco), offering insights into the early days of oil prospecting in the Kingdom and the character of its people. Lippman's book is a frank look at the ebb and flow of Saudi-American relations beginning with Aramco's early days.

MIDDLE EAST AND WORLD OIL

Barger, Thomas C. "Energy Policies of the World: Arab States of the Persian Gulf." In *Energy Policies of the World*. Vol. 1. Gerard J. Mangone, editor. Newark, N.J., 1976.

Longrigg, Stephen Hemsley. *Oil in the Middle East: Its Discovery and Development*. 3rd ed. London, 1968.

Nawwab, Ismail I., Peter C. Speers and Paul F Hoye, editors. *Saudi Aramco and Its World, Arabia and the Middle East*. Dhahran, 1995.

Nicolas Sarkis. *Arab Oil and Gas Directory*. Paris, 1994.

Owen, Edgar W. *Trek of the Oil Finders*, Tulsa, 1975.

Oxley, Owen. *Saudi Arabia, The Great Adventure: The Americans Who Helped a Remote Desert Kingdom Become One of the Richest Nations in the World*. London, 2006.

PennWell Publishing. *International Petroleum Encyclopedia*. Tulsa, Okla., 1994.

Philby, Harry St. John B. *Arabian Oil Ventures*. Washington, 1964.

Pledge, Thomas A. *Saudi Aramco and Its People: A History of Training*. Houston, Texas, 1998.

Stegner, Wallace. *Discovery!* Beirut, 1971.

Stocking, George W. *Middle East Oil: A Study in Political and Economic Controversy*. Nashville, Tenn., 1970.

Tughendhat, Christopher. *Oil: The Biggest Business*. London, 1968.

Turner, Louis. *Oil Companies in the International System*. London, 1978.

Yergin, Daniel. *The Prize: The Epic Quest for Oil, Money and Power*. New York, 1991.

Longrigg, Stocking and Tughendhat present surveys, each with its own strength. Longrigg provides the most detail; Tughendhat is easiest to read and the widest ranging. *Arabian Oil Ventures* contains Philby's story of the negotiation of what became the Aramco concession and of Major Frank Holmes's earlier concession covering much the same area. Stegner tells the story of Aramco's pioneering days. The books published by PennWell and Nicolas Sarkis are solid reference works. Barger's work, although now dated, provides a useful summary of developments during OPEC's early years and the evolution of oil industry-government relations up to 1975. The book edited by Nawwab, et al., was originally developed as a handbook to familiarize Aramco's foreign employees with the land in which they lived, the wider Arab and Muslim worlds, and the oil industry. Pledge's book tells the story of Saudi Aramco's extensive training program for Saudis.

BEDOUINS, OASIS DWELLERS, AND SAILORS

Agius, Dionisius A. *In the Wake of the Dhow: The Arabian Gulf and Oman*. Reading, U.K., 2002.

_____. *Seafaring in the Arabian Gulf and Oman. The People of the Dhow.* London, 2005.

Cole, Donald Powell. *Nomads of the Nomads: The Al Murrah Bedouin of the Empty Quarter*. Arlington Heights, Ill., 1975.

Dickson, H. R. P. *The Arab of the Desert: A Glimpse into Badawin Life in Kuwait and Saudi Arabia*. London, 1949.

Ferdinand, Klaus. *Bedouins of Qatar*. London, 1993.

Hawkins, Clifford W. *The Dhow: An Illustrated History of the Dhow and Its World*. Lymington, Hants, U.K., 1977.

Hobbs, Joseph J. *Bedouin Life in the Egyptian Wilderness*. Austin, Texas, 1989.

Hourani, George F. *Arab Seafaring in the Indian Ocean in Ancient and Early Medieval Times*. Princeton, 1951.

Keohane, Alan. *Bedouin: Nomads of the Desert*, London, 1994.

Lancaster, William. *The Rwala Bedouin Today*. 2nd ed. Cambridge, 1997.

Ma Huan. *Ying-yai sheng-lan: 'The Overall Survey of the Ocean's Shores'* [1433]. Translated by Feng Ch'eng-Chün. Cambridge, 1970.

Musil, Alois. *The Manners and Customs of the Rwala Bedouins*. New York, 1928.

Risso, Patricia. *Merchants and Faith: Muslim Commerce and Culture in the Indian Ocean*. Boulder, Colo., San Francisco and Oxford, 1995.

Silveira, Humberto da. *Bedu*, Lausanne, Switzerland, 1994.

Thesiger, Wilfred. *Arabian Sands*. London, 1985. (Braille edition, 1976.)

Tibbetts, G.R. *Arab Navigation in the Indian Ocean before the Coming of the Portuguese, Being a translation of Kitab al-Fawa'id fi Usul 'Ilm al-Bahr wa-l-Qawa'id of Ahmad ibn Majid*. London, 1971.

Villiers, Alan J., *Sons of Sindbad*, London, 1940. (Published as *Sons of Sinbad*, New York.) London, 2006.

_____. *Sons of Sindbad: The Photographs*, London, 2006.

Thesiger's work is considered a classic. It describes the Bedouins of southern Arabia with great perception. Dickson is rich in material on the people of eastern Arabia. Villiers gives a popular account of the life of the Arab sailor, while Hawkins describes and illustrates the ships he sails. Musil's work is a classic of Arabian ethnography, preserving a picture of Arabian life in the early 20th century. Ferdinand focuses on the material culture and handicrafts of his subjects. Hobbs details the environmental relations of Bedouins who were modern migrants from northeastern Saudi Arabia to eastern Egypt. The translations of works by Ma Huan and Ahmad ibn Majid shed light on Arabia's early role as a seafaring and trading hub.

NATURAL HISTORY

Allen, Mark. *Falconry in Arabia*. London, 1980.

Baron, Stanley. *The Desert Locust*. London, 1972.

Basson, Philip W., John E. Burchard, John T. Hardy, and Andrew R. G. Price. *Biotopes of the Western Arabian Gulf: Marine Life and Environments of Saudi Arabia*. 2nd ed. Dhahran, 1981.

Benson, S. Vere. *Birds of Lebanon and the Jordan Area*. London and New York, 1970.

Bundy, G.; R. J. Connor, and J. O. Harrison. *Birds of the Eastern Province of Saudi Arabia*. London, 1989. [Published in association with Saudi Aramco.]

Burton, John J. S., *Cultivated Outdoor Plants of Saudi Aramco*. Dammam, Saudi Arabia, 2001.

_____. *Urban Pest Control: The Saudi Aramco Experience*. Dammam, Saudi Arabia, 2001.

Buttiker, William. *Wildlife of Saudi Arabia and Its Neighbors*. London, 1990.

Chaudhary, Shaukat Ali, editor. *Flora of the Kingdom of Saudi Arabia, Illustrated*. 3 vols. Riyadh, 1999-2001.

Cloudsley-Thompson, J. I., and M. J. Chadwick, *Life in Deserts*, London. 1964.

Collenette, Sheila. *An Illustrated Guide to the Flowers of Saudi Arabia*. London, 1986.

Cornes, M.D. and C.D., *The Wild Flowering Plants of Bahrain*. London, 1989.

Gasperetti, John, "Snakes of Arabia." In *Fauna of Saudi Arabia*. Vol. 9, pp. 169-450. Basel, Switzerland, 1989.

Harrison, David L., and Paul J. J. Bates. *The Mammals of Arabia*. 2nd ed. Sevenoaks, U.K., 1991.

Hollom, P. A. D., R. F. Porter, S. Christensen, and Ian Willis. Birds *of the Middle East and North Africa*. Calton, U.K., 1988.

Jennings, Michael C. *An Interim Atlas of Breeding Birds of Arabia*. Riyadh, 1995.

Krupp, F. A., Abdulaziz Abuzinada, and Iyad A. Nader. *A Marine Wildlife Sanctuary for the Arabian Gulf*. Riyadh, 1996.

Larsen, Torben B. *Butterflies of Saudi Arabia and its Neighbors*. London, 1984.

Lebling, Robert, and Donna Pepperdine. *Natural Remedies of Arabia*. London, 2006.

Mandaville, James P. *Flora of Eastern Saudi Arabia*. London and New York, 1990.

McKinnon, Michael. *Arabia: Sand, Sea, Sky*. London, 1990.

McKinnon, Michael, and Peter Vine. *Tides of War*. London, 1991.

Miller, Anthony G., and T.A. Cope. *Flora of the Arabian Peninsula and Socotra*. Vol. 1. Edinburgh, 1996.

Miller, Anthony G., and Miranda Morris. *Plants of Dhofar*. Muscat, Oman, 1998.

Mountfort, Guy. *Portrait of a Desert*. London, 1965.

Price, Mark R. *Animal Re-introduction: The Arabian Oryx in Oman*. Cambridge, 1989.

Saint Jalm, M., and Y. van Heezik. *Propagation of Houbara Bustard*. London, 1996.

Walker, D. H., and A. R. Pittaway. *Insects of Eastern Arabia*. London, 1987.

Western, A.R. *The Flora of the United Arab Emirates: An Introduction*. Abui Dhabia, 1989.

Wood, J. R. I., and Hugo Haig-Thomas, *A Handbook of the Yemen Flora*. Kew, U.K., 1997.

Works on the flora and fauna of Arabia have proliferated in recent years. The book on marine life in the Arabian Gulf by Basson and others is a well-illustrated account useful to both general readers and professionals. Readers seeking detailed accounts of fauna should refer to the journal series *Fauna of Saudi Arabia*, co-published by the National Commission of Wildlife Conservation and Development, Riyadh. Books on plants range from illustrated technical manuals with keys (Chaudhary, Mandaville, Miller and Cope, and Wood) to those comprised mainly of identified photographs (Collenette and Burton). Miller and Cope's work is a projected six-volume definitive flora of the entire Arabian Peninsula; one volume had been published by the end of 2005. The flora volume edited by Chaudhary is published by the Saudi Arabian National Herbarium, Riyadh. The beautifully illustrated book by Miller and Morris, which exists also in an Arabic edition, contains much information on medicinal and other uses of plants in southern Oman. The book by Lebling and Pepperdine is a valuable survey of medicinal plants of the Arabian Peninsula.

Acknowledgments

A Land Transformed, like other works of similar size and complexity, is the result of contributions from scores of people other than the editors and writers cited on the title page. First and foremost, this book would not have been possible without the unfailing support of Saudi Aramco management in Dhahran, Saudi Arabia, and Aramco Services Company in Houston, Texas. Mazen I. Snobar, Mustafa A. Jalali, Jamil F. Al Dandany, Deya A. Elyas, Mohammad A. Mulla and Nassir A. al-Nafisee all deserve mention for their encouragement and assistance. Nor could this book have been produced without reference to the valuable work of the scholars and editors who contributed to previous editions. In particular, we would like to credit George S. Rentz, Ismail I. Nawwab, John A. Sabini, Peter I. Speers, Paul F. Hoye, William Tracy and Jane Waldron Grutz.

Special thanks is owed to the individuals who wrote or worked on sidebars for the book: Saudi Aramco geologist Robert F. Lindsay, "Geology of Arabia," and retired Saudi Aramco geophysicist Richard Hastings-James, "The Search for Oil and Gas"; Kay Hardy Campbell, "Music"; James P. Mandaville, "Climate"; Paul J. Nance, "Handicrafts"; and Ni'mah I. Nawwab, "Saudi Women Today." Many other individuals went out of their way to answer our questions and assist in other aspects of the project with courtesy and clarity. Among them were: Michelle M. Alireza, Osama Alkadi, Robert Arndt, Mohammad Aslam, Debbie S. Clark, Dick Doughty, Ed Escamilla, Yusef Fadlalla, Richard Ford, Khalid Al-Ghamdi, Charles V. Hudson, Sami H. Juraifani, Thomas H. Keith, Dhafer al-Koheji, Robert Lebling, Thomas Lippman, David Lugo, Jack Moore, Khalid A. En-Najjar, Gregory Noakes, Abdullah H. Okab, Ali Osseiran, Kyle Pakka, Honorio S. Pangan, Eleanor Parker, Janis Patton, Michael Romaro, Steve Sawyer, Tariq Shuja, Joseph Thazhath, Fuad Therman, David Tschanz and Alex Wyllie.

A Land Transformed was designed by Pentagram Design, Inc., in Austin, Texas, which also created the charts and diagrams. Many of the maps were developed by Saudi Aramco's Cartography Department and by Mapping Specialists of Madison, Wisconsin. Polly Koch and J. Naomi Linzer, respectively, did valuable proofreading and indexing work.

Most of the photographs, illustrations and other images reproduced in this volume came from the archives of the Saudi Aramco Photo Lab Unit, from the Saudi Aramco World Public Affairs Digital Image Archive (PADIA) or were acquired through Feldman & Associates Photo Research in Northfield, Illinois, or William Facey in London.

For those who helped in any way with this book and are overlooked in these acknowledgments, please know that our appreciation for your help is not diminished by the oversight.

PHOTO CREDITS

ii-iii George Steinmetz; vi-vii Abdulla Y. al-Dobais/Saudi Aramco; viii-ix Gunnar Bemert; xiv-xv AP/Wide World Photos; xvi-xvii Shaikh M. Amin/Saudi Aramco; xviii-xix Peter Sanders Photographic Library; xx-xxi Richard Doughty/Aramco Services Company; xxiv-1 Thomas F. Walters/Saudi Aramco; 1 Peter MacDiarmid/Reuters/Corbis; 2-3 Karl S. Twitchell, K.S. Twitchell Collection/Saudi Aramco; 4 (tr) Steineke Collection/Saudi Aramco; 4 (bc) Steineke Collection/Saudi Aramco; 5 Robert Azzi/PADIA; 8 Ilo Battigelli; 9 (bl) Gertrude Bell Photographic Archive, University of Newcastle-upon-Tyne/Bell; 9 (tr) Andrew Thompson; 9 (cr) Andrew Thompson; 10-11 Karl S. Twitchell, K.S. Twitchell Collection/Saudi Aramco; 12 (bl) Hussain A. Ramadan/Saudi Aramco; 12 (br) Karl S. Twitchell, K.S. Twitchell Collection/Saudi Aramco; 13 Dorothy Miller/Saudi Aramco; 14-15 Karl S. Twitchell, K.S. Twitchell Collection/Saudi Aramco; 15 (cr) Ilo Battigelli; 15 (br) Ilo Battigelli; 16 (tl) Dorothy Miller/Saudi Aramco; 16 (cl) Conway Library, Courtauld Institute of Art, London; 17 (tl) Victoria & Albert Museum, London/Art Resource, NY; 17 (cr) William Facey; 17 (br) William Facey; 18 Shaikh M. Amin/Saudi Aramco; 19 Abdulla Y. al-Dobais/Saudi Aramco; 20 Wendy Cocker; 21 Ilo Battigelli; 23 Ilo Battigelli; 24-25 Bassignac Gilles/Gamma Press, Inc.; 26-27 Juris Zarins; 27 Juris Zarins; 28-29 John Herbert; 30 (tl) Andrew Thompson; 30 (cl) Norman Whalen/PADIA; 31 David W. Pease/ PADIA; 32 (t) Bibliothèque des Arts Décoratifs Paris/Dagli Orti/Art Archive; 32 (br) Middle East Centre Archive, St Antony's College, Oxford. Freya Stark Collection Kuwait Alb No 44.; 33 (tc) William Facey; 33 (c) Steve Raymer/National Geographic Image Collection; 33 (cr) William Facey; 33 (tr) William Facey; 33 (br) William Facey; 35 Ilo Battigelli; 37 British Museum; 38-39 Row 1: (l) Andrea Pistolesi/TIPS Images, (cl) Penny Tweedie/Woodfin Camp & Associates, (cr) Paul Doyle/Alamy Images, (r) Shaikh M. Amin/Saudi Aramco; Row 2: (l) AP/Wide World Photos, (cl) Peter Sanders Photographic Library, (cr) Paul Doyle/Alamy Images, (r) David South/ImageState; Row 3: (l) Israel Images/Alamy Images, (c) Abdulla Y. al-Dobais/Saudi Aramco, (r) Thorne Anderson/ PADIA; row 4: (l) Bill Lyons/Alamy Images, (cl) Getty Images, (cr) Jamal Saidi/JS/ABP Sport-Soccer Doha/Reuters, (r) Ed Kashi/Corbis; 41 (tr) William Facey; 41 (cr) William Facey; 42 (cl) Hussain A. Ramadan/Saudi Aramco; 42 (bl) William Facey; 42-43 Karl S. Twitchell, K.S. Twitchell Collection/Saudi Aramco; 44-45 William Facey; 46 William Facey; 47 William Facey; 48-49 John Herbert; 50 (bl) John Herbert; 50 (br) John Herbert; 50 (c) John Herbert; 52 Hussain A. Ramadan/Saudi Aramco; 53 Thomas F. Walters/Saudi Aramco; 54 Abdulla Y. al-Dobais/Saudi Aramco; 56-57 King Faisal Center for Research and Islamic Studies; 57 Mehmet Biber; 58-59 Kazuyoshi Nomachi/HAGA/The Image Works, Inc.; 61 Museum fuer Angewandte Kunst, Vienna, Austria/Erich Lessing/Art Resource, NY; 62 King Faisal Center for Research and Islamic Studies; 64 Peter Sanders/HAGA/The Image Works, Inc.; 66 Harper Collins Publishers/Art Archive; 67 King Faisal Center for Research and Islamic Studies; 68 Giraudon/Art Resource, NY; 70 Peter Sanders Photographic Library; 71 Roger Wood/Corbis; 72 Jane Sweeney/Art Directors & TRIP Photo Library; 73 Norman MacDonald/Saudi Aramco; 74-75 Michael Maslan Historic Photographs/Corbis; 77 *The Arabian Sun*/Saudi Aramco, and Makki al-Bahrani; 78 Vanessa Stamford/PADIA; 79 Egyptian Museum Cairo/Dagli Orti/Art Archive; 80 King Faisal Center for Research and Islamic Studies; 81 Werner Forman/Art Resource, NY; 82 The Granger Collection, New York; 83 Peter Sanders Photographic Library; 84 Norman MacDonald/Saudi Aramco; 85 Golestan Palace, Tehran, Iran/Werner Forman/Art Resource, NY; 86 Bibliothèque Nationale, Paris, France/Art Resource, NY; 88-89 Courtesy of the Bukhari Collection of Antique Maps of Arabia; 89 Tor Eigeland/PADIA; 90-91 Historical Picture Archive/Corbis; 93 Tor Eigeland/PADIA; 94 (tl) John Herbert; 94-95 Patricia Barbor; 97 Helene Rogers/Art Directors & TRIP Photo Library; 97 (br) The British Museum/HIP-Topham/The Image Works, Inc.; 97 (c) The British Museum/HIP/The Image Works, Inc.; 97 (cr) The British Museum/HIP-Topham/The Image Works, Inc.; 97 (tc) The British Museum/HIP-Topham/The Image Works, Inc.; 97 (tr) John Herbert; 98 Norman MacDonald/Saudi Aramco; 99 Norman MacDonald/Saudi Aramco; 100 Steineke Collection/Saudi Aramco; 101 Bibliothèque Nationale, Paris, France/Art Resource, NY; 103 The Granger Collection, New York; 104 Norman MacDonald/Saudi Aramco; 106 Norman MacDonald/Saudi Aramco; 107 M. & E. Bernheim/Woodfin Camp & Associates; 108 Eric Hansen/PADIA; 109 HIP/Art Resource, NY; 110-111 Bibliothèque Nationale, Paris, France/Bridgeman Art Library; 112 Snark/Art Resource, NY; 113 Bibliothèque Nationale, Paris, France/Bridgeman Art Library; 114-115 W.H.I. Shakespear, March 1911/Royal Geographical Society Picture Library; 115 Faisal I. al-Dossary/Saudi Aramco; 116-117 Hussain A. Ramadan/Saudi Aramco; 118 Steineke Collection/Saudi Aramco; 119 Hussain A. Ramadan/Saudi Aramco; 120 Shaikh M. Amin/Saudi Aramco; 122 (bc) *The Travels of Ali Bey,* 1816; 122 (c) Time & Life Pictures/Getty Images; 122 (cr) Private Collection/Bridgeman Art Library; 123 Rodney Searight Collection/Victoria and Albert Museum; 124-125 Hussain A. Ramadan/Saudi Aramco; 126 Rodney Searight Collection/Victoria and Albert Museum; 127 Ilo Battigelli; 128 (c) National Portrait Gallery, London; 128 (bc) Mansell Collection/Time Life Pictures/Getty Images; 129 (tr) Heather Colyer Ross; 129 (cr) Burnett H. Moody and Ahmad Montakh/Saudi Aramco; 130-131 Arnold Heims/Image Archive ETH-Bibliothek, Zurich; 132-133 Abdulla Y. al-Dobais/

Saudi Aramco; 135 W.H.I. Shakespear/Royal Geographical Society Picture Library; 136 R.E. Cheesman, 1923-24/Royal Geographical Society Picture Library; 137 Ilo Battigelli; 138 Mansell/Time & Life Pictures/Getty Images; 139 Royal Geographical Society; 140-14 Gertrude Bell Photographic Archive, University of Newcastle-upon-Tyne/Bell, 1914; 142 HRP Dickson/Popperfoto/ClassicStock.com; 143 Steineke Collection/Saudi Aramco; 144-145 Abdulla Y. al-Dobais/Saudi Aramco; 145 J.W. "Soak" Hoover/Saudi Aramco; 146-147 Owen Oxley; 148 Steineke Collection/Saudi Aramco; 149 Thomas F. Walters/Saudi Aramco; 150-151 Bettmann/Corbis; 153 Saudi Aramco; 154 Saudi Aramco; 155 Thomas F. Walters/Saudi Aramco; 156 Norman MacDonald/Saudi Aramco; 157 Saudi Aramco; 158 Owen Oxley; 159 Aramco Services Company; 160 and 161 Norman MacDonald/Saudi Aramco; 162 Hulton-Deutsch Collection/Corbis; 163 Gunnar Bemert; 164 (tr) Michael J. Isaac/Saudi Aramco; 164 (b) Burnett H. Moody/Saudi Aramco; 165 Hussain A. Ramadan/Saudi Aramco; 166 Courtesy of The Royal Commission for Jubail & Yanbu'; 167 Bettmann/Corbis; 168 Robert Azzi/PADIA; 169 Khaled Fazaa/AFP/Getty Images; 170 Abdulla Y. al-Dobais/Saudi Aramco; 171 Peter Sanders Photographic Library; 172-173 Abdulaziz M. al-Moaiweed/Saudi Aramco; 176 Ni'mah Isma'il Nawwab; 177 (t) Abdulla Y. al-Dobais/Saudi Aramco; 177 (b) Reuters/Corbis; 178 (t) Hadi A. Al-Makayyal/Saudi Aramco; 178 (b) Ramin Talaie/Corbis; 179 Saudi Aramco; 180-181 Abu Abdul Aziz Studio/Saudi Aramco; 182-183 Michael McKinnon; 183 James P. Mandaville, Jr.; 184-185 Michael McKinnon; 186 Peter Harrigan/PADIA; 188 (cl) James P. Mandaville, Jr.; 188 (tl) James P. Mandaville, Jr.; 188 (tr) Mike Hill and Mike Hill, Jr./PADIA; 189 (cl) James P. Mandaville, Jr.; 189 (tc) Wendy Cocker; 189 (tl) George Steinmetz; 189 (tr) Peter Harrigan/PADIA; 190 Michael McKinnon; 191 Michael McKinnon; 193 Worldspec/NASA / Alamy Images; 194 (cr) Gunnar Bemert; 194 (tl) Michael McKinnon; 194 (tr) Mohammad al-Shihri/Saudi Aramco; 195 (cl) Mohammad al-Shihri/Saudi Aramco; 195 (tl) Michael McKinnon; 195 (tr) Michael McKinnon; 196 (tl) Michael McKinnon; 196 (tr) Michael McKinnon; 197 Owen Oxley; 198-199 Mark Mercer/Saudi Aramco; 199 Steineke Collection/Saudi Aramco; 200-201 Sarah Leen/National Geographic Image Collection; 202 Saudi Aramco; 204 Karl S. Twitchell, K.S. Twitchell Collection/Saudi Aramco; 205 The Granger Collection, New York; 207 Saudi Aramco; 208 Hulton Archive/Getty Images; 209 Bettmann Archives/Corbis; 211 Steineke Collection/Saudi Aramco; 212-213 Karl S. Twitchell, K.S. Twitchell Collection/ Saudi Aramco; 214 Oberlin College Archives; 215 Karl S. Twitchell, K.S. Twitchell Collection/Saudi Aramco; 216 Steineke Collection/Saudi Aramco; 217 Images copyrighted by Chevron Texaco Corporation and used with permission; 218 Saudi Aramco; 219 Aramco Services Company; 220-221 Schuyler B. "Krug" Henry/Saudi Aramco; 222 J.W. "Soak" Hoover/Saudi Aramco; 223 Richard G. Kerr/Saudi Aramco; 224 Saudi Aramco; 225 Steineke Collection/Saudi Aramco; 226 Richard G. Kerr/Saudi Aramco; 228 Lester Hilyard/Saudi Aramco; 229 Saudi Aramco; 230-231 Don M.McCleod/Saudi Aramco; 232 Cecil Green/Saudi Aramco; 233 Don M. McCleod/Saudi Aramco; 234 Thomas F. Walters/Saudi Aramco; 236-237 Ilo Battigelli; 238-239 Richard Finnie/Saudi Aramco; 240 James MacPherson/Saudi Aramco; 241 Bettmann/Corbis; 242 (cl) Owen Oxley/Saudi Aramco; 242 (bl) Fred Porrett/Saudi Aramco; 242-243 (bc) Robert Yarnall Richie; 244 Saudi Aramco; 245 Thomas F. Walters/Saudi Aramco; 246-247 Thomas F. Walters/Saudi Aramco; 248 Thomas F. Walters/Saudi Aramco; 249 (t) Pat K. Moody/Saudi Aramco; 249 (cr) Shaikh M. Amin/Saudi Aramco; 250 (cr) Ali M. Khalifa/Saudi Aramco; 250 (tl) NDM/Saudi Aramco; 250 (tr) Thomas F. Walters/Saudi Aramco; 251 Thomas F. Walters/Saudi Aramco; 252-253 Shaikh M. Amin/Saudi Aramco; 254 Tor Eigeland/PADIA; 255 Shaikh M. Amin/Saudi Aramco; 256 Hussain A. Ramadan/Saudi Aramco; 257 Saudi Aramco; 258 (tl) Jacques Langevin/Saudi Aramco; 258-259 Michael J. Isaac/Saudi Aramco; 260-261 AP/Wide World Photos; 262 (t) Ken Childress/Herring Design/Saudi Aramco; 262 (cr) Adrian Wayne/Saudi Aramco; 263 Abdulla Y. al-Dobais/Saudi Aramco; 264 Stan Honda/AFP/Getty Images; 265 Saudi Aramco; 268-269 Abdulla Y. al-Dobais/Saudi Aramco; 269 (tr) Abdulla Y. al-Dobais/Saudi Aramco; 269 (cr) 300 Abdulla Y. al-Dobais/Saudi Aramco; 269 (br) Abdulla Y. al-Dobais/ Saudi Aramco; 270-271 Courtesy of Showa Shell Sekiyu K.K.; 273 Faisal I. al-Dossary/ Saudi Aramco; 274 Hadi al-Makkayal/Saudi Aramco; 278-279 Ken Childress/Herring Design/Saudi Aramco; 280 Courtesy of Showa Shell Sekiyu K.K.; 281 Faisal I. al-Dossary/Saudi Aramco; 282 (c) Saudi Aramco; 282 (bl) Courtesy of Petron Corporation; 282 (br) Courtesy of Motiva Enterprises LLC; 283 Saudi Aramco; 284 Hussain A. Ramadan/Saudi Aramco; 285 Hussain A. Ramadan/Saudi Aramco; 286-287 Abdulaziz M. al-Moaiweed/Saudi Aramco; 289 Abdulla Y. al-Dobais/Saudi Aramco; 290 Shaikh M. Amin/Saudi Aramco; 291 (tl) Saudi Aramco; 291 (cl) Faisal I. al-Dossary/Saudi Aramco; 291 (br) Ken Childress/Herring Design/Saudi Aramco; 291 (cr) Mahmoud al-Hashem/Saudi Aramco; 291 (tr) Abu Abdul Aziz Studio/Saudi Aramco; 292 (tl) Sam Pierson/Aramco Services Company; 292 (bl) Abdulla Y. al-Dobais/Saudi Aramco; 292-293 Abu Abdul Aziz Studio/Saudi Aramco; 294 Ken Childress/Herring Design/Saudi Aramco; 295 Hadi A. al-Makayyl/Saudi Aramco; 296-297 Hussain A. Ramadan/Saudi Aramco; 298-299 Abdulla Y. al-Dobais/Saudi Aramco; 300-301 Faisal I. al-Dossary/Saudi Aramco; 302-303 Courtesy of Motiva Enterprises LLC; 304-305 Hussain A. Ramadan/Saudi Aramco.